D1302778

Energy Policies and the Greenhouse Effect
Volume Two: Country Studies and Technical Options

ENERGY POLICIES AND THE GREENHOUSE EFFECT
VolumeTwo: Country Studies and Technical Options

**Michael Grubb, Peter Brackley, Michèle Ledic, Ajay Mathur,
Steve Rayner, Jeremy Russell, Akira Tanabe**

The Royal Institute of International Affairs
Dartmouth

A CIP catalogue record to this book is available from the British Library.

Published by Dartmouth Publishing Company, Gower House, Croft Road, Aldershot, Hants, GU11 3HR, England

Dartmouth Publishing Company, Old Post Road, Brookfield, Vermont 05036, USA

ISBN 1 85521 198 X

Cover by Twenty Twenty Design

Printed in Great Britain by
Billing & Sons Ltd, Worcester

Contents

Figures

Text Boxes

Foreword

The second volume of this book represents the culmination of nearly four years of research on the Greenhouse Effect by the Energy and Environmental Programme. The publication of Volume 1 last year, followed our shorter reports in 1988, 1989 and 1990 on: 'Issues for Policymakers', 'Negotiating Targets', and 'Formulating a Convention'.

Volume 2 represents the intellectual underpinning of the *Policy Appraisal* volume, yet can be read independently. It contains the technical, analytical and country analysis in support of the conclusions on the policies - both national and international - necessary to reduce greenhouse gas emissions. It was not our intention to produce such a large work at the outset of the project. The final product reflects the evolutionary and iterative nature of a large research study.

We owe a considerable debt to our case study authors; particularly to those whose chapters were complete in early 1990 and who graciously accepted the delay entailed in dividing the work to allow for the introduction of additional material. All the country studies fed into Volume 1 and in turn could draw upon it in final draft. Preliminary technical assessments were conducted in the early stages, but the authors could not draw upon the complete technology review chapters.

Michael Grubb has carried the study through to an extremely successful conclusion. During the past three years, he has become an internationally-recognised authority on this subject. The workload involved - both for Michael and the staff supporting him - has been an order of magnitude greater than could have been predicted at the outset. The success of their efforts has been largely responsible for placing our Programme, and the name of Chatham House, in the forefront of policy research on the greenhouse effect.

Jonathan Stern, April 1991

About the Lead Author

Dr Michael Grubb is a Research Fellow at the Energy and Environmental Programme of the Royal Institute of International Affairs, where he is leading studies on the implications of the greenhouse effect, and on emerging energy technologies. Following publication of his report *The Greenhouse Effect: Negotiating Targets* (RIIA), 1989) he was appointed as an adviser to the United Nations Environment Programme, and has been involved in working groups of the Intergovernmental Panel on Climate Change and the World Energy Council. His studies prior to joining the Institute resulted in a range of publications on renewable energy sources and on electricity system operation and planning.

Research by the Energy and Environmental Programme is supported by generous contributions of finance and professional advice from the following organisations:

Arthur D. Little • British Coal • British Gas
British Nuclear Fuels • British Petroleum • Caltex
Chubu Electric Power Co • Department of Energy
Eastern Electricity • East Midlands Electricity • ELF (UK)
Enterprise Oil • Esso • Idemitsu International
Japan National Oil Corporation • Kuwait Petroleum International
LASMO • National Energy Administration, Sweden
National Grid • National Power • Neste
Petroleos de Venezuela (UK)
Petroleum Economics • PowerGen • Sedgwick Energy • Shell
Statoil • Tokyo Electric Power Co
United Kingdom Atomic Energy Authority

Acknowledgments

Many have helped with this work. In addition to those acknowledged in Volume 1 and by the individual authors in this volume, particular contributions to Volume 2 have been made by Ian Smart (Chapter 1), Bernard Giovannini, Bill Chandler, Ian Brown and Linda Taylor (Chapter 2), Bob Williams (Chapters 2 and 3), Walter Patterson (Chapter 3), and Gordon McKerron (Chapter 4). Gerald Leach and Les Shorrock provided key input for Chapter 4. My thanks for their contributions; the book would have been poorer, and shorter, without them. I am indebted to the case study authors, who have laboured long on their work, and responded so well to a wide variety of comments. The studies are their own creations, but they cannot be held responsible for my interpretation of their results. I hope they think the final product to be a fitting tribute to their efforts. Matthew Tickle provided valuable assistance, Rosina Pullman edited the text, and Nicola Steen transformed it to the printed page, created the illustrations, carefully read the work, and generally oversaw the process. Above all I am indebted to my wife, Anne-Christine, for her patience, understanding and support throughout.

Michael Grubb

Acronyms, units, and conversion factors used in text

Acronyms:
GDP   Gross Domestic Product
IPCC Intergovernmental Panel on Climate Change
NGOs Non-governmental organizations
OECD Organisation for Economic Cooperation and
      Development

Primary units in this study:
tC   tonne of carbon
GtC   Gigatonnes (billion tonnes) of carbon
Mtoe Million tonnes of oil equivalent (industrial unit of energy)

Prefixes:

Kilo (Thousand)	k
Mega (Million)	M
Giga (Billion, milliard)	G,B
Tera (Trillion)	T
Peta (Quadrillion)	P

Energy units and conversion factors:
1 kilocalorie (kcal)   = 4.2kJ (kilojoule)
1 British Thermal Unit (Btu)= 1.05kJ
1 quad   = 10^{15}Btu = 1.05EJ = 10^{10} therms
1 terawatt-hour (TWh)   = 3.6PJ
1 tonne oil equivalent (toe)[*] = 10400 Mcal = 44.6 GJ GHV*
1 barrel oil   = 0.136tonnes
1000m^3 nat gas equiv[*]   = 9555 Mcal = 40GJ = 0.90toe GHV
1 tonne coal equivalent[*]   = 7220 Mcal= 30.4GJ= 0.68toe GHV
Other units:
1km   = 3330 feet = 0.62 miles
1km^2 = 100 hectares = 247 acres
1m^3 = 1000 litres = 220 Imperial gallons = 264 US gallons

* Energy units use international/World Energy Council standard definitions based on Gross Heating Values (GHV), ie. including the energy content of condensed steam from combustion (see Appendix 1).

Summary and Conclusions

The impact of greenhouse gas abatement policies (examined in Volume 1, *Policy Appraisal*), will be determined by the resources and technologies available, and the constraints of national energy, economic and political systems. The world has abundant energy resources: proven oil and gas reserves could last for many decades, and more will be discovered; coal could last for hundreds of years; nuclear and renewable resources in total exceed conceivable human demands. However, dependence on distant and/or concentrated resources increases costs and environmental impacts, and creates economic and political risks. The key constraints are those of resource distribution, technical adequacy, and environmental impact.

Improving the efficiency of energy use offers the largest and cheapest potential for limiting emissions and other problems associated with energy systems. Substituting identified and cost-effective technologies in OECD countries could in principle increase the efficiency of electricity use by up to 50%, and of other applications by 15-40% over the next two decades. Fully optimising energy systems would yield larger savings, but it is far from clear how much of this potential can be tapped. Technologies and options for greater efficiency will continue to improve.

Advanced gas turbine systems can substantially improve electrical generating efficiencies, both from gas and from coal via gasifiers; these technologies can be extended to using biomass fuels, and also broaden opportunities for using waste heat from power generation. New technologies will also lower the cost of liquid fuels from biomass. Other renewable technologies have advanced rapidly; some are already competitive in good locations, and many will become so if fossil fuel prices rise in real terms. New nuclear technologies could lower costs and reduce other obstacles to nuclear expansion. But of all these opportunities, only gas-fired combined cycle plant are sufficiently developed to expand on a large scale without government support in the 1990s.

Analytical techniques are not yet adequate to assess abatement strategies with any precision. 'Top-down' analysis based on general macroeconomic relationships cannot sufficiently reflect the microeconomic determinants of energy demand, and the potential for very low cost savings available from modifying the operation of energy markets. 'Bottom-up' analysis of systems yields much better understanding of technical opportunities and their costs especially concerning efficiency improvements, but cannot reflect the realities of energy market behaviour and price responses. Combined approaches are better, but complex. Overall, various technical analyses suggest that a concerted mix of policies could probably reduce CO_2 emissions from most developed economies at a rate averaging up to 1% annually for at least a couple of decades at little or no net economic cost.

Case studies of different countries emphasize large national differences. The United Kingdom/European Community study notes considerable scope for limiting emissions, from improved efficiency in buildings especially and fuel switching towards gas and a mix of renewable sources. Given the dominance of free market economic philosophy, the central issue concerns the willingness of government to pursue, and the public to accept, policies to improve efficiency, to sustain energy price rises, and to support non-fossil sources. Reluctance concerning domestic measures contrasts with official recognition of the greenhouse effect as a serious problem, and the greater willingness in some other European countries to intervene for environmental ends. Strong East-West and North-South tensions within Europe over the form, rate and distribution of responses are likely but overall the EC is likely to pursue abatement measures and to continue leading the international process.

The US economic philosophy parallels the UK's reluctance to intervene, but instead of this being tempered by scientific concerns and international links, it is reinforced by the historical abundance of cheap fossil fuels, and the physical and institutional consequences of this. The US study recognises substantial cost-effective opportunities for improving efficiency but states that gas resources are significantly constrained whilst all non-fossil options are inadequate. The extent of investment in existing infrastructure and the openness of the political process to a wide variety of conflicting pressures and special interest lobbies make likely responses slow, hard fought, and dominated by political and industrial considerations. The author advocates a flexible approach, with investment abroad offsetting domestic abatement pressures.

The Japanese analysis reflects unique conflicts: a conservative society in which many doubt the need for, and fear the consequences of, CO_2 constraints on an already efficient economy; but which could yet respond forcefully, as it did to the oil shocks. Dependence on foreign energy resources has created an attitude that energy is not to be squandered, and a readiness to accept government action to that end. There is scope for more efficiency and non-fossil sources, and the close relationship between government and industry provides the means for achieving this. Japanese experience with efficient technologies makes internationalization of greenhouse responses an opportunity as well as a challenge.

In stark contrast, the USSR's huge energy infrastructure contains immense inertia despite political upheavals. Like the US, the USSR has developed in energy abundance. The infrastructure is fundamentally driven by supply, and the economic system cannot easily stimulate the myriad decentralised decisions needed to exploit the very large technical potential for improving efficiency. Price reform might extend to energy but only if it is first successfully accomplished in other areas, accompanied by deeper changes. Yet the growing focus on gas and non-fossil sources, and the pressing need for improved efficiency, will anyway limit emissions. Greenhouse concerns are peripheral and the extent and pace of reform highly uncertain, but the Soviet Union is already embarked on a de facto abatement course.

Chinese industry similarly reflects its economic path and current stresses, and pressures for general economic reform which could reduce energy losses in heavy industry and lessen the exclusive supply-orientation of commercial energy developments. But the low starting point, the vast rural population, and the dominance of coal resources make rapid CO_2 growth inevitable. Emissions growth would be lessened by diversion of resources to more gas exploration and development and hydro, and improved rural biomass use and regionalization of responses could be important; but more substantial abatement would require fundamental reform, and would still be swamped by pressures for increased coal-based supply.

India also reflects the complexities and constraints of poverty, but much like Japan, the greenhouse effect is seen both as threat and opportunity. Transferring resources from supply to end-use improvements could aid development, but is politically and managerially extremely difficult. Coal is the prime domestic resource, gas requires imports and infrastructure, biomass resources are already heavily exploited, and non-fossil sources are too capital-intensive - but all would help reduce dependence on oil. Chronic shortage of capital and hard currency also hamper efficiency improvements in industry and electricity supply especially, and impede development of good public transport. The scope for limiting emissions may be considerable, but much would depend directly or indirectly on expanded and redirected foreign assistance, and on reduced debt pressures.

Taken together, these studies emphasize the extent to which abatement depends upon political and institutional factors. The attitude of different countries is frequently the inverse of what might be expected from an objective appraisal of technical opportunities: more efficient countries, with more limited additional opportunities for abatement, are amongst the most willing to act to limit emissions further.

This points to perhaps the broadest conclusion from these studies. Responding to the greenhouse effect has been almost universally presented as an issue of trading off the costs of adapting to climate change against the costs of emissions abatement. This is wholly inadequate. The environmental costs are unknown and may be dominated by inherently unquantifiable risks. Conversely, limiting emissions is not primarily a matter of economic costs, but of culture, institutions, and politics in the broadest sense.

PART I: TECHNICAL OPTIONS

Energy Resources and Systems

Concerns about limits of global fossil fuel resources have receded. At 1990 rates of use, proven oil reserves would last over 40 years, gas 60 years, and coal for several hundred years. Economic reserves will expand if prices rise, and with improved extraction and exploration techniques. Large unconventional sources of both oil and gas are also available, at higher cost. Uranium resources are adequate to support expansion of nuclear power for many decades, and much more if additional nuclear fuel were to be 'bred' in fast reactors. Resources for fusion power are essentially unlimited. Global renewable energy resources similarly exceed conceivable human needs, and though most of the conversion routes available greatly limit the amount which can be exploited, the potential is still very large.

The energy problem is not one of inadequate resources, but of their distribution, the technical and infrastructural requirements for exploiting them, and the environmental impacts of doing so. The heavy concentration of oil in the Middle East, including most recent discoveries, implies further increasing dependence on that region. Gas is more widespread but the biggest deposits of conventional gas are also relatively concentrated in a few key regions. Many countries have coal resources, though the global total is dominated by China, the US and the USSR. Some renewable resources, notably hydro and geothermal, are also unevenly distributed, though the major diffuse renewable resources of solar, biomass and wind energy are widespread.

Dependence on distant and/or concentrated resources involves political risks which are well known, and increases costs and environmental impacts. Significant energy is used in pumping gas over long distances or liquefying it for shipping, and although overhead electricity cables are cheaper, the relative losses in transmission are larger. Long distance transport amplifies political risks if the systems cross many national boundaries. Other constraints of electricity systems, including the relatively high cost of storage, may also limit the ability to exploit some distant or highly variable sources of non-fossil power. However, the difficulties posed by the short-term variability of some renewable sources are much less severe than is often assumed; with the possible exception of photovoltaics, the key constraints will generally not concern these system aspects, but site availability and economic viability.

In 1972, *Limits to Growth*[1] offered a warning that by the end of the century the fossil fuel resources on which the world depends, notably oil, could approach exhaustion. In the event, by the early 1990s, concerns about the adequacy of fossil fuel resources have largely receded, and their place has been taken by concerns about the global environmental consequences of continued reliance upon fossil fuels. Widely differing attitudes persist about how fossil fuel prices may vary as resources are exploited and, consequently, the economic background against which alternatives will be competing. Opinions also differ concerning the commercially feasible resources of many proposed alternatives, even if adequate technologies are developed, and doubts are raised about other difficulties, such as the constraints of transportation and (for many renewable resources) technical constraints due to their variability. This chapter seeks to clarify some of these issues by reviewing energy resources and the constraints of energy systems.

1.1 Fossil fuel reserves and resources

It is convenient to summarize the amount of a given fossil fuel available with a single number, but inevitably misleading. The presence of some fossil deposits may have been proven, their characteristics known, and the costs of exploitation may be low; others may be based on more speculative data, or may require much greater effort and cost to extract them than could be justified at current prices. Other resources may simply be inferred from general geological data where a given area has never fully been probed. As a result, analysts have traditionally drawn a distinction between proven reserves, which are known deposits exploitable at (or near) current prices using current technology; and estimated total resources. Table 1.1 shows estimates of global fossil fuel reserves and resources. Various other categories and sub-definitions exist; all, inevitably, have some ambiguity. In general, price rises, technological development, and further exploration move deposits from the resources category to becoming proven reserves, and in practice total resources also increase as both the technical and geographical frontiers of exploration expand.

Coal deposits are particularly hard to classify. The quality varies greatly, from pure hard metallurgical coals to dirty brown mixtures with more dirt than fuel. Deposits similarly vary from seams many metres

---

[1] D.H.Meadows et al, *Limits to Growth*, Universe, 1972.

Table 1.1 Global fossil fuels: resources, reserves and current production (Btoe)

	Solids	Liquids	Gas
Estimated resources in place, 1987[a]	7081	307	243
Proven reserves, 1989[b]	722	137	102
Production, 1989[b]	2.2	3.1	1.7

[a]Estimated from World Energy Council; *1989 Survey of Energy Resources*, WEC, London, 1989; [b] *BP Statistical Review of World Energy*, BP, London,1990.

thick near the surface, which can be stripped out in huge volumes at minimal cost, to complex narrow seams at great depth, which may be extremely expensive to exploit. Often, the extent of coalfields is speculative, and the amount which might be extracted at a given cost is even more uncertain.

All these caveats cannot obscure the fact that there is an enormous amount of coal in the world. The proved recoverable reserves of hard coal reported to the World Energy Conference total over 1,000 billion tonnes (Bt), compared with annual consumption little over 3Bt; the estimated additional 'amount in place' is 5-10 times larger.[2] Globally, the amount of coal which could be extracted at costs not greatly above current levels therefore probably amounts to between several hundred and several thousand years' consumption at present levels.

Furthermore, coal is relatively evenly distributed. Although the global total is dominated by deposits in China, the US, and the USSR, many other regions have substantial reserves, as indicated in Figure 1.1. For these reasons, coal is widely seen as the major long-term fossil energy resource. Many regard its eventual return to being the global fuel of choice as a matter not of whether, but when - with that being determined primarily by the vagaries of oil and gas availability.

Oil resources are geologically much less complex than coal. Reservoirs are marked by fairly clear boundaries and, once mapped, it is a relatively

[2] World Energy Council, *1989 Survey of Energy Resources*, WEC, London, 1989.

Figure 1.1 Global distribution of proven coal reserves, Mtoe

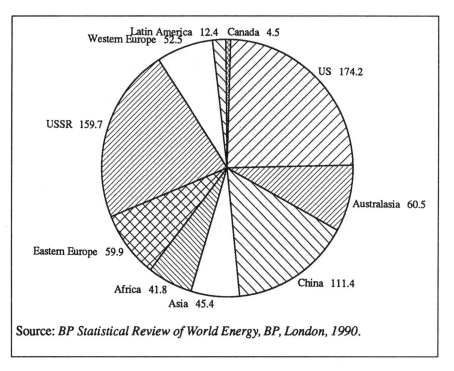

Western Europe 52.5   Latin America 12.4   Canada 4.5

US 174.2

USSR 159.7

Australasia 60.5

Eastern Europe 59.9

China 111.4

Africa 41.8

Asia 45.4

Source: *BP Statistical Review of World Energy, BP, London, 1990.*

easy process to drill a well and extract the oil. The gap between proven reserves and estimated resources is therefore much smaller (often barely a factor of two) and the quantities are better defined. Despite this, firm figures have proved elusive. Reserves and resources have climbed steadily as exploration continues, and reclassification of resources raised the figure for proven reserves by 1989 to nearly 140Bt - more than forty times the 1990 annual production of just over 3Bt.[3] These figures reflect application of current technology. Reserves are likely to be further increased by the development of better techniques for exploration and extraction, including methods for extracting more oil from existing reservoirs.

However, oil deposits are very unevenly distributed as illustrated in Figure 1.2. Global reserves remain dominated by those in the Middle East, and two thirds of the 'new' reserves identified over the two decades

[3] ibid.

Figure 1.2 Global distribution of proven oil reserves, Mtoe

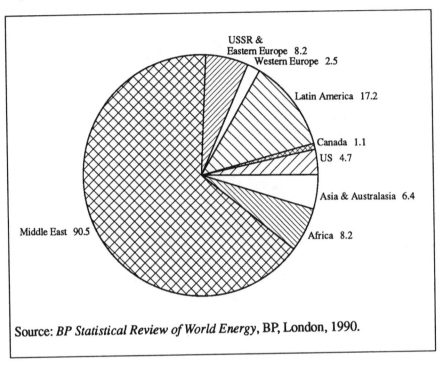

Source: *BP Statistical Review of World Energy*, BP, London, 1990.

1969-89 were located in that region.[4] The eruption of the Gulf crisis in 1990 again made the world nervous of over-dependence on the area, and efforts to keep energy supplies well diversified are likely to be maintained. This may make governments anxious if global oil consumption rises much above current levels. This, conversely, may mean that global reserves persist, at reasonable levels and costs, for several more decades though they will become steadily more concentrated in the Middle East.

If prices did rise much in the longer term, tar sands and oil shales could offer large additional sources of oil. Technologies for extracting such deposits and converting them to usable oil have been demonstrated, but

[4] *BP Statistical Review of World Energy*, BP, London, 1990. A fuller discussion of petroleum resource characteristics, distributions and production futures is given in C.D.Masters, D.H.Root and E.D.Attanasi, 'World Oil and Gas Resources - Future Production Realities', *Annual Review of Energy 15*, 1990, pp.23-51.

they would appear to be of commercial interest only at oil prices more than twice those existing in the late 1980s.[5] The resources, however, are vast: in the US, the only country to have surveyed such resources in detail, it is estimated that the recoverable energy in oil shales is of the same order as the US coal reserves, themselves the second largest in the world.[6]

Among the conventional fuels, the one with the biggest potential for displacing both oil and coal in the short to medium term is now widely seen to be natural gas. While coal and oil reserves have grown steadily, those for gas have expanded dramatically; reserve estimates almost doubled during the 1980s, and now amount to 120BCM (billion cubic metres) - approaching the energy content of oil reserves, and some sixty times current annual gas production. The estimated total resources more than doubled in the thirty years to 1990, and are still more than twice the proven reserves. The geographical spread of known gas resources has also increased, to 85 countries by 1989 compared with about 40 in 1960.

These factors, combined with the steady development of gas-using technology and infrastructure, have transformed the outlook for gas from being a secondary and sometimes unwanted by-product of oil extraction, to being a major global fuel in its own right, which over coming decades might well surpass oil. Since gas has been less thoroughly explored than oil or coal, many expect the proven reserves to carry on expanding relatively rapidly. However, total reserves seem likely to remain dominated by those in the Soviet Union and Middle East (Figure 1.3), and there are concerns that long term heavy reliance on gas could lead to over-dependence on these regions (Volume 1, section 5.1).[7]

In addition to conventional gas deposits, there are various forms of 'unconventional' gas resources. These include gas trapped in tight sands and shale, in coal seams, and geopressurized gas. Information on these is scarce but a review of such resources in the US in 1980 estimated that such unconventional resources were probably comparable to total

[5] A broad discussion of unconventional oil resources is given in G.Foley, *The Energy Question*, Penguin, (Third Edition, 1987). Recent efforts to exploit Venezuelan heavy oil by emulsifying have resulted in a commercial product, Orimulsion, which is being marketed as a liquid competitor to coal for power generation, but it cannot substitute for oil.
[6] WEC, *1989 Survey of Energy Resources*, op.cit, Ch.3
[7] Michael Grubb, *Energy Policies and the Greenhouse Effect, Volume 1: Policy Appraisal*, Dartmouth/Gower, 1990, section 5.1. Hereafter referred to as Volume 1.

Figure 1.3 Global distribution of proven gas reserves, Mtoe

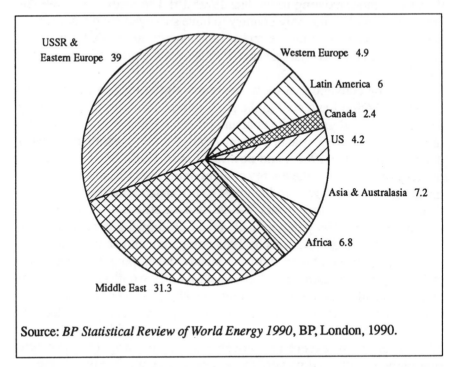

Source: *BP Statistical Review of World Energy 1990*, BP, London, 1990.

conventional gas resources.[8] In addition, ice-bound methane deposits at high latitudes form a potentially enormous resource.[9] Theories about the earth's mantle being a source of natural gas, instead of exclusively organic formation, remain unproven (and an exploratory well in Sweden has yielded ambiguous results); but whatever the origin, there is probably much further gas to be discovered at depth. How much of these unconventional resources it may be practical to exploit at reasonable cost remains unknown, but some proponents argue that gas resources could eventually exceed even those of coal.[10]

---

[8] National Petroleum Council, *Unconventional Gas Sources*, NPC, Washington, 1980.
[9] Estimates of total quantity of methane in hydrates vary by a factor of more than a thousand, from 2,000 to 5,000,000Bt; a review is given in K.Kvenvolden and L.Barnard, 'Methane Hydrates and Global Climate', *Global Biogeochemical Cycles 2*, 1988, pp.221-229.
[10] G.J.MacDonald, 'The Future of Methane as an Energy Resource', *Annual Review of Energy 15*, 1990, pp.53-81.

A review of global energy resources at the opening of the 1990s thus stands in sharp contrast to those presented twenty years earlier. Despite the politically-driven upheavals in the oil market, new discoveries and the overall march of technologies for locating and extracting fossil fuels more cheaply, mean that the spectre of resource shortages has largely receded. Contrary to the fears which then dominated popular debates,[11] there is a widespread belief that fossil resources will prove adequate to support global economic expansion for many more decades at acceptable costs. Another twenty years could perhaps reverse the picture again if growth is rapid and oil and gas reserves do not expand significantly (though this could not really apply to coal), but environmental constraints now loom larger.

Environmental issues now dominate the debate. Using a sizeable fraction of the world's fossil resources, it is now widely believed, would bring changes to climate and ecosystems unprecedented since the last ice age at least, with consequences and risks which are far from fully understood. If environment is the constraint, the very abundance of fossil fuels becomes a handicap. Markets cannot be relied upon to drive the price up and to constrain demand; policies are required not merely to try and manage volatile markets, but to change them fundamentally in the face of the strong economic interests of those who possess and profit from the resources. Furthermore, if policies do hold consumption down while technical improvements and exploration continue to boost reserves and reduce extraction costs, prices also fall so that the task of making alternatives competitive becomes all the harder. Though in the short and medium term various factors may limit the importance of this price reaction (see Volume 1, section 5.4), if environmental constraints are critical, in the long term the sheer abundance of fossil fuels, especially coal, could turn out to be as much a global curse as a blessing.

---

[11] For the sake of the record it should be emphasized that many economists never accepted the fears about major energy resource crises; from Marshall's Principles of Economics at the turn of the century onwards, neo-classical economics had emphasized the extent to which market responses, incorporating technical and organizational ingenuity, could be relied upon to react to and circumvent resource constraints. For a recent discussion of the development of resource economics, and the extent to which global environmental constraints differ, see E.B.Barbier, *Economics, Natural-Resource Scarcity, and Development*, Earthscan, London, 1989.

1.2 Nuclear fuels

In the last few decades, perceptions of uranium resource availability for nuclear power have followed a remarkably similar pattern to those concerning oil and gas, but to an even greater extent. In the early 1960s, proven uranium reserves were barely adequate to meet the demand implied by projections of rapid nuclear expansion even to the end of the century. This was the key argument for the development of fast breeder reactors (FBRs), which use uranium about fifty times more efficiently than conventional thermal reactors (see Chapter 3). By the end of the 1980s, uranium discoveries combined with stagnation of nuclear power development had created an excess which, from the point of view of FBR proponents, was embarrassing.

Uranium deposits are widely distributed. In addition to reserves which might be exploited for their own sake, considerable amounts are sometimes recoverable as a by-product of other mineral extraction, notably of gold, phosphates, and copper. Unlike fossil fuels, reserves are generally classified explicitly in terms of the price of extraction, which are closely related to the concentration.[12] Proven resources below $130/kgU and outside the former Centrally Planned Economies (CPEs) amount to around 2.4MtU, with at least as much again estimated but not proven. This compares with annual production in the late 1980s of under 40,000 tonnes. Magnitudes appear similar in the former CPEs.[13] Reserves below $130/kgU thus appear sufficient to meet current demand for over 100 years, and exploration has more or less ceased. Greatly expanded use of nuclear power could exhaust currently identified reserves in a few decades, but new sources are likely to be found if there is pressure on resources. Better extraction technologies could also reduce costs, though equally, raised environmental standards might drive them up.

The rationale for FBRs, originally one of necessity given limits on feasible uranium resources, had already by the 1980s turned into one of long-term economics; the price of uranium would rise as cheap resources

[12] Uranium statistics now commonly cite 'reasonably assured resources' (RAR) at below $130/kgU - a level which would have little impact on the overall costs of thermal nuclear power -as 'known resources'. Separate estimates of RAR below $80/kgU are often given. Technical advances combined with stagnation in nuclear capacity led to the 'spot' traded price declining steadily during the 1980s, to barely $25/kgU.
[13] All figures, WEC, *1989 Survey of Energy Resources*, op.cit.

were exhausted to the point where the much higher efficiency (in uranium terms) of the FBR would make it economic despite the greater difficulty and cost of the technology. This in turn now looks a dubious argument. *If* conventional nuclear power revives on a large scale, *if* new cheap uranium reserves are not found and improved techniques do not make extraction much cheaper, and *if* the problems and fears of the plutonium economy can be overcome, FBRs could emerge as cheaper than thermal reactors; but given these qualifications, and the scale of potential problems associated with FBRs, this hardly seems likely.[14]

Nuclear resources of a different order would be tapped by fusion power. Rather than seeking to split uranium, fusion could in principle be fuelled by the deuterium isotope of hydrogen. Water would become an energy source: the theoretical resource amounts to perhaps fifty billion years of current global energy consumption.[15] The deuterium-tritium fusion reaction, which occurs at lower temperatures and thus may be easier to exploit, requires lithium as a fuel to produce the tritium; this might limit the resource to 2,000 years of current global energy consumption. However, seduced by such numbers, the resources poured into the international research effort have tended to downplay questions of economic feasibility and environmental impact, which as discussed in Chapter 3, place the real constraints on fusion. Hopes for 'cold fusion' as a power source appear to have evaporated.[16]

1.3 Renewable energy resources

Figure 1.4 illustrates global renewable energy flows.[17] The figures may be compared with global energy consumption, including non-commercial sources, of around 10,000Mtoe/yr (about 450EJ/yr,

[14] An extensive review of the issues in Fast Breeder Reactor development, including submissions from a wide range of viewpoints, is given in the report by the House of Commons Select Committee on Energy, *The Fast Breeder Reactor, Energy Committee's Fifth Report*, HMSO, 1990. The Committee recommended against continuing fast reactor development. See discussion in Chapter 3, section 3.2.
[15] J.T.McMullan, R.Morgan, R.B.Murray, *Energy Resources*, Edward Arnold, London, 1983.
[16] F.Close, 'Cold fusion I: the discovery that never was', and J.Bockris, 'Cold fusion II: the story continues', both in *New Scientist*, 19 January 1991, give differing views on the 'cold fusion' saga. Neither argues that it is likely to provide a viable large-scale power source.
[17] B.Sorenson, *Renewable Energy*, Academic Press, 1979, gives a detailed technical analysis of renewable energy flows.

Figure 1.4 Global renewable energy flows (TW)

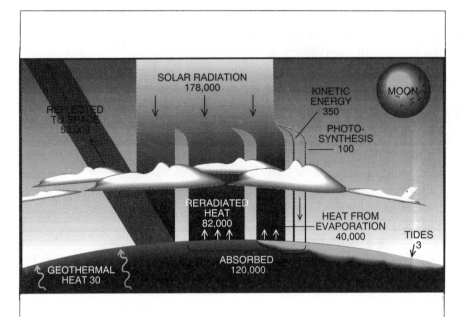

Source: Ged R.Davis, 'Energy for Planet Earth', *Scientific American*,
September 1990.

equal to an average power of over 14TW). The rate of solar input is over
12,000 times current human demands. Of this, 30% is immediately
reflected and nearly half is converted directly to heat and re-radiated as
infra-red radiation. The great majority of the rest is taken up in the
hydrological cycle, and the tiny fraction of this which falls as rain or
snow over high ground and can be captured in running off forms the
hydro resource, which is equivalent to over 20% of current global energy
use.[18] The atmospheric heat gradients drive the winds, which dissipate
13,000EJ/yr; about one per cent of this is converted into waves. Finally,
some 3,500EJ/yr - perhaps eight times global energy consumption - is

[18] The World Energy Council 1989 survey estimates a gross theoretical capability of
over 25,000TWh/yr (90EJ output), of which about 10,000TWh/yr (36EJ output, or
100EJ of fossil input equivalent) is estimated as 'exploitable capability' given current
costs and conditions, WEC, op.cit.

absorbed in photosynthesis every year.[19] To this list, in principle, should be added the large ocean resources arising from heat gradients and ocean streams, the osmotic resource arising from the differing salt content of river and sea water, and the vapour pressure resources from the heating of desert air.

The solar input represents the physical limit to the energy available from solar-derived renewables. This is not the case for tidal and geothermal energy.[20] Tidal energy schemes work by increasing the dissipation of tidal energy at shorelines, so the natural rate of dissipation (the number in Figure 1.4) does not represent the theoretical limit. Geothermal energy similarly does not rely on the continuous natural heat flow, but generally extracts, at a rate much faster than natural replacements, heat which has accumulated over centuries in water (aquifers) or hot rocks as a result of tidal friction and natural radioactive decay. Consequently geothermal energy is not a renewable source, although it is usually included as such. It is most easily exploited from aquifers, but this resource is probably fairly small.[21] Pressurized brines, at greater depth, present a largely unknown resource. The theoretical resource from tapping hot rocks or even magmas is immense (the heat energy contained in the top few kilometres of rock worldwide is many times larger even than world uranium resources exploited with breeder reactors) but only a very small portion of this could conceivably be tapped. For these sources, the technical and resource characteristics are too uncertain to allow more meaningful estimates.

It is clear that, globally, renewable and geothermal energy resources are more than adequate to meet any conceivable human needs. The extent to which these resources can be tapped, in an environmentally acceptable

---

[19] Some sources give different figures. This figure, and that of Figure 1.4, reflect estimates from detailed primary research (eg. R.H.Windacker and G.Lykens, 'Primary Productivity of the Biosphere', in H.Leith and R.H.Widd, *The Biosphere and Man*, Springer-Verland, New York, 1975; D.O.Hall, private communication).

[20] In theory, some solar-derived resources can also be extracted at greater than the natural rate of dissipation, but this is not relevant in practice.

[21] Few areas have been surveyed for aquifer resources unless water breaches the surface in hot springs. The *World Energy Survey* of the 1978 World Energy Conference estimated a resource to 3km depth of over 1,000GW operating for 100 years.The 1989 survey stated '.. 10GW represents an ambitious but realistic target' (yielding about 0.1% of global energy). The economics would vary very widely, as would efficiency, with temperature and assumed maximum depth of exploitation.

manner without excessive costs, is one of the great unknowns in energy projections. In practice, attempts to estimate the exploitable resources are scattered, and do not form part of mainstream energy literature. The authors of the country case studies presented later in this book were invited to make particular effort to find information on these questions, with mixed success. Chapter 3 of this volume summarizes some of the relevant technologies, and Volume 1, section 5.6, summarizes some possible implications if various renewable technologies were to be successfully applied. More specific resource issues are usefully framed in terms of the three main types of renewable sources delineated there.

Activity-dependent renewables are those which depend on the level of human activity. One form is the general wastes from human activity. Table 1.2 lists the estimated energy available from such residues in the US, and costs of collection;[22] the UK and Japanese studies also give some estimates of the potential from wastes. Domestic and industrial wastes such as paper, tyres, plastics, waste food etc. contain energy amounting to a few per cent of demand. If wastes are dumped, some of this is slowly transformed into methane; tapping this forms a simple but very inefficient way of recovering the energy in wastes, with a plausible contribution of 1-2% of electricity in developed economies. Direct combustion of wastes would yield several times as much energy but is more complex both for logistic and environmental reasons - for as long as land-fill sites are easily found. Agricultural wastes are generally easier to exploit and may contribute as much energy. Such wastes, in the form of straw, dung, etc., form the bulk of biomass energy use in many developing countries, but the conversion, generally by burning for heat and light, is very inefficient. The effective exploitation of waste and biomass resources as countries develop depends upon the use of better technologies, some of which are reviewed in Chapter 3.

Direct solar heating of space and water are also activity-dependent, since they are tied directly to narrowly defined end uses. In sunny areas, the solar energy incident upon houses is sufficient to meet a major part of hot water requirements even after all conversion losses, but the potential falls off rapidly in colder regions. Solar space heating using

[22] $1/GJ = $6/boe (barrel oil equivalent) = $44.6/toe. The resource figures compare with US energy demand of about 80EJ; conversion losses, particularly for transport fuels, mean that raw biomass resources cannot substitute for an equivalent amount of fossil energy (see Chapter 3).

Table 1.2 Potential biomass energy supplies in the US

Feedstock	Net raw biomass resources[a] (EJ/yr)	(Mtoe/yr)	Cost ($/GJ) Current	Target
Residues				
Logging residues	0.8	18	>3	<2
Urban wood wastes and land clearing	1.2	27	2	2
Forest manufacturing residues	2.1	47	1	<1
Environmentally-collectible				
Agricultural residues	2.0	45	1-2	1
Municipal solid & industrial food waste	2.4	54	2-3	<1.5
Animal wastes	0.5	11	4	3.5
Subtotal	**8.9**	**200**		
Biomass from existing forest				
Commercial forest wood	4.5	101	<2	<2
Improved forest management	4.5	101	<2	
Shift 25% of wood industry to energy	0.5	11	2	2
Subtotal	**9.5**	**213**		
Biomass from energy crops				
Agricultural oil seed	0.3	7		
Wood energy crops	3.2	72	3	2
Herbaceous energy crops				
Lignocellulosics	5.5	123	4	2
New energy oil seed	0.4	9		
Aquatic energy crops				
Micro-algae	0.3	7		
Macro-algae	1.1	25	3.5	2
Subtotal	**10.8**	**242**		
Total	**29.3**	**657**		

[a] Biomass supplies net of estimated losses in production and handling, before conversion to liquid fuels or electricity.
Source: Table 2.4-3, p.85, in W. Fulkerson et al, *Energy Technology R&D: What Could Make a Difference?*, Vol.2, Part 2, Supply Technology, ORNL-6541, Oak Ridge National Laboratory, Oak Ridge Tennessee, December 1989.

architectural features is more important in colder climates because of the longer heating season, but the contribution is generally limited to a modest fraction of space heating requirements, depending partly on the insulation levels. The seasonal mismatch in most areas means that inter-seasonal storage would be required for the solar heating contribution to rise much above one or two per cent of global energy demand.

Fundamental constraints appear to limit the feasible contribution from 'activity-dependent' renewables to 5-15% of total energy demand in most developed economies. The use of these resources is also particularly closely tied to other societal issues such as waste management, town and building planning and practice, and the nature and organization of agriculture.

Concentrated renewables, in which natural processes lead to a convenient concentration of resources, in many respects lie at the opposite end of the spectrum. Examples include hydro, tidal, and geothermal energy. The global resources have been discussed above, and they tend to be the most unevenly distributed of the renewables. Hydro energy is concentrated in and around mountain regions. Tidal estuary energy depends upon the combination of local and regional coastal topography.[23] Deposits of water which are large enough and hot enough to exploit as geothermal aquifers occur in various locations. Where these coincide with cities, the water can be used directly for heating (as in Paris), but most of the potential is seen to lie in deposits hot enough to generate electricity. Hot dry rock energy is similarly seen primarily as an electricity source because of limits on direct heat transport. Granite rocks and some special anomalies provide a better than average resource, but by far the greatest economic potential lies in geologically active regions, especially volcanic areas.

The contributions available from such concentrated renewables vary widely, from being quite negligible in many flat or dry, geologically stable inland countries, to being capabable of supplying a large part of national electricity demand. In global terms, hydro can (and does) make a important contribution, but barring fundamental breakthroughs, the

---

[23] Suggestions have been made for tapping ocean streams, including tidal streams, and for exploiting tidal motion away from estuaries. These would be exploiting new and very large resources, but research has not advanced much beyond the stage of general concept.

global contribution of concentrated renewables will clearly be limited, to perhaps not much more than activity-dependent renewables.

In general, such concentrated renewables have the most in common with fossil energy resources, with potentially large-scale systems required for exploiting the energy and transporting it from source to application. Debates in the UK over proposals for the Severn Tidal Barrage, and suggestions of importing Icelandic geothermal and hydro electricity (see UK/EC Chapter), may be indicative of future debates over this kind of resource.

Diffuse renewables comprise the third category. These encompass the primary solar resource and its many derivatives, such as biomass, wind, waves, ocean thermal gradients, and assorted other forms. These have the least in common with conventional energy deposits, and their nature poses special difficulties for exploitation and assessment. The two ocean-based derivatives could in principle make large contributions in countries near suitable ocean regions, but this would be small in global terms and engineering difficulties seem likely greatly to limit even this. From a global perspective, the key diffuse renewables are thus biomass, wind, and above all the conversion of direct solar energy to more flexible forms - either electricity, or hydrogen, which is a flexible and in many respects an environmentally ideal fuel, as it produces only water when burnt.[24]

Feasible contributions would depend on conversion efficiencies and acceptable siting densities. The discussion in Volume 1 (especially Figure 5.4) suggests that the contribution from biomass and wind could range from being marginal to making a large contribution, depending on a variety of conditions. For sparsely populated countries such as the USSR and US, wind resources comfortably exceed plausible electricity demand,[25] and in principle there could be spare for substantial exports (see also the country chapters). Biomass resources, including dedicated energy crops, are of a similar order. Table 1.2 shows estimates of the biomass potential from existing forests and potential energy crops in the US; together with residues, the raw resource is about 30% of US primary

---

[24] A recent overview of studies on the 'hydrogen economy' is given in D.Fisher, *Options for Reducing Greenhouse Gas Emissions*, Stockholm Environment Institute, 1990 (Chapter 4c).
[25] See for example the US and Soviet chapters, and C.J.Weinberg and R.H.Williams et al, 'Energy from the Sun', *Scientific American*, September 1990.

energy demand (itself twice the average per-capita energy demand of many other OECD countries). There are many complexities and debates surrounding the use of such resources on this scale, and depending on assumptions the exploitable resource can vary considerably as compared with such central estimates. For more densely populated countries, wind and biomass resources could be important, especially in relation to electricity supplies, but they rarely approach the scale of projected total energy demand. The UK and Japanese case studies consider how these resources combined with other renewables might relate to total demand in these more densely populated countries.

Generation from direct solar power using thermal cycles could also make large contributions in some locations, but the need for direct sunlight and the much lower efficiency of the conversion process limits the apparent resource advantage of direct solar power over wind and biomass for this technology. The real potential of the raw solar resource can only be tapped by technologies for tapping diffuse solar radiation with a conversion efficiency well above the one or two per cent of complete biomass systems. The primary option is photovoltaics (PV) - solar cells. This and various other renewable technologies are discussed in Chapter 3; PV appears 'promising but uncertain' - developing rapidly, but with major improvements still required for bulk supplies. Even if these and more are achieved, the siting constraints on PV may be stronger than for wind or biomass, and the lack of any heat-based stage means that, unlike some solar thermal systems, PV output necessarily follows slavishly the strength of the incident radiation and its diurnal and seasonal cycles. For very large contributions, therefore, another stage of conversion to a storable form, incurring further costs and losses, would be required (see section 1.5 below).

This brief review of renewable energy resources and the principal technical constraints on their deployment reveals a complex picture. The cascade of natural conversion in the global energy system gives many and varying opportunities for exploiting renewable resources, suited to different human uses and circumstances. Moving up the cascade towards the primary resources increases the theoretical energy available, but also increases the extent to which the characteristics, technological requirements and constraints differ fundamentally from those of conventional energy sources, and this poses considerable and varied challenges. In combination, the different renewables form a large resource with a useful geographical spread, but the extent to which they can be exploited depends not only upon the resources and conversion technologies; these and other options will depend equally upon the ability of energy systems to overcome mismatches in both space and time.

1.4 Energy systems: transport issues

Many aspects of responses to the greenhouse effect will depend upon such system issues. Geographical mismatches demand transport infrastructure (and can imply heavy dependence on key regions, considered in Volume 1); temporal mismatches demand storage or other ways of managing system dynamics. Biomass, being both ubiquitous and fairly easily stored, may be the least dependent upon these aspects, and the much more readily exploited coal resources come a close second. Many countries can rely predominantly on domestic coal reserves, and international coal trade is a small, but growing, fraction of global consumption. Coal transport is not easy, primarily because of the bulk which need to be handled and transferred, but once loaded on to trains and ships, transport does not involve great costs or losses even over large distances, and as infrastructure develops, the vast surface reserves of coal are becoming more accessible. Oil is of course very unevenly distributed, but it is by far the easiest fuel to transport and store. Widespread use of any other energy resources cannot easily be divorced from system considerations.

Transport of natural gas through pipelines is technically straightforward, but large (and hence expensive) pipes are required, and significant energy can be used in pumping gas large distances. The Soviet case study reports that the gas industry, the 'star performer' of the Soviet economy since the late 1970s, will itself consume an estimated 12% of the increased natural gas production up to the end of the century, simply on pumping the output west. There are no simple answers to questions about transport costs, which vary with pipe size, climatic and terrain conditions. However, gas developments have consumed a large share of Soviet energy investments which by 1988 accounted for a startling 24% of all centralized investment, and Wood-Collins[26] estimates that major

---

[26] John Wood-Collins, 'An Overview of Europe's Gas Supply Options', *Special Supplement to Gas Matters*, February 1989; cited in Jonathan P. Stern, *European Gas Markets: Challenge and Opportunity in the 1990s*, RIIA/Dartmouth, Aldershot, 1990, p.68.

supply expansions to European gas markets would require an assured delivered price above $25 per barrel oil equivalent (substantially above world fossil fuel prices in the late 1980s). This reflects in large measure the costs of transport infrastructure over the two to five thousand kilometres from the cheaply exploited reserves of the USSR, Middle East and Africa to West Europe.

In addition, with many pumps, joints and valves, long distance transport involves a potential for leakage which poses safety problems and, along with the energy losses, adds to the radiative and other impacts of gas (see Appendix 2).

But the difficulties of pipeline transport are not just those of engineering, environmental impact, and costs. Stern notes of possible new pipelines to Europe that:[27]

> Although challenging, these [physical] aspects are dwarfed by the political and security problems of pipelines crossing many countries. Generally speaking, political uncertainties multiply exponentially with the number of borders crossed. Gas exports from Africa and the Middle East would need to flow from and through regions of exceptional political turbulence. All pipelines would need to cross at least three borders before reaching central Europe and the potential for political problems between any two Middle Eastern or African countries would be considerable. Nor should political difficulties between European countries be entirely ignored.

Similar remarks may apply to the immense Soviet reserves if the Union does disintegrate to a significant degree. If there were pipelines to southern Asia, for example from Soviet or Iranian resources, these could face equal uncertainties.

The political drawbacks could be greatly reduced by using liquified natural gas (LNG) from a diversity of sources, shipped much like oil. It is a commercial technology: nearly a quarter of international gas trade in 1989 was by LNG, most to Japan from Indonesia, but with significant movements also from Africa to Europe. The drawbacks are those of costs, losses, and safety. Liquefaction can require 10-20% of the energy in the gas and this, combined with other losses, may substantially offset the greenhouse benefits arising from lower carbon content of gas compared with oil, irrespective of methane leakages (see Appendix 2). Also, LNG terminals form a major potential industrial safety hazard (though the

[27] Jonathan P.Stern, *European Gas Markets*, op.cit, p.60

record has been relatively good to date), and the prospects for LNG could look very different if there were a major disaster.

Many similar issues could apply to any serious development of the environmentally most benign fuel, hydrogen. Hydrogen can probably be transported through natural gas pipelines, at two-thirds the overall rate of energy throughput, if valves and pumps are replaced to make seals adequate to contain the much smaller hydrogen molecules.[28] How many redundant gas pipelines would be available near areas suitable for producing hydrogen from non-fossil electricity sources (such as desert areas using PV) must be open to question, as would the management of the switch over; but some hydrogen can be mixed in with natural gas, and new pipelines might share some existing rights of way. Gas pipelines from some offshore areas might also be suitable for carrying hydrogen from other sources as the gas resources deplete: offshore wind, wave energy, and sea-based nuclear reactors have all been suggested. Other means of transporting hydrogen would presumably be required in other cases.

None of this should be taken as suggesting that long-distance gas transport faces insuperable difficulties. To date the political difficulties experienced with gas pipelines have been trivial compared with those of wholesale dependence on Middle Eastern oil, for example. But transport is not a negligible issue, and consideration of resources cannot be divorced from such system considerations.

The fastest-growing form of international energy trade is electricity. Overhead lines are much cheaper to build than major pipelines. Power is traded regularly among utilities in Europe and in the US, and small amounts are already transferred over several thousand kilometres across both the North American and Soviet systems. Most of the transfers are across direct alternating current (AC) connections linking neighbouring utilities, which have developed as much for reasons of overall system

---

[28] C.Carlson, 'An assessment of the potential future market in Sweden for hydrogen as an energy carrier', *International Journal of Hydrogen Energy*, Vol.7, No.10, pp.821-29. The lower energy density of hydrogen (as compared with natural gas) is partly offset by its lower viscosity. For recent discussions of hydrogen transport engineering and economics see J.M.Ogden and R.H.Williams, *Solar Hydrogen*, World Resources Institute, Washington, 1989, and Chapter 4c in D. Fisher, ed, *Options for Reducing Greenhouse Gas Emissions*, op.cit. The latter source states that significant problems may arise from reactions between hydrogen and the material usually used in gas pipes.

management (with transfers in either direction according to generating and demand conditions) as for actual bulk trade. AC connections require the operation of the connected systems to be synchronized; in effect, the two sides become one system. This and related factors, including the higher losses associated with AC transmission, limit the practical extent of long-distance AC trade. By converting the AC to direct current, these and other problems can be overcome. The cost of AC/DC power conversion has declined with developments in power electronics, and DC links are steadily expanding; examples include the 2,000MW undersea link from France to the UK completed in 1986. Undersea cables are expensive, but DC overhead lines are no more expensive than AC.

However, unlike most forms of fossil energy transport, the losses for a given power and line characteristic increase at least in proportion to distance, and reducing the line losses increases the costs per unit length. The penalties of distance thus increase much faster than with fossil energy transport.[29] Large transfers over a thousand kilometres involve considerable costs and losses, and over more than a few thousand kilometres appear most unpromising. Some hopes have been expressed that superconducting technologies might create a breakthrough, but as discussed in Chapter 2 this appears improbable.

Engineering economics aside, other factors would limit the enthusiasm of most countries for heavy dependence on electricity imports. If a high percentage of power came through any one channel (or indeed from any one source), the stability of the system would be jeopardised if that input collapsed. Large lines, crossing several borders, would be subject to the same kind of political risks as discussed above for pipelines. Given the immense strategic importance of electricity and the inability to stockpile it, the political sensitivities involved may be even greater than for fossil fuel imports. The option to import fossil fuels with which to generate domestically is likely to ensure that electricity in most countries retains a strong domestic generating component.

All these factors limit the economic and political feasibility of extensive dependence on electricity from large external centres of non-fossil power, be they nuclear 'islands' or massive geothermal or

---

[29] A 'rule of thumb' sometimes adopted for comparing long distance gas and electricity transport (eg. for studies of possible hydrogen schemes) is that electrical losses are twice those of gas pumping, and electricity is twice as valuable, because of the conversion losses (R.H.Williams, private communication).

desert-based PV schemes, though all might feature to some degree. However, a greater obstacle to major inputs from sources such as wind and PV is generally held to be another characteristic: their variability, combined with the difficulty of storage.

1.5 Electricity system dynamics and the role of variable power sources

Renewable sources of electricity, such as wind, solar, wave and tidal energy, differ from most conventional power sources in being 'variable': their output follows the fluctuations of the natural cycles. This appears to be a serious drawback, and it is widely assumed that storage would be required to make much use of such sources.

Many systems already have some electricity storage, in the form of systems for pumping water into high reservoirs, from which it flows down through generators (these are sometimes associated with existing hydro schemes). These have generally been constructed for two purposes: for system regulation, using the unique capabilities of hydro generation for responding very rapidly to changes in the system; and to help meet peak loads, and so avoid the costs of building and operating dedicated peaking plants. However, the costs of dedicated storage are relatively high, with capital costs in the region $500-$1,500/kW, and 20-25% of the energy is lost in the conversion processes.[30] Attaining a high storage capacity and efficiency often requires a high head, which can make pumped storage schemes environmentally sensitive, though there have been proposals for schemes which rely on underground caverns for the lower reservoir, reducing this objection. Other options for storage might include large batteries and super-conducting magnets, but neither appears promising as a more economic approach to large-scale electricity storage for power systems.

Consequently, if storage really were a central requirement in backing up variable power sources, this would be a serious penalty; for sources which may anyway struggle to be competitive, it would be the coup de grace. However, the difficulty of utilizing variable sources, and the need

---

[30] A review of hydro and other storage technologies is given in D.Fisher, *Options for Reducing Greenhouse Gas Emissions*, op.cit.

for storage, tends to have been greatly overplayed when variable sources feed into large power systems.[31]

On small systems, variability can certainly pose major difficulties. The output from just a few wind turbines clustered on one site, for example, may generate a substantial fraction of the total power. The output may be very variable, sometimes fluctuating widely within a few minutes. The rest of the system, which might well amount to a few diesel stations, has to alter its output rapidly to follow the changes, with individual units repeatedly shut down and restarted, which can waste a great deal of fuel and increase maintenance requirements. Careful control strategies may be required to prevent system collapse. Integration of variable sources such as wind and wave on small diesel systems can consequently pose severe problems. The high cost of alternate supplies may well justify such projects, and continuing research is leading to major improvements, but the operational losses on such systems can still be substantial.

But the global consumption of fossil fuels for power generation is dominated by large power systems, on which the problems of integrating variable sources are trivial in comparison. If variable sources account for only a small part of the installed capacity - a 'small system penetration' - fluctuations are lost among the variations in the demand for electricity. Large systems have a greater capacity for absorbing variations, and most have hydroelectric units or gas turbines that can respond quickly as conditions change in the network. Significant renewable capacities would involve many different units, spread out over many sites, which tends to smooth out the variations: relative swings in the power are reduced, predictability increased, and the overall distribution becomes much more favourable with far fewer occasions of near zero or peak output.

There still could be occasions without power from variable sources, so that some 'backup' is still required if the capacity of variable sources rises much above the level of general statistical fluctuations in peak

[31] This discussion is drawn from a broader study of the issues involved in integrating renewable electricity sources on power systems, including the possible role of 'limited energy plants' and the issues on smaller systems, in M.J.Grubb, 'The Integration of Renewable Electricity Sources on Power Systems', *Energy Policy*, June 1991. A technical analysis is given in M.J.Grubb, 'The Value of Variable Sources on Power Systems', *IEE Proceedings C*, Institution of Electrical Engineers, London, February 1991; for a more popular exposition see 'The Wind of Change', *New Scientist*, 17 March 1988.

demand and the availability of conventional power stations.[32] Yet this backup need not be provided by storage. Technologies such as gas turbines are cheaper to build. Connections with other power systems can also prove a source of peak reserve; one of the major reasons for many existing interconnections. Furthermore, if improvements in end-use efficiency do stabilize or even reduce electricity demand in developed economies, systems may have redundant capacity which can usefully serve as backup. Hydro power stations and biomass electricity systems may also provide opportunities for cheap backup, because although it may be costly to increase the total energy available, the incremental cost of adding generating capacity alone may be low. The key questions therefore do not concern backup options considered in isolation, but rather the overall capital and fuel costs and savings taking into account the need for adequate security of system operation. Extensive use of variable sources increases the value of storage, and vice versa, but storage is in no sense a central element.

These issues have been examined extensively elsewhere.[33] Based primarily on modelling studies of wind and tidal energy on the UK electricity system, it was concluded that:

* The energy from variable sources is usually as valuable as that from equivalent conventional stations, in terms of both fuel and capacity savings, when they form a small fraction (up to 5-10%) of the total generating capacity.

* It seems highly unlikely that the use of variable sources on large power systems will ever be seriously inhibited by bulk system limitations. In many cases, contributions of perhaps 20% of the demand could be obtained from one type of variable source with only a modest reduction in the value of the energy, and contributions of 40-50% of demand would seem to be feasible before the penalties become necessarily intolerable, even neglecting storage and possible

---

[32] In practice, the capacity of a variable source typically has to rise to around 5% of the installed capacity of thermal stations before the statistics of its variation become significantly different from those of conventional power stations - which can also fail. Variable sources therefore can serve to displace some conventional capacity without loss of reliability.

[33] A detailed comparison of wind energy modelling studies is given in M.J.Grubb, 'The Economic Value of Wind Energy at Higher Power System Penetrations: An Analysis of Models, Sensitivities and Assumptions', *Wind Engineering*, Vol.12, No.1, 1988.

power exchanges with other systems. By using combinations of different variable sources, hydro, storage, and/or trade, there is no technical reason why large systems should not derive well over half of their power from variable sources.

It is uncertain how far the quantitative conclusions apply if the only significant renewable source is PV. Since the output from installations several hundreds of kilometres apart would still be closely correlated, large capacities would involve correspondingly large power swings, with significant power produced for perhaps only a third of the time. The economic limits on PV would depend strongly on the diurnal and seasonal characteristics of demand on the system, and storage with a capacity sufficient to replace much of the lost supply at least across the common evening peak in electricity demand might make a large difference. Even without such storage, however, considerable amounts of fossil fuel could be displaced by PV if systems developed to accommodate it.

The real difficulties come with attempts to construct systems with variable supplies alone (eg. wind-solar-battery). The possibility of long periods without adequate input from the variable sources means that very large and expensive storage capacities are required if reliability is to be maintained; except for small-scale remote supplies, such systems appear completely impractical. However, with widespread availability of natural gas, and growing interest in gasification of biomass fuels for power generation (Chapter 3) many power systems may in any case develop a substantial resource of plant with low greenhouse gas emissions, and low capital but moderate to high fuel costs. These are exactly the characteristics required for low-cost 'backup' of variable power sources. To put it another way, if the system has much plant which is cheap to build but expensive to run, variable sources are very valuable just as fuel savers. Their short-term value of reducing coal and oil bills could in principle transform into a long-term role of helping further to limit emissions and extend gas and/or limited biomass applications. The variability of renewable electricity sources is often cited as a major obstacle, but in reality it seems likely to be one of the least significant constraints when such sources are integrated on large power systems.

1.6 Conclusions

Global economic development faces many challenges but an overall shortage of energy resources is not one of them. All the fossil resources can last several decades at expanding rates of use, and coal - and probably gas and oil if unconventional sources are exploited, at additional cost - could meet growing consumption throughout the 21st century. Nuclear resources appear equally unconstrained, and the renewable resources in combination are large enough to meet likely global demand indefinitely. Various constraints on energy systems, as well as the availability of economically competitive technologies, limit the extent to which these simple resource figures can be translated into exploitable reserves. None of the system constraints are such as to rule any source out, but in general the economic, environmental, and political costs of relying on a given source in a given region grow rapidly as the distance and/or scale of dependence increases. The nature of some of these constraints have been examined in this chapter as general background to the question of altering energy systems. Overall, such constraints place a premium on maintaining diversity of supplies, and on the use of local or regional resources.

With current technologies, for many countries there is a tension between these objectives and those of limiting greenhouse gas emissions, since coal is the most widespread of fossil resources and oil the most easily transported and stored. Electricity system constraints may also limit the ability to exploit some distant or highly variable sources of non-fossil power, though the main obstacles at present are more basic issues of economic viability. Chapter 3 examines energy supply and conversion technologies, including the options which might ease these tensions. Limiting energy demand by improving the efficiency of energy use, however, eases both environmental and systemic pressures, and the technical options for improving end-use efficiency are examined first.

Technologies for Efficient Energy Use

Many general technologies exist for improving the efficiency with which energy is used. Heating requirements can be reduced by better controls, vacuum and other insulating panels, and advanced window technologies, whilst heat can be supplied more efficiently by using condensing boilers and heat pumps, and by tapping spare heat especially from modern small-scale power plant. Advances in electric motor drives and optimisation of pumping systems can yield large savings, especially by using integrated adjustable speed drives for applications with varying loads. Superconductors are unlikely to yield significant energy savings, but broad applications of modern electronics in sensors and control systems for industry, building energy management, and metering technologies can optimise energy use. Improved industrial processes include membrane separation, electrothermal techniques, and new catalyst applications, whilst new material technologies offer savings in both production and applications.

The potential impact appears particularly large in buildings, which account for about half of OECD CO_2 emissions. In most OECD countries, heating demand in new buildings can be more than halved from recent averages using measures which pay back in a few years. Simple roof and water system insulation and draught-proofing can improve existing buildings, but the costs of more extensive retrofitting varies widely and can be high. Better motors, insulation and design can more than halve consumption in most electrical appliances, while for lighting, new technologies and better design and control can achieve still larger gains. Such improvements can also pay back in a few years.

There are many options for further improving vehicle efficiency, and cars with half the current average fuel use can be produced for little extra cost, but trade-offs against various aspects of vehicle performance mean that estimates of the market potential vary widely. However, improvements in new cars of around 20% over the next decade, and possibly a doubling of efficiency in the long term, seem plausible. Obtaining larger reductions would require a move towards other fuels, with the most promising candidate for obtaining large CO_2 reductions being electric cars powered by hydrogen fuel cells. The diversity of industrial activities makes potential improvement difficult to assess, but most industrial processes are as yet far from theoretical efficiency limits.

These assessments relate to developed market economies. In the former centrally-planned economies the technical potential for improved energy efficiency is larger, but in these and developing countries the options are constrained by capital shortages and other factors. In many developing countries improved stoves are important in reducing pressures on forests and other biomass.

The rate of efficiency improvement is constrained by stock turnover, but few electrical applications, vehicles or building heating systems, last longer than 20 years. Overall, identified and cost-effective technologies in the OECD countries could in principle increase the efficiency of electricity use by up to 50%, and other applications by 15-40%, over the next two decades. Even after such improvements, energy use would still be at least ten times the thermodynamic minimum required for the services delivered, suggesting that efficiency could continue to increase throughout the next century.

Some of the technical options will be taken up anyway by market responses. Others cannot be realised because of hidden costs in achieving them, or the impact of consumer preferences. The rest can in principle be tapped but only if market conditions alter. The critical uncertainties concern how much of the potential can be tapped by policy changes.

Improved energy efficiency is the one option which simultaneously helps to reduce almost all the problems associated with energy provision: energy security, balance of payments, visual impact and land use, and more general impacts at the local, regional and global level. The extent of efficiency improvements after the oil price shocks surprised many analysts, and has helped to increase appreciation of the potential importance of efficiency, though it is certainly not a new discovery.[1] This chapter attempts to give a broad overview of the principal options for improving efficiency, and the impact which they might have given various constraints, focusing on the efficiency of 'final' energy use, or the 'end-use' efficiency. 'Final' is something of a misnomer, because physically the energy usually undergoes several further transformations before being dissipated as heat, but it is final in the sense of commercial transactions and energy industry statistics. Because of this such end-use efficiency has generally received less attention than supply issues, which are covered in the next chapter. However, concern about the economic and environmental consequences of excessive energy consumption has led to a gathering interest and steadily growing literature concerning the options and potential impact.

The literature includes several voluminous surveys. Comprehensive listings of technologies and suppliers, though focused mainly on the US, are given in the Lovins/RMI Competitek reports.[2] The Energy Technology Support Unit (ETSU) in the UK conducted an extensive review covering both supply and demand side technologies.[3] Giovannini and Pain provide a broad review of the literature and comparison of different sectors and technologies across different

---

[1] Many of the themes currently discussed were already identified by the mid-1970s. Authors such as Lovins (A.B.Lovins, *Soft Energy Paths*, Penguin, Harmondsworth, 1977) and Chapman (P.Chapman, *Fuel's Paradise*, Penguin, Harmondsworth, 1975) laid great stress on minimising energy consumption through both technical and social adjustments; and energy conservation became an acknowledged field of energy studies following the oil price shocks, as indicated for example by papers in the *Annual Review of Energy*, Annual Reviews Inc, Vol.1, 1976.

[2] For example A.B.Lovins, *The State of the Art: Drive Power*, Competitek, Rocky Mountain Institute, Colorado, 1989.

[3] UK Department of Energy, *Background Papers Relevant to the 1986 Appraisal of UK Energy Research, Development and Demonstration*, ETSU-R-43, HMSO, London, 1987.

countries, and derive implied 'optimal' efficiency targets.[4] Studies by the IEA provide a useful review of national programmes and earlier work, including some policy issues.[5]

Most of these, and many other studies, are primarily reviews of efficiency data on available or proposed technologies, and sometimes cost and other performance issues. A major programme to assess energy technology R&D needs included volumes both on end-use technologies and on cross-cutting technologies.[6] The physical, engineering, economic and marketing issues underlying electricity technologies were extensively analysed for a congress sponsored by the Vattenfall utility in Sweden.[7] Various studies have attempted to bring the apparent technology potentials together to assess the possible implications for energy demand in particular sectors and/or countries,[8] the most comprehensive international analysis being that of the End Use Global Energy Project which resulted in the *Energy for a Sustainable World* reports[9] reviewed briefly in Volume 1, section 7.1.

Whilst sectoral estimates of energy demand by fuel are readily available, aggregated data on current end uses are incomplete. Estimates of the distribution of final energy demand in the OECD in 1986 are illustrated in Figure 2.1. Heating accounted for well over half, and transport for nearly another third, of final demand. Electricity in all accounted for around 15% of final demand (the largest components being electric drives and lighting), but because of the conversion losses, this

[4] B.Giovannini and D.Pain, *Scientific and Technical Arguments for the Optimal Use of Energy*, Centre Universitaire d'Etude des Problèmes de l'Energie (CUEPE), Université de Genève; Update 2.2, April 1990.

[5] International Energy Agency, *Technologies for Energy Efficiency and Fuel Switching* (various national reports), IEA/OECD, Paris, 1988.

[6] W.Fulkerson et al, *Energy Technology R&D: What Could Make a Difference?*, ORNL-6541, Oak Ridge National Laboratory, Oak Ridge, Tennessee, December 1989.

[7] T.B.Johansson, B.Bodlund, R.H.Williams (eds), *Electricity: Efficient End-Use and New Generation Technologies, and Their Planning Implications*, Lund University Press, Lund, Sweden, 1989.

[8] A extensive collection and summary of various sectorial studies is given by the IEA in IEA, *Energy Conservation in IEA Countries*, IEA/OECD, 1987. This does however omit some of the most radical and optimistic assessments, notably those of Lovins (see ref.2) and Olivier (D.Olivier and H.Miall, *Energy Efficient Futures: Opening the Solar Option*, Earth Resources Research Ltd, London, 1983).

[9] J.Goldemberg, T.B.Johansson, A.K.N.Reddy, R.H.Williams, *Energy for a Sustainable World*: summary report, World Resources Institute, Washington DC, 1987; book, Wiley/Eastern, New Delhi, 1987.

Figure 2.1 Final OECD energy use 1986

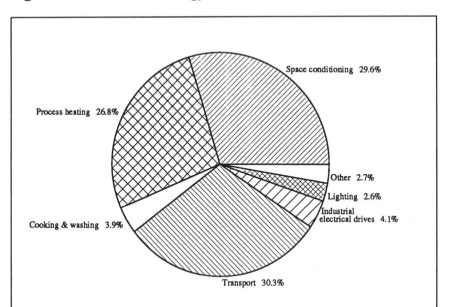

Note: Because of conversion losses, the importance of electricity in terms of primary energy and carbon emissions is about twice that indicated in the chart. Electricity supplies all electric drives, lighting and 'other', about 10% of space conditioning and process heating, and 60% of cooking and washing.

Source: N.Nakicenovic, IIASA, Laxenburg, Austria, private communication.

equated to nearly a third of primary inputs. As discussed in Volume 1, section 6.1, transport and electricity production each account for about a third of OECD carbon emissions, and both are growing relative to other applications; heating is less carbon intensive.

Structuring a review of efficiency options is complicated by the interrelated nature of many of the technologies and applications. Important technologies appear in many different guises and sectors. Heating is required for space and water, appliances such as washers and cookers, and many industrial applications. Modern electronics finds applications throughout all sectors, including electric motor drives, whose applications in turn range from industrial fans and power tools to electric vehicles and a wide variety of home appliances.

To span these complexities this review falls into three parts. Sections 2.1-2.3 cover the main generic energy technologies surrounding heat supply, electrical applications, and industrial processes. Sections 2.4-2.7 then detail the consequences of these and more specific techniques for end-use applications in different sectors: buildings, transport, and industry, and special applications in non-OECD countries. Finally, sections 2.8-2.9 examine the broader issues and implications: the context and possible impact of such technological opportunities, and the long-term limits on efficiency improvements.

2.1 Generic technologies for heat supply and demand

Perhaps the most ubiquitous energy use is that of 'low-grade' (low temperature) heating, which spans applications ranging from the space heating of buildings to the hot water requirements of showers, clothes and dish washers, etc. The most common means of supplying heat is to use fuels or electricity directly. Direct electric heating is inefficient because of the losses in generation; using fuels directly often requires about a third as much energy overall, especially if modern efficient boiler systems are used. Where piped natural gas is available, this offers a convenient source, and modern developments have also greatly improved the attractiveness of traditionally cumbersome and rather inefficient coal stoves.

Using spare heat

Probably the greatest opportunities for improving the efficiency of heat supply is simply to use heat which is already available. Designing buildings to capture maximum sunlight is one option, of particular interest in high latitude areas where overheating is rarely a problem and long winters can better offset the added costs. Also, many industries produce considerable amounts of spare heat, and 'cascading' heat from different processes, all the way down to space heating of industrial buildings, as been an important focus of industrial efforts since 1973, with applications still spreading. Subway and sewage systems also generate heat which is rarely captured. The energy consumed by electrical goods also helps to heat - or overheat - surroundings.[10] But

---

[10] As the efficiency of electrical goods is increased, the free heat gains are reduced. This is generally a secondary but still significant effect. Increasing the efficiency of electrical goods increases space heating requirements, but reduces cooling demands in

undoubtedly the greatest source of waste heat is from electricity generation.

The key technical difficulty facing such *combined heat and power (CHP)* applications has traditionally been that of mismatching scales; the pursuit of scale efficiencies in power generation has led to stations which reject heat sufficient for up to a million homes. Distributing and using such enormous quantities of heat is both complex and costly, with considerable losses. While institutional factors have been of immense importance in determining whether or not heat from smaller stations has been used (Volume 1, section 4.7), the key technical factor which could make widespread use of such waste heat practical is the reversal of the former trend towards large power stations. An increasing appreciation of the diseconomies of over-sized power stations, combined with various technical developments have greatly increased the efficiency and overall attractiveness of much smaller-scale generation, particularly from natural gas (Chapter 3).

Schemes for producing electricity and industrial heat have grown steadily in recent years, and studies in the UK suggest that if a reasonable price can be obtained for the electricity produced, gas-fired internal combustion engines sized to meet the heat demand in many service sector buildings, from hospitals to hotels, would be economically attractive.[11] The potential for energy savings, if this were realized, would be very large indeed;[12] and there is even talk of systems small enough to meet heating demand in households, or at least small blocks of flats, selling spare electricity to the grid. If such systems do meet their potential, and regulatory systems do evolve to accommodate them as discussed in Volume 1, section 6.2, the major portion of building heating loads might be obtained as a by-product of electricity generation (or vice versa). However, it is uncertain how small such applications can really go, and district heating schemes also become more costly as the density

---

hot regions and many commercial buildings where the losses from computers, photocopiers etc already overheat premises during working hours.
[11] R.D.Evans, *Environmental and Economic Implications of Small-Scale CHP*, Energy and Environment Paper No.2, Energy Technology Support Unit, Harwell, Oxon, 1990. The study reports that starting from a theoretical maximum of around 50% of electricity supply, 'a reasonable estimate is that viable CHP potential could be at least 10 per cent of total electricity demand', and that 'at the moment, market penetration of small-scale CHP is limited by non-economic barriers' (p.6).
[12] ibid.

of heating demand declines - as from more efficient buildings, for example.

Smart heat: heat pumps

At the opposite end of the size scale, *heat pumps* offer an important alternative. Although the direct use of electricity is usually inefficient, the laws of thermodynamics which limit the efficiency of producing electricity from fossil fuels via heat also apply in reverse; high grade energy such as electricity can be used to 'pump' heat by evaporating a working fluid in a low temperature 'source' environment, and using higher pressures to condense the vapour at a higher temperature 'sink' where it gives off heat. The heat transfer can exceed the input of high-grade energy by a factor which increases rapidly as the temperature difference falls.

Heat pumps have been widely canvassed as a way of making electricity both economically and environmentally competitive. However, the considerable resources devoted to promoting them have to date yielded less than many hoped, the greatest penetration being in Sweden with 100,000 units installed. The capital costs are considerable, and unlike other heating equipment, they increase rapidly with the maximum load, so heat pumps are best used for applications with fairly constant loads, which may apply to water heating, but rarely for space heating. Since they have much in common with air conditioners (and other refrigeration cycles), heat pumps, often backed up by conventional systems to give adequate heat in cold periods, can be of benefit for heating where cooling is also required (eg. winter cooling, summer air conditioning). Apart from this, one recent detailed assessment[13] gives a somewhat pessimistic outlook for heat pumps for domestic space heating, concluding that they can only be attractive in rather well insulated buildings where electricity is little more expensive than fossil fuels (conditions almost unique to Sweden). However, this review does note various other applications where currently-available heat pump technology could be attractive, and major improvements over existing systems seem plausible. The Oak Ridge review notes that 'the coefficient of performance theoretically could be more than doubled', and focuses upon thermally-activated heat pumps which 'could be fuelled by a variety of fuels or even solar collectors'.[14] A major Japanese

[13] Thore Berntsson, 'Heat Pumps', in T.B.Johansson et al, *Electricity*, op.cit.
[14] Fulkerson et al, *Energy Technology R&D*, Vol.1, op.cit., p.70.

development programme has focused upon advanced heat pumps combined with condensed heat storage, so that problems of both system sizing and timing can be overcome, thus allowing moderately-sized systems to use night-time electricity to meet daytime heating loads. Costs are not yet available, but the reported performance is startling.[15]

Insulating technologies

In principle, maintaining a small temperature difference across a partition - wall, ceiling, fridge casing, etc - need consume very little energy. In practice, conductive losses still account for a large fraction of heat losses. The first steps to improve efficiency are to ensure adequate seals and to minimise conduction through supporting structures, but better insulating materials are a key to reducing heating requirements.

Conventional foams remain one of the best materials for general insulation. Many are blown with CFCs, but replacements of broadly comparable performance have been developed. Better insulation can be obtained simply with thicker layers where feasible, and if wall cavities exist, insulating foams can be injected to reduce heat losses. However, constraints on thickness and weight combined with the need to phase out CFCs have renewed interest in other insulation options. Most approaches to highly insulating narrow panels use a vacuum in some form. *Compact vacuum* insulation relies on laser-welded metal envelopes with internal glass supports to maintain a high vacuum. With *vacuum powder* insulation, a special insulating powder also provides the strength to maintain a moderate vacuum. *Aerogel* is a transparent insulating solid which can likewise maintain an partial vacuum. Such technologies provide better insulation with less thickness. The costs are higher than with conventional foams, but would come down with bulk production, and some forms also provide strength which could be usefully exploited.[16]

---

[15] 'The super heat pump energy-accumulation systems' performance is epoch-making, in that it: double-increases (sic) the efficiency; triples the temperature rise (up to 300 deg.C); and reduces the equipment size by a factor or ten, by using high-density chemical heat storage', Dr Eng. Takao Kashiwagi, 'Present status and future prospects of advanced energy technology for solving global environmental problems', in *Europe-Japan Global Environmental Technology Seminar 1990*, JETRO, Tokyo, 1990, p.48.

[16] For discussion see Fulkerson et al, *Energy Technology R&D*, op.cit., Vol.2, part 1, pp.38-43.

Table 2.1 Insulation performance of different types of window

Window type	Heat loss $(W/m^2/K)$	Status
Single pane	6	Commercial
Double pane	3	Commercial
+ low emittance coating	1.8	Commercial
+ gas filling	1.5	Commercial
Evacuated double pane (silica aerogel spacer)	~0.5	Research

Source: C.G.Granqvist, 'Energy-Efficient Windows: Options with Present and Forthcoming Technology', in T.B.Johansson et al (eds), *Electricity*, op.cit.

Windows usually provide poor insulation compared with their surroundings. As illustrated in Table 2.1, simple double-glazing can halve window losses, while selective coatings and gas filling can halve them again. Evacuating the space between the double panes, and filling it with aerogel spacers (still at the research state) may reduce losses to a tenth of standard single-pane windows, to levels often less than those of the walls around them. The economics of these depend heavily on the application, climate, and area of window involved. As retrofits in domestic dwellings, even double-glazing is often quite a costly step (though it is often undertaken for reasons of comfort, noise insulation, etc, and it tends to be marketed more aggressively than other insluation measures). For new installations, the economics of special coatings at least seem attractive. Further opportunities are provided by 'switchable' coatings in which the characteristics can be altered (by an electric field) according to the heating requirements.[17]

[17] For an extensive review see C.G.Granqvist, 'Energy-Efficient Windows: Options with Present and Forthcoming Technology', in T.B.Johansson et al, (eds), *Electricity*, op.cit.

2.2 Electricity technologies and motive power

The key technical developments which make options such as small-scale CHP and heat pumps feasible are not primarily those of heat or mechanical technologies, but concern electronics. Control systems apply modern computing and sensor technologies to control finely the performance of such systems to match the loads upon them and optimize operation, and to register automatically the energy consumption and outputs. Power electronics, in which solid state devices carry large currents, developed rapidly during the 1980s and offer compact, cheap and reliable alternatives to mechanical relays, switches and valves; this enables small and varying power sources to be connected with grids, with full electrical interfacing and production, at far lower costs and greater reliability than would previously have been possible. Their application to small-scale CHP is obvious, but power electronics could permeate a far wider range of electrical applications than this, not just because of their greater efficiency, but because of overall superior performance.[18] Foremost among the energy impacts may be that on electrical motors and drive systems.

Electric motor drives

The key facts concerning electrical motor drives have been succinctly expressed by Baldwin:[19]

> Electric motors are the workhorses of modern industrial society. They run home refrigerators; drive office heating and ventilation systems; power industries' pumps, fans, and compressors; and keep cities' water supplies flowing ... Electric motors typically account for 2/3 of all electricity use. Although individual components in electricity motor drive systems perform relatively well, passing through the many devices of a system can reduce the delivered energy to as little as 5-10% of the input fossil fuel. Numerous technologies are being developed to reduce these losses ...

Table 2.2 shows the breakdown of average losses for pumping in the US. Overall losses are divided roughly equally between those of

[18] Powertechnics magazine predicted in 1987 that the future use of power integrated circuits (PICs) in power converters would reduce costs buy 25%, mass by 40% and volume by 50% (J.D.Shephard, ed., *Powertechnics*, Vol.3, No.8, 1987, p.8; reported in Fulkerson et al, *Energy Technology R&D*, Vol.2, Part 3, op.cit.)
[19] S.F.Baldwin, 'Energy-Efficient Electric Motor Drive Systems', in T.B.Johansson et al (eds), *Electricity*, p.21, op.cit.

Table 2.2 US Average pumping system losses from coal power generation*

Location	Efficiency (output as % input of device)	Remainder, % of starting total
Electric plant	30	30.0
Transmission & Distribution	92	27.6
Power transformers	96	26.5
Electric motors	88	23.3
Shaft couplings	98	22.9
Pump	72	16.5
Pump throttling*	86	14.1
Piping system	80	11.3

* Note: The figures include constant load, unthrottled systems. The losses in most throttled systems would be higher than indicated here.

Source: Baldwin, 'Energy-Efficient Electrical Motor Drive Systems', op.cit.

generation, and the rest of the system. Motors themselves are a significant source of loss, often because of poor design and maintenance. Better motor design, using better materials, can often improve performance by several percentage points; Baldwin notes that the costs are greater, but his data indicates that for heavily used applications 'even scrapping a working motor and replacing it with an efficient model would have a simple payback of just over 5 years'.[20]

However, other components of the system usually account for greater losses. Many of these losses arise from the need to meet variable loads, because the traditional electric motor is a somewhat inflexible device; the rotational speed is driven by the grid frequency, and operation at part load can be very inefficient. Throttling and other control systems are designed to dissipate energy, and produce back pressures and variations which reduce the efficiency of pumping, while the piping also needs to be designed to withstand the pressures and other fluctuations involved.

[20] ibid, p.27.

Modern power electronics has given rise to practical and efficient Adjustable Speed Drives (ASDs) which can change the speed and power of the motor directly, while various modern control and sensing systems can establish fine control of system conditions. This and related changes can greatly improve the overall performance. The costs appear attractive for most new variable-load installations and many retrofits, and the components can now be integrated into a power integrated circuit, further increasing reliability and reducing costs.

Baldwin, whilst declining to make estimates of the total potential owing to the inadequacy of available data, offers various examples of achievable and broadly economic savings of over 50% in variable load applications.[21] EPRI estimated a 'maximum technical potential' by 2000 of 28-45% of industrial motor drive savings;[22] Lovins suggests aggregate savings of a third to a half.[23] The uncertainties concerning industrial drives are relatively modest; given the breadth of applications also in domestic appliances and building services, each with different engineering and market characteristics, the difficulty of making a full assessment becomes obvious, but given the ubiquitous nature of motor drives in non-industrial applications the potential is clearly important.

System technologies and superconductivity

Advances in power electronics open ways to improve the overall economic and energy efficiency of electricity systems themselves. Modern devices can help to match power flows in the system and reduce the costs and losses in distribution networks, for example. In addition they open the possibility of 'dynamic' pricing of electricity, in which electronic meters can reflect an electricity price which may vary according to the production costs on the system, and register consumption at the corresponding times - a more sophisticated version of arrangements already made with some large industrial consumers. Such meters can automatically disconnect some interruptible loads (such as fridges), and display the current price for consumers to react to if they wish. This reduces demand on the higher cost - and usually less efficient - generating stations, and can increase the scope for higher efficiency

[21] ibid, p.46.
[22] Electric Power Research Institute, *Efficient Electricity Use: Estimates of Maximum Energy Savings*, EPRI CU-6746, California, March 1990.
[23] A.B.Lovins, 'End-Use/Least Cost Investment Strategies', *14th Congress of the World Energy Conference*, Montreal, September 1989.

baseload plant and renewable sources. The consequent reduction in peak demand also reduces the need for new power stations.

In popular imagination, mundane issues of better heat supply and motor system optimization pale beside the grand technology image of superconductors, especially since the discovery of 'high temperature' superconductors which can carry currents with zero loss at temperatures as high (sic) as -150 °C (compared with below -260 °C for traditional superconductors), well within the range of liquid nitrogen. However, although superconductors could undoubtedly be used in some applications to reduce losses, in reality there is little to suggest that they will ever play a large role. In the first place, the losses in conventional copper conductors are usually quite small relative to other losses. Second, above a certain strength of current or magnetic field, superconducting properties always break down, limiting the potential range of applications in power systems. Third, even 'high temperature' superconductors still need extensive cooling, which adds considerably to the costs - and consumes energy. Fourthly, the ability to fashion most superconducting materials into configurations useful for generators or wires, to date has been very limited. The realistic potential seems negligible.[24]

The future for energy efficiency lies not with superconductors but the ubiquitous semiconductor. Some of the potential impacts of power semiconductors have already been noted; in the more common guise of the computer chip, the technology opens up possibilities of optimization in the design and control of energy supply and use which would be inconceivable without them. The overall impacts are, by their nature, impossible to quantify at present, and will take time to realize, but even a cursory analysis of technology, combined with the theoretical limits

---

[24] The potential savings are examined exhaustively in Bergsjo and Gertmar, 'Superconductivity and the Efficient Use of Energy', in Johansson et al (eds), *Electricity*, op.cit. Widespread use of superconductors in major generators and power transformers, which at least in principle could be feasible at the temperature of the current generation of 'high temperature' superconductors, are estimated to save up to 0.5% of current electricity consumption in the US; apart from this, 'no electrical savings worth mentioning seem feasible from superconducting magnetic energy storage and distribution or from a general use of liquid nitrogen temperature superconductors' (p.389). Even if room temperature devices were discovered with suitable properties for uses such as general motors and distribution (currently complete speculation) this would save only about 5% of US electrical consumption.

discussed above, indicate that greatly enhanced design and control capabilities - if coupled with incentives to apply them - could be at the heart of many further improvements in efficiency in almost all sectors.

2.3 Materials and industrial processes

Industrial energy use spans a very wide range of processes, many of which are very specific to the process requirements. However, some generic technologies stand out as having potentially widespread impact.

Improved *materials technology* can save energy both by reducing the energy used in manufacturing the materials suitable for a given application, and by producing materials whose properties can lead to energy savings elsewhere. Continuing improvements in specific processes are being made, as discussed above, but the broadest potential probably comes from substitution of metals by other materials which require far less energy in manufacture, including strong ceramics and corrosion free plastics. An extensive review documents the growth of such materials,[25] and the Oak Ridge review indicates continuing areas of improvement, which are steady rather than spectacular. Improved materials can also reduce energy use in varied applications: ceramic engines are one option being developed in Japan, whilst advanced material surface treatments can reduce frictional losses.

Separation processes are estimated to account for about 20% of industrial energy use.[26] Much of this arises from the energy requirements of distillation. Whilst improvements to distillation processes are still quite feasible, major savings might be realised through the use of alternative approaches. Membranes can be made permeable to molecules of a certain characteristic or size, and applied in various ways to separating components, sometimes coupled with either chemical or electrical stimulation.[27] Although membranes have already been applied to some aqueous solutions, 'the application .. to nonaqueous solutions, gaseous systems, and gas-liquid systems is promising, but relatively unexplored'.[28] Other little-explored options for much lower

[25] R.H.Williams, E.D.Larson, and M.H.Ross, 'Materials, Affluence, and Industrial Energy Use', *Annual Review of Energy* 12, Annual Reviews Inc, 1987.
[26] W.Fulkerson,et al, *Energy Technology R&D*, Vol.1, p.72. The figure applies to the US but is probably typical for developed economies.
[27] Membrane Applications Centre, *The Membrane Alternative and its Implications for Industry*, Conference Proceedings, University of Bath, UK, 1990.
[28] W.Fulkerson et al, (eds), *Energy Technology R&D*, op.cit., Vol.2, part 3, p.97.

energy consumption include superfluid extraction and various advanced methods of solvent extraction and leaching.

Various *electrothermal processes*, for depositing heat within materials and on surfaces in finely controlled conditions, can both improve general performance and increase energy efficiency more than enough to offset electrical generation losses.[29] Continuing advances in understanding of *catalysts* is steadily expanding the range of chemical conversion processes which can be accelerated, carried out at lower temperatures, or otherwise altered to lower energy requirements. Advances in *biotechnology* could yield large energy savings in chemical and paper processes,[30] though the most promising applications lie more in energy conversion than in end use - and potentially in enhancing CO_2 fixation.

But perhaps the broadest scope for savings comes from adapting the opportunities discussed in the preceeding sections to the special characteristics of industrial processes. Electrical developments open many possibilities for improved sensors and monitoring, to optimise conditions within what were previously 'black box' processes. Small-scale power generation and interfacing technologies expand the scope for industrial CHP, and industrial heat management is a field in its own right, where studies indicate large remaining potential savings from optimising heat flows to reduce the final heat dissipated to a minimum. The continued march of innovation for improving industrial efficiency has not run out of steam. The key questions concern the potential impacts and the role, if any, which policy could play in accelerating such developments, as discussed below.

In all, the technical developments outlined in the sections above could be at the heart of many further improvements in all sectors. To these more specific applications we now turn.

2.4 Energy in buildings: heating, appliances, and lighting

Buildings typically account for 30-50% of total energy demand in developed economies. Building energy use is beset by pervasive failures of market incentives to use energy efficiently. Building purchasers usually rate energy consumption as a very minor issue; most indeed have

[29] H.Schaefer and M.Rudolph, 'New Electrothermal Processes', and S.Eketorp, 'Electrotechnologies and Steelmaking', both in Johansson, *Electricity*, op.cit.
[30] These and other advanced options are discussed in Fulkerson et al, *Energy Technology R&D*, Vol.2, part 3, op.cit.

little or no idea of the energy performance of properties. There is little incentive for builders to design or construct efficient houses. Many similar factors apply to consumer purchases of appliances for houses. In many countries, opportunities for improving efficiency with paybacks of 2-4 years or less - let alone 10 years - are rife (see for example the UK, US and Soviet case studies). The building sector is thus an obvious sector for potential efficiency gains.

Heating requirements

In terms of overall energy requirements, few end uses display such important disparities as low-grade heating and cooling for buildings. In principle, maintaining a small temperature difference between the inside and outside of buildings need take little or no energy, and indeed many 'zero energy' houses have been demonstrated which rely on the free heat gains from daylight and people and equipment inside the building to offset through thick insulation and small air exchanges the small loss of heat. In practice, space heating forms the largest single energy use in many OECD countries, while other forms of low-grade heating, and space cooling, may in total consume as much again.

Simple draught-proofing and some insulation on roofs and walls can go a long way to reducing losses in many older buildings especially. Adding further insulation becomes rapidly more expensive, for steadily declining gains, and can face problems of weathering and space on walls and floors, and weight on roofs; details vary considerably according to the stock. Substantial improvements have already been obtained in existing buildings; heating intensities in OECD countries declined by 20-30% through the decade 1970-80.[31] This was largely as a result of simple draught-proofing and loft insulation. In some Scandinavian countries, nearly all such opportunities were exploited in the aftermath of the oil shocks, but in most other countries substantial cheap opportunities remain, as discussed below.

More advanced opportunities for improving insulation, including windows, have been summarised above. The need for ventilation, for comfort and to prevent the accumulation of various gases (including the radioactive radon), limits the degree to which insulation could make sense, but currently few buildings approach such limits. For substantial future improvements there is a strong distinction between new and

[31] L.Schipper and A.Ketoff, 'Home Energy Use in 9 OECD Countries', 1960-80, *Energy Policy*, June 1983.

existing buildings. For new buildings, different studies vary in their coverage of the options considered, and many are hazy about the dividing line between the technically possible, socially practical, and economic; the last in any case varies according to energy price projections, which are notoriously fickle, and the ever-present uncertainties concerning the discount rate chosen. If economics is largely disregarded, estimates suggest a maximum practical reduction in heating requirements of 70-90% below current levels, depending somewhat on the stock.[32] Giovannini and Pain suggest 'optimal' standards for the year 2000 at levels which are comparable to those of new Swedish standards,[33] and which equate to about 30% of the current OECD average heating intensity. The Danish Ministry of Energy reports that a reduction of 25-30% in new buildings, over the existing high levels in Denmark, 'would not entail increased [net] costs.'[34] Although some ground may be lost through the removal of CFCs, some of the special insulation technologies discussed above could be applied to buildings to improve the situation further.[35]

The situation for existing buildings is very different. Although very large savings are often technically achievable, the costs and disruption of retrofitting more than basic insulation and draught-proofing can be substantial unless major renovations are being carried out anyway. Estimates published by the Danish Ministry of Housing conclude that

[32] This equates to the 'service efficiency' discussed below. A study from IIASA (Nakicenovic *Technological Progress, Structural Change, and Efficient Energy Use*, Final report, 700/76.716/9, IIASA, Laxenburg, Austria, 1989, p.178.) reports various estimates of between 10% and 16%. Estimates from Scandinavian countries tend to be 20-30%, largely because of the much greater efficiency of the current stock.

[33] B.Giovannini and D.Pain, *Scientific and Technical Arguments for the Optimal Use of Energy*, op.cit., p.67. The suggested figures are $180MJ/m^2/yr$ for single family homes and $150MJ/m^2/yr$ for multiple-family homes in temperate climates, reducing by about 25% after 25 years. Variations in climate and building practice mean that Swedish standards are not necessarily transferrable to other countries, but are nevertheless indicative.

[34] Danish Ministry of Energy, *Energy 2000*, Danish Energy Agency, April 1990.

[35] '[Highly insulating] composite walls and foam cores could sharply reduce construction costs as well as energy requirements. The pending ban on CFCs, a prime component of most of the present foams, suggest that substitutes such as evacuated panels should be developed to avoid a drop in the efficiency of new buildings. Active systems are another possibility. For instance, windows with switchable emissivity (opaque on winter nights, transparent during the day) could produce major savings' (Fulkerson et al, *Energy Technology R&D*, Vol.1, op.cit., p.71).

reducing overall residential heating demand by over 50% from current levels by 2030 would be technically possible, but quite expensive; but that about 60% of these savings could be obtained at little net extra cost.[36]

Low-grade heating in the commercial and industrial sectors has been less studied, and the issues and possibilities are more difficult to assess because of the very wide range of building types. The intensity of heating and cooling demand per unit of floor area tends to be higher in the service sector than in the domestic. This and the larger scale overall may bring other options to the fore, such as CHP and the use of building control systems which optimise the distribution and timing of heating and cooling.[37]

Despite the importance of technical improvements, the role of human behaviour and management systems - as well as the importance of building size - should not be overlooked. Poor controls, especially in multi-user buildings where the occupant is not paying the heating costs, or where energy is very cheap or even not metered, can lead to occupants controlling temperatures by opening windows. Much of the difference in heating intensities between the US and continental Europe can be attributed to a combination of larger homes in the US with expectations of shirt-sleeve temperatures in winter and extensive chilling in summer, sometimes combined with a lack of automatic timing controls on heating systems. Considerable short-term savings have been realized simply by creating better awareness of energy use and needs, both for space and water heating; and good controls, to provide the right amount of service at the right time, would clearly yield further savings.

Finally, as noted in the previous section, the range of options for supplying a given heating load can offer considerable further opportunities for reducing overall energy requirements and/or carbon emissions, by using direct fuel heating (especially gas in condensing boilers) or electric heat pumps in preference to direct electrical heating, and by tapping waste heat supplies and free solar gains where feasible. In all, the opportunities for reducing emissions associated with building space and water heating are clearly considerable.

[36] Danish Ministry of Energy, op.cit., p.52. It is not clear if these figures include water heating.
[37] International Energy Agency, *Energy for Buidings: Microprocessor Technology*, IEA/OECD, Paris, 1986.

Many similar issues apply to building air conditioning loads, which respond similarly to improved insulation and controls. Selective window coatings which can transmit visible light but block infra-red (heat) radiation, and the experimental windows which can react to conditions to vary their transmission of heat as appropriate, are of particular relevance to this. Various improvements in air conditioners themselves also appear feasible, and the replacement of CFCs (often the working fluid) does not appear to be as difficult or costly, in energy or economic terms, as once feared. Better understanding of opportunities in the local environment can also reduce demands; trees provide improved shading, while on a broader scale, the 'heat islands' generated by large cities in hot regions can be alleviated by increasing the number of trees and the light reflecting surface area.

Lighting
Although heating tends to dominate the final energy demand in many buildings, electricity use in lighting and appliances is often just as important in terms of CO_2 emissions and, unlike heating loads, their use is still growing rapidly. Although lighting is generally a minor component of demand in homes and industry (usually under 10%), it is much more important in services; overall, McGowan[38] estimates that lighting consumes 8-17% of electricity in industrialized countries. The overall growth in lighting use shows little sign of abating, but in some countries, efficiency improvements have been sufficient to hold lighting energy demand nearly constant. Although the basic efficiency of the dominant technologies - incandescent bulbs and fluorescent tubes - has improved little in the past few decades, most new service applications have used fluorescent tubes, while fixtures, design and control have improved.

There appears to be considerable further scope for improvement simply by better reflectors and coatings; these opportunities are reviewed by McGowan.[39] But the recent upsurge in interest has been stimulated by the development of more advanced technologies, which offer prospects that efficiency improvements could accelerate rather than slow down. The range of lighting technologies and performance is shown in Figure

[38] T.McGowan, 'Energy-Efficient Lighting', in Johanssen et al (eds), *Electricity*, op.cit.
[39] ibid.

Figure 2.2 Efficiency and output of different lighting technologies

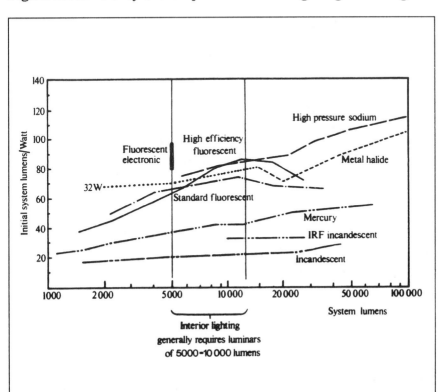

Fluoresent electronic bulbs can provide 80-100 lumens/Watt across a range of output.

Source: T.McGowan, 'Energy Efficient Lighting', in Johansson et al (eds), *Electricity*, Lund University Press, Lund, Sweden, 1989.

2.2. Glenny[40] highlights 'three changes made possible by advances in technology [which] offer the greatest potential for energy saving whilst maintaining lighting standards': i) A change from filament lamps to

[40] T.Glenny, 'Efficient lighting technologies', in M.Grubb et al, *Emerging Energy Technologies: Impacts and Policy Implications*, forthcoming, Dartmouth, Aldershot, 1991.

compact fluorescent lamps (CFLs). CFLs have folded arc tubes in a compact design which can fit into conventional incandescent light sockets. ii) A change of fluorescent lighting from mains-frequency to high-frequency, using *electronic ballasts* (the electric control and interface system) in place of conventional electro-mechanical devices. iii) The introduction of *needs control* for lighting, ie. according to the need for light at a given time and place.

As indicated in Figure 2.2, CFLs are generally 3 to 5 times as efficient as incandescent bulbs, and they last up to eight times as long. They are however much more expensive, often by a factor of 10 to 20. On a conventional, discounted cash flow analysis, this is not a significant economic obstacle; Eyre notes in a report for the UK Department of Energy that:[41]

> Where lighting is currently provided by filament bulbs, using an 8% discount rate typical of electricity supply, it would be cost effective to use CFLs in each location where operating time exceeds 250 hours/yr. These locations are estimated to account for 93% of the energy use. The economically achievable savings are therefore 71%, or 5.3TWh/yr.

Costs are expected to fall as sales increase, with most sources estimating reductions of 20-40%. But the problem remains that consumers rarely make choices on the basis of discounted cash flow analysis, least of all at an 8% rate. For most, the idea of paying over $10 for a bulb is unacceptable. In addition, CFLs may not fit readily in all conventional fittings, some dislike the style or the type of light produced, and they cannot be readily dimmed. CFLs with electronic ballasts are smaller and give still better light quality, but are more expensive still. The issues are therefore more complex than for most of the appliances discussed below; in addition to extensive indifference concerning efficiency, for lighting, the large opportunities are matched by very real obstacles. Either direct utility funding, or financial assistance of one form or another, is clearly needed overcome them.

---

[41] N.Eyre, *The Abatement of Gaseous Emissions by Energy Efficient Lighting*, Energy and Environment Paper No.2, Energy Technology Support Unit, Harwell, UK, p.4. The report notes (p.20) that 'it is the reductions in electricity which provide 90% of the cost savings; only 10% is due to the savings in filament bulb costs. The analysis is therefore robust against an alternative of 'long life' filament bulbs.'

Persuading services and industry to replace filament bulbs may somewhat simpler, but these sectors already tend to rely more upon traditional forms of fluorescent lights. Again, various options including better conventional fittings and ballasts, lamp temperature optimization and special coatings can all improve performance. However, the greatest interest centres around using electronic ballasts in place of conventional mechanically-operated ones. This not only reduces the ballast losses, but it enables the bulb to operate at high frequency, improving efficiency by 25-30% over standard fluorescents across a wide range of light outputs. Given the large role of fluorescent lighting in services, this represents a large savings, and the incremental costs are small compared with those of replacing incandescent bulbs by CFLs: 'the extra cost...is usually recovered within the lifetime of the first lamp...at present discrete components are used... but the next few years should see the introduction of Integrated Circuits which will enable reductions in both size and cost.'[42]

However, 'still more significant are the control capabilities which can be designed into electronic ballasts...adjustable output and a full range of programmed functions are practical even on a luminaire-by-luminaire basis. Control strategies that might be employed include: compensating for normal light output depreciation...(minimizing overdesign); reacting to daylight; adjusting the output of individual luminaires according to task; personnel sensing; lighting scheduling and architectural dimming.'[43]

This emphasizes the third item highlighted by Glenny, namely the overall control of lighting systems. Options are illustrated schematically in Figure 2.3. McGowan continues that 'Reported studies have measured lighting energy savings from 32-52% with the implementation of just two (scheduling and daylight integration) of the strategies.' Another report[44] indicates that dimming devices and occupancy sensors are could both save 20-40% of lighting energy, with paybacks of 2-3 years. This points to the importance of modern technologies applied with reference to the whole system and the actual energy service needs. Combined with the options for technical lamp efficiency improvements,

[42] T.Glenny, *High-Efficiency Lighting*, op.cit.
[43] T.McGowan, 'Energy-Efficient Lighting', op.cit., p.74.
[44] R.Bergton and A.H.Rosenfeld, 'Energy for Buildings and Homes', *Scientific American*, September 1990.

Figure 2.3 Efficient lighting design

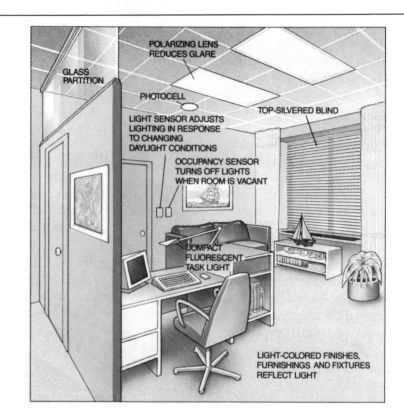

Even from exisiting fluorescent systems, fixture improvements can more than halve energy consumption, and large gains could be obtained through intelligent controls and room design.

Source: Arnold P.Pickett, Clark W.Gellings and Amory B.Lovins, 'Efficient Use of Electricity', *Scientific American*, September 1990.

the potential for long-term economic efficiency improvements in lighting appears to be immense - well over 50% as compared with current practice.

Electrical appliances

It is estimated that appliances excluding lighting account for 30-50% of all electricity consumption in OECD countries,[45] with most of this relating to 'white goods' - fridges, freezers, clothes and dish washers, electric cookers etc. Appliance use, and their electricity consumption, continues to grow in all countries, but a number of the most important applications now appear to have reached saturation point at least for domestic consumers in developed economies. Refrigerators and freezers are a very important component, frequently consuming as much as all other household uses combined in homes which have both. In principle, sufficient insulation could limit the energy requirement to that required to cool inserted food and to cool air entering when the door is opened; in practice, this only accounts for 10-20% of consumption, the rest being lost through the walls. Better insulation can thus greatly increase efficiencies, and further gains are possible by improvements in the heat pump cycle and the motor used to drive it. Cooking on a hotplate is likewise a very inefficient process, with about 15% of the energy typically being transferred to the food, and ovens are frequently oversized and poorly insulated; pressure cookers, smaller ovens with better insulation, and microwave ovens offer large efficiency gains. For washing machines, it is very difficult to judge the potential improvement, because the basic energy requirements depend heavily on the process and requirements, but substantial improvements appear possible, for example with the use of lower temperature detergents;[46] also, with a major energy requirement being heat, the implied CO_2 emissions may depend strongly upon the heat source.

The technical opportunities for improving efficiency have been closely investigated, especially since the pioneering work of Norgard,[47] which included laboratory tests which in some cases have already led to commercial products. Ten years later, Norgard produced an extensive analysis of efficiency options in electrical appliances, from which Table 2.3 is drawn, which compares the consumption of current average stock,

[45] J.S.Norgard, 'Low Electricity Appliances - Options for the Future', in Johansson et al (eds), *Electricity*, op.cit.

[46] For a discussion of cradle-to-grave efficiencies in washing machines see, 'Reincarnation in the design studio', *Financial Times*, 3 April 1991.

[47] J.S.Norgard, 'Improved Efficiency in Domestic Electricity Use, *Energy Policy*, March 1979.

Table 2.3 Estimated potential for improved efficiency in electrical appliances (Denmark)

Type of end-use technology	All sectors consumption 1988 kWh/capita (Denmark)	Intensity index			
		Average sold 1988	Best available 1988	Efficiency avanced	Efficiency advanced +heat subst
Refrigerator	150	0.75	0.25	0.14	0.14
Freezer	235	0.80	0.35	0.20	0.20
Combined F/F	90	0.80	0.55	0.20	0.20
Clothes washer	175	0.75	0.60	0.00	0.10
Dish washer	90	0.72	0.62	0.33	0.07
Clothes dryer	65	0.85	0.67	0.35	0.20
Elec-cooking	340	0.93	0.57	0.40	0.00
Heat distribution	270	0.75	0.25	0.13	0.13
Ventilation	500	0.80	0.55	0.15	0.15
Miscellaneous	425	0.90	0.70	0.50	0.50
Lighting	860	0.85	0.35	0.20	0.20
All appliances + light	3200	0.81	0.47	0.26	0.20

Source: J.S.Norgard, 'Low Electricity Appliance Options for the Future', in Johansson et al, *Electricity*, Lund Univeristy Press, Lund, Sweden, 1989, p165.

Note: Results of this analysis are here expressed in terms of the intensity indices, ie., the intensities obtainable relative to the average of the units in use in the base year 1988. Heat subst indicates the electrical use if all heating is supplied from other sources (this is speculative, and for some cases impractical). For discussion and reference to other studies and countries see text.

average sold, and best available in 1988, with Norgard's estimates of advanced efficiency models. Though these may tend towards an upper bound on potential improvements, studies by analysts in other countries have led to similarly impressive conclusions: potential savings from today's average stock are of the order of 50-80%.[48]

Applying his estimates to current consumption patterns, Norgard estimates that in Denmark, 'the present [1986] level of electrical services... can be maintained while using only 26% of present electricity consumption.'[49] Furthermore, 'the estimated added costs... corresponds to an average price of approximately 2.5USc/kWh saved' - considerably cheaper than electricity costs in many countries, though the marginal costs of the last incremental savings are not reported and must be quite high. Giovannini and Pain broadly support Norgard's analysis with the exception of cooking (because of the importance of consumer behaviour), whilst raising some unresolved doubts about how far they may apply to very different appliance sizes and the nature of future trends in consumer preferences; they also confirm that the extra 'embodied energy' in the extra materials used is usually trivial compared with the lifetime operational savings.[50]

The Danish Ministry of Energy support estimates of almost comparable magnitudes in studies for the Danish energy scenarios: 'it seems technically possible to halve electricity consumption in households over the next 40 years; if nothing is done it would rise by about 13%.'[51] If these savings are broken down into three stages of equal magnitude, the cost are respectively negative or negligible, below 0.15DK/kWh and 0.15-0.35; 'in general these costs are lower than the socio-economic costs of producing 1kWh of electricity.'[52] Overall in the Danish government scenarios, net savings from electricity efficiency improvements largely offset the added costs of the projected building retrofit programme. Other cost estimates are detailed in the study for the UK Department of Energy,

---

[48] See for example the review by Giovannin and Pain, *Optimal Energy Use*, op.cit., Chapter 4; UK Department of Energy, 'Energy Efficiency in Domestic Electric Appliances', HMSO, London, 1988; and various publications from the American Council for an Energy Efficient Economy, Washington.

[49] Norgard, 'Low Electricity Appliances', op.cit., p.125.

[50] B.Giovannini and D.Pain, *Scientific and Technical Arguments for the Optimal Use of Energy*, op. cit., p.84.

[51] Danish Ministry of Energy, *Energy 2000*, op.cit., p.53.

[52] ibid, p.54.

Table 2.4 Costs and benefits of move to world best practice in UK domestic appliances

	Fridge	Light	Washing machine	Tumble drier	Dish washer	Cooker	Others	Total
Extra cost of world best appliance, £m	1500	1700	1000	620	90	1200	-	6100
Annual value of saved electricity, £m/yr	500	370	130	70	40	280	130	1500
Simple payback to consumer, yrs	3	4.7	7.7	8.9	2.3	4.3	-	4.1
Annual elec savings, % total demand	3.2	2.3	0.8	0.7	0.2	1.8	0.8	10.0
Reduction in peak elec demand, %	2.1	2.9	1.0	0.8	0.2	2.3	1.0	10.4
National CO_2 savings,%	1.6	1.2	0.3	0.3	0.1	0.9	0.4	4.8

Source: Derived from UK Department of Energy, *Energy Efficiency in Domestic Electric Appliances*, HMSO, 1989, London, (Table 10.2).

the key economic results of which are detailed in Table 2.4; they indicate that the world best appliances in the most important applications would generally pay back the extra costs in 3-4 years; the overall impact of moving to world best appliances would be to save around £1,500m/yr for an added capital investment of £6000m, while reducing total electricity demand by about 10% and UK carbon emissions by nearly 5%.

The fact that such large energy savings can be achieved at little cost points to the almost total absence of energy cost as a factor in the appliance business. Herring[53] examines data on fridge and freezer models available in the UK and concludes that 'there is no consistent relationship between efficiency and unit cost; more efficient models are often cheaper than less efficient models; in the most popular size range, efficiency can vary by up to 3:1 ... for refrigerators, the most efficient model costs the same as the least efficient.' Most consumers are wholly unaware of operating costs, and companies have had little interest in efficiency issues; insulation levels in fridges and freezers, for example, have been determined more by the need to avoid excessive cooler sizes, and to maintain coolness during power failures, than for any reasons associated with energy costs.

However, in general the literature says little about the non-economic tradeoffs, of which there are clearly some. Efficient fridges, freezers and ovens require greater insulation thickness especially with the elimination of CFCs (unless vacuum insulation is used), and for some consumers this could be very awkward. Despite this caveat, appliances offer one of the most obvious areas for cost-effective energy savings of all, and much of this could clearly be tapped by the use of a variety of the measures discussed in Volume 1, Chapter 4.

2.5 Transport

Transport accounts for nearly a third of all final energy consumption in the OECD, and has been the most rapidly growing sector of all in most countries. Over 80% of transport energy in the OECD is taken by road vehicles. The thermal basis of the internal combustion engine limits the feasible fuel-to-power conversion efficiency which, combined with losses in the drive, results in typical efficiencies of around 20%. Average on-road vehicle efficiency can be improved by improving traffic flow and by limiting maximum speeds; Figure 2.4 shows how consumption varies with speed for a range of vehicle types. Also, as the figure emphasizes, the size and weight of vehicles is very important. However, even within the confines of the petrol car, there are still important opportunities for improving efficiencies.

[53] H.Herring, 'The Potential for Energy Savings in Domestic Appliances', in M.Grubb et al, *Emerging Energy Technologies: Impacts and Policy Implications*, op.cit.

Figure 2.4 Energy consumption/CO$_2$ emission characteristics for different car types

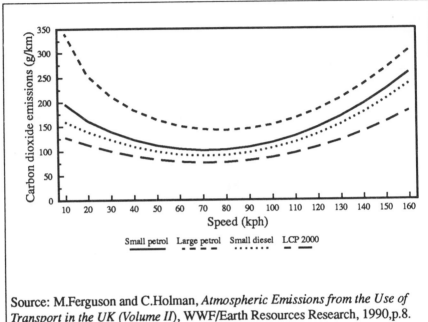

Source: M.Ferguson and C.Holman, *Atmospheric Emissions from the Use of Transport in the UK (Volume II)*, WWF/Earth Resources Research, 1990,p.8.

Technical options for increasing petroleum vehicle efficiencies

Bleviss identifies seven potential technical avenues for improving vehicle performance.[54]

Improved engine efficiency, arising mostly from better startup and part-load operation and management, reducing frictional losses, improved design and better oils, and improved combustion characteristics which can be obtained using electronic controls and catalysts, and extend to stratified and 'lean burn' technologies which are claimed to improve engine efficiency by about 20%. Diesel engines are generally about 10% more efficient than petrol engines, and can in principle can be further improved by direct injection (currently only applied to heavy duty vehicles).

[54] D.L.Bleviss, *The New Oil Crisis and Fuel Economy Technologies*, Quorum Books, 1988, (as cited in Giovannini and Pain, *Optimal Energy Use*, op. cit., pp.182-187).

Improved transmission efficiency. Potential improvements of 5-20% are claimed for discrete transmission, but the largest gains would come from continuously variable transmission systems, which allow engine operation to be kept at optimal points (various systems have been demonstrated).

Weight reduction. A weight reduction of 10% improves efficiency by 4-5% in general driving, and 7-8% in urban conditions. Better design and materials can reduce weight, but clear constraints are posed by the need to maintain adequate strength and safety.

Reduced aerodynamic drag. Recent years have seen much sleeker designs, but there is still considerable variation in the drag performance of new vehicles and some further improvements would be possible. In the extreme, according to General Motors,[55] 'the technical feasibility of a half-width personal vehicle, called the "lean machine", has been confirmed by GM. It can provide up to 150mpg [64km/l] without compromising comfort or acceleration performance. They should be very attractive to the commuter, but their effective use will require coordination with local traffic officials.'

Engine start-stop and startup. Fuel can be saved by switching the engine off when the vehicle is stationary or decelerating. Some countries already encourage drivers to do this at traffic lights, and some cars now have automatic stop-start systems, the most successful of which is said to yield 10-20% savings in city driving, though safety - or more likely, consumer perception of safety - may slow or prevent the application of such technologies. Adding a flywheel improves performance and reduces battery strain, and can even allow regenerative braking (still at the research stage), but does add to weight and costs. Other options identified by Bleviss are reduced tyre resistance and improved accessory efficiency (eg. of power windows, air conditioning).

These improvements are not additive, but the overall theoretical potential for improving vehicle efficiency is still considerable, and this has been demonstrated by various prototype vehicles detailed in the

---

[55] A.J.Sobey, 'Energy Use in Transportation: 2000 and Beyond', in *Proc Workshop on Energy Efficiency and Structural Change: Implications for the Greenhouse Problem*, (LBL-25716) Lawrence Berkeley Laboratory, Oakland, 1988. 150mpg (US) is more than five times the current US average on-the-road car performance. Because of the confusion engendered by the difference between US and Imperial gallons, all statistics in this book are converted to metric units: 1 mile per US gallon = 0.426 kilometres per litre (1 litre = 0.22 Imperial gallon = 0.264 US gallon).

literature,[56] with efficiencies at least double and in some cases three or four times today's averages.

Achievable impacts

However, translating technological and economic possibilities to realisable impacts is much more complex for vehicles than most other energy areas, because of the impact of consumer tastes. In Europe for example, vehicle technology improved steadily during the 1980s, but consumers exploited this by buying more powerful cars, rather than more efficient ones; the average efficiency scarcely changed.[57] Beyond a certain point there are clear trade-offs between efficiency and other aspects of performance such as maximum power and crash protection.

Given this, studies differ widely about the practical market potential. Sobey states that 'with respect to fuel efficiency, we may be close to the economic limits.'[58] In stark contrast, Lovins cites various high-efficiency prototypes, including two with three times today's efficiency for little or no extra costs, and states that 'most offer comfort, performance, crashworthiness, and [non-CO_2] emissions comparable or superior to those of standard cars today.'[59] Difiglio et al examine the potential of existing technologies to improve efficiency without changing anything to the characteristics as perceived by the consumer, and estimate achievable fleet improvements in US cars to be 17% by 1995 and 20-25% in 2000.[60] These figures have been contested by an engineer's team of General Motors, Ford and Chrysler, who estimate

[56] Bleviss *The New Oil Crisis and Fuel Economy Technologies*, op.cit
[57] C.Holman, 'Efficient Vehicle Technologies', in M.Grubb et al, *Emerging Energy Technologies: Impacts and Policy Implications*, op.cit.
[58] A.Sobey, 'Energy Use in Transport: 2000 and Beyond', op.cit.
[59] A.B.Lovins, 'End-Use/Least Cost Investment Strategies', op.cit.
[60] C.DiFiglio, K.G.Duleep and D.L.Greene, 'Cost Effectiveness of Future Fuel Economy Improvements', *The Energy Journal*, Vol.11 No.1, 1990.This analysis was extended by other analysts and applied to estimating the marginal cost curve of incremental efficiency improvemnts, from which it was estimated that 'if average automobile size and accelaration performance were held constant at their 1987 levels, new car fuel economy could cost-effectively be improved to 43.8mpg at an average cost of 53 cents per gallon saved'. This represents a 50% increase in new car efficiency as compared with the 1987 base vehicle, at a marginal cost of around $1.24/gallon (M.Ledbetter and M.Ross, 'A supply curve of conserved energy for automobiles', American Council for an Energy-Efficient Economy, Washington DC, 1990).

achievable savings to be less than half these estimates.[61] Schipper writes that:[62]

> While many high MPG prototypes exist, the challenge of the next decade appears to be the improvement of more conventional, ie., family-type, cars that dominate present markets ... The 1990 auto fleets in Europe average about [11.1 km/l], those in N. America about [9.5 km/l]. These could be improved to about [17 km/l] at less than a 10% increase in vehicle cost, if energy were the only consideration ... more realistic figures might be [15.3 km/l] for the U.S. and Europe. Since these figures are 'test' values, they must be adjusted by about 10% for the U.S. and as much as 15% for Europe.

These estimates equate to improvements of around 45% in the US fleet (partly through the elimination of older vehicles) and 20% in European fleets over 1990s. Looking to the longer term, Giovannini and Pain[63] state that 'experts usually estimate the long term potential to be 50-60% of today's consumption' (ie. roughly a doubling of current efficiencies) based on prototypes and additional research.

One of the difficulties for achieving such savings, quite apart from the over-riding importance of consumer tastes, is that fuel costs become of still less concern as efficiency is improved. Figure 2.5 shows for a range of oil prices how the total costs involved in owning a vehicle, with a given mileage, vary as the efficiency improves. The diagram indicates that life-cycle costs remain almost constant for more than a doubling of efficiency. This represents a massive variation in terms of national energy security and environmental impacts, but even to well-informed consumers concerned about life-cycle costs it appears as an economic 'plateau of indifference'. Fantastic oil tax levels might required to drive such improvements by price alone, while setting binding standards to reach such levels might be almost as difficult politically. The 'guzzler to sipper' transfer of capital costs discussed in Volume 1 and elsewhere[64]

[61] W.V.Bussman, 'Potential Gains in Fuel Economy', in *Energy and Environment in the 21st Century,* Conference Proceedings, MIT, 1990.

[62] L.Schipper, 'Improved energy efficiency in the industrialised countries: past achievements, CO_2 emission prospects', *Energy Policy,* March 1991

[63] B.Giovannini and D.Pain, *Optimal Energy Use,* op.cit., p.189.

[64] Since completing Volume 1, a more detailed study of such 'revenue neutral' incentive schemes has been published: J.Koomey and A.H.Rosenfeld, 'Revenue-neutral incentives for efficiency and environmental quality', *Contemporary Policy Issues,* Vol.VIII, July 1990.

Figure 2.5 Total cost of motoring for different efficiencies and fuel prices

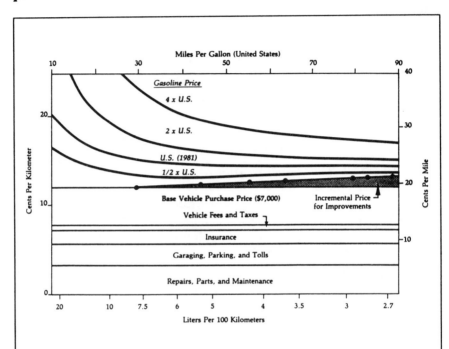

Source: F.von Hippel and B.G.Levi, 'Automative Fuel Efficiency: The Opportunity and Weakness of Existing Market Incentives', Resources and Conservation, 1983.

might be the only practical way of even approaching such improvements in the vehicle market.

Alternative transport options

In considering transport options, the savings offered by other modes of ground transport should not be neglected; as Figure 2.6 indicates, these can offer very large savings. However, although congestion and developments in transport policy designed to tackle it and urban pollution may (as discussed in Volume 1) assist more efficient modes, and otherwise help to limit the almost universally projected continued growth in car use, they seem unlikely to halt it completely. Carbon emissions

Figure 2.6 Estimated energy consumption of different transport modes in London

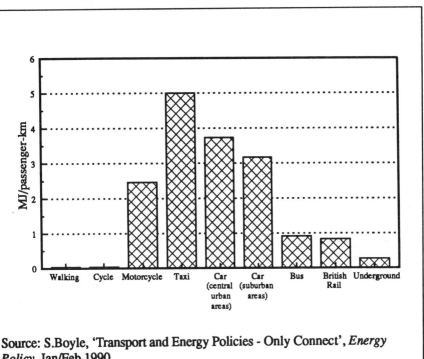

Source: S.Boyle, 'Transport and Energy Policies - Only Connect', *Energy Policy*, Jan/Feb 1990.

from transport seem set to grow despite the most optimistic projections of car efficiency, certainly on a global basis and perhaps even within the developed economies, for as long as vehicles remain based on the petroleum-fired internal combustion engine.

A wide variety of alternative vehicle fuels have been proposed, and many tested: ethanol; methanol; natural gas used as liquid (LNG) or compressed (CNG); electric vehicles; and hydrogen vehicles. Sperling and Deluchi[65] review performance characterics including greenhouse

[65] D.Sperling and M.A.DeLuchi, 'Transportation Energy Futures', *Annual Review of Energy 1989*, No.14, pp.375-424. More extensive studies of alternative vehicle technologies are given in D.Sperling, (ed.), *Alternative Transportation Fuels*, Quorum Books, Westport, Connecticut, 1989.

gas emissions. Of those which rely on the internal combustion engine, methanol gives a substantial increase in CO_2 emissions as compared with petroleum if it is derived from coal, and little or no change if derived from natural gas, while natural gas cars offer 15-20% savings. Natural gas vehicles offer potentially significant reductions, but competing uses combined with resource constraints may squeeze it out; it seems likely that the economic and environmental benefits of using gas in power stations, discussed in Chapter 3, will usually exceed its application to transport, and in few areas could gas sustain major contributions to both sectors, but it could form an important bridge to other gaseous fuels. Without more radical changes in vehicle design, major reductions in CO_2 emissions can only be achieved from biomass fuels, principally ethanol or methanol. Biomass resources and conversion are discussed in the next chapter. Despite the relatively promising economic prospects, the combination of efficiency losses at all stages - biomass production from solar energy (1-2%), conversion to ethanol (50%), and use in internal combustion engines (20%) - means that the overall contribution of liquid fuels from biomass is clearly constrained. Achieving major global impacts will require routes with much higher efficiencies.

The environmental benefits of electric vehicles (EVs) have attracted great interest. The main motivation, apart from selling electricity, has been to avoid the local pollutants and oil dependence of traditional cars. However, the electric drive also circumvents the inefficiencies of the internal combustion engine, and carries certain other advantages arising from the ease of power control and startup, and possibly even the use of regenerative braking to recapture some of the energy lost in braking, for example.[66] Use of adjustable speed drives using modern power electronics offers the prospect of drive trains which are not only much more efficient but altogether simpler, with fewer moving parts, lower weight and maintenance costs, etc. By 1989, recognition of these factors was leading analysts to revise estimates that electric vehicles would be

[66] M.DeLuchi, Q.Wang, and D.Sperling, 'Electric Vehicles: Performance, Life-Cycle Costs, Emissions, and Recharging Requirements', *Transportation Research A*, Vol.23A, No.3, 1989; pp.255-278. Table 6 indicates that the complete power train of EV prototypes is typically 5-6 times more efficient than that of 'comparable' internal combustion cars, which reflects in part the added benefits of the lighter drive train etc.

more costly than petrol cars,[67] and it appears increasingly probable that EVs may actually be cheaper on a life-cycle basis.

The higher efficiency of EVs can more than offset the losses in electricity generation. Sperling and Deluchi[68] estimate that the overall CO_2 emissions from current electric vehicles are roughly equal to those from conventional cars if the electricity is drawn from the average power generating mix in the US, and that savings would be about 18% if the electricity came from a modern gas power plant. Other sources suggest savings as high as 60% if the electricity is drawn from modern gas plant, partly because of higher assumed electric vehicle efficiency incorporating recent developments.[69]

Electric vehicles, however, have one critical Achilles' heel: the battery. Conventional lead-acid batteries are hopelessly heavy. Even with one of the most advanced batteries for EVs developed to date (Na-S), the battery is ten times the weight and seven times the size of a gasoline tank, for half the vehicle range.[70] There are also serious unresolved concerns about battery lifetimes given repeated charging, the acceptability of the slow charging rates, and even the environmental consequences of such large-scale battery production and disposal. Reducing dependence on batteries has led some manufacturers to examine combined systems, with batteries for town driving and petroleum for distance driving.

In all, attitudes towards EVs have tended to oscillate over the years, but with the cumulation of improvements and the appearance of more viable prototypes based on them such as the General Motors *Impact*, interest has grown again: the most detailed study to date concludes that 'no longer does successful commercialization depend on technical breakthroughs'.[71] It does however still clearly require substantial improvement, and doubts about the market realities for EVs persist.[72]

---

[67] ibid.

[68] D.Sperling and M.A.DeLuchi, 'Transportation Energy Futures', op.cit.

[69] J.Smith, personal communication. Such differences reflect a problem of all comparisons of alternate fuelled vehicles - frequently the greatest uncertainty concerns not the characteristics of the different fuels, but the relative efficiencies assumed for the different vehicles.

[70] D.Sperling and M.A.DeLuchi, 'Transportation Energy Futures', op.cit.

[71] Deluchi et al, *Electric Vehicles*, op.cit.

[72] For a thoughtful and critical survey of electric vehicle developments see C.Clarke, 'All wired up and ready to go', *Financial Times Energy Economist*, January 1990.

The other main potential route by which non-fossil power might be utilised is through hydrogen, which can be obtained by gasifying biomass at about 80% efficiency, or from the electrolysis of water for example by technologies such as wind energy or PV, discussed in the next chapter. Use of hydrogen in internal combustion engines would require some redesign of the engine, but the major change would be in the storage system. Compressed hydrogen gas and liquid hydrogen contain about 3 times as much energy as petroleum fuels for a given *weight*, but they take up several times as much *space*, and the storage container adds much bulk and weight, and there are certain other obstacles.[73] Metal hydride storage (combining hydrogen with metals in a form from which it can easily be dissociated) overcomes some of the problems, but adds others (including weight). A review concludes that 'all hydrogen storage systems are bulky and costly and will remain so, even with major advances,' and suggests that gasoline prices would have to rise to at least US$0.8/l for hydrogen to have any chance of being competitive with this.[74] The analysis of Ogden and Williams is not dissimilar, but offers a different interpretation: the bulk and cost of storage means that hydrogen places the emphasis on vehicle efficiency - but if efficient vehicles are used, they argue that hydrogen is one of the most promising alternatives.[75]

In fact, by far the most promising approach to non-fossil fuelled transport may in fact come from a marriage of the two apparently disparate 'alternative' approaches. By using the hydrogen not in an internal combustion engine, but to produce electricity in a fuel cell which then drives an electric motor, all the losses and drawbacks of the internal combustion engine are circumvented and replaced by the simplicity and efficiency of the electric drive train, whilst retaining a storage system which weighs a small fraction of even the most advanced batteries and may be recharged almost as quickly as a tank. Despite the added conversion, if vehicles take advantage of recent advances in fuel-cell technology and variable speed electric drives, they apear to be more promising than either route alone. With the greater efficiency and lower

---

[73] A extensive discussion of hydrogen storage for cars is given in J.M.Ogden and R.H.Williams, *Solar Hydrogen: Moving Beyond Fossil Fuels*, World Resources Institute, Washington, October 1989.
[74] D.Sperling and M.A.DeLuchi, 'Transportation Energy Futures', op.cit.
[75] J.Ogden and R.H.Williams, *Solar Hydrogen*, op.cit.

vehicle weight, such vehicles might compete even if the hydrogen were much more expensive than petroleum, so that non-fossil sources may indeed come economically within reach.

At the time of writing interest in such vehicles is only just emerging, and no test vehicles are available. The claims have therefore yet to be tested. But of all the 'alternative' vehicles proposed so far, such combined vehicles appear to offer the best prospects for meeting the high efficiency for alternative vehicles in a greenhouse-constrained world and, almost incidentally, a ready application to non-fossil energy sources.[76]

The rapid growth in air transport, which already accounts for over 10% of OECD transport energy consumption, could make its contribution to CO_2 emissions hard to ignore. However, fuel is an important component of airline costs and manufacturers have paid much attention to it, and aircraft efficiency has improved rapidly, at nearly 3.5%/yr; specific efficiencies over time are illustrated in Figure 2.7. There can be little expectation of 'free' gains to be had, except in the area of traffic and load control which are driven by concerns other than those of energy. However, if fuel prices rise, further improvements, of up to 50%, may be stimulated through the use of propfan engines; the costs both of development and the engines themselves led to their development being abandoned during the oil price decline of the 1980s. Various more incremental improvements in air flight management and technology could offer less dramatic, but still significant improvements. The only realistic alternative to current jet fuels may be other liquid fuels from biomass.

2.6 Industry

Analysing energy consumption and potential savings in industry is an extremely complex task because of the wide variety of characteristics and processes involved and also because confidentiality limits the data available on costs and performance. The extent to which energy costs are significant in processes or products also varies greatly, so market behaviour is similarly diverse. This section therefore does not attempt to list the individual possibilities, but rather to give a broader discussion with some examples from key industries and processes.

Industrial energy efficiency can be improved in several fundamentally different ways. *Better housekeeping* can range from simply paying more

[76] M.DeLuchi and R.H.Williams, personal communication.

Figure 2.7 Aircraft fuel consumption: average trends and specific aircraft

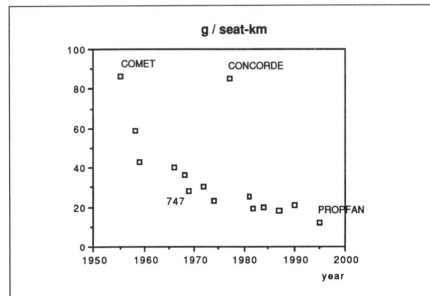

Source: B.Giovannini and D.Pain, *Scientific and Technical Arguments for the Optimal Use of Energy*, CUEPE, Université de Genève, updated April 1990.

attention to energy issues (eg. switching lights and other equipment off when not needed) to fuller assessments of the scope for reducing losses without equipment changes, which may involve formal energy managers. *Energy investments* may be defined as those which have energy saving as a major rationale without actually changing the industrial processes involved; this could include, for example, investing in more efficient motors, heat exchangers or heat cascading to make fuller use of heat generated by primary processes. Frequently, opportunities may exist which are not considered if energy use is not a central component of the costs. *Process changes* in contrast are those which involve substantive changes in the industrial process employed, which could be undertaken for a variety of reasons including energy efficiency. *Recycling* from later stages of manufacturing may be considered as part of process options, but when it involves recovering sold material it involves many other issues. Similar remarks apply to *material substitution* and *changes of output specification*, which may again have considerable energy implications.

Different issues are raised by each of these. Underlying each, to a much greater extent than in most other sectors, lies the critical question regarding apparently cost-effective options for improving efficiency; why haven't they already been adopted? In some cases, especially with reference to energy costs which are a small part of overall business costs and which fall outside the main activity, managers may often evaluate options - or ignore them - in much the same way as domestic consumers, especially at times of low or falling energy prices. This applies particularly to 'housekeeping' measures, but also often to larger-scale investments aimed explicitly at improving efficiency. Skea reports that:

The relatively short payback periods required in industry, and sometimes low take-up rates for apparently profitable investments, are due not only to poor information flows but are also an inevitable consequence of capital budgeting procedures in major companies. 'Optional' investments in energy efficiency are viewed as discretionary and must take second place to investment in long term productive capacity. Consequently, the short payback period is used most commonly as a capital rationing device...'[77]

Indeed, in estimating take-up of more efficient technologies, the UK's Energy Technology Support Unit apply much higher discount rates to 'non-process' investments. More generally, Giovannini and Pain[78] report studies which 'found that firms are concerned about energy management whenever their energy cost share is above 5% or when the total energy consumption is above 120TJ/yr (at 1986 prices)'. Other analysts noted that the biggest changes in industrial energy efficiency trends following the oil price shocks occurred in the *less* energy intensive industries: 'we reason that while raw materials producers were always sensitive to fuel-saving opportunities ... light industries paid scant attention to energy, particularly fuels for space and process heat or steam raising. After the oil price shocks, however, light industries discovered a myriad of fuel savings opportunities.'[79]

[77] J.Skea, *A Case Study of the Potential for Reducing Carbon Dioxide Emissions in the UK*, Science Policy Reseach Unit Special Report, SPRU, Surrey, June 1990.
[78] B.Giovannini and D.Pain, *Optimal Energy Use*, op.cit., p.132
[79] R.Howarth, L.Schipper, P.Duerr, 'Manufacturing Oil and Energy Use in Eight OECD Countries,' LBL-27887, Lawrence Berkeley Laboratory, 1990.

Table 2.5 Energy cost shares for typical production units, processes or industries (1982-86 data)

Process	Energy cost, % total
Oil refining, distillery	55-70
Gypsum plaster processing	40-60
Cement works - wet	40-50
Cement works - dry	30-35
Iron and steelworks	25-40
Paper and board	25
Air transport	20-30
Aluminium metallurgy	20-30
Sugar	16
Synthetic fibres and textile finishing	12-20
Glass works	10-20
Brewing and malting	5-7
Bread and flour	4
Agriculture, cereals, etc	3-5
Car assembly	2-3
Printing	2-3
Electronic appliance assembly	1-2
Service industries, banking, insurance	0.5-1

Source: derived from Giovannini and Pain, *Optimal Energy Use*, op.cit.

Table 2.5 shows the fraction of costs attributable to energy consumption in various industries, at the prices of the early 1980s. This suggests that the great majority of industrial consumption was in industries where the costs were significant (though it does not follow that all components of energy costs would be considered). With the relatively low prices since the early 1980s, the figures in Table 2.5 could be as much as halved, and there are indications that many intermediate industries have again relegated energy efficiency to the backwaters of management attention. There is thus undoubtedly a significant degree of 'efficiency gap' in industrial energy use, though it is probably smaller than in other sectors.

It does not follow that the overall potential for efficiency improvements is small, or even that achieving it need be costly. As illustrated by the discussion of generic technologies in section 2.4, the steady march of technology continues to produce new ways of improving processes, and there is always a lag in taking these up, particularly those (the majority) which are best introduced when equipment is replaced; all reviews note many opportunities for improving efficiency even in many well-established, energy intensive processes, which can pay back in a few years at most.[80] Most industrial processes are not yet close to theoretical limits, and steady improvements continue. Most of the technologies discussed earlier in this chapter can help to improve industrial efficiency: cascading heat from higher temperature processes to lower ones; cogeneration; better motor drive systems; improved lighting; and the general industrial technologies of improved materials, separation techniques, electrothermal processes, and catalytic and various other techniques, together with a wide variety of applications of modern sensors and control systems. These are all applied to some extent at present, and future improvements will often be no more than a continuation of past trends.

There is further potential for improvement even in heavy material process industries. Ross and Steinmeyer report that 'as carried out in even the most efficient plants, basic operations, such as the separation of oxygen from air and the production ethylene and petrochemical feedstocks, expend between four and six times the thermodynamic minimum. Furthermore, many industrial processes that now consume vast amounts of energy, such production of metal parts in particular shapes or the attachement of one part to another, theoretically require no energy at all.'[81] Table 2.6 compares various current and projected performances for steelmaking, an energy-intensive industrial process, and Giovannini and Pain show trends in various energy-intensive industries of which only aluminium production has yet approached to near a factor of two of the theoretical minimum.

However, it does seem likely that further improvements in most of the energy-intensive industries will become more and more difficult, and even the theoretical limits on efficiency would still imply substantial

---

[80] For example, Energy Efficiency Office, *Energy Use and Energy Efficiency in UK Manufacturing Industry up to the year 2000*, Energy Efficiency Series 3, HMSO, London, 1984; Giovannini and Pain, *Optimal Energy Use*, op.cit.
[81] M.H.Ross and D.Steinmeyer, 'Energy for Industry', *Scientific American*, September 1990.

Table 2.6 Iron and steel smelting process

Country/Process	Energy consumption[1] GJ/tonne
US average, 1987	21.7
Swedish average, 1983	16.3
Japanese average,[2] 1987	15.4
Swedish planned, 1983 assessment	15.1
Swedish possible, 1983 assessment	13.0
Elred process	11.9
Plasma melt	8.7
Theoretical minimum	3.9

[1]Energy consumption, including final electricity, adjusted for a 50:50 mix of scrap and ore. The plasma melt process is 50% electric, much higher than others.
[2] Japanese average derived from Japanese case study, adjusted for different input mix.

Source: J.Goldenburg et al, *Energy for Sustainable World*, World Resources Institute, Washington DC, p.68; Japanese case study.

energy consumption if materials use continues to grow exponentially. It is for this reason that the actual trends and pressures in material use itself are so important. For reasons discussion in Volume 1, section 6.4, there are strong grounds for believing that trends in developed economies will themselves tend to limit, and possibly reduce, raw material processing. This is partly because of the increased pressures for materials recycling, which frequently saves energy;[82] the main constraints have often been the difficulties of collection and separation from other wastes, but the overall pressures for improved waste handling are overcoming such obstacles. More important is the steadily declining importance of bulk materials in developed economies. The energy consumption in major

[82] Ross and Steinmeyer, 'Energy for Industry', op.cit., indicate the following energy savings from recycling: aluminium, 75%; glass, 30%; steel, 30%; plastic, 50% (theoretical - not in use).

energy-intensive industrial processes has already declined sharply in OECD countries, and this trend seems likely to continue almost irrespective of technical process efficiency improvements.

2.7 Energy efficiency in transition economies and developing countries

The discussion above has focused upon the technical options for improving efficiency primarily within the context of developed economies. Though some of the options are similar in other economies, widely differing circumstances can affect the technical menu and relative importance of different options.

In the 'transition economies' of Eastern Europe and the Soviet Union, the industrial sector dominates demand, focusing on heavy industry. The economic focus on production targets, combined with extensive energy subsidies, means that relatively little attention has been paid to energy efficiency (see Chapter 8). The overall economic pressures on existing industries as markets are opened up are likely to dominate over any explicit industrial issues, though the gradual replacement of old industry will provide many opportunities for bringing in much more efficient industrial processes, such as those outlined in the previous section.

Domestic demand accounts for most of the rest. Frequently, the efficiency of *supply* is greater than that in OECD countries, because of the widespread use of large-scale CHP, for which the key issues are ones of institutional capabilities rather than conventional economic incentives (Volume 1, section 4.7). However, these gains are more than offset by the inefficiencies in use. The opportunities for improved insulation, lighting and appliances are all immense. In many transition economies, potentially major improvements may be obtained from metering and control techniques; some houses have no metering, others do but lack thermostatic controls, so that the easiest way of controlling temperature is to open windows (a problem not unknown in developed economies, especially in service buildings).

Transport and services are comparatively under-developed areas of energy demand in the transition economies; many of the technical options discussed above will be available as these sectors develop, and much may depend on the choices made.

In most developing countries, transport and services demand are similarly small compared with OECD countries, but are far from negligible; many Third World cities suffer from traffic congestion just as much as elsewhere, and transport accounts for about 15% of fossil CO_2 emissions from non-OECD countries overall, and is growing very fast. The vehicle stock tends to be older than in developed economies, and maintenance is often poor, because of both institutional and financial constraints on regular vehicle testing and tuning. To the extent that these constraints can be overcome, better maintenance, and biasing growth towards the more efficient end of the vehicle range, would both help to limit emissions growth and be economically beneficial.

Tales of gross industrial inefficiency are especially prevalent in many developing countries, reflecting similar institutional and financial constraints. Reform is often difficult because capital is so scarce; that which is available is usually swallowed up in the attempt to keep pace with growing demand. These and other constraints are discussed in Volume 1, section 6.5, and in the Indian and Chinese case studies. Without such an extensive legacy of inefficient industry as is found in the transition economies, and faster growth, the potential impact of ensuring efficient processes in new industries would be large. The capital restrictions and other differing circumstances - for example, climate and the differing kinds of product requirements - may imply some differences in the technical options, but to a large extent the dominant demand occurs in heavy processing industries. Also, losses in electricity systems are frequently very high though how much this is due to technical inefficiencies remains unclear.

The area in which efficiency options for developing countries differ most radically concern the domestic sector. In central urban areas, the pattern may be not unlike that in industrial countries, though often with considerable air conditioning loads. Such demands may be profligate in comparison with the rest of the population, but the numbers involved are so small that energy use in shanty towns and rural areas may be more important in absolute terms, and certainly affects a far greater population. The dominant energy sources are respectively often charcoal (firewood) and fuelwood burned directly in stoves for heating, cooking and light.

The efficiency of such stoves is often low, around 5-15%,[83] and the requirement for fuelwood and charcoal can place great strains on wood

---

[83] Stove efficiency is hard to define and even harder to measure, and it can vary considerably with the care of use, which in turn depends upon the difficulty of gathering the firewood. For a general critique see Jas Gill, 'Improved stoves in developing

supply. Much effort has been devoted to designing and disseminating improved stoves, with mixed results. Foreign designs have often failed to take account of the multi-purpose applications of traditional stoves, and the various constraints on manageable cost and complexity for those who use such fuels because they cannot afford anything else. Support for local efforts, combining engineering and marketing experiments and evaluation, are yielding substantial improvements; East African designs for example have yielded improvements of 15-40% over traditional charcoal stoves, and are selling through normal commercial channels.[84] Indian programmes are also leading to improvements (see Indian case study), though none meet the heights of earlier expectations. The obstacles to improving rural fuelwood use are greater, and the nature of the fuel and application inevitably limits the efficiency. Test designs can readily double efficiencies, but approaching anywhere near this in the field would require sustained effort and government support to overcome the initial cost hurdle.

Larger efficiency improvements would require a move to completely different processes. Liquid fuels and electricity can be used in cheap appliances at several times the efficiency of wood stoves. Advanced biomass technologies for liquid fuels or electricity, discussed in the Chapter 3, are too complex and costly to replace household demand in many developing countries until economic development creates the resources and infrastructure which could accommodate them. Liquid fuels from simpler fermentation are possible, but especially at the oil prices of the late 1980s, subsidising kerosene or LPG would be much cheaper, and is potentially a significant option for reducing pressures on firewood. To the extent that the displaced wood involved net deforestation, CO_2 emissions would be substantially reduced. Obviously, many other factors affect the choice, but the statistics are impressive: displacing all the firewood consumed globally in this way would add little over 2% and 5% to world energy and oil demand respectively.[85]

---

countries: a critique', *Energy Policy*, 15(2), April 1987. The Indian study cites average stove efficiencies of around 8%; quoted African figures tend to be nearer 10-12%. It is not clear if these reflect real variations or differing definitions.
[84] Dominic Walubengo (ed.), 'Proceedings of International Biomass Course', Nairobi, Keyna, Kenya Energy and Environment Organisation, Nairobi, 1989.
[85] Derived from statistics provided by G.Leach (private communication). Per-capita fuelwood use is estimated to be 0.15-0.26toe, at an efficiency of 10-15%. This compares

As the poorer countries develop, they tend to move away from existing patterns of energy towards those of more developed economies. Much may depend upon the extent to which they can adopt some of the more efficient advanced technologies as they do so, a question examined briefly in Volume 1, section 6.5. It depends upon many factors - including the extent to which developed economies learn how to exploit more efficient technologies.

2.8 Potential, constraints and economic context

The technical potential for improving overall energy efficiency is difficult to assess precisely. This is partly because, besides the general uncertainties in future trends and sectoral shares of different activities, there are many complexities and interactions involved. For example, making appliances more efficient reduces incidental 'heat gains' (though this is usually a relatively small effect), and improved traffic flow management reduces the scope for technical efficiency improvements, some of which arise from improved part load and start/stop characteristics. In other cases, savings are multiplicative, the most obvious examples being combinations of more efficient heat supplies (CHP or heat pumps) with better building insulation, better lamps with more intelligent lighting control systems, and better motor drive systems with improvement in the systems they are driving, be it fridge insulation or industrial processes.

These interactions also complicate economic assessment. Applications which are multiplicative are frequently in economic competition; reducing the need for lighting, heating or mechanical energy reduces the returns on systems which provide them more efficiently. There are however important exceptions: reduced heat requirements make super heat pumps or solar heating more feasible, and better vehicle efficiency greatly improves the prospects for most alternative fuels.

The primary obstacles to improving efficiency do not appear to be those of costs in the conventional economic sense of discounted net present value. The great majority of improvements discussed would provide handsome returns as compared with most energy supply investments, but

with kerosene and LPG stoves at 40-50%, so that displacing fuelwood use by an estimated 3 billion people would require 130-225Mtoe, compared with global commercial energy and oil consumption in 1989 of 8,000Mtoe and 3,100Mtoe respectively.

are not taken up for a variety of the reasons discussed in this chapter and in Volume 1, Chapter 4. Overall, the economic potential, if assessed by comparing existing stock with the 'optimal' at discount rates of around 7-10%, appears to be very large. 'Optimal' energy use in new buildings could more than halve consumption of both heat and electricity as compared with current stock in most countries. Potential economic savings in industry are frequently of the order of 20-40% (some claim higher when full system opportunities are considered). Transport, as noted, is more hotly disputed because of uncertainties about safety and performance tradeoffs; the estimates reported suggest potential improvements of 15-25% in new vehicles over the next decade, but the long-term economic potential is clearly much larger, depending somewhat upon the impact of consumer choice.

Using a discount rate closer to the actual realized return on energy supply investments (which has generally been well below 7-10%) - and closer to the social discount rate of 2-3% (with or without shadow capital costing as discussed in Volume 1, section 3.2) - would boost the estimates of economic potential further.

Volume 1, Chapter 7, reports various sectorial studies, including those reviewed by the IEA.[86] Figures of 15-50% economic savings are consistently found, (with the higher figures again relating to building energy demand and electrical applications) consistent with the analysis of technologies and applications presented in this chapter.

Such figures neglect the critical element of time. Costs are clearly much higher if improvements have to be retrofitted or if stocks prematurely replaced, so the real economic potential increases steadily as the time horizon lengthens. Few domestic boilers, vehicles or electrical applications last much longer than 20 years. Over such a period, some natural opportunities would also arise for retrofitting building stock and long-lived industrial processes though the potential is certainly reduced by the persistence of oil stock. This indicates that economic efficiency improvements of up to 50% in electrical applications, and 15-40% in other uses, might be available over a period of two decades. The question of the rate of impact of efficiency improvement is considered more closely through modelling studies in Chapter 4.

The discussion above notes that many of these improvements are not being taken up by existing energy markets. Yet such efficiency

---

[86] International Energy Agency, *Energy Conservation in IEA Countries*, Paris 1987.

improvements would, if they could be realized, reduce energy supply costs by 1-3% of GNP in most OECD countries - and of the order of $100bn in the US economy alone. The additional capital expenditure involved would amount to only a small fraction of the cumulative savings. It has to be said that if savings of this order really are available but untapped in developed market economies, then conventional economics has an awful lot of explaining to do. Most economists would accept that various market imperfections, and delays in implementation, could create some cost-effective opportunities, but find it hard to believe that the 'efficiency gap' can possibly be as large as these figures imply in economies which have, for all their faults, demonstrated the unique power of market economics. Most simply either disbelieve such claims, or conclude that some important factors have been omitted which mean that most of the apparent 'efficiency gap' is illusory. These same factors, it is reasoned, mean that the real savings available are far smaller than the simple engineering cost statistics imply. There are certainly many potential candidates for explaining away the apparent 'efficiency gap', and Figure 2.8 shows a useful way of illustrating them.[87]

The total height of the column represents the apparent 'engineering' potential for cost-effective savings. At the top, consumer dislikes (eg. of some fluorescent lights), unavoidable hidden costs and other barriers reduce the amount which is genuinely available; also, some of the apparent savings from efficiency improvements would be lost to 'rebound' (or 'take-back') in products where improvements in efficiency, and hence lowered operating costs, encourage consumers to use them more. The rest of the column represents savings which could in principle be tapped with net benefit, and is divided into three components: those which would be realized through natural take-up without any alterations in energy markets; those which would incur a real cost but which are justified on grounds of non-greenhouse externalities which should in principle be 'internalized' in energy costs (this has not been considered in any detail); and those which can only be realized if the microeconomic conditions are changed, for example by using the kind of policy instruments discussed in Volume 1, Chapter 4. The overall potential - the size of the column - increases over time as stock turns over (and as better techniques are developed).

---

[87]The author is grateful to J.Edmonds and R.Richels for suggesting this way of illustrating the issues.

Figure 2.8 Energy efficiency: engineering potential and realizable gains - a classification

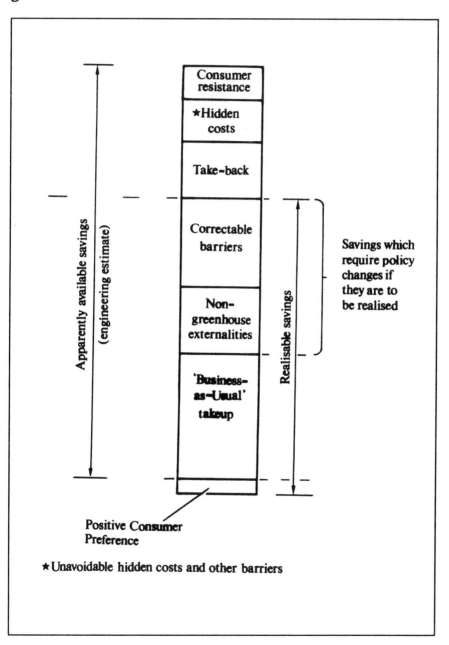

The critical question is then not only whether estimates of the potential for improved efficiency are correct, but how they are divided into the different components. How much is illusory because of irremovable hidden costs and market imperfections, 'takeback', or consumer opposition? How much of the remainder would be taken up anyway in the absence of policy changes? And how much can only be realized through policy changes to change the microeconomic character of energy decisions, and to incorporate externalities (not considered here)? The answers to these questions are not known in detail. There are reasons to suppose that 'takeback' is relatively small for most policy-driven efficiency improvements (Volume 1, section 4.2), and consumer preference seems an important factor only for cars (where it is already taken into account in most credible estimates) and possibly lighting. The nature of the general market imperfections and hidden costs, and the extent to which they might be reduced, seems particularly complex because they appear to involve not only simple market obstacles, but far more subtle aspects of real-life human and market behaviour. The immense and perceptive Oak Ridge study of energy technology concludes with a final section on 'non-hardware R&D needs', primarily concerned with social science understanding of energy decisionmaking. After discussing public attitudes to risk, uncertainty, and techniques for resolving conflicts, the study reviews research on 'how markets work' and reports:

The most commonly used economic theories are relatively poor representations of the way market decisions are made. Traditional assumptions about market behaviour based on logical postulates about 'rationality' have generally not been supported by observations of actual behaviour. For example 'rational expectations' theories have not been validated by testing, nor have life cycle costing hypotheses... Markets do not place a very high value on collective or long-term benefits...the research literature suggests that, whenever collective goods are provided through a market mechanism, they will be chronically undersupplied or underfinanced relative to actual individual preference for them. Information is a classic example of such collective goods. Moreover ... market decisions ... place little value on long term benefits ... this situation narrows the focus of market decisions in ways that may not only be socially dysfunctional but also economically noncompetitive in the long run.[88]

Stripped of the jargon, there is ample evidence that people do not behave quite in the way that economic theory predicts. In the field of energy provision, representing as it does the cumulative impact of billions of decisions which involve operating expenditures which at the personal level are marginal, but which have economic and environmental repercussions over decades and even centuries, this can lead to potentially very serious distortions.

Doubtless, some of the hidden costs and market imperfections are unavoidable; their scale is uncertain, and to some extent a matter of definition.[89] Also, substantial efficiency improvements will occur even in the absence of policy changes. Yet overall, the pervasive nature of the market imperfections discussed in this study suggest that a large fraction of the potential savings will remain untapped without applying the kind of policy instruments discussed in Volume 1, Chapter 4, together perhaps with still more advanced ways of changing the microeconomic context of energy decisions.

2.9 How far can efficiency go?

In concluding, two general points need to be stressed. First, efficiency improvements cannot automatically be equated with reducing absolute demand. Aggregate energy efficiency improves radically as countries industrialize, but this is much more than offset by the immense growth in *applications* of commercial energy. Improved technical efficiency means merely that a given level of services can be met with lower energy requirements than would otherwise have been the case.

Projections of declining energy consumption thus rest as much on beliefs about the saturation of energy applications as on efficiency improvements. The question of the extent to which energy applications may saturate in developed economies is discussed in Volume 1, Chapter 6, and taken further in Chapter 4 of this volume.

[88] W.Fulkerson et al, *Energy Technology R&D*, op.cit., p.129.
[89] For example, perfect consumer behaviour in terms of never leaving lights on or doors open, and always optimally maintaining equipment, would clearly yield 'cost effective' savings, but little could be done to turn these hypothetical savings into reality. Whether these are added as potential but unachievable savings, or ignored entirely, is largely a matter of semantics.

Finally, one unavoidable limitation of long-term energy and efficiency projections is that they inevitably reflect current technical understanding Going back 50 years to what people might have speculated in 1940 abou energy use and efficiency in 1990 reveals just how difficult and uncertain such a projection is bound to be. Many studies of CO_2 emissions projec energy use throughout the next century. Given the impossibility o projecting meaningfully all the technologies which might be in use, ca anything be said about theoretical limits to efficiency improvements?

To address these issues, the second law of thermodynamics can be use to calculate the minimum theoretical amount of work required to perforn a given task (as opposed to the first law, which merely states that tota energy is conserved). The fundamental unit for second-law analysis i not energy but 'exergy' (see box), and 'exergy efficiency' is defined a the ratio of the minimum theoretical work required to that actuall consumed.

The distinction between energy and exergy is important theoreticall but in practice they only differ significantly concerning heat supply because heat is a lower 'grade' of energy, to which other forms of energ are eventually transformed. Transforming heat to higher quality energ such as motion or electricity involves unavoidable energy losses (whicl depend on the temperatures involved) dictated by thermodynami principles. Thus thermal power stations, which boil water to raise stear to drive turbines, are fundamentally limited to efficiencies of aroun 60%; car engines, which use the pressure of combustion heat to drive th pistons, are similarly limited. Many practical constraints on therma processes limit these efficiencies further. The same laws dictate th potential for heat pumps to transfer heat from lower to higher temperatur reservoirs, with the heat transferred being several times the input c high-quality energy.

The value of energy and exergy efficiency analysis however is not onl that it identifies theoretical limits to improvements, but it can highligl the steps in energy systems which involve the greatest losses. A repor from IIASA[90] provides a comprehensive discussion and review c literature, and derives estimates of exergy efficiencies for energ provision in the OECD.

For direct applications of fossil fuels, the primary energy is usuall converted to secondary energy (where conversion is required at all) an

Energy, Exergy, and Efficiency

Exergy, or available work, is sometimes described as a measure of energy quality. The American Institute of Physics (*Efficient Use of Energy*, AIP Conference Proceedings No.25, AIP, New York) define exergy as:

> The maximum work that can be provided by a system (or by fuel) as it proceeds (by any path) to a specified final state in thermodynamic equilibrium with the atmosphere; interaction with the atmosphere is permitted, but work done on the atmosphere is not counted.

The exergy value of motion, chemical energy, and electricity are all quite close to the energy content; they are 'high grade' forms, and there is little practical difference between energy and exergy efficiencies for processes converting between these forms. Heat is a 'low grade' energy form; the available work, and hence exergy value, is lower than the energy content, and depends on the temperature relative to the reference state (eg. the atmosphere). The maximum theoretical efficiency of converting heat at temperature T_1 to work is $(T_1-T_0)/T_1$, where T_0 is the reference temperature and temperatures are expressed in degrees Kelvin, ie. degrees centigrade + 273. Thus, the exergy value of heat at temperatures not far from atmospheric temperatures is much lower than its energy value.

The exergy value of fossil fuels lies between the gross and net heating values (Appendix 1), since the energy in the steam produced by combustion can contribute work, but is itself thermal energy with irreducible losses incurred in exploiting it.

delivered as final energy at relatively high efficiencies, the major losses being in petroleum refining, the transport of coal and its transformation to coke, and pumping and liquefaction and regasification of natural gas. For electricity, the conversion and distribution losses combined generally limit the overall primary-to-secondary efficiency to about 30%. Technologies for improving electricity conversion are considered in the next chapter. However, even the losses of electricity conversion can be small compared with those of the final stages, which IIASA break down into two components.

First is the conversion of final energy to useful energy - the conversion from the fuel as delivered to the energy as physically applied. For example, internal combustion engines convert chemical energy to mechanical energy with a maximum efficiency of about 33%, and after other losses less than 20% of the energy in the petroleum is delivered to the wheels - the final to useful conversion. For lighting, incandescent bulbs convert about 4% of the electricity supplied into visible radiant energy, while fluorescent lamps may reach 20-30%.[91] For heat supply, the final-to-useful *energy* conversion is often quite high, perhaps 80-90% for boilers, and nearly 100% for electrical immersion, but in the most common application of heating to only a few tens of degrees above the outside air temperature (if that), the *exergy* efficiency is very low. Direct heating to maintain a temperature difference of 20 degrees has an exergy efficiency of about 6.5%; with an electric heat pump operating at an exergy efficiency of 30% (typical for current heat pump technology), the final-to-useful efficiency is 22% after other losses, but including the electricity generation losses reduces the overall primary to useful exergy efficiency to around 8%.[92]

Finally, the *service efficiency* reflects the efficiency with which the useful energy is used to provide the desired service. In practice this can be very difficult to estimate, and somewhat arbitrary bounds have to be drawn. The IIASA report estimates service efficiencies by examining the best applications of existing practical technology; for example, the practical maximum extent of building insulation (with reference to consumer convenience and acceptance, but not economics) might reduce heating needs to 10-15% of actual use, whilst much of the light output from bulbs is also wasted, being obstructed or illuminating unwanted areas. These factors represent service efficiencies. They are inevitably uncertain, but the main message is again to emphasize further theoretical scope for improving end-use efficiency. IIASA's estimates for the exergy efficiencies of conversion from primary energy to final, useful, and actual service application for the OECD overall are illustrated in Figure 2.9. Overall, the authors estimate a primary-to-service efficiency of

[91] ibid, p.155.
[92] ibid, p.171.

Figure 2.9 Estimated exergy efficiencies in OECD countries for 1986

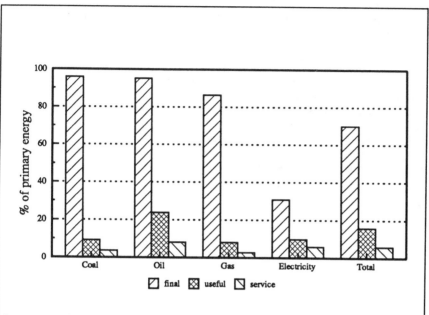

Source: Nakicenovic et al, *Technological Progress, Structural Change, and Efficient Energy Use*, Final report, 700/76.716/9, IIASA, Laxenburg, Austria, 1989, p.213.

around 6%, consistent with (indeed, somewhat higher than) some of the other reported estimates.

Such analysis in itself says nothing about the realisable scope for improving efficiency, which depends upon the technical and economic feasibility and desirability of technologies for improving efficiency, but it does serve to emphasize that current energy systems have approached nowhere near the theoretical limits, and point to the main areas where major improvements might be found.

Consequently there is no reason to suppose that estimates such as those indicated in this chapter and elsewhere represent a fixed potential which will be exhausted given time. In most countries, there were substantial efficiency improvements in the fifteen years following the first oil price shock, but the potential remains just as large as it was assessed to be then.[93] Rather like oil itself, energy efficiency appears to be a distinctly limited resource which in reality never runs out, and there appear to be no physical reasons why efficiency should not continue to improve for most of the next century.

[93] The UK industrial sector had by 1990 achieved most of the efficiency potential identified in 1980 by the Department of Energy's projection to 2000, but the remaining potential in 1990 appeared almost as large, and 1990 estimates from the Department's research unit suggested a larger remaining economy-wide potential than the total potential identified by either official or independent studies a decade earlier. See, G.Leach and Z.Nowak, *Cutting carbon dioxide emissions from Poland and the United Kingdom*, Stockholm Environment Institute, 1990; and European Commission, 'The CO_2 Crash Programme' DGXII, Brussels, 1991.

Supply-side changes can reduce CO_2 emissions by improving the efficiency of energy conversion and by moving to lower or zero carbon sources. The main opportunities for improving conversion efficiency lie in electricity generation. The monolithic steam turbine is restricted to efficiencies of little over 35% and has reached its zenith; future developments will focus on advanced gas turbine cycles. When fired by natural gas, large combined cycle plants can reach efficiencies over 45%, at capital costs well below those of major steam plants. Existing steam-injected cycles offer lower costs for smaller applications, at efficiencies still above 40%. Further modifications of steam injected cycles offer the prospect of efficiencies approaching 50% at low cost.

Many different fuels can be used to power gas turbines. Fluidized bed combustion of coal can be used to drive gas turbines directly, and offers one of several ways of gasifying the coal. Coal conversion adds to the capital cost and reduces the efficiency by several points as compared with gas systems, but is still likely to offer gains over steam thermal systems; pollutant control is also much easier. Fuel cells offer an alternative approach and could yield efficiencies above 50%, but high costs may restrict them to relatively small applications.

Biomass may be considered as the renewable equivalent of fossil fuels: it is available in many different forms, which can be transformed to a wide range of products. Traditional methods of exploitation greatly restrict its feasible contribution as societies develop, but modern technologies could transform its prospects. Two key options are likely to be enzymatic processes for producing liquid fuels, especially alcoho and gasification for power generation from advanced gas turbine cycles Careful management of biomass resources can boost yield considerably, and successful application of these and supplementar techniques could re-establish biomass as an important component c energy supplies.

The costs and performance of nuclear power already varies considerabl between countries, according to the design and management, an incremental developments should continue to improve performanc slowly. Fundamentally new approaches based on modular and passivel safe designs could increase both the market and public acceptability c nuclear power. There is little prospect that fast breeder reactors can b economically feasible when the full requirements are accounted for. Th outlook for fusion power is even worse.

Renewable energy technologies are many and diverse. Hydro resource and geothermal aquifers are already widely exploited, and furthe opportunities remain, including the wide use of micro-hydro sites Projection of other renewables is difficult because relatively so little ha been spent on them, and experience is limited. However, wind energy an solar thermal power developed rapidly during the 1980s and are alread competitive for grid-based generation in some areas. The costs of sola cells, which offer the largest single potential of any renewabl technology, have likewise fallen dramatically and they may approac competitiveness during the 1990s. Other renewables could become ver important in some locations.

The key uncertainties are not just those of technical advances, but o background fossil fuel prices. Production costs from the cheapest foss reserves are so low that there is little prospect of alternatives bein cheaper. Rather, developments in renewable technologies especially wi moderate the costs of non-fossil strategies: the technologies can enter i and when fossil fuel prices rise above the low levels of the late 1980s, o if relatively modest carbon taxes are applied.

Although all fossil fuels are finite resources, for the reasons discussed in Chapter 1 there is little sign that resource constraints will fundamentally limit the use of any of them over the next few decades, and there are pressures on all three for expanded use. Gas use seems set to grow along with the continuing development of infrastructure and technologies for gas use. Oil may, depending somewhat on price, continue to retreat from 'non-premium' markets - but the global expansion in transport and petrochemicals demand could easily more than offset this. Coal is under pressure in many areas, but it is the largest resource of all and in many developing countries especially - above all China - it forms the backbone of plans for economic development, particularly for meeting what continues as explosive growth in electricity demand.

Faced with this situation, there are two broad technical approaches to trying to limit the use of carbon in energy supplies, beyond the attempts to limit final energy demand discussed in the previous chapter. One is to increase the efficiency of energy conversion from the primary extraction to the delivered energy. Since, as discussed in Chapter 2, the efficiency of delivering fossil fuels is already high, this is only an important option with respect to electricity, where there are potentially large gains if the inherent losses of the steam-turbine cycle can be circumvented. The other option is to change the mix of fossil fuels used: increased use of natural gas, within the constraints noted; nuclear power; and coming full circle by returning to the use of renewable energy sources, but in a form which can meet the needs of modern societies. This chapter examines these options.

3.1 Generating electricity from fossil fuels: technical options

Steam Turbines. Since the birth of electricity systems, generation has been dominated by steam turbines. The steam engine, in which coal was used to raise steam, to provide the pressure for mechanical energy of all forms, had been the key energy conversion technology of the industrial revolution; adding a generator to it was a natural and relatively easy step. The history of electricity generation ever since - including nuclear power - has been described as that of 101 ways of boiling water.

Efficiencies increased steadily over more than half a century to the early 1960s, as the working temperatures and pressures of steam turbines were raised. But since then, despite ever increasing size and complexity, efficiencies in most developed economies have been more or less static at little over 35% (Gross Heating Value, GHV).[1] Though higher temperatures and pressures are possible, they have not proved economically worthwhile, because of the greater operational difficulties, stresses, and requirements for special materials to withstand such conditions.

Even as some of the finest examples are still being completed, the conventional steam power station is at the end of its development path. The final blow in developed economies is likely to be the rise of environmental concerns, notably those over emissions of sulphur dioxide and nitrogen oxides. Cleaning these substances from the flue gases is possible, but expensive. Environmental concerns have combined with economic forces and fundamental technical constraints to bring a plethora of other options to centre stage.

One option is to keep the steam system intact, but to change fundamentally the nature of the boiler by using an *atmospheric fluidized bed combustor* (AFBC).[2] In this, a dense bed of burning coal and other particles are kept 'fluidized' by a continuing updraft of air. Coal is continuously fed in from one side, and ash removed from the bottom. The coal burns in a steady and controlled fashion, with heat being transferred so rapidly that the high flame temperatures which create NOx in conventional boilers are not reached. Furthermore, it is easy to introduce limestone into the bed to absorb sulphur, and there are certain other advantages over conventional coal boilers. Though various difficulties have been encountered, AFBCs are already commercially available for industrial applications, and are being commercialized for use as 'retrofit' alternatives to post-combustion scrubbing of conventional boiler flue gases, particularly in the US. Because they rely on the steam cycle, AFBCs do not increase efficiency above that of conventional boilers, though they can avoid the efficiency losses associated with flue gas clean-up.

---

[1] All generating efficiencies in this chapter are quoted on the basis of Gross Heating Values. Net Heating Values yield efficiencies about 3% higher for coal (ie. about 1 percentage point from current levels), and 10% higher for gas; see Appendix 1.
[2] An excellent overview of all the coal technologies discussed in this chapter, including description of operation, manufacturers and (1990) market status, is given in W.Patterson, *Coal Use Technology in a Changing Environment*, Financial Times Management Report, FTBI, London, 1990. More technical references are given as cited.

A major development from this is the *pressurized fluidized bed combustor* (PFBC), in which the bed is operated under considerable pressure. This can improve the operating characteristics of the bed, but more importantly, it opens the option of using higher temperatures and pressures than is available in steam cycles. The extra energy can be captured using a gas turbine; and gas turbines now form technical path in themselves.

Gas turbines. Gas turbines for aircraft and industry have developed steadily since the Second World War , but for electricity production they were considered the poor relation of the steam turbine. Rather than being driven by injected steam, gaseous fuel burns in air which has been pressurized by a compressor, producing powerful expansion which drives the turbine directly. This enables higher pressures and temperatures to be used directly. However, whereas in the steam turbine, steam can be condensed to produce a low temperature and low pressure exhaust, with gas turbines there is no way of condensing the exhaust. The potential efficiency advantage of high temperatures is more than offset by the energy lost through the exhaust, and conventional gas turbines are less efficient than steam turbines. They are however inherently simpler, lighter, and cheaper, because of the absence of the complex steam cycle.

The biggest application of gas turbines to date has been for jet engines, where the lightness and high power have made them the only practical option. They have also been common in many industrial applications, particularly where there is a use for the high exhaust temperatures for combined heat and power. For bulk power generation, many were constructed during the 1950s and 1960s to help meet the rapid growth in demand, and to run on cheap oil products. Gas turbines have continued to have an important role as peaking plants on electricity systems: their low capital costs and rapid response (they can usually start from cold in a few minutes) makes them suitable for meeting demand surges and peaks.

However, the lower efficiency and need for clean premium fuels - natural gas or light oil distillates - meant that the typical attitude of utility operators, especially since the oil price shocks, has been that 'the only good gas turbine is one that doesn't have to run'.[3] But during the 1980s,

[3] Quoted in R.H.Williams and E.D.Larsen, 'Aeroderivative Turbines for Stationary Power', *Annual Review of Energy*, Vol.13, 1988.

Figure 3.1 Combined cycle plant with coal gasification

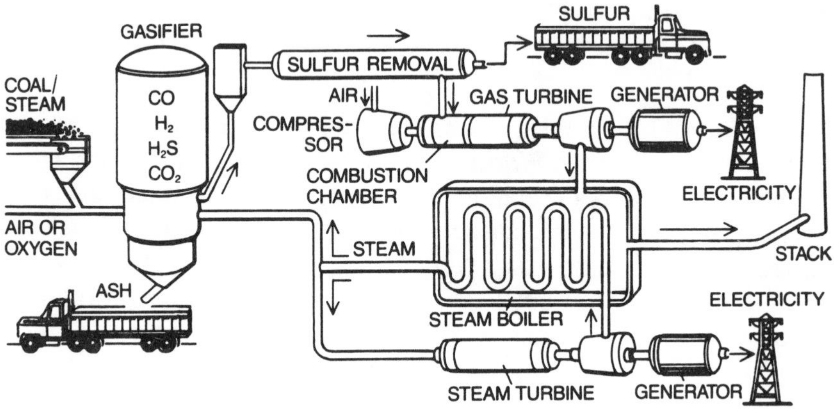

Source: W.Fulkerson, R.R.Judkins and M.K.Sanghvi, 'Energy From Fossil Fuels', *Scientific American*, September 1990.

gas turbines began to emerge as a highly competitive option, on the basis of improved basic operating performance combined with a range of simple modifications to the power cycle used that can dramatically boost the power and efficiency available.

Of these modifications, the simplest is the *combined cycle* plant. The hot outlet gases from the gas turbine are used to raise steam to feed into a conventional steam turbine; Figure 3.1 shows an illustration of a combined cycle plant powered by coal gasification, discussed below. By thus combining the high inlet temperature of a gas turbine with the low outlet temperature of a steam turbine, the overall efficiency is raised well above that of either. With natural gas as the fuel, figures of over 45% efficiency are cited. Although the capital costs are much higher than those of simple gas turbines, the lower steam temperatures and pressures mean that the capital costs are typically well below those of the monolithic modern steam power plant.

The reason perhaps why such a simple and obvious idea was not developed earlier is because natural gas was, until the 1980s, widely perceived to be a scarce and costly fuel with little future, and oil distillates were likewise considered too limited and expensive to be used widely to displace coal power generation (though many steam plants were built to use heavy fuel oil during the oil boom of the 1960s). Indeed, an EC directive in 1975 explicitly banned the use of natural gas for power generation in an attempt to conserve what then seemed very limited resources for premium applications. As described in Chapter 1, the situation now seems very different in many regions. The EC directive was repealed in 1990, and related constraints have been removed elsewhere during the 1980s.

Gas-fired combined cycle plant had to wait until the mid-1980s before they were commercially developed and available. By 1990 they were widely recognized to be more efficient, cheaper to build, and - because of the high efficiency and relatively low industrial gas prices - even cheaper to run in many areas than conventional coal plant. The increasing liberalization of electricity industries has given them further impetus - small private generating companies appreciate above all the low capital cost and short construction time. Also, the input contains scarcely any sulphur, and the process produces a fraction of the NO_x produced by conventional steam turbines. Where plentiful cheap natural gas exists, it is hard to see what can stand in the way of combined cycle technology.[4]

Except, perhaps, still better applications of gas turbines. The steam which can be raised by the exhaust gases does not have to be used in a steam turbine. It can instead be injected back into the combustor and gas turbine itself, at the temperature and pressure of the compressed air.[5] This greatly increases the mass flow through the turbine section and, in a process reminiscent of turbocharging a car engine, leads to a great boost in power - and efficiency, as compared with a conventional gas turbine, since the exhaust gases are then cooler. By avoiding the steam turbine

---

[4]'Will gas turbine technology dethrone King Coal?', *Gas Matters*, 30 November, 1989, gives data on the cost and performance of various gas turbine systems, and the threshold prices for competiveness against coal.

[5] Injecting steam to boost power and efficiency should not be confused with the long-established practice of injecting small amounts of steam into the combustion chamber to help suppress NO_x formation.

stage entirely, the capital costs are lower than for a combined cycle, though the efficiency - typically around 40% - is not as high.

One reason for interest in such 'Steam Injected Gas Turbines' (STIGs) is that, while combined cycle plants use heavy-duty industrial gas turbines, STIGs can better utilize aeroderivative engines, which are designed for higher mass flows, lower outlet temperatures - and for great reliability and ease of maintenance. Immense R&D has already been invested in aeroengines. As a result, 'most of the relatively low technology cycle modifications available for improving performance [for ground-based power generation] remain largely unexploited, even though enormous high-technology advances have been made'.[6]

For small-scale applications STIGs have another inherent advantage, because large plant are required to take full advantage of economies of scale in the steam part of combined cycle plant - their efficiency falls and relative costs increase for plant sizes below about 400MW. For applications below about 100MW, STIGs are probably preferable on nearly all counts; but they probably cannot compete with the higher efficiency of large-scale combined cycle plant. However, interest has been sustained by the recognition that further simple modifications can substantially improve on the basic STIG cycle. Simply by cooling the air compressed in the first stage of the compressor (a fraction of which is then directed to cooling the turbine blades), greater inlet temperatures can be used, and the efficiency raised to be comparable to that of large combined cycle plant, still at lower capital cost than combined cycle plant.

Such *Intercooled Steam Injected Gas Turbines* (ISTIGs), illustrated in Figure 3.2, are not a proven technology. The likely performance gains above those of large combined cycle plant are modest, and this probably helps to explain why no companies are yet committed to their full-scale development. But they have many of the other potential advantages of STIG technology, as summarized by Williams and Larson,[7] and successful development seems likely.[8]

---

[6] R.H.Williams and E.D.Larson, 'Expanding Roles for Gas Turbines in Power Generation', in T.B.Johansson et al (eds), *Electricity: Efficient End-Use and New Generation Technologies, and Their Planning Implications*, Lund University Press, Lund, Sweden, 1989, p.520.

[7] 'An ISTIG has several advantages over a combined cycle unit: it is simpler, requiring no steam turbine, condenser, or cooling tower; pollution controls would be less costly..; the small unit capacity implies flexibility in capacity planning, improved reliability,

Figure 3.2 Intercooled steam injected gas turbine (ISTIG) system

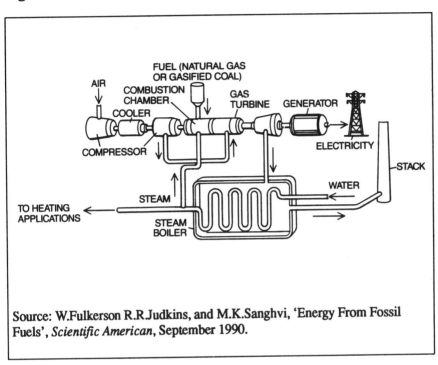

Source: W.Fulkerson R.R.Judkins, and M.K.Sanghvi, 'Energy From Fossil Fuels', *Scientific American*, September 1990.

The capital cost, efficiency and pollution performance of these various technologies is illustrated in Table 3.1. Further developments could improve the performance of both combined cycle and ISTIG plants. The

and ease of maintenance through lease-pool arrangements; their small size also makes themgood candidates for cost cutting innovations and the economies of mass production; and [they] will continue to benefit quickly from expected continuing improvements in jet engine technology.' (Williams and Larson, 'Expanding roles for gas turbines in power generation', op.cit., p.532). Other possible advantages, eg. for biomass applications, are noted in the text of this and the following section.
[8] W.Fulkerson et al, *Energy Technology R&D: What Could Make A Difference?*, ORNL-6541, ORNL, Tennesee, 1989. Volume 1: Synthesis Report; Volume 2, in three parts. This major technology assessment by the US Oak Ridge National Laboratory reports that: 'The ISITG cost and efficiency projections cited by Larson and Williams are supported by a wide range of authors in industry and academia ... the major obstacle for the wide-scale implementation of ISTIG appears to be the lack of a development sponsor. This obstacle, in turn, is closely tied to current market competition with combined cycle systems.' (Vol. 2, Part 2, p.43)

Table 3.1 Performance of modern natural gas power generation cycles

	Capital cost ($/Kw)	Efficiency (%,GHV)	NO_x (mg/MJe)	CO_2 (kgC/kWh)
Gas turbine	200-300	30	100	0.17
Steam turbine	760	36	180	0.14
Combined cycle	520	47	15	0.10
STIG	410	40	15	0.12
ISTIG	400	47	10	0.10
Advanced fuel cell	600-800	50-55	5-20	0.09-0.10

Source: W.Fulkerson, et al, 'Energy from Fossil Fuels', *Scientific American*, September 1990, except gas turbine data, from various sources.

'Kalina Cycle' can raise the efficiency of steam turbine cycles by 10-20% by using a mixture of ammonia and water which varies in composition throughout the cycle.[9] An upper temperature limit may make the Kalina Cycle particularly appropriate for combined cycle plants. However, it is achieved at the cost of greatly increased complexity and has yet to be demonstrated satisfactorily. In ISTIGs, some of the spare energy in the steam output can be recovered by 'chemical recuperation', in which the input fuel is reformed to a mixture of H, CO and CO_2, boosting the efficiency further.[10]

[9] W.Fulkerson et al, *Energy Technology R&D: What Could Make A Difference?*, op.cit., Volume 2 Part 2, pp.46-47.
[10] Williams and Larson, 'Expanding roles for gas turbines in power generation', op.cit.

Non-thermal cycles. Impressive as these developments and possibilities are, none seem likely to be capable of turning more than half the energy available into electricity.[11] Attempts to go further have to circumvent the fundamental constraints of the thermodynamic cycle.

One approach, which attracted considerable attention and investment during the 1960s especially, is that of magnetohydrodynamics (MHD), in which particles are ionized and accelerated by magnets to induce electric current directly. Despite considerable research efforts, results have not been promising.[12] More hopeful is the fuel cell, the principles of which have been known for almost as long as electricity itself. It is the inverse of water electrolysis, in which water is split into hydrogen and oxygen. In a fuel cell, electrodes are placed in an solution (the electrolyte), and a fuel rich in hydrogen is fed to one electrode while an oxidant (usually air or pure oxygen) is fed to the other. Hydrogen ions migrate in the electrolyte to react with oxygen at the other electrode, producing a voltage difference and electrical current if an external circuit is connected, directly from the chemical energy of the fuel.[13] There are still inherent limitations on the efficiency of the process, but these are not as severe as those of the thermodynamic cycle. Heat is produced, which must be drawn off; some of it can be used in processing the primary fuel into a hydrogen-rich gas suitable for introducing into the fuel cell. According to Blomen, 'fuel processing systems can be designed to produce either pure hydrogen or synthesis gas of variable composition, from almost any hydrocarbon fuel. While natural gas is most commonly

---

[11] Kalina Cycles and chemically-recuperated ISTIGs fired by natural gas might yield all-round efficiencies of about 50% on a GHV basis. Higher efficiencies quoted are usually on the basis of net heating values (NHV): for gas, 50% GHV corresponds to around 55% NHV.

[12] A recent review of MHD is given by G.F.Morrison, *Coal-Fired MHD*, IEACR/06, IEA Coal Research, London, 1988. W.Fulkerson et al, *Energy Technology R&D: What Could Make A Difference?*, op.cit., draws on this and states that 'Overall plant efficiency for large, mature MHD plants are projected to be in the range of 50 to 60%, although 40 to 45% is probably more realistic for early commercial plants... the potential for a small reduction in cost will probably not justify the risk required to develop the technology'. (Vol. 2, Part 2, p.48).

[13] A detailed technical review of fuel cells is given in L.Blomen, 'Fuel Cells', in T.B.Johansson et al (eds), *Electricity*, op.cit. A brief and highly readable account of fuel cells and their potential applications is G.Stein, 'Unlocking the fuel cell's potential', *SCRAM*, Bulletin No.76, SCRAM, Edinburgh, April/May 1990.

used, other fuels have been studied as well, including pure methane, biogas, LPG, naphtha, and coal (via gasification)'.[14]

Like batteries, to which they are closely related, fuel cells tend to come in very small sizes. To date they have been used in various mobile applications, including spacecraft. Fuel cells can generally vary their output very rapidly, and can run just as efficiently at part loads, unlike most thermal cycles. This, in combination with their smaller size, silent operation, and almost complete lack of gaseous emissions from the cell itself, may make them particularly suitable for small CHP applications.

Fuels cells come in several very different forms, of which two have been fairly well developed. Alkali fuel cells have been used in many space missions. They cannot tolerate carbon oxides and require pure hydrogen as a fuel - fed off cylinders of pure hydrogen and oxygen, the only products are heat, electricity, and drinking water, with the electricity produced at efficiencies of up to 60%. Systems of up to 50kW (ie. one ten-thousandth of typical power station scales) have been developed, but the need for pure hydrogen fundamentally limits their applicability to hydrocarbon fuels.

The phosphoric acid fuel cell (PAFC) is the best established and most widely applied. The largest demonstration units have been two 4.5MW plants built by United Technology Corporation in Tokyo and New York, the former of which has demonstrated performance well enough for UTC to proceed with commercialization plans. Currently however their efficiency is around 40%, and development is not expected to push efficiency above the level of advanced gas turbine cycles. The requirement for costly materials make the capital costs around $2,000-$3,000/kW.

For power system applications the greatest interest is being expressed in molten carbonate fuel cells (MCFCs). These operate at high temperatures and cell efficiencies of 55-65%. There are many uncertainties and practical difficulties, and the only systems tested to date are R&D cells with a maximum 25kW output. The figures in Table 3.1 assume broadly successful development of such advanced fuel cells.

The outlook for fuel cells is thus uncertain.[15] The relative economics depend upon the size of the system, the nature of the operating conditions,

---

[14] L.Blomen, 'Fuel Cells', op.cit., p.631.
[15] Blomen, ibid, presents calculations to show that 'MCFC fuel cells can be economic even at current performance levels', and projects substantial cost reductions from mass

the extent to which the waste heat is used, and the temperature at which it is required. For limited small scale applications PAFCs can already be economic, but they are clearly not a bulk power source. For large scale power applications, the realizable advantages even of carbonate cells seems likely to be marginal, at least unless more speculative approaches prove good.[16] What probably would make fuel cells come into their own on a large scale would be if hydrogen fuels were developed, when they might well provide the most efficient and attractive means of conversion - including, as noted in the previous chapter, the most efficient means of powering vehicles yet conceived.

Coal gasification and CO_2 removal. Gas turbine technologies, and possibly fuel cells in the longer term, seem set to play a central role in future power generation. When operated with natural gas, all the technologies discussed above produce less than half the CO_2 produced by a conventional coal-fired power station of the same output. But natural gas is not available everywhere, and large-scale electricity expansion based upon it, especially if it included extensive retrofitting or displacement of coal generation, could strain gas resources and make gas prices volatile, as discussed in Volume 1, Chapter 5. To what extent can the advantages of gas turbines and fuel cells be applied to other fuels, especially coal?

As noted above, pressurized fluidized beds are one way of extracting the energy of coal into a high pressure and temperature gas stream which can power a turbine. Efficiencies of just over 40% may be attainable, but there are inherent difficulties and costs arising from the nature of the bed combustion process and from the volume of material which must withstand the high temperature and pressure gas stream. Another approach, which many consider more promising at least for new plant (as opposed to 'repowering' of old plant), is to gasify the coal into products which can be burnt directly in a gas turbine. Three main gasification techniques exist, (each with many detailed variants), and a few fundamentally different approaches have been proposed; a review

production (much more so than for ISTIGs, where most of the components are either already proven or adaptations of technologies proven at scale); but this inevitably involves an extensive extrapolation from existing experience, and somewhat pessimistic cost estimates for competing technologies, (p.653).
[16] W.Fulkerson et al, *Energy Technology R&D*, Vol.1, op.cit., notes various other advanced cycles as 'interesting possibilities', (p.74).

is given by Peters.[17] Despite advances, the overall additional handling and processing requirements for the coal (as illustrated schematically in Figure 3.1 above) inevitably incur extra costs as compared with direct use of natural gas, and some of the energy in the coal has to be consumed or otherwise lost in the gasification process.

Figure 3.3 illustrates one estimate of the economics of the various coal cycles (together with biomass, discussed in the next section), which suggests that PFBCs and IGCCs may not compete against conventional steam plant, but that there are clear advantages for coal ISTIGs, which would be available also at much lower capacities. Table 3.2, using data from another (and more recent) source, shows simplified cost and pollution performance estimates. This suggests that all the new cycles may present significant cost as well as environmental improvements over traditional steam systems; in some cases they may be economically attractive for 'repowering' plant as an alternative to fitting equipment to scrub acid pollutants from the stack gases. However, in all cases the capital costs are higher, and the efficiencies are several points lower, than for equivalent gas fired plant, while CO_2 emissions are about twice as high. Irrespective of environmental factors, in new power stations the outlook for coal is contingent upon the limited availability and higher price of natural gas.

One other feature of coal gasification technology has been noted in Volume 1, Chapter 1, section 1.6. If oxygen is used for gasification instead of air, a shift reaction employing steam can transfer nearly all the energy in the coal to hydrogen and CO_2. This yields a concentrated stream of CO_2 which can then be largely removed by a process of physical absorption into a concentrated liquid stream, that can be pumped away from the power plant. The process is far cheaper than trying to remove CO_2 from stack gases, with initial estimates suggesting that the separation process may add only 10-20% to the costs. These estimates

---

[17] W.Peters, 'Coal Gasification Technologies for Combined Cycle Power Generation', in T.B.Johansson et al (eds), *Electricity*, op.cit. The main types are: i) pressurized fluidized beds in which the coal is not burnt but instead converted, using steam and oxygen, into suitable volatile gases; this requires moderately pulverized coal fed in a continuous stream; ii) a 'fixed' bed (as distinct from fluidized) through which reaction gases flow; fixed beds can take almost any form of solid fuel, and in the form of the Lurgi process are probably the most widely applied to date; iii) entrained flow, in which extremely fine coal particles are converted as they are blown along in a gas stream, with the slag dropping out of the flow.

Figure 3.3 Projected energy costs from various coal and biomass electricity systems

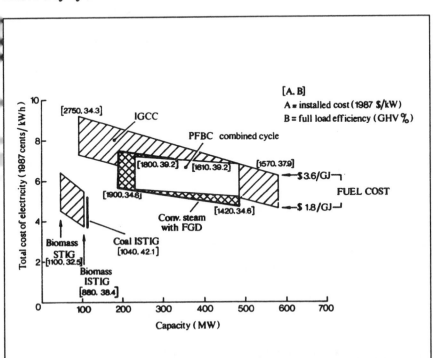

The figures shows estimated cost of energy (with the capital cost and efficiency in brackets) over a range of plant sizes and fuel costs. The lower coal cost of 1.8$/GJ is the average utility price projected for 1995 by the US Department of Energy. For the range of biomass costs and other assumptions see source.

Source: E.D.Larson et al, 'Biomass Gasification'; T.B.Johansson et al (eds), *Electricity*, p.720, Lund University Press, Sweden, 1989.

are inevitably rather uncertain, but a high tax on emitted CO_2, for example, could well make such a process more competitive with natural gas than any other coal plant - depending very much on the costs of disposal, if indeed there is anywhere to put it at all. This, as noted in Volume 1, is the bigger problem, and CO_2 removal is at best a partial solution.

Table 3.2 Performance of modern coal-based power generation

	Capital cost ($/kW)	Efficiency (%,GHV)	NO_x (mg/MJe)	CO_2 (kgC/kWh)
Steam turbine	1600	34	300	0.25
Combined cycle*	1700	42	25	0.20
PFBC	1200	42	60	0.19
STIG*	1300	36	25	0.24
ISTIG*	1030	42	20	0.20
Advanced fuel cell	1000-1500	45-52	10-35	0.17-0.19

* Using coal gasification technologies

Source: W.Fulkerson, et al, 'Energy from Fossil Fuels', op.cit.

Fossil fuel generating technologies: conclusions

Technologies for more efficient generation display an impressive variety. There seems little doubt that the monolithic steam turbine reached its limits during the 1960s; but the process of deploying alternatives is only just beginning. In areas with access to relatively cheap natural gas, new construction seems likely to be dominated by gas turbine cycles. Other areas will continue to rely on coal steam turbines for a while, but even this seems likely to be slowly displaced by more advanced systems based on fluidized beds or gasification with gas turbine cycles, perhaps including retrofits as an alternative to the costs of flue gas scrubbing. These will all increase efficiency and thereby reduce CO_2 emissions. The technical developments have other implications, however. Smarter often means smaller as well, with the extreme being the fuel cell. This further broadens the scope and economic potential for CHP applications, yielding much greater overall efficiency because the ejected heat is not wasted.

The implications for CO_2 emissions of these various options are sketched in Figure 3.4, which illustrates emissions from plants which are already commercially demonstrated. Going from current average coal-fired steam turbines to either the best available natural gas combined cycle, or to the best CHP applications of coal-fired PFBC, reduces CO_2 emissions by nearly 60%. Going further to the best CHP applications of natural gas may reduce emissions by another 30%.

In most developed economies with access to adequate natural gas, these developments alone could slow or even halt completely the growth of CO_2 emissions from electricity production. Modest policies and institutional reforms, as discussed in Volume 1 (especially section 6.2), might well turn this into a slow decline even if demand continues to grow. In developing countries the picture is less promising, partly as they often have little infrastructure for exploiting gas resources, and may lack the technical basis to utilize more efficient coal technologies; indeed, other steps, such as upgrading transmission systems, may in any case often take higher priority.

Overall, improving the efficiency of fossil-fuelled generating technologies, and especially moves towards natural gas, could make a very important contribution. But gas is not inexhaustible and in some areas is unavailable or distinctly limited, and the scope for further improvements in generating efficiency are clearly limited. Halting the global growth in electricity-related CO_2 emissions, particularly in the longer term, will require much besides. The rest of this chapter considers options which produce little or no CO_2.

3.2 Biomass production and conversion

Biomass can be converted to liquid fuel via ethanol or [to] electricity via gas turbines, besides more conventional uses for heat and gas. It can also become the basis of a modern chemical industry via synthesis gas. Biomass should be considered a renewable equivalent to fossil fuel.[18]

In the greenhouse debate to date, discussion of biomass has concentrated mostly upon the role of deforestation as a net source of CO_2, and on reforestation as a means of absorbing it. The contribution of permanent

[18] D.O.Hall, 'The Importance of Balancing CO_2 Budgets', *Proc. Conf. on Biomass for Utility Applications*, Electric Power Research Institute, Palo Alto, October 1990.

Figure 3.4 CO₂ emissions from commercially-available power plant

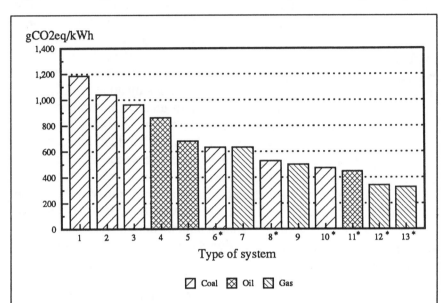

1. Average conventional steam turbine (coal, Eff.34%)
2. Best steam turbine (coal, Eff.39%)
3. Pressurized fluidized bed combustion (PFBC) (coal, Eff.42%)
4. Average conventional steam turbine (oil, Eff.38%)
5. Best available combined-cycle gas turbine (oil, Eff. 48%)
6. Cogeneration: average conventional steam turbine (coal, Eff.78%, E/H=0.5)
7. Average combined cycle turbine (natural gas, Eff.36%)
8. Cogeneration: best available steam turbine (coal., Eff. 83% E/H = 0.6)
9. Best available combined-cycle gas turbine (natural gas, Eff.45%)
10. Cogeneration: pressurized fluidized bed (coal, Eff.86%, E/H = 0.65)
11. Cogeneration: best available steam turbine(oil, Eff.81%. E/H = 0.60)
12. Cogeneration: steam- infected gas turbine (nat gas, Eff.75%, E/H = 0.80)
13. Cogeneration: best available combined-cycle gas turbine (natural gas, Eff. 77%, E/H = 1.0)

* Cogeneration plants, displacing heat produced from same fuel at 85% GHV boiler efficiency.

Source: E.Mills, D.Wilson, T.B.Johansson, 'Beginning to reduce greenhouse gas emissions need not be expensive', *Second World Climate Conference*, WMO/UNEP, Geneva, November, 1990.

reforestation is ultimately limited by the land available, and it faces some important managerial difficulties; limits on plausible contributions have been discussed briefly in Volume 1.[19] However, for a given carbon content, dry wood contains almost as much energy as coal. If it can be used as fuel to displace coal, at comparable efficiency of use, burning it is therefore as effective at limiting CO_2 as leaving it standing. In practice there are powerful reasons for believing that if biomass growing is to have a major role in limiting CO_2 accumulation, it will have to be primarily through the use of biomass energy rather than through forests for accumulating carbon.[20]

Existing biomass uses and resources. Volume 1 noted that for 80% of the human population, biomass is the most important single energy source. Burnt in stoves, it supplies cooking energy, heat, and light to approximately 4 billion people. However, these same people generally use less than a tenth as much energy as people in more developed economies. Currently available biomass resources in developing countries are often already stretched, and although (as noted in the previous chapter) the efficiency of stoves can be increased, even with such improvements, biomass applied in this way cannot conceivably meet energy demands as countries industrialize; the resources are too limited, and for growing urban populations, the real cost is also often much higher than for fossil fuels. The future for biomass as an energy resource depends upon better techniques - to increase the amount available, the efficiency with which it is used, and to lower the costs of more efficient use to economically practical levels.

Biomass in developing countries has been developed for many uses other than stoves. Biogas digesters, in which residues (usually animal dung) ferment to produce gas have been widely promoted. As indicated

[19] For example, although grants could be given for planting forests, it is difficult to see how effective incentives to then manage them over a period of decades could be maintained if there were no explicit value in the product. The land areas required for long-term absorption, and the limits this places on the likely contribution, have been noted in Volume 1, Chapter 1, p.24.

[20] ibid. In addition to these factors, biomass for energy will tend to focus on a higher rate of growth (and hence absorption) than in the long-rotation forests suggested for permanent accumulation, and much biomass energy can be derived from land which is not suitable for permanent forests (D.O.Hall, H.E.Mynick and R.H.Williams, *Carbon Sequestration Versus Fossil Fuel Substitution*, PU/CEES Report No.255, Princeton University, 1990).

in the Chinese and Indian case studies these have met with mixed success, but have certainly not met the high hopes expressed by some, and the conversion efficiencies remain rather low. Various processes have been used to produce liquid fuels from biomass, the most notable case being the Brazilian national programme to produce ethanol from sugar cane. Whilst this has helped to insulate that country from the turbulence of the world's oil markets, it has been at a relatively high financial cost.[21] Experience with this and various other programmes is described by Gowen.[22]

In developed economies, biomass digesters and a variety of other conversion processes, including simple burning in open hearths or small industrial boilers, have been applied on a small scale.[23] Landfill gas is now being exploited by drilling into waste tips (see UK chapter). Domestic and industrial wastes especially are already being burnt to drive steam power stations, often with sophisticated systems both for recovering energy and preventing pollutants from entering the atmosphere, and straw burning forms a significant part of Denmark's renewable energy plans.

Such technologies are far from insignificant but, excepting the important contribution from burning off methane rather than letting it escape to the atmosphere, they are directed more at alleviating waste problems than at alleviating the greenhouse effect, and they do not form viable ways of exploiting most forest residues or potential biomass crops.

---

[21] Most studies estimate Brazilian ethanol production costs at $0.23-0.30/l (US$36-46/bbl), more than twice the world oil prices of the mid to late 1980s. However, given the benefits of the programme in providing rural employment and saving foreign exchange, and other factors, debates about its overall value continue, see for example M.M.Gowen, 'Biofuel v fossil fuel economics in developing countries', *Energy Policy*, October 1989. A.de Oliveira, 'Reassessing the Brazilian alcohol programme', *Energy Policy*, January/February 1991, argues that parts of the programme are clearly competitive, while others are not, and the components need to be separated.

[22] ibid. Gowen concludes that 'The breadth of biofuel substitution [with current technologies in developing countries] is certainly less than envisaged... the future challenge is to focus on environmentally sound, and economically justifiable, advanced biofuel systems'.

[23] For an excellent if somewhat dated review of biomass sources and conversion technologies applied or tested by the early 1980s see M.Flood, *Solar Prospects*, Wildwood House/FoE, London, 1983; a more recent UK review is given in M.A.Laughton (ed.), *Renewable Energy Sources*, Watt Committee Report No.22, Elsevier, London.

As discussed in Chapter 1, new biomass resources can be very significant in relation to total demand, and can be made available at costs ranging from $1/GJ to $4/GJ, with the Oak Ridge study suggesting that improved techniques might bring these costs down to the range of $2/GJ or less, equivalent in raw energy terms to the low oil prices of the late 1980s ($2/GJ = $12/boe).[24]

For making such biomass viable on a much larger scale, interest is focusing on two areas where technical advances may offer great improvements: advanced electricity cycles and new liquid fuel processes.

Biomass electricity cycles. Biomass, as noted above, is already used to raise steam in conventional power stations. Because biomass is bulky and obtained from dispersed sites, plants are usually relatively small - well under 50MW - and cannot take advantage of the economies of scale available for large steam plants. Costs tend to be high and efficiencies (typically 20-25%) low compared with coal plants. However, biomass is well placed to take advantage of developments in gas turbine cycles described in the previous section. Like coal, biomass can be gasified into volatile gases suitable for burning in a gas turbine, but it has two crucial advantages: it is much more reactive than coal, so that it can be gasified at a lower temperature; and it contains little or no sulphur, so the additional expense and loss associated with sulphur removal is avoided.

Biomass gasification is not itself a new process, but gasification suitable for high-performance gas turbine stations is. Although far more effort has been expended on research into coal gasification, suitable biomass processes can to a large extent draw on such research; indeed, biomass gasification could well reach commercial demonstration first, the costs seem almost certain to be lower, and the efficiency could be comparable or higher.[25] This is not to minimize the uncertainties and potential difficulties associated with such a varied resource for using

[24] 1GJ (GHV) = 0.0224toe = 0.165 boe (barrel of oil equivalent). Figures in this chapter have not been converted to oil equivalents as all the sources drawn upon use Systeme Internationale units (GJ, EJ, etc).
[25] E.D.Larsen, P.Svenningsson, I.Bjerle, 'Biomass Gasification for Gas Turbine Power Generation', in T.B.Johansson et al (eds), *Electricity*, op.cit., discuss the various issues in detail. Their economic analysis uses a gasification efficiency derived from an industrial pilot plant, which 'indicated lower gasification efficiency than with coal. However, there is no obvious reason why biomass gasification efficiency... should not be as least as high as for coal', p.719.

such an application, but the prospects if sufficient R&D is applied do seem relatively good.

Because biomass is such a dispersed resource, it would be used in relatively small stations - perhaps 5-50MW sited in the centre of associated biomass collection areas, managed by a small station staff. For reasons of scale this would of necessity require ISTIG technology rather than combined cycle, which for reasons indicated in the previous section introduces further elements both of uncertainty and potential. Cost estimates for this technology are illustrated in Figure 3.3, which suggests that if such systems were successfully developed, biomass electricity at least from forest residues would be competitive with any form of sulphur-free coal generation. Figure 3.5 presents other estimates in terms of the cost of displacing CO_2 emissions from coal priced at $1.8/GJ, as a function of the biomass price, drawn from Hall et al.[26] On these estimates, biomass gasification would be competitive with coal even from successfully developed coal gasification/ISTIG plants for biomass costs below about $2/GJ, and would cost about $75 per tonne of carbon offset for biomass at $4/GJ. Even at biomass costs of $4/GJ the process could just break even against conventional coal steam plant because of the lower capital costs.

It is an open question how much confidence can be placed in cost estimates before a technology is developed, but many of the component technologies are known and proven at scale, and the assessments contain elements of pessimism as well as optimism. Certainly, the analysis suggests that biomass cannot be excluded as a possible large-scale source of electricity over a range of technical and environmental assumptions. The major obstacle at present appears to be that the heavy electrical industry is poorly structured to promote or pursue interest in biomass, while those involved in biomass do not have the capital or technical expertise to undertake such a development programme.

Liquid fuels from biomass. As noted above, interest in obtaining liquid fuels from biomass has a long tradition. Despite the considerable investments to date (relative to many other biomass conversion processes), there are still a wide range of candidates for biofuel processes, and apparently considerable potential for future

---

[26] Hall et al, *Carbon Sequestration Versus Fossil Fuel Substitution*, op.cit.

Figure 3.5 Cost of carbon abatement from alternative biomass applications in the US

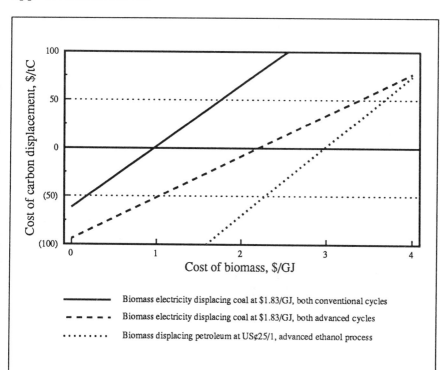

Notes: Negative values imply net economic savings from using biomass
Advanced processes not yet proven
Costs compare with sequestering by reforestation estimated at $15-50/tC in the US
Coal costs correspond to delivered costs in US West North Central
Gasoline price is US DOE projection (1989) of wholesale price in 2000
For other assumptions and discussion of biomass costs see text and source

Data source: D.O.Hall, H.E.Mynick and R.H.Williams, *Carbon Sequestration Versus Fossil Fuel Substitution*, PU/CEES Report No.255, Princeton University, 1990.

improvements. Some plant can produce natural oils which resemble diesel fuels, though some upgrading is usually still required. Wood and other biomass can be liquefied and processed to gasoline by techniques similar to those used for liquefying coal; the Oak Ridge technology assessment describes low temperature, high pressure catalyzed thermochemical processes for this as being 'potentially a high payoff area of research, but many problems have to be solved'.[27] But many analysts believe that ethanol production has the greatest potential. The Oak Ridge analysis summarizes some of the issues:

> Ethanol is produced by fermentation. Wood and herbaceous products have greater ultimate potential for the production of ethanol than food crops, but the fermentation process is more difficult ... among various processes under development, the enzymatic process appears to hold the most promise, although it is the least developed.[28]

Taking a similar view, Hall et al state that 'there appear to be major opportunities for displacing fossil CO_2 emissions with biomass at negative cost. The indicated economics are especially promising for ethanol derived from lignocellulosic feedstocks (eg. wood) using enzymatic hydrolysis.'[29] The potential conversion efficiency is estimated to be just over 50%.

Along with the estimates for biomass gasification, Figure 3.5 illustrates the calculations of Hall et al of the costs of carbon abatement if ethanol displaces gasoline priced at 25c/l (the ethanol could be blended in with existing gasoline, or cars can be converted to operate on ethanol alone). On these estimates, ethanol would be competitive with gasoline for biomass costs below $3/GJ (corresponding to the estimate by the US Department of Energy studies, on which they are based). At $4/GJ, the costs of CO_2 displacement again rise to about $75/tC. The steeper slope of the line reflects the fact that a tonne of biomass applied in this way displaces less carbon than for either sequestration alone, or for displacing coal-based electricity.[30] The conclusion seems to be that, if R&D efforts are devoted to developing modern biomass technologies and

[27] W.Fulkerson et al, *Energy Technology R&D*, op.cit., Vol.1, p.80.
[28] ibid, p.79.
[29] Hall et al, *Carbon Sequestration Versus Fossil Fuel Substitution*, op.cit., p.11.
[30] This reflects both the lower carbon content of gasoline and the lower relative efficiency of the displacement (biomass conversion at about 53% compared with oil refining at about 90%).

expectations are realized, then biomass from various sources may be competitive on quite a large scale.

Biomass yields, costs, and impacts. The economic feasibility of biomass depends heavily on the cost of the raw biomass. For many existing sources, notably various residues and forest wastes (from both commercial and indigenous forests), costs already look competitive, and these could provide a not inconsiderable resource, as suggested in Chapter 1 (Table 1.2). In particular, some industries generate large amounts of biomass waste. Studies have indicated an immense potential for producing electricity from sugarcane residues - so large that, as one analysis put it, the industries could become primarily electricity producers with sugar as a valuable by-product.[31] The potential in forestry and pulp and paper industries is also large.[32]

In addition, experience with some existing forest plantations suggests that relatively low costs can be achieved, especially in warmer and wetter regions of the world; Larson et al cite costs from a range of developing countries of between \$1/GJ and \$2/GJ, which also reflect exchange rate effects and low labour costs. But biomass resources are already quite stretched and used for varied applications in many developing countries (see for example the Indian case study), and in most temperate zones and developed economies, the costs of plantation forests look higher. There are also important constraints on suitable land. Even if improved technologies for use are developed successfully, the overall economic potential with current yields is clearly limited on a global scale,[33] with

[31] J.M.Ogden, R.H.Williams, and M.E.Fulmer, 'Cogeneration Applications of Biomass Gasifier/Gas Turbine Technologies in the Cane Sugar and Alcohol Industries', *Proc. Conf. on Energy and Environment in the 21st Century*, MIT Press, Cambridge, MA, 1990.

[32] E.D.Larson, 'Biomass-Gasifier/Gas Turbine Application in the Pulp and Paper Industry: an Initial Strategy for Reducing Electric Utility CO_2 Emissions', *Proc. 9th EPRI Conference on Coal Gasification Power Plants*, EPRI, Palo Alto, CA, October 1990.

[33] A global long-term energy modelling study by the Environmental Protection Agency included some scenarios with biomass production totalling over 200EJ/yr by 2050, well over half current global energy consumption. A discussion by Williams (R.H.Williams, 'Biomass Energy Strategies for Coping with the Greenhouse Problem', Princeton University, 1989) examined this and concluded that it 'may be feasible to realise this ambitious target', but that it would require substantially improved yields as well as better conversion technologies, while much of the biomass would have to located in developing countries, probably requiring large resource transfers. Williams also

more severe constraints in particular regions; in Europe, for example, economic biomass contributions would probably at most total 10% of total primary energy demand based on current yields.[34]

There is therefore considerable interest in possibilities for increasing yields of forests and other potential energy crops, both to increase the amount available and to lower the costs. The potential to increase the yield of unmanaged forests is certainly large. Long-term experiments in Sweden have shown that in most forests, trees grow at rates far below their natural potential level, that nutrient availability is usually the most important limiting factor, and that optimizing nutrient availability can result in 4- to 6-fold increases in yield.[35] The forestry industry has already learnt how to exploit certain species and conditions to give high yields. These often include intensive fertilizers and monocultures, which have attracted strong environmental criticism. In some cases however good results have also been achieved and Hall et al suggest that high forest yields can be attained without such drawbacks by interplanting trees of different species with different nutrient characteristics.[36] Compared with yields of a few tonnes per hectare (if that) in existing temperate forests, these authors state that yields of 9-12 tonnes/ha/yr in temperate and 20-30 tonnes/ha/yr in tropical regions are feasible with existing technology.[37]

Even higher yields are feasible with herbaceous crops (such as sugarcane), some species of which are also suited for growing on marginal lands not well suited to forestry or conventional agriculture. All will be constrained by competing uses for land and residues, and more general environmental considerations: different discussions can give very different impressions, sometimes from surprising quarters.[38]

---

concluded that extensive research would be required to reach more definitive conclusions concerning the realistic global biomass potential.

[34] D.O.Hall and F.Fossil-Calle, 'Biomass, Bioenergy and Agriculture in Europe', *7th Canadian Bioenergy Research and Development Seminar*, Ottawa, Canada, April 1989.

[35] Hall et al, *Carbon Sequestration Versus Fossil Fuel Substitution*, op.cit., p.17.

[36] ibid, p.17: optimising nutrients 'could make it possible to achieve high yields with existing species and clones, thus facilitating the incorporation of pest resistance and other desirable characteristics, and the maintenance of a diverse landscape mosaic. To the extent that croplands and wastelands would be converted to energy crops in this way, it may be feasible not only to maintain but to improve biological diversity.'

[37] ibid, p.6.

[38] The Oak Ridge technology review (Fulkerson et al, *Energy Technology R&D*, op.cit., Vol.2 Part 2, pp.82-99) exudes enthusiasm about the potential for biomass in US

Increasing biomass yields, perhaps dramatically, and thereby also reducing costs, is clearly possible given time and experience, as the possibilities seem so varied and relatively so little effort has been explicitly devoted towards modernizing biomass; but the trade-offs are complex. Hall et al conclude:

The biomass sources used for energy will probably be a diverse mix of residues, increased production from existing forests, and wood or herbaceous crops planted for energy purposes on unforested land or understocked forested land. The appropriate mix will be determined by economics, water and land resources availability, and constraints posed by environmental and soil conservation considerations ... The techniques and technologies for growing biomass and converting it into modern energy carriers must be more fully developed, and new industrial infrastructure must be evolved in order to realize the full potential for bioenergy. Despite such challenges, bioenergy industries could be launched in the decades immediately ahead, starting off using residues from agriculture and forest products industries ... if at the same time the R&D needed on the sustainable production and conversion of biomass is given high priority, and if policies are adopted to nurture the development of bioenergy industries, these industries will be able to innovate and diversify as they grow and mature.[39]

3.3 Nuclear energy

The technology, economics and safety issues involved in nuclear power are subjects about which vast amounts have been written, and this chapter makes no attempt to cover the same ground. It is clear that the economics of nuclear power vary widely between different countries, and that these variations depend more upon institutional, managerial and political factors, and the degree of government commitment, than the technology itself.

A recent review from the International Energy Agency concludes that nuclear power, now consisting almost entirely of Pressurized Water

energy supplies. The review by the Stockholm Environment Institute (D.Fisher (ed.), *Options for Reducing Greenhouse Gas Emissions*, Stockholm Environment Institute, 1990) sounds a more cautious note, while acknowledging an important role for biomass.
[39] Hall et al, *Carbon Sequestration Versus Fossil Fuel Substitution*, op.cit., pp.9- 21.

Reactors, is still cheaper than coal in many countries under standard utility investment criteria. There have been various critiques of such figures; some of the broad issues in dispute have been noted in Volume 1 (Box, section 5.5). The real comparison remains uncertain, partly because utility accounting practices and fuel price projections vary. It seems likely that the rise in nuclear costs experienced in many countries has passed its zenith (though even this is uncertain), and that if new reactors are ordered, future developments could serve to reduce costs, particularly for those countries where the costs have been exceptionally high. Advanced light water reactors could incorporate a number of evolutionary improvements to lower the cost and improve reliability.[40]

Conversely, however, the profile of 'back end' costs of decommissioning and waste handling are likely to grow, as these problems have to be faced on a larger scale. Overall, although the cost of nuclear power may be expected to reduce somewhat, so that it would remain, or could become, a positive item on the balance sheet of public utilities, there seems little prospect that refinements of existing nuclear technology could make nuclear power attractive to private generators in a competitive market without strong government support, at least unless the price of all fossil fuels did rise greatly.

The analysis in Volume 1, section 5.5, suggests that in practice, the cost and performance of nuclear generating technologies is probably a secondary issue in determining the future for conventional designs; its prospects depend more upon public confidence and political and institutional factors than technical ones, though these certainly do include the evolving regulatory frameworks for the electricity industry, and the suitability of nuclear technology within them. On these scores, as discussed in Volume 1, the prospects do not look promising. Surveying such factors, the Oak Ridge analysis argues that 'a fundamental reexamination of the nation's Civilian Reactor Program is needed to respond to today's conditions and to prepare for the future'.[41] Their foremost suggestion concerned fundamentally new reactor designs.

---

[40] K.E.Stahlkopf, J.C.DeVine, and W.R.Sugnet, 'US ALWR Programme Sets Out Utility Requirements for the Future', *Nuclear Engineering International*, 33 (412), pp.16-19.
[41] W.Fulkerson et al, *Energy Technology R&D*, op.cit., Vol.2 Part 2, p.52.

Alternative reactor designs. Two factors are seen to bedevil existing nuclear power station designs: the public is afraid of them, partly because of the 'doomsday' scenario of complete core meltdown; and they are too large, too long in construction, and generally entail too much financial commitment and risk, to be embraced by private utilities. The two factors are to an extent interlinked: fears about meltdown possibilities have led to an extraordinary complexity of in-depth safety features which have added much to costs, and public opposition often delays construction and startup. In a bid to overcome these limitations, various proposals have been made for radically new reactor designs, which are designed to be 'passively', or 'inherently' safe: the structure ensures that the core could not melt even in the event of complete loss of coolant.

One of the first such designs was the PIUS (Process Inherent Ultimately Safe) reactor proposed in Sweden. Other designs followed, by most of the major manufacturers, including even 'super-safe' reactors for district heating.[42] Probably the most promising of these designs is the Modular High Temperature Gas Reactor (MHTGR), of which different forms have been proposed in Germany and the US. The basic idea would be to have a much smaller core than in current PWRs, cooled by gas and with the fuel made from ceramic or other temperature-resistant materials, so that even if the cooling system were breached completely, natural convection would be sufficient to keep the temperature below the core's melting point, and radioactivity could not escape. Also, the reactor cores would be barely a tenth the power of existing commercial PWRs, and hence the reactors could be 'modular', entailing much smaller financial risk. Based on a traditional steam cycle, economies of scale suggest a need for several such modules driving a central steam turbine, with efficiency limited to about 35%. Further improvements have been proposed, whereby the output of such modules would instead be used to drive a gas turbine, with a total plant size of around 100MW and efficiency of over 45%. Proponents claim that such a reactor could produce electricity for about 4.5¢/kWh with a capital cost of $1,000/kW.[43]

[42] NEI, Reports in *Nuclear Engineering International*, September 1988.
[43] L.M.Lidsky, D.D.Lanning, J.E.Staudt, X.L.Yan, H.Kaburaki, M.Mori, 'A Direct-Cycle Gas Turbine Power Plant for Near-Term Application', 10th International HTGR Conference, San Diego, California, 1988. Costs cited in P.E.Gray, 'Nuclear Reactors Everyone Will Love', *Wall Street Journal*, 17 August, 1989.

If such a technology were successfully developed and demonstrated, it might dramatically change the outlook for nuclear power. But it might not. Serious concerns about decommissioning, waste and proliferation would remain (the last of these might be amplified); such a development on its own would be far from meeting the criteria suggested by some analysts as necessary for a nuclear revival.[44] Furthermore there is little sign at present that the industry is prepared to embark upon potentially costly new development programmes when, as far as many in the industry are concerned, there are no guarantees that it will result in a more marketable product, and the process of development might even jeopardize acceptance of the existing and proven technology.

If the nuclear industry did revive successfully and expand rapidly, there might after a few decades be a need for fast breeder reactors (FBRs) to make much more efficient use of proven uranium reserves. However, FBRs suffer from all the problems of conventional reactors but writ larger still. The fundamental process consists of fast neutrons (ie. ones not slowed by a moderator, as in a conventional thermal reactor) turning the dominant U-238 into plutonium. Fast neutrons interact with fissile nuclei far less readily than slow ones, so that to sustain a reaction, much higher densities of fissile material are required, and the fuel is packed much more tightly into a tiny core. The only way to extract such heat from such a small volume is with liquid metal, and for various reasons, liquid sodium is the prime candidate. This has a number of drawbacks. Sodium reacts violently with both air and water, so that any leaks are potentially very serious. To compound this, sodium itself becomes radioactive when irradiated with neutrons in the core, so that it has to pass through a heat exchanger to another sodium circuit, which then passes its heat on to water in a second heat exchanger to produce steam to drive the turbine. Integrity in both heat exchangers is vital, but difficult to achieve. In addition, the reaction itself is far more volatile than the thermal nuclear reaction, requiring much faster control responses. To cap all this, high-grade plutonium must be separated in reprocessing facilities, which raises a whole range of chemical, radioactive, proliferation and security difficulties.

FBRs are thus a complex and unforgiving technology. The only full scale FBR in the world (the French 'Superphoenix') has had a very poor

---

[44] For example, R.H.Williams and H.A.Feiveson, 'How to Expand Nuclear Without Proliferation', *Bulletin of the Atomic Scientists*, April 1990.

operating record to date (caused partly by a series of sodium leaks), and even if it worked to specification it would be several times as expensive as conventional nuclear power. With tens of billions of dollars spent on the technology worldwide, the US abandoned its FBR programme in the late 1970s; the UK has followed suit a decade later. In this author's view, there is no realistic prospect that FBRs will be either economically viable or politically acceptable.

Nuclear fusion. To many who have reached similar conclusions, the greatest hopes for a long-term energy source lie at the opposite end of the atomic scale, with nuclear fusion. Instead of splitting heavy elements like uranium, the aim is to fuse light ones such as hydrogen. Such fusion can release a great deal of energy, but the problem is to overcome the strong repulsive force between the nuclei. This can be achieved if the atoms can be heated to temperatures of several million degrees, when the nuclei are travelling fast enough to cause some to fuse in collisions. The main approach to achieving this so far explored is with magnetic confinement, using a reaction of deuterium (hydrogen-2) and tritium (hydrogen-3). Deuterium occurs as a natural variant of normal hydrogen (about 1 in 6,000); tritium, which is unstable and so does not occur naturally, can easily be manufactured by bombarding lithium with neutrons. Somewhat like the FBR, the idea is to have a central reaction core surrounded by a blanket which manufactures new fuel from relatively common elements. The resource is then essentially unlimited.

Holding out the promise of limitless power from sea water, with no radioactive products from the reaction itself, fusion has held appeal for scientists and public alike. Unfortunately, as with most attractive myths, contrary facts have had a hard time breaking through. After more than 30 years of fusion research, the problem is not that we don't know how to build fusion reactors: it is that we do. And even with a string of highly optimistic assumptions, the cost of energy from the most popular and advanced candidate fusion technology appears to be many times that of fission power. The reasons are unfortunately quite fundamental ones. Basic physics sets a limit to feasible densities in such magnetically-confined plasmas, and experience has shown that a large number of superimposed magnetic fields are required to keep the plasma stable long enough for any useful reaction to develop. These two factors alone seem sufficient to indicate that any reactor based upon external magnetic confinement would be many times the size of an equivalent fission reactor, and many times as expensive. Obviously, the technology will advance past various physical signposts, but in other technologies, economic potential is usually considered a relevant criterion.[45] Britain's leading nuclear proponent Lord Marshall neatly expressed the doubts in 1987:

> Sometime this century the fusion physicists will succeed in getting more energy out of the plasma than energy they have put into the plasma. Some time in the following three decades they will succeed in getting more energy out of the machine than energy they have put into the machine. However, in my opinion, they will not succeed in getting more money out of the machine than money they have put in.[46]

To cap this, although the reaction itself produces no radioactive products, the reactions which occur in the blanket and shielding, as the fast neutrons are stopped, produce a range of highly radioactive products, which need to be replaced as the fast neutrons rapidly destroy the integrity of the reactor walls. Also, the preferred fuel of tritium is itself radioactive (half the tritium nuclei decay every 12 years), and dangerous because it is easily taken up by organisms, through water.[47]

Naturally not everyone accepts such a pessimistic view, as evidenced by the fact that world-wide funding has exceeded $20bn and fusion is still the largest single item in the EC energy R&D research budget.[48] But as far as the present author can judge, the main practical result of over 30 years of expensive research has been to rule out, for all practical purposes, every approach to magnetically confined fusion power so far considered.

---

[45] A detailed critique of approaches to nuclear fusion was given by the report *Criteria for the Assessment of European Fusion Research*, EP-STOA, European Parliament, Luxembourg, May 1988. The most in-depth, and ultimately non-committal study, has been: Office of Technology Assessment, *Starpower: The US and the International Quest for Fusion Energy*, US Congress, OTA, October 1987.

[46] House of Lords Select Committee on Science and Technology, *Research and Development in Nuclear Power*, HL Paper 14-1, HMSO, 1987: Volume 1, p.17.

[47] The STOA report gives details of environmental aspects: for a brief review, see A.Atkinson, 'The Environmental Impact of Fusion Power', *Energy Policy*, June 1989, pp.277-288.

[48] More enthusiastic assessments are given for example by the Oak Ridge technology assessment (Fulkerson et al, *Energy Technology R&D*, op.cit., Vol.2 Part 2. pp.63-76). Articles and an ascerbic exchange of views on fusion occurred in *Energy Policy* (Issues: 17(1), February 1989; 17(4), August 1989; 18(5), June 1990; 18(10), December 1990).

With *inertial confinement,* the aim is to create an intense implosion of fusion material so that temperatures and pressures soar to levels sufficient for a fusion reaction, and sheer inertia sustains this for long enough for useful energy to be released. The only practical means of approaching this seems to be to fire an intense laser beam evenly over the surface of a small fusible pellet. To ensure timing to within a million-millionth of a second, a single laser beam has to be used, split into many elements by mirrors before being focused from all sides on to the pellet. Basic difficulties include those of creating mirrors which would not move, distort or degrade under the impact of the laser beam and fusion reaction, and various problems in common with magnetic confinement associated with harnessing the reaction and managing the radiation. The research has been mostly confined to the US, where most of it is classified because of various military connections, so progress cannot really be judged. The Oak Ridge review states that it 'may eventually lead to commercial power',[49] but there seem few reasons for taking a more optimistic view than for magnetically confined fusion.

Another approach, *Z-pinch fusion,* was in fact the first proposed, but it was rejected as impossible in the 1950s. If a powerful electric current is focused in a very narrow stream in a plasma, it creates a magnetic field which could in principle 'pinch' the plasma stream long enough for fusion to occur. An electric arc struck between two electrodes can create such conditions if a powerful enough and sharp enough voltage pulse is applied. Advances in general pulsed power engineering over the last two decades have made such voltage pulses feasible, but major unsolved problems remain. The plasma stream is inherently unstable, and so far there has been no demonstration that it could survive long enough to create useful fusion conditions. Also, the electrodes would erode very rapidly under the intense heat and neutron irradiation, and the management and radiological problems of working with Tritium remain. As yet, Z-pinch reactors have barely left the drawing board. The fourth and final theoretical approach so far identified would be to create 'mu-mesons' in a particle accelerator to catalyze a fusion reaction, to which similar remarks apply.[50] Excitement about the possibilities for

---

[49] Fulkerson et al, *Energy Technology R&D*, op.cit., Vol.2 Part 2, p.72.
[50] S.E.Jones, 'Muon-Catalyzed Fusion: Where Do We Go From Here?', *Scientific American*, 257(1), 1987, pp.84-89.

'cold fusion' dissipated as leading research groups proved unable to reproduce the results initially reported in 1989 (Chapter 1, footnote 16).

Fusion involves fascinating and fundamental research, and the value of this should not be lightly discounted. Also, as for any technology, the possibility of fundamental breakthroughs can never be ruled out, though these seem unlikely to come from large-scale demonstration of existing ideas. But overall, the emotional appeal of fusion as a limitless energy source does not yet seem to be matched by any economically feasible approach.

3.4 Renewable sources for primary heat and electricity

Renewable energy sources cover a far more diverse range than fossil or nuclear sources. They comprise six major energy resources (four derived from solar energy, plus tidal power, and geothermal power if that is included), and several minor derivatives which could be tapped through scores of different technologies. The resources have been discussed in Chapter 1. Some of the principal technological categories are illustrated in Table 3.3; each could be subdivided into many distinct technologies. The table serves to emphasize that renewable energy technologies cover a very diverse range: from ideas still on the drawing board to well-developed technologies; from local and small-scale systems, through intermediate-scale dispersed and centralized applications, up to the large civil engineering projects of hydro and offshore developments, and even solar satellites.

Biomass, being a form of stored hydrocarbon energy which can be converted in various ways using technologies which are often closely related to conventional processes, has much in common with fossil fuels and has been considered above. Some other technologies produce heat directly, but these have limited (though often locally important) applications. Almost all the others, especially those which in principle could play a large role in displacing fossil fuels, produce electricity as the primary product.

This section does not attempt to describe such a wide range of specific technologies or to analyze their prospects in any depth. This is partly because many of the technologies themselves are still developing so rapidly, and the issues involved in deploying them are so poorly understood, that any such assessments would be speculative; certainly, extensive discussion would be required to touch upon all the important

Table 3.3 Principal renewable energy categories

Hydro

Large scale	Elec	Developed, often economic, widely deployed
Micro hydro	E	Developed, usually economic, not widely deployed

Solar

Passive heating	Heat	Developed, usually economic, mixed deployment
Active heating	H	Developed, variable economics & deployment
Central thermal	E	Large test stations, results not favourable
Dispersed thermal	E	Commercialized, still improving.
Photovoltaic	E	Rapidly developing, varied projections
Solar ponds	E	Demonstrated, not economic at present
PV-Hydrogen	Fuel	Components proven; economics speculative.

Wind

Pumping mechanical		Developed, deployed in remote areas
Onshore turbines	E	Recently developed, still improving, early deployment
Offshore turbines	E	Some trial stations, varied projections

Biomass (Agricultural & forest residues & surpluses, domestic & industrial wastes, biomass crops)

Direct combustion	H	Widely used but inefficient
Decomposition/ hydrogenation/ fermentation etc	F	Various demonstrated, usually not economic at present
Gasification	F, E	Unproven but promising

Geothermal

Aquifers	H, E	Proven, often economic
Hot dry rock	H, E	Exploratory schemes, mixed results

Tidal

Estuary dams	E	Proven; heavily depend ent on financing assumptions
Streams	E	Speculative

Wave

Shore-based	E	Test stations, favourable results.
Deep water	E	Wide variety of devices; pilots but no prototypes tested

---

Others: Ocean thermal energy; dew point energy; salt gradients; solar satellites.

---

issues and possibilities. Also, as well as there being other reviews which readers can consult,[51] publications due in 1992 provide unprecedented surveys of renewable energy technologies and prospects.[52] Instead, this section summarizes developments and issues in the two main non-biomass 'diffuse' technologies of photovoltaics and wind, notes briefly salient features of other renewables, and suggests broader conclusions which may be drawn at this stage.

Solar cells or *photovoltaics* (PV), in which solar radiation is converted directly to electricity by semiconductors, represent by far the largest single renewable potential. There are many different varieties, and an assessment illustrates many of the issues and continuing uncertainties in renewables.

From one perspective, it is not hard to present arguments to suggest that PV has little real prospect for major energy supplies. Despite being by far the best supported of all renewable energy sources to date, with around $2bn of government money and considerable private investment, the costs are still at least three times the level required to produce baseload grid electricity competitively even in sunny areas, and many of the cells degrade significantly in real operating conditions. Also, for many temperate countries solar energy is poorly suited to needs: in the UK, for example, 5/6 of the solar energy falls during the summer months, whereas electricity demand peaks strongly in the winter, and peak electricity demand is frequently after winter sunset. Furthermore, the

[51] General technical reviews and assessments of renewable sources include: the International Energy Agency study *Renewable Sources of Energy*, IEA/OECD, Paris, 1987; R.H.Taylor, *Alternative Sources for the Generation of Electricity*, Adam Hilger, Bristol, 1987; and the earlier and simpler D.Deudney and C.Flavin, *Renewable Energy - the Power to Choose*, W.W.Norton and Company, New York. More recent technical assessments are included in W.Fulkerson et al, *Energy Technology R&D*, op.cit., Volume 2 Part 2, and D.Fischer (ed.), *Options for Reducing Greenhouse Gas Emissions*, op.cit. Ramage (J.Ramage, *Energy - a Guidebook*, Oxford University Press, 1983 and various reprints) gives excellent if dated description and discussion of most renewables.

[52] Especially recommended is the two-volume collection of studies commissioned for the 1992 UN Conference on Environment and Development (R.H.Williams, T.B.Johnasson, A.K.Reddy, *Renewable Energy*, forthcoming, January 1992). Also, the World Energy Council is conducting a study of renewable energy sources for its own 1992 conference. Forthcoming studies edited or produced by the present author will also contain more detailed analysis of some options than is possible within the confines of this volume (M.Grubb (ed.), *Emerging Energy Technologies: Impacts and Policy Implications*, RIIA/Dartmouth, forthcoming 1991).

manufacture of PV is a capital-intensive, high-technology process, so it appears poorly suited to developing countries where some of the greatest resources and potential applications lie. All this paints a rather bleak picture.

On the other hand, an opposite view can be made equally persuasively. In comparison with the money spent on conventional energy sources, $2bn is relatively little and no-one should expect a mature energy source to emerge from such expenditure; nuclear proponents argue that they can still make large improvements despite much longer development and R&D expenditures totalling perhaps a hundred times that on PV. More pointedly, PV is improving very rapidly. Figure 3.6 shows the trends in cell efficiency and manufacturing costs over the 1980s, and projections by Japanese industry of the prospects in the 1990s. During the 1980s, cell efficiencies roughly doubled and costs reduced by a factor of five, and there are many clear possibilities for further improvement.

In addition to technical advances, the potential for economies of scale in manufacture is immense. Figure 3.7 shows various manufacturer's estimates of how costs would reduce with increasing production volumes. Few production facilities at present are much above 1MW/yr (10^6 peak Watts/yr), so savings from improved technology will be multiplied by those from increasing production volumes. Many of those involved argue that the goals for grid competitiveness can be reached through a range of foreseeable developments in amorphous silicon cell technology within the next five years,[53] though the Oak Ridge review is more cautious.[54]

Another feature of PV is its suitability for a wide range of markets. Although volume production lowers manufacturing costs, the individual units can be very small, so that PV is particularly appropriate for many non-grid applications. Even in a country such as the UK, there are many such possibilities: in addition to various familiar micro-electronic applications, Hill[55] reports that PV is frequently the most

[53] D.Carlson, 'Low cost power from thin-film photovoltaics', in T.B.Johansson et al (eds), *Electricity*, op.cit.; R.Hill, 'Review of Photovoltaics', in M.J.Grubb (ed.), *Emerging Energy Technologies*, forthcoming, op.cit.

[54] W.Fulkerson et al, *Energy Technology R&D*, reports the US DoE five-year goals as being to achieve costs (with standard US utility financing) of 6¢/kWh in desert regions, and 10c/kWh in other southern areas, but suggests that this may be optimistic, and not enough for general grid competitiveness.

[55] R.Hill, 'Review of Photovoltaics', op.cit.

Figure 3.6 Commercial development of photovoltaics in Japan

(a) Conversion efficiencies of various cell types, 1982-1992

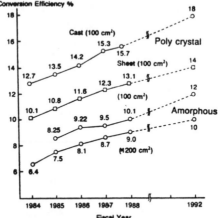

(b) Cost trends (yen/Wp), 1974-1990 and projection to 2000

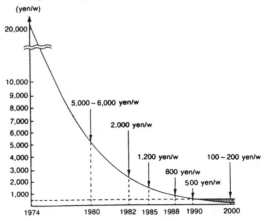

Note: 1000yen = US$7.20 at 1989 exchange rates

Source: T.Kashiwagi, 'Present Status and Future Prospects of Advanced
Energy Technology for Solving Global Environmental Problems',
Europe-Japan The Global Environmental Technology Seminar 1990, JETRO,
Tokyo, November, 1990.

Figure 3.7 PV costs as a function of annual production volume

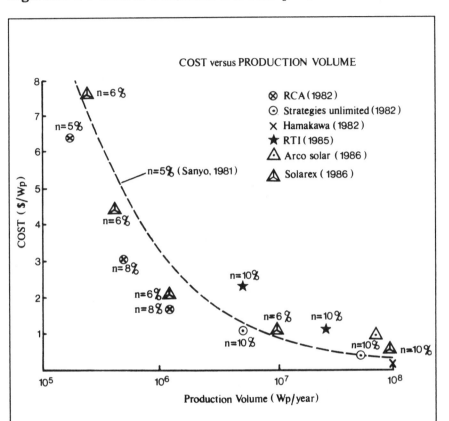

Note: The figure shows estimates of how PV production costs will vary with the size of production line established, in annual peak Watts (Wp) produced. Each symbol represents a different estimate; n is the conversion efficiency. The costs decrease sharply to less than $2/Wp for plant with capacities exceeding a few MWp/yr, and continue to decline for higher production volumes.

Source: D.E.Carlson, 'Low-Cost Power From Thin-Film Photovoltaics'; Johannson et al (eds), *Electricity*, p.619, Lund University Press, Sweden, 1989.

cost-effective option for communication repeater stations, cathodic protection of various structures, motorway signs and telephone points, boats and caravans, as well as isolated dwellings: 'it is now cheaper to install a PV lighting unit in a shed at the bottom of the garden rather than pay to have a mains cable'. In developing countries the potential applications are much larger still, and can provide invaluable services for mobile or remote refrigeration, lighting, etc. In such applications, PV competes with copper cable rather than baseload electricity, or small diesel sets, and does so with increasing ease. Such applications represent considerable markets, which are growing rapidly as the price falls, and can displace inefficiently used fossil fuel or wood.

Although solar cell manufacture requires high technology, once in place, maintenance (when required at all) is usually very simple, consisting mostly of cleaning and mending broken connecting wires. Also, PV does not suffer from the long lead times of most power plants, and produces minimal environmental damage in deployment. Despite being capital intensive, PV is thus an unusually suitable and low-risk technology for use in aid and development programmes. This could rapidly expand from experience with remote applications to grid-based peaking and then perhaps baseload uses as costs reduce and new capacity is required - and perhaps as technology transfers develop as part of attempts to forge a global approach to tackling global environmental problems.

Even the drawbacks of seasonal and daily variations of solar electricity are perhaps exaggerated. This is partly because of the general factors discussed in Chapter 1, but also because in many of the areas with the best resources for grid-based PV - which include much of the world's population - electricity demand is or may become loosely correlated with the solar input, because cooling is more important than heating. For the longer term, producing hydrogen from PV in desert areas has been proposed as one of the most promising ways of displacing oil with electricity in transport, with eventual costs estimated at $1.70 to $2.40/gallon of petroleum equivalent.[56] An alternative transport application might be to use stand-alone PV units at car parks, homes, garages or automated roadside filling points, to charge batteries for

[56] Measured in US gallons. See J.M.Ogden and R.H.Williams, *Solar Hydrogen - Moving Beyond Fossil Fuels*, World Resources Institute, Washington DC, 1989, p.63.

electric cars or perhaps to generate hydrogen for hydrogen vehicles - possibilities which do not seem to have been explored.

PV is by no means the only way of generating electricity from solar radiation. Indeed, dispersed solar thermal systems, in which parabolic mirrors focus sunlight to heat a fluid in a narrow tube, which then drives a conventional turbine cycle, is cheaper and has developed faster than PV, and has been commercialized as a reliable peaking plant technology in the sun and financing conditions of California. On a global scale its applications are more limited than PV, because it requires direct sunlight and larger units, and the scope for further development may be limited; but it is still an important technology. Solar ponds, in which salt gradients are used to stabilize large solar-induced temperature differences in ponds (which then drive a conventional turbine), provide automatic storage, and they are again currently cheaper than PV.

In fact, as indicated in Figure 3.8, PV is the most costly of the major diffuse renewable energy technologies, and its costs have not declined as rapidly as some others. Perhaps the most striking developments have occurred in *wind energy*, which provides an example of particular interest. Nearly all studies during the 1970s concluded that wind energy could not be a large-scale economic source of power. For some, wind energy retains the image of a primitive, medieval technology not fit for the modern age, and yet the technology advanced very rapidly during the 1980s; just ten years after rejecting it as one of the least promising renewable sources, the UK Department of Energy's programme managers wrote that 'the Department of Energy now regards large-scale generation from wind energy as a serious option',[57] with an estimated contribution by 2025 of up to 10% of current generation.[58]

Although government-led R&D played a significant part, the major developments occurred through the creation of a market for small and medium-sized machines in the US, when a favourable regulatory regime combined with generous Federal and State tax incentives which made wind energy in some areas - particularly California - an attractive private investment even at the then high costs. Installation rates in California rose from 10MW/yr in 1981 to 400MW/yr in 1984, with a cumulative

[57] L.Bedford and D.Page, *The UK Department of Energy's Wind Energy Programme - a Progress Report*, EC Wind Energy Conference, Herning, June 1988.
[58] HMSO, *Renewable Energy in the UK: The Way Forward*, Energy Paper No.55, London, 1988.

Figure 3.8 Renewable electricity production costs: trends and projections

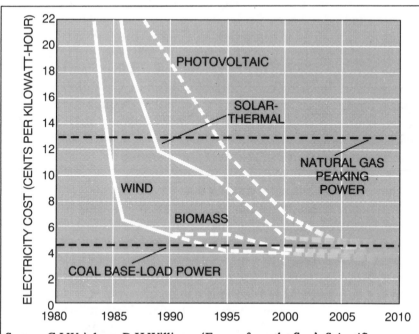

Source: C.J.Weinberg, R.H.Williams, 'Energy from the Sun', *Scientific American*, September 1990.

investment by 1986 of about $2bn. In this brief period the mean size of commercial units doubled, performance improved dramatically, and costs fell sharply, mostly as a result of applying advanced materials and control systems and a better understanding of wind turbine dynamics and stresses. The fall in oil prices and removal of tax credits then greatly tightened the market at a time when several large companies had put substantial capital into new machines, creating incentives to further cost and price cuts.

In Denmark, the leading manufacturing country, wind energy is regarded as economic resource, with 350MW installed by 1990 feeding an official target of 2,000MW (to generate 10% of electricity) by

2000.[59] In 1988 the UK's Central Electricity Generating Board stated that at very good sites in Britain, modern wind turbines could generate electricity more cheaply than either nuclear or coal stations.[60] Avenues expected to give further substantial improvements have been identified.[61]

Although the performance of many of the early Californian wind farms has been very poor, with the market base and finance available, several companies gained rapid experience. Windfarms from the best manufacturers in the US and Europe have had several years operation at more than 90% availability, with some above 95% - higher than most large-scale steam plant. This has been possible in part because the small unit size limits the overall complexity of the system and allows a rapid product cycle in which the lessons from failures can be quickly incorporated. Furthermore, when problems do occur most components can be quickly replaced. It is such a young technology that the long-term reliability is still unproven, but even if major components do fail, they can generally be replaced without great difficulty or cost, compared to failures in large thermal plant. Some manufacturers now offer a complete 10-year performance guarantee on their turbines, a striking contrast to the cost-plus arrangements for most conventional power stations.

Except at very good sites, or when it competes against very high cost power (such as isolated diesel plant), wind energy is still more expensive than conventional coal power sources (depending somewhat on the financing assumptions). But in many areas the gap is small, and is still narrowing. Gas combined cycle plants present a much stiffer challenge.

---

[59] For a recent EC review of progress and costs see H.N.Nacfaire and K.Diamantaras, *The EC's Demonstration Programme for Wind Energy and Community Energy Policy*, European Wind Energy Conference & Exhibition, Glasgow, Peter Peregrinus, 1989, and other papers in this volume. A recent US cost review is given in J.M.Cohen et al, 'A methodology for computing wind turbine cost using utility economic assumptions', *Windpower '89*, SERI/TP-257-3628, Arlington, VA, March 1990.

[60] CEGB, Hinkley Point C power station public enquiry, *Proof of Evidence on Comparison of Non-Fossil Options*, CEGB 6, CEGB, 1988.

[61] The major Oak Ridge technology assessment states that, in the context of the relatively poorer wind resources of the US, 'cost-effective and extremely competitive wind systems are attainable within the next five to ten years...high temperature power semiconductors can significantly "leap frog"...today's wind control systems' (W.Fulkerson et al, *Energy Technology R&D*, op.cit., Vol.2. Other developments expected include improved airfoils and structural dynamics.

Wind resources and integration have already been discussed in Chapter 1. The physical resources are large, and various attempts to take account of realistic siting constraints have resulted in a wide range of estimates, because they inevitably rely on largely subjective estimates of what constitutes 'acceptable' sites and siting densities. Many people, pointing to the size of wind turbines and concerns about noise, electromagnetic interference and other worries, believe that planning objections to siting will heavily constrain the practical resource. Others argue that wind farms can be made very attractive, that the other objections raised amount to no more than scare stories (certainly, most noise and interference difficulties to date have been easily overcome by better technology and siting), and that wind will prove much more acceptable than conventional sources. If the latter is correct, planning procedures will simply weed out inappropriate sites and leave a large acceptable resource. Another option might be to go offshore, where stronger and more constant winds help to offset the extra engineering requirements - this application is less developed, with more uncertain costs. In either case, in many relatively sparsely populated countries such as the US, or in those with usually good onshore and/or offshore resources, such as the UK, wind energy could in principle become a major component of electricity supply.

The projections of technology costs in Figure 3.8 are obviously uncertain, but are based on detailed engineering calculations of the effects of foreseeable improvement and economies of scale. They suggest that within fifteen years, all the major diffuse renewables could become roughly competitive with coal-based power generation.

The focus on these technologies in this chapter is not to suggest that they are the only important renewables - far from it. *Large-scale hydro* dams already supply about 15% of the world's electricity often at low cost, and could supply considerably more depending very much on environmental constraints, as discussed in some of the country studies. Much smaller *'micro-hydro'* schemes can be equally cheap, and are much less exploited. *Tidal energy* is another form of hydro energy, rather more limited and rarely exploited at present. Some coastal inlets are of a shape which naturally amplifies the effect of tides, building up water heads of many meters; by placing dams across such estuaries the energy of the tides, sometimes thousands of megawatts, can be captured. Most of the technology is conventional, though the application is largely new and there are environmental concerns. There have also been some speculative proposals for tapping tidal streams in ocean channels. All large hydro schemes are capital intensive, with long construction times and very long lifetimes, so the economics depend very heavily on the financing assumptions (see UK chapter for further comments on tidal power).

Geothermal energy, in which heat is extracted directly from the earth's crust, comes in two fundamentally different forms. The first, in which hot underground reservoirs (*geothermal aquifers*) are tapped to provide a source of hot water or steam, has been in use for many years in areas where such reservoirs are easily reached. Like tidal energy, the technology is largely conventional, but the applications are novel and overall resources are limited (see Chapter 1). The second form does not rely on such reservoirs. *Hot Dry Rock* (HDR) geothermal relies instead upon drilling two or more boreholes several kilometres deep into hot rocks, fracturing the rock surface between them, and circulating water through the system to extract the heat of the rocks. Though it is simple in theory, in practice a number of major technical problems have to be overcome. It is most attractive in areas where the heat gradient in the surface rocks is unusually high, but in general has a wider potential than aquifers.

Wave energy is another source which divides into two distinct forms, one small in potential but often feasible, the other larger in potential and highly uncertain at present. *Shore-based wave* power can be tapped by a number of fairly simple technologies, and Norway has demonstrated machines which it has now exported. The resource, however, is limited by the energy incident upon suitable shorelines, and many constraints upon siting. *Deep water wave* energy, by contrast, would involve much more complex technology operating in a far harsher environment, but the energy density and total resource is much larger. The problems of achieving economic deep water machines are formidable, but developments over the last five years have suggested that official British pronouncements of the death of wave power prospects were premature (see Chapter 5). Cables might be used to bring the power to shore or, conceivably, machines might be used to generate hydrogen, perhaps in the region of offshore gas fields where existing infrastructure and experience could be drawn upon as natural gas production declines.

What conclusions might be drawn from this medley of technical options and promising but uncertain predictions? Certainly, it would be premature to conclude that renewables will provide an economic and painless solution to greenhouse concerns. The projections of Figure 3.8 suggest only that large-scale renewables may be marginally competitive with coal generation at typical US prices. Although it seems a relatively common experience for mainstream projections to be unduly pessimistic when a technology is still in the phase of rapid and innovative development because many possibilities are overlooked, it is equally common for supporters' assessments to be over-optimistic when it comes to actual deployment of favoured designs - because practical complications are also overlooked. Though such problems tend to be greatest for large and complex engineering projects, there is no reason to suppose that renewables will be entirely immune. Also, and ironically, many renewables will undoubtedly face substantial environmental constraints: hydro, waste combustion, windfarms, geothermal aquifers, and high-yield forestry have all already raised environmental opposition, and there is little doubt that the same would apply at least to tidal and shore-based wave energy, and probably others as well. Much may depend on how far such opposition limits practical exploitation.

Yet the converse attitude, that renewables have little or no role to play in limiting greenhouse gas emissions, is more indefensible. The developments are impressive, and the fact that much remains to be learned simply means that the projections are uncertain, not that they can be ignored, as appears to be the case in many energy policy developments and studies of CO_2 abatement costs. Much has to be learned not only about the technologies themselves, but about the possible constraints on their deployment, and how the many diverse characteristics of different renewables may best fit into energy systems. Any individual renewable technology taken on its own, even PV, has a limited potential for displacing fossil fuels. Taken in combinations which complement and match national demand and resource conditions, in association with other activities, energy trade, and perhaps storage, their role may be substantial. The science of understanding the real potential for renewables is in its infancy, but it is likely to be one of the central themes in developing long-term responses to the greenhouse effect.

3.5 Conclusions

Any technical review is a product of its time, and conclusions may alter as technologies progress and new problems and new ideas emerge. But at the opening of the 1990s, the following seem clear.

The greatest opportunities lie in electricity production, where a whole panoply of options seem likely to be attractive given the right local conditions. Gas turbines, used in combined cycle or ISTIG plants, and fuelled by natural gas or gasified coal or biomass, seem likely to be a mainstay of future supplies. All would help to reduce greenhouse gas emissions by varying amounts, depending on the fuel and whether the waste heat is utilized. Fuel cells, with a similar variety of fuelling options, could also compete for smaller-scale applications. If the costs of nuclear power can be reduced as many claim and if other obstacles can be overcome, perhaps through the use of modular gas-cooled reactors and other improvements, nuclear might yet make a spectacular recovery in some areas at least. Wind in windy regions, solar thermal and later PV in sunny regions, and a host of locally concentrated renewables also show quite good prospects for being economic set against conventional coal generating costs and price projections.

In transport the options are more limited, but advanced processes for producing ethanol from biomass might well compete against conventional oil price projections, while systems for powering vehicles from non-fossil sources either by electricity or hydrogen - perhaps from decentralized PV or other sources - could be among the most attractive possibilities if oil prices rise above those of the early 1990s, or if and where environmental or other constraints force a move away from oil products.

There are some clear examples of non-fossil options which appear to be economic but which are not taken up because of various market obstacles. The most notable cases concern waste and various biomass residues, but other examples include some solar heating and the use of good wind and mini-hydro sites. Changing regulatory environments could do much to help exploit such opportunities, and financial incentives could help to overcome obvious hurdles to initial development and deployment of all small-scale renewables. But the details of market imperfections play a relatively much smaller role in supply than in end-use. Indeed, it may be that the most important questions and uncertainties relate neither to this nor even to the characteristics of 'alternative' technologies themselves, but rather concern the price of the fossil fuels which they are seeking to displace.

Traditionally, most fossil fuel price projections have forecast steady price increases, as demand rises and reserves are depleted, forcing moves towards higher cost and more distant and/or geographically concentrated resources. If this is the correct background, then the outlook for a whole range of alternative sources and generating technologies, nearly all of which (excepting coal conversion to liquid fuels) reduce greenhouse gas emissions, seems quite promising, and the need for additional incentives such as carbon taxes may be limited. Yet the history of fossil fuel prices has, albeit with some spectacular exceptions, tended to proceed in the opposite direction. Improvements in technologies for production, transport and conversion, combined with the discovery of new resources, have led to prices falling, and in real terms the production costs of all fossil fuels are now as low as they have ever been. Much depends on future consumption levels, and in turn, on the extent to which prices reflect production costs.

Coal is generally the most expensive of fossil fuels to produce and process. Although developments of large strip mined coal deposits and automated techniques for deep mining certainly help to lower costs, it is plausible that various non-fossil sources could compete against coal in many regions, or at least that removing subsidies or a fairly modest carbon tax could create such a situation.

For gas the situation is more complex. Extraction is usually relatively cheap, and with the advent of advanced gas turbines there is little prospect that either coal or non-fossil sources could produce power more cheaply than regionally produced gas. If price is the only tool, high taxes on fossil fuels might be required to give other sources an edge when it comes to new capacity. But as discussed in Chapter 1, long distance transport of gas can be relatively costly, and can entail various political risks: to the extent that gas prices decouple from production costs, or production moves to exploit distant or unconventional, high cost resources, the situation would be very different.

Similar remarks apply even more aptly to oil. Both production and transport costs are low from the major land-based reserves; even in hostile environments such as the North Sea, production costs fell sharply with efforts to keep such sources economic at the low oil prices of the late 1980s. The capability of the major oil producers to undercut any serious competition is almost unlimited, as long as reserves and production capacity can meet the demand. As history demonstrates, the oil world is much more complex than this suggests, but the point remains that in the absence of government action to keep prices high, for reasons of environment or energy security, the economic feasibility of a technology such as ethanol from biomass depends as much upon the actions of OPEC - and government policy towards the dangers of oil dependence - as it does upon advances in enzymatic conversion processes.

Thus, even if non-fossil sources do develop to become competitive against traditional fossil fuel price projections, as seems increasingly feasible, it does not necessarily follow that they will be deployed on a large scale without government support. It is indeed impossible to project the overall economics of alternative supply sources not only because the technologies are still developing, but because they are chasing the moving and inherently uncertain target of fossil fuel prices - which are themselves to an important extent politically determined. What can however be said with some confidence is that natural gas will play an important role, while the march of non-fossil technologies will make the costs of moving away from carbon-based fuels less than many current projections assume. The deployment of such technologies would in turn help to lower the costs of whatever fossil supplies are still employed; and that alone would be no small achievement.

Energy forecasting has a poor track record. Since the mid-1960s, most projections of total demand extending more than a few years ahead have proved too high. Analysing the reasons reveals several important lessons. The extent and/or impact of price changes were underestimated, partly through a failure to examine the technical options available for improving energy efficiency, given incentives. The impact of structural change within industry was largely overlooked. The saturation of various end-uses was often neglected. Long-run projections, at least of prices, were too heavily influenced by recent trends. Modelling complexity has not to date yielded success.

Many uncertainties are irremovable, implying a need for a range of scenarios in exploring possible futures. Within this, improved modelling techniques can reveal much. Models can be broadly divided into 'top-down' models which aggregate energy behaviour, estimated primarily on the basis of past trends and price responses, and 'bottom-up' models which focus on the physical applications of energy and technical options. Each has strengths and weaknesses. Top-down models provide the best single approach for estimating the impact of price changes and supply-side developments over time, and have been widely developed and applied. Bottom-up analysis is required for understanding the underlying pressures on future energy demand, and the potential impact of different low-cost technologies for improving efficiency, particularly in energy use.

Both perspectives are required to obtain a good understanding of energy prospects and options, but a consistent modelling combination is extremely difficult. Bottom-up analysis is the most suitable single approach for examining the range of future possibilities and emission abatement strategies including exploitation of the 'efficiency gap'.

Case studies of bottom-up analysis applied to the UK suggest a very wide range of technically plausible futures. Ten years ahead, carbon emissions from different scenarios differ by more than 20%, and forty years ahead the range spans a factor of three. The lowest levels reflect widespread implementation of abatement technologies and moderate growth in applications, and highlight the widespread nature of changes which would be required; there are no dominant technical fixes. However, the central importance of transport and electricity production in long-run CO_2 emissions emerge clearly.

These scenarios are largely subjective in their estimates of feasible rates of change and do not explicitly represent policy impacts. A detailed modelling study of specific microeconomic policy changes (standards) applied to the UK domestic sector suggests that these could reduce domestic sector CO_2 emissions by 1-2% annually over the first decade or two, exploiting only techniques and technologies which are known to be cost-effective. These results cannot be widely extrapolated, but related information is available for some other sectors and countries.

In general, modelling studies carried out to date are not adequate to estimate accurately the potential rate and costs of CO_2 abatement overall. However, drawing on the available results and data suggests that it may be possible to reduce OECD carbon emissions from current levels by up to 1%/yr for a couple of decades at little or no net economic loss, if suitable measures are taken. New techniques and/or non-fossil sources would be required to maintain such reductions thereafter, increasing uncertainties in both achievable rates and costs. Even within the OECD there would be substantial national and regional variation in achievable rates of abatement; the prospects and potentials in other economies are very different, and are still more uncertain.

The previous chapters have discussed many technical options for limiting emissions of greenhouse gases. In analyzing energy policy responses to the greenhouse effect, the central technical questions concern the impact which such technologies and other changes might have on overall energy supply and demand, and associated emissions, when introduced into energy systems. Conditions vary greatly between countries, but there are issues of methodology and assumptions which are common to many energy systems. This chapter discusses these common issues, and presents some modelling studies which illustrate themes of particular relevance to questions concerning carbon emission trends, abatement strategies, and costs.

4.1 Energy forecasting: lessons from the track record

Assessing the possible impact of different policies on greenhouse gas emissions requires quantitative projections of the energy economy. The nature of energy development and the greenhouse effect means that a long-term view is needed. Unfortunately, perhaps the only consistent theme to emerge from past experience of energy projections is that predictions have usually been wrong - often spectacularly so. Before developing projections it is instructive to consider some lessons from past experience of energy forecasting.

Energy projections in the 1960s and 1970s almost all projected rapidly growing energy demand for the decades ahead. Most national forecasts made before 1975 foresaw energy use increasing by at least 50%, in some cases doubling, over the period 1970-1990, with continuous exponential increase thereafter. Set against this, from the mid 1970s especially, some studies appeared arguing for 'low energy futures' in which energy demand could be lower, and might even fall. Aspects of this debate, and some of the key studies, have been summarized in Volume 1, Chapter 7.

It is a matter of history that the development of energy demand during the 1970s and 1980s, especially in OECD countries, was closer to the hopes of low energy enthusiasts than to the official projections of the 1970s. Total UK energy demand in 1989, for example, was just below that of 1973, very close to Leach's 'low energy strategy' projection.[1] However, when examined closely it is apparent that even those which did get close to the right numbers were right partly for the wrong reasons. Outside Japan and some European countries, few of the conservation

---

[1] G.Leach, *A Low Energy Strategy for the UK*, Science Reviews Ltd, London, 1979.

policies advocated were in fact adopted. In the UK, none foresaw the massive industrial restructuring of the early 1980s; Leach's study was one of the few which pointed at all to the possible large impact of structural changes on energy demand. The UK experience was extreme in this respect but the pattern of almost constant energy demand was repeated throughout the OECD from 1973-1986.[2]

Why were so many studies so wrong? The question can be answered at two levels, namely the political and the technical. Many have argued that the energy projections of the 1970s were anything but objective science, being more in the realm of tools for justifying particular political outlooks.[3] Projections by those representing the interests of major energy suppliers - which often included governments and energy ministries - sought to emphasize the importance of the energy sector and to justify large supply developments; it is perhaps not so surprising that such a culture inclined to high projections. Conversely, lower energy demand projections were essential if the anti-nuclear lobby was to offer any kind of alternative. In some countries with open political systems, there arose a compromise of 'negotiated energy futures';[4] in others, the divisions simply deepened.

Yet such a political explanation is of little practical help. Most of those developing energy projections - on both sides - believed they were conducting an objective analysis. The fact that they were so widely different, and in most cases so wrong, point to a serious limitation in the basic assumptions and/or tools used. One source of error was that most analysts were using projections of GDP growth that turned out to be too high. This points to inherent uncertainties in the background economic projections, about which little can be done by energy analysts. However, it is readily apparent that most of the studies would still have projected rapid energy growth even given accurate GDP projections, and there were many other sources of error. The question of why so many projections proved so inaccurate gives a number of useful technical insights which may be summarized as follows:

---

[2] Total OECD primary energy demand in 1986 was 3546Mtoe, compared to 3327Mtoe in 1973 (Source: *Energy Policies and Programmes of IEA Countries*, 1987 Review, IEA/OECD, Paris, 1988).

[3] See T.Baumgartner and A.Midttun, *The Politics of Energy Forecasting*, Clarendon Press, Oxford, 1987.

[4] ibid.

* Few of the earlier studies foresaw the large oil price rises of the 1970s, and even the later studies greatly underestimated the relevant *price elasticity of energy demand*, ie. the extent to which demand would respond to large rises in price. The price elasticities were mostly estimated from relatively small price fluctuations around a low base price, and on this basis were judged to be small. This proved a very poor guide to the response to a large price shock. Since 1973, estimates of energy price elasticities have varied widely, and these variations can have major implications for projections.[5]

* Many projections ignored *saturation effects*. For many energy uses there is a clear limit to the desire for energy services, more or less irrespective of price and wealth - ie. demand *saturates*. People for example do not have an infinite desire for lighting or refrigeration, but seek a standard of comfort which, once achieved, ceases to form a significant growth area. Perhaps the most striking case is that of heating demand - people do not want to roast just because they are richer. Figure 4.1, which shows household energy expenditure in the UK across a wide range of income, shows this clearly. It is clearly incorrect to suppose that energy demand will increase uniformly with rising income (as, by implication, did many energy studies). Beyond a given level the relationship between wealth and energy use for comfort is broken. Most energy demand sectors are, ultimately, subject to such saturation; the discussion in Volume 1, Chapter 6, argues that even transport and industrial demand may approach saturation as societies develop further, beyond the state of current OECD economies.

* Projections also failed to foresee the extent and implications of *structural change* within the economy. The potential impact of shifts between different industries, and between manufacturing and services, can have a major impact on energy demand and carbon emissions quite independent of total GDP. In practice, over the 1970s

---

[5] Pearce argued in 1980 that ' ... values of 0.25 characterize UK elasticities before 1973. Given the much higher price now, elementary economic theory dictates that the elasticity will itself be higher ... [we conclude] that long run price elasticities may differ by a factor between two and three from the value implied in the official forecasts. Making only a modest adjustment reduces [projected] energy demand in the year 2000 by 15% while raising the elasticity by a factor of just over two actually eliminated the growth in primary energy demand altogether', (D.Pearce, 'Energy Conservation and Official UK Energy Forecasts', *Energy Policy*, September 1980).

Figure 4.1 Energy saturation: direct energy expenditure in households as a function of income (UK)

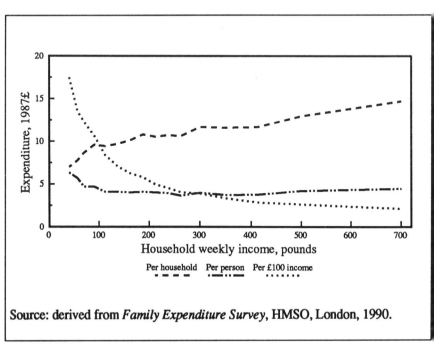

Source: derived from *Family Expenditure Survey*, HMSO, London, 1990.

and 1980s, heavy industries in OECD countries became relatively much less important, with more economic activity concentrated in less energy intensive industries and in services. The extent to which this was driven by prices, and the role played by migration of heavy industries to developing countries, is still unclear; but Volume 1, section 6.4 notes powerful reasons for supposing that the trend towards lower aggregate intensity in industrial energy use is a fundamental one, which will continue in the long term.

* *Technical change,* and related responses to price changes and other constraints, can be very important. The years after 1973 saw a rapid improvement in industrial and transport efficiencies. The dire predictions of the 'Limits to Growth' study[6] melted away as industries explored and discovered new resources, developed less material-intensive products, found techniques for exploiting

[6] D.H.Meadows et al, *Limits to Growth*, Universe, 1972.

lower-grade ores, and developed substitutes for the scarcer materials. Conversely, the oil price collapse of 1986 stimulated a dramatic fall in the cost of drilling rigs as offshore operators struggled to remain competitive.

* Projections have tended to be *influenced too heavily by recent developments*. In the aftermath of the 1973 and 1979 price shocks, most analysts foresaw ever-rising energy prices. Following the collapse of oil prices in 1986, there was a belief that low prices would persist throughout the 1990s. By the mid-1980s most analysts had radically reduced their forecasts of energy demand from those of the early and mid-1970s. Following the rapid upturn in demand in many countries in the late 1980s, forecasts were revised upwards again. The 1990/91 Gulf crisis may provide yet further examples.[7] This applies not only to the short term but to projections ten, twenty or even fifty years ahead, and illustrates the inadequacy of our understanding of the factors which really determine long-run energy price and demand.

* Finally, an impressive lesson is that *sophistication does not equal success*. Complex computer-based projections are only as good as the assumptions which underlie them. The 'Energy in a Finite World' studies cited in Volume 1, section 7.1 were a pinnacle of complex computer forecasting, but there is little evidence that this made them more accurate; as noted there, it was shown several years later that entirely different results, particularly concerning supply choices, could have been obtained from modest alterations in assumptions which were in any case largely arbitrary. In energy planning there is a danger that excessive complexity may do no more than hide critical assumptions beneath a veneer of sophistication.

Armed with these lessons from the past, how can one approach the still more complex problem of assessing the possible responses to the greenhouse effect?

---

[7] The crisis has led some to project higher oil prices for the 1990s and beyond. The real medium to long-term impact could well be the opposite if Kuwaiti and Iraqi production rejoins expanded output elsewhere, with further efforts at diversification having been stimulated in importing countries.

4.2 The use and abuse of scenarios

Because the past has taught humility with respect to predicting the future, it is now common to use 'scenarios' to project energy developments, to cover a number of possible futures. Scenarios can be conceived in a number of ways. Often they are used to express a range of uncertainty concerning key variables: for example, GDP and energy growth forecasts are often made in this manner, with high, middle and low forecasts, with each developed in great detail to form an internally consistent view of the future.

One difficulty with this approach is that, because of the amount of information and analysis involved, there can be a tendency to focus on the middle scenario as representative. This can undermine the main objective of using scenarios in the first place. More generally, the problem is not that key parameters are numerically uncertain, but that often the future turns out to be radically different from anything that people had considered likely. Scenarios which simply vary a few key numbers may give limited insight into possible surprises and the policy options which may be open for affecting the course of developments.

An alternative is to use scenarios not so much as predictions under uncertainty but as tools for broadening understanding of what could happen, and for aiding analysis of major policy options. The psychology of 'high, middle and low' is then not very relevant. The focus is upon possibilities and potential rather than 'most likely' predictions; upon mechanisms rather than numbers; and upon the relative consequences of different policy decisions. This approach has been used increasingly in the oil industry, for example, to assess the risks associated with large-scale, long-term investments.

In more broad-ranging analysis of national policies relating to emissions, the distinction between the approaches is sharper still. The primary issue is not predicting the future. The key questions concern how, and by how much, policy and behaviour changes can alter the future energy economy, and the costs involved. Frequently it is sufficient to take a baseline case and to use other scenarios to assess the impact of different policy strategies on this. This is the approach used in the country studies in this book. It does not imply that the baseline 'business-as-usual' scenarios are necessarily considered to be accurate predictions, merely that they form a plausible reference from which to make comparisons.

For many purposes it is useful to draw a clear distinction between the short and the long term in energy analysis. In the short term - which in the context of energy systems means anything within the next ten years or so - it would be expensive to write off existing supply investments or to deploy major new technologies on a large scale. The major options on this timescale lie in affecting: the take-up of goods which have a high turnover rate (which mostly relate to energy demand rather than supply); the speed of applying retrofits (usually for conservation) to longer-term stock; energy-related aspects of consumer behaviour (eg. through price changes); and the choice of technology (mostly from existing options) where new investments are required because of growing demand or the retirement of old plant, or are economically attractive enough to displace older plant.

In the longer term, the scope is much wider. A large proportion of existing installations may be replaced, and a much wider range of technologies may be available including many which are in prototype or which at least can be constructed on current knowledge but are not yet commercially developed. Larger institutional and economic changes can also be conceived. Separating the short and long term also means that scenarios can focus on particular 'target years', greatly easing the analytic burden and presentation.

Authors of the country studies in this project were therefore asked to prepare illustrative scenarios of the energy system for the years 2000 and 2030. In the short term, options are sufficiently constrained that only two principal scenarios are required. In the long term, to reflect the greater scope for changes in both fuels and efficiency, four scenarios are used. The basic scenarios are listed in the box. Each, of course, can be supplemented by discussion of the sensitivity of results to various assumptions.

4.3 Bottom-up or top-down analysis?

There are two broad analytic approaches to making energy projections, commonly known as 'top down' and 'bottom up'. The gulf between high and low demand projections can often - though not always - be attributed to the analytic approach used, so it is important to understand the differences.

Top-down analysis relies on extrapolating from general macroeconomic properties of energy systems, usually estimated on the

Definition of country study scenarios

Scenarios are defined by the primary consumption of each fuel in a target year. Six scenarios were used:

Short-term scenarios year 2000:

2000A	**Business-as-usual**
2000B	**Abatement policies**

Long-term scenarios year 2030:

2030Ai	**Business-as-usual**
2030Aii	**Business-as-usual energy demand, with fuel switching to limit carbon emissions**
2030Bi	**Policies for high energy efficiency**
2030Bii	**Policies for both high energy efficiency and fuel switching to limit carbon emissions**

basis of past behaviour; for many purposes it is synonymous with 'macroeconomic modelling', though the latter is often given a much narrower meaning, confined to models which reflect investment and employment linkages throughout the full economy. Top-down analysis embodies prices and economic growth as the critical determinants of energy behaviour. Historical data is generally used to estimate the relations between growth, prices, and energy demand (often separately for different sectors). By including estimates of how much one fuel will substitute for another for a given price difference ('cross-substitution elasticities'), interfuel competition can be modelled. Projecting GDP and prices then gives an estimate of future demand, and projecting technology costs enables the take-up of different supply technologies to be estimated; the effects of technology development or subsidies can be expressed in terms of price changes. Generally, such models are designed to 'choose' supply technologies in the future so as to minimize the total costs of the energy system over time.

Many different top-down models have been developed and applied to a wide variety of energy issues, and various reviews and conference collections provide a guide and discussion of the major models available.[8] A review from the OECD examines models which have been applied to the greenhouse issue, and gives an idea of the wide variety available, and some of their strengths and weaknesses.[9]

Volume 1, section 8.2, noted several major difficulties facing energy modelling, two of which are of specific concern for top-down models. First, the lack of any detail in representing the end uses of energy means that the impact of more efficient end-use technologies cannot be satisfactorily included. It is difficult or impossible to represent major changes in the behaviour of energy markets - including those which might be introduced by regulatory measures designed to exploit the 'efficiency gap'. Analyses using most top-down models almost by definition conclude that costs will be incurred in limiting emissions - or in making any other changes to the energy system - since in optimizing the baseline projection, the models assume that any measures which are cost-effective in their own right will be taken up anyway. Abatement scenarios are then perturbations to the optimal solution. But as discussed in Volume 1, there is a great deal of evidence to suggest that in the real world, business-as-usual conditions are far from optimal, and measures to improve efficiency can reduce both costs and emissions.

Second, the models tend to 'project the past' in terms of the various elasticities, estimated from historical observation, which relate prices and GDP to demand. This can lead to substantial errors, partly because

---

[8] C.J.Hitch, ed., *Modelling Energy-Economy Interaction: Five Approaches*, Resources for the Future, Washington DC, 1977; J.A.Edmonds and J.M.Reilly, 'Global Energy and CO_2 to the year 2000', *The Energy Journal*, Vol.4 pp.21-47, 1983; L.Bergman, 'Energy policy modeling: a survey of general equilibrium approaches', *Journal of Policy Modeling*, Vol.10, No.3, pp.377-399, 1988; *MIT/GSEL Workshop on Economic/Energy/Environmental Modeling for Climate Change Policy Analysis*, Washington, October 1990; J.Edmonds and D.W.Barns, 'Factors Affecting the Long-Term Cost of Global Fossil Fuel CO_2 Emissions Reduction', Battelle Pacific Northwest Laboratory, Washington DC, 1990. An Energy Modelling Forum directed from Stanford University, US, regularly reviews and compares developments in top-down models.

[9] P.Hoeller, A.Dean and J.Nicolaisen, 'A Survey of Studies of the Costs of Reducing Greenhouse Gas Emissions', OECD Department of Economics and Statistics, Working Paper No.89, OECD, Paris, 1990. The review examines fourteen modelling studies, falling into five broad categories. Differences include their geographical coverage, division and linkages between regions; the time-span modelled; the detail with which the energy sector is disaggregated; the form and detail of linkages between the energy sector and the rest of the economy; and the detail with which the broader economy is modelled.

it is very difficult to separate the impact of prices from many other factors which affect historical energy demand, and partly because it depends upon future reactions being similar to those in the past. Saturation of demand in various energy sectors, as noted above, is one particular and important reason why this may not be the case. Some of these effects can in principle be incorporated in top-down models, but only at the cost of considerable complexity. In reality, long-run elasticities, which reflect technological reactions to higher energy prices, are fundamentally uncertain as noted above. Even if they could be convincingly derived from historical data, there would be few grounds for assuming the same values to apply decades ahead. Yet macroeconomic models for long-term energy analysis rely fundamentally upon such elasticities. As a tool for prediction, top-down modelling, applied in isolation, thus becomes rapidly more questionable the further ahead it is applied, and as a tool for assessing policy measures other than general economic instruments it may be very limited.

Bottom-up analysis contrasts with the top-down approach by concentrating on the structure of energy demand - how energy is actually used. For example, space heat demand in residential buildings, commercial sector lighting demand, electricity use in the metals industries, etc, are all accounted for separately, and the total is derived as the sum of the parts. Obviously the level of breakdown can vary greatly.

The approach can be used for making forecasts by projecting each activity (often on the basis of existing trends or more detailed behavioural studies), and incorporating with each expected changes in the efficiency of energy use in providing the service demanded. This, too, necessarily requires subjective judgements on various aspects. However, the approach naturally separates, as far as possible, the impact of structural developments and changes in the factors driving demand for energy services, from the impact of efficiency improvements. Saturation effects are incorporated inherently, and the impact of deploying different technologies, or of changing fuels in different end-use sectors, can be readily studied. Consequently the potential scope for, and limits to, various technical changes in the energy sector can be better judged than with top-down modelling. All round, bottom-up analysis gives a much better insight into the activities and technological factors which determine energy demand, and the sectors upon which policy for limiting demand might best focus.

There are however several drawbacks to such analysis. There is no explicit role for prices - and as noted, prices have proved to be very important in determining demand, on all timescales. Some price effects can be incorporated indirectly through estimates of the impact of price changes on energy performance at the level of detailed end use, estimated either subjectively or on the basis of both historical and cross-country comparisons, but this is not very satisfactory. Also, when used for projection, there is a substantial subjective element in judging how different end uses may change, and if new and unforeseen end uses arise, a bottom-up analysis will underestimate the potential growth in demand. There is no macroeconomic context to reflect the interactions between the energy sector and the broader economy (top-down models also vary greatly in this respect). A practical difficulty is often that a bottom-up analysis requires a great deal of data, which may simply not be available at the level of detail required. Finally, many bottom-up studies do not contain any explicit time element; they look at snapshots of energy systems, with little or no data on how rapidly changes from one state to another can reasonably occur, with such constraints estimated externally. However, some of the most sophisticated technology-based models do explicitly incorporate time; when applied to optimizing energy sector developments including end-use options such models often have difficulty projecting any energy growth, since much more efficient technologies are steadily taken up as stock turns over.[10]

At root of the debate between these approaches - and much else - are the questions: to what extent does energy behave as a traditional economic commodity, with price as the main factor determining a near-optimal investment pattern; and to what extent does the pervasive nature of energy as a crucial but financially often very minor component in other activities, together with various other quirks of the energy business, invalidate traditional economic assumptions of market behaviour and optimality? Much of the discussion in Volume 1 highlighted special features of energy systems as well as reasons for

---

[10] An example occurs with a recent application of the MARKAL model (S.C.Morris, B.D.Solomon, D.Hill, J.Lee, G.Goldstein, 'A Least Cost Energy Analysis of US CO_2 Reduction Options', in J.W.Tester and N.Ferrari, (eds), *Energy and Environment in the 21st Century*, MIT Press, Cambridge, MA, 1990).

believing that the past may be a poor guide to the future, and earlier chapters in this volume demonstrated clear technical opportunities for large savings at low costs, which are not taken up due to varied market imperfections. These observations underline doubts about the suitability of simple top-down analysis. In the past, most energy projections have used top-down modelling. Bottom-up analysis appears to have a better track record, though the experience is more limited and it is arguable that this is to an extent an accident of trends over 1975-85, when price rises for once made consumers pay more attention to the technological opportunities, as identified in bottom-up studies.

There are many variants on these two broad classes of modelling approaches, and the most appropriate technique clearly varies with the question being addressed. As in other areas, much of the skill lies in selecting 'horses for courses'.[11] In principle a combination of methods would be ideal. At a sufficient level of sophistication the approaches should merge,[12] but the sheer complexity involved, and lack of relevant data, would reduce the value of such an attempt; better insight might be gained by comparing carefully the reasons for differences between simpler top-down and bottom-up studies of the same problem.

Some recent studies of the potential for limiting carbon emissions have used another approach to combining top-down and bottom-up methods.[13] A top-down projection of energy demand - usually resulting in a prediction of substantial growth - forms a base case. The

---

[11] This point emerges clearly from the OECD review cited above (P.Hoeller et al, 'A Survey of Studies of the Costs of Reducing Greenhouse Gas Emissions', op.cit.) and from Fisher, who categorises modelling approaches and the applications to which they are best suited (J.Fisher, 'Advantages and Disadvantages of Modelling Approaches', Workshop on the Uses and Limits of Economic Models as Tools for Assessing Climate Change Policies, Alliance to Save Energy, Washington DC, 1991).

[12] Price elasticities can be attached to the various end uses in a bottom-up model, so that the effect of prices can be incorporated. However this may exceed the data available - the response of different end uses to price changes is often very speculative, especially in the long run. Saturation effects can be imposed in a top-down model if the projections are sufficiently disaggrated, and elasticities can be altered over time to reflect more detailed studies of how energy markets may change; but this can rapidly become unmanageably complex, and faces the same data problem.

[13] For example, E.Haites, 'Canada: Opportunities for Carbon Emissions Control', in W.Chandler, (ed.), *Carbon Emission Control Strategies: Case Studies in International Cooperation*, World Wildlife Fund and the Conservation Foundation, Baltimore, MD, 1990.

potential savings, derived from a detailed end-use analysis, are then subtracted from the projection. Despite its growing popularity this mixed approach has substantial drawbacks. First, some of the explicit savings identified may implicitly be taken up in the projection, which generally includes some allowance for increasing energy efficiency; unless there is an attempt to 'net out' these savings, they may be counted twice. On the other hand, there is no analysis of the potential for limiting the demand increases which account for the projected growth - indeed, the top-down modelling may give little indication of the actual use to which the additional energy is put. Consequently some potential savings - those from increasing the uptake of more efficient technologies in areas of new demand growth, which may be some of the easiest savings to realize - are omitted entirely. Such analysis thus potentially double counts some opportunities and neglects others. Attempting to net out the former results in a systematic tendency to underestimate potential savings.

Alternatively, bottom-up and top-down models can be used complementarily: bottom-up studies can be used to help formulate input assumptions concerning energy demand and price responses for input into top-down models, disaggregated at least by sector. The top-down model can then then introduce the macroeconomic framework, reflect more consistently the impact of and influences on price changes, model supply side developments (which seem more amenable to conventional economic analysis), and introduce an explicit and coherent time element. Some top-down models enable many aspects of demand to be defined externally, giving this flexibility, but it is hard to define the 'interface' consistently. The IIASA 'Energy in a Finite World' studies attempted a direct linkage, but consistent feedbacks between the models was not achieved (Volume 1, section 7.1).

A simpler approach is to specify within a top-down model a rate of non-price-induced efficiency changes over time, as used in a number of recent modelling applications including the widely-cited Manne and Richels model (Volume 1, section 8.2). This perhaps comes as close to an integrated methodology as any yet developed. Confusion can arise because the somewhat mis-named parameter of 'autonomous [non-price] energy efficiency improvements' combines the impact of several different factors: *structural change* due to the changing patterns of economic growth; *technological change*, improving technological efficiencies irrespective of price rises; and *policy changes* which increase the take-up of more efficient technologies, through the kind of measures discussed in Volume 1, Chapter 4. This approach does however at least give the capability of incorporating non-price induced changes, and thus has the virtue of helping to transfer the focus of debate from the model structure towards the assumptions. Experience has indeed proved the rate of autonomous efficiency improvements to be a key issue, and a prime focus of debate (Volume 1, section 8.2), centred upon how to assess and interpret adequately the technological opportunities for greater efficiency, saturation, and structural change. Whilst careful interpretation of past trends gives some important insights concerning past rates of improvement, this requirement nevertheless leads back to bottom-up analysis as a key component in understanding future possibilities.

In the absence of facilities for combining bottom-up studies with sufficiently sophisticated top-down models, a full bottom-up analysis of energy demand by end use seems, despite its limitations, to be the most appropriate single method for exploring scenarios of the potential for growth and savings in carbon emissions, and in particular for assessing the potential for relatively low-cost savings which might be achieved by end-use efficiency improvements. Unfortunately for most of the countries in this study it is impossible because of the lack of data on energy end uses, and because end-use analysis has tended to receive relatively little attention compared to the more traditional top-down approaches. Therefore, the rest of this chapter presents and analyses two forms of detailed end-use analysis, applied to the UK, and draws upon these to make general observations about the potential for and relative importance of abatement opportunities in different energy sectors.

4.4 Illustrative end-use analysis for the UK

This section develops and analyses end-use scenarios for the UK, taking the structure of demand in 1987 as a base year.[14] The breakdown used, shown in Table 4.1, reflects the data available and is a compromise between relevant detail and manageable complexity. A great deal of information can be derived from this alone. The data emphasizes, for

[14] Data elements from studies of 1985, 86 and 87 were amalgamated, with suitable scaling, to obtain the full breakdown shown in Table 4.1. In 1988 and 1989 total energy consumption was roughly constant, as were carbon emissions, with growth in transport offset by decline in domestic energy use.

example, that no one sector dominates energy demand in Britain, so that any substantial attempts to limit emissions will have to address a wide variety of actors and processes; but that space heating demand within the domestic and service sectors, and private cars, are major direct users of fossil fuels, while domestic appliances and commercial lighting consume much electricity, suggesting these as candidates for particular attention.

Such issues and other aspects of the UK energy economy are discussed more fully in the UK/EC country study (Chapter 5), and some of the underlying assumptions which are common to this and all the country studies are summarized at the end of this chapter. In this section, the emphasis is upon the general conclusions that can be gained from using such an end-use breakdown in constructing future scenarios.

Table 4.1 shows data as entered on a spreadsheet calculator, which makes manipulation of the data for creating different scenarios and for sensitivity studies a relatively simple task. For forming a projection, each end-use is determined as a product of two factors:

* A primary *activity level*, which reflects the single most important quantity determining the final demand for the associated services. For example, domestic demand for cooking and appliances is driven by the number of people; demand for space and water heating is driven by the number of dwellings (domestic) or floor area (services); whilst the primary variable in personal transport is the distance driven.

* An *energy intensity*, which indicates the energy delivered for the end use per unit of activity level. This itself is a product of the demand for the end-use service per unit of activity, and the technical energy productivity in delivering the required service.

The scenarios all assume growth in primary activity levels - population, GDP, floor areas, total transport requirements, etc. There is some variation in these when they might reasonably be affected by policy - for example, the relative use of different means of transport. However, the underlying features of the economy - population and GDP - are the same across different scenarios for a given date. The scenarios are therefore not intended to span the full range of possible outcomes, since population and (to a much greater extent) GDP are uncertain; rather, the scenarios are intended to illustrate possible developments in response to the greenhouse effect and other pressures on the energy system, as a basis for the policy discussion, whilst keeping the fundamental assumptions about the level and nature of economic activity constant.

Table 4.1 Illustration of end-use spreadsheet analysis: the structure of UK energy demand 1987 (PJ, GHV)

Demand drivers and end uses

	Service 58%	Industry 42%
GDP:417 £1987bn		

Domestic: Number of households, millions (Mhh):	20.8
Population, millions (Mp):	56.8
Commercial & institutional, value added, £bn	242
Total floor area, square km (km²)	700

Industrial GDP, value added

Metals, £bn	3
Minerals & chemicals, £bn	12.1
Other, £bn	160

Transport

Car etc: Billion vehicle km (BV-km):	269
Road goods: Billion tonne km (Bt-km):	114
Other road: Billion passenger km (BP-km):	35
Air: Billion passenger km (BP-km):	5
Rail: B-pass-km + B-tonne-km (BPt-km):	57

	Energy intens	Total ener	Heat	Coal	Oil	Gas	Elec
			Fuel breakdown, %				
Agriculture (Source: OECD)	-	55	0	2	67	5	27

Energy industries

Energy industries: use and losses

	PE/I	Coal	Oil	Gas	Elec
Coal	-	94	-	-	22
Oil	-	-	226	20	13
Gas	-	-	-	208	-
Elec industry	672	2133	205	10	85
Industry gen	57	71	69	18	

Electricity and heat generation

	PE/I	Coal	Oil	Gas	Elec output	Heat output
Elec by output:%	1.8	69.7	8.1	0.4	-	

Electric plant generation, PJ

	PE/I	Coal	Oil	Gas	Elec output	Heat output
Elec industry	212	738	72	3.6	1026	
Ind CHP	-	17	9	6	31	60
Ind direct	20	6	14	1	40	

Electric plant generation, TWh

	PE/I	Coal	Oil	Gas	Elec output	Heat output
Elec industry	59	205	20	1.0	285.0	
Ind CHP	-	4.6	2.3	1.6	8.5	
Ind direct	5.7	1.5	3.9	0.2	11.1	

Gross production (demand+losses),   304TWh

Elec intensity, by end use:15.5%,   by primary 35.8%

Ind & services, % CHP 2.2%,   % non-fossil 0.1%

Structure of energy demand and carbon emissions

Delivered energy

Delivered energy	Coal	Oil	Gas	Elec	Direct heat	Other	Total
Domestic	240	104	1082	358	0		
Industry	382	597	594	366	60		
Services	51	177	287	239	3		
Transport	0.4	1750	0	12	0		
Total delivered	673	2628	1963	975	63	3	9050

Total primary energy requirements

	PE/I	Coal	Oil	Gas	Other	Total
TPER, PJ	728	2971	3129	2219	3	9050
TPER, Mtoe	16	67	70	50	0	203

Carbon emissions

by end use, Mt:	Coal	Oil	Gas	Elec	Total
Carbon, Mt/TJ inc OU	25.3	20.2	16.3	61.0	
Domestic	6.1	2.1	17.7	21.8	47.7
Industry	9.7	12.0	9.7	22.3	53.7
Services	1.3	3.6	4.7	14.6	24.1
Transport	0.0	35.3	0.0	0.7	36.0
Total	17.0	53.0	32.1	59.5	161.5

- Indicates data not known or not applicable

PE/I = Primary (nuclear and renewable) and imported electricity.

Domestic (Source: Gerald Leach)

Space heat, Mhh	49.9	1039	0	21	8	73	7
Hot water, Mhh	17.7	368	0	5	5	70	20
Cooking, Mp	2.1	119	0	5	1	51	43
Lighting, Mp	0.5	29	0	0	0	0	100
Fridges, Mhh	3.0	62	0	0	0	0	100
Other, GDP	0.2	70	0	0	0	0	100

Industry (Sources: Energy, OECD; Other, Leach)

Metals, £bn	122	365	-	58	8	17	17
Mins &chems, £bn	60	727	-	10	43	34	13
Other, £bn	5	793	-	12	28	36	24

Commercial & institutional services (Source: ACE/EEO)

Space heating, km²	0.66	460	-	9	33	49	9
Hot water, km²	0.10	73	0	11	31	39	18
Lighting, km²	0.12	86	0	0	0	0	100
Cooking, km²	0.07	51	0	0	2	64	35
Air cond, km²	0.03	22	0	0	0	0	100
Other, £bn	0.25	61	0	0	1	2	98

Transport (Source: Leach)

Car etc, BV-km	3.4	925	0	0	0	100	0
Road goods, Bt-km	3.8	429	0	0	0	100	0
Other road, BV-km	14.7	52	0	0	0	99	1
Air, BP-km	53.5	267	0	0	0	100	0
Rail, BPt-km	0.76	43	0	1	0	73	27
Water	-	46	0	0	0	99	0

Both activity levels and the intensities may be affected implicitly by price rises, and the values adopted reflect subjective views on prices and their impact, rather than modelling results based formally on elasticities (which as noted are frequently very uncertain). The objective is more to reflect the technical options for the energy system, than the (uncertain) behaviour of energy markets.

Technical assumptions are estimated with reference to the technology discussions of this volume (Chapters 2 and 3), and from more detailed studies of UK energy sectors. Inevitably there is some subjective judgement in developing scenarios; they are intended as tools around which to base a discussion, not as specific predictions. Nevertheless, care is taken to develop scenarios which are as far as possible internally consistent, and which in the author's judgement could be technically and logistically possible, though perhaps far from easy to achieve. The main assumptions are summarized in the boxes, and Table 4.2 shows the key scenario outputs. The UK/EC chapter draws some comparisons with other studies, and discusses the resource and policy implications of the scenarios. There follows a brief summary of the main technical themes of the different scenarios and some key technical insights to emerge from the analysis.

Short-term scenarios

In both the short-term scenarios (year 2000), GDP grows by 25% from the base 1987 level with a slower growth in household numbers and service floor area. Other common changes, in both demand and supply, reflect existing or generally recognized trends and prospects, for example: further GDP shifts from manufacturing towards services; moves from solids to gas for heating and growth of electricity especially in the service sector; and the retirement of ageing nuclear plants.

The 2000A scenario reflects a business-as-usual approach, with no particular measures taken to limit demand or otherwise to curb greenhouse gas emissions. There is some improvement in the efficiency of space heating, with better new houses and some continuing insulation projects in older buildings. Energy efficiency in some other areas - for example refrigeration and industrial process - also improves owing to the general development and introduction of more efficient stock. In many other cases however, with no particular pressures for improvement, efficiency is static, and energy use increases in line with growing demand for the services.

Short-term scenarios: key assumptions

Activity levels - see text

2000A: Business-as-usual. As compared with 1987:

Domestic sector
 * Space heating and refrigeration intensities (energy/household) fall by 10% as stocks improve
 * Water heating, lighting and cooking intensities (energy/person) remain constant
 * The use of other appliances increases, resulting in a 10% increase in intensities (energy/person)

Industrial sector
 * The division of value added between metals, minerals and chemicals, and others, remains constant
 * Energy intensities (energy/value added) fall by 10% in each category

Service sector
 * Space heating intensity (energy/m^2) falls by 10%
 * Air conditioning intensity (energy/m^2) grows by 100%
 * Other intensities (energy/value added) remain constant

Transport
 * Private car use and air transport grows by 35%, roughly in line with government projections
 * Other road uses grow by 20%
 * Other transport use remains constant
 * The average energy intensity (energy/vehicle-km) of private transport reduces by just 5%, with technical improvements being offset by more powerful cars and add-ons, including the small efficiency penalty of catalytic convertors. Intensities for other transport falls by 10%.

2000B: Emissions abatement. As compared with 1987:

Domestic sector
  * Heating intensities fall by 20% following building
regulations and increased retrofitting measures
  * Refrigeration intensity falls by 20%
  * Lighting intensity falls by 40%
  * Other intensities remain constant

Industrial sector
  * There is a 15% value-added switch from metals into other
  materials
  * Energy intensities fall by 25%

Service sector
  * Heating, lighting and cooking intensities change as in the
  domestic sector
  * Air conditioning growth is limited and based on more
  efficient technologies, giving a 50% intensity increase
  * 'Other services' intensity falls by 15%

Transport
  * Growth in private car and air use is moderated a little, with
  a 30% increase in each
  * Road goods transport increases as before
  * Other road uses (eg. buses) and rail use increase 40%
  * The average energy intensity of private cars falls by 20%,
  and that of all other modes of transport by 15%

Electricity and heat
  * Power station own-use and system losses are reduced by
  10%
  * The use of CHP increases to provide 5% of total electricity
  requirements.

2030A: Scenarios: key assumptions

Activity levels - see text

2030Ai: Business-as-usual + support for coal as compared with 1987:

Domestic sector
   * Space and water heating intensities stay constant at the 1987 level, as improvements are offset by moves to bigger houses with lax standards
   * Lighting, cooking and refrigeration intensities fall by 20%
   * Other appliances intensity, including air conditioning, increases by 20%
   * Convenient coal technologies combined with the long-run price trend result in a slight growth in solid fuel use as oil retreats

Industrial sector
   * Metals and other energy-intensive industries retain their 1987 share of GDP
   * Energy intensities fall by 30% throughout industry

Service sector
   * Intensities change as in the domestic sector, except:
   * There is a large growth in air conditioning, partly in response to the warming climate, for which the energy demand is 9 times the 1987 level.
   * Energy intensity in other services (eg. computers, entertainments) is constant, with technical advances being offset by expansion of more general services
   * The fuel mix shifts as for the domestic sector

Transport
   * Private car use and air transport (passenger-km) doubles, roughly in line with government projections
   * Other road, and rail, use increase by 50%
   * Energy intensity in all transport declines by 20%

Electricity generation
  * Following privatization of the industry, electricity
  generation remains the province of commercial decisions.
  Present oil and nuclear stations reach the end of their life and
  no more are built; nor is there any construction of tidal or
  other large renewable energy schemes, or of large CHP
  schemes. Markets are wary of the prospects for gas prices: of
  the total 425TWh input, 70% is from coal, 20% gas, and 10%
  renewables and imports
  * Industrial cogeneration accounts for 10% of the total
  electricity
  * Average generation efficiencies are 43% for coal and 47%
  for gas, and four points lower in terms of electrical output for
  small and large-scale CHP schemes.

Scenario 2030Aii: Emissions abatement through fuel
switching

  * Domestic consumers and services focus on gas and direct
  heating from CHP and some passive solar measures
  * The coal industry, with government backing, develops
  large-scale CHP in several cities in an attempt to retain its
  market, generating 25TWh/yr.
  * There is some shift from metals to other materials
  * 160TWh of electricity is obtained from non-fossil sources
  and imports, and only 20% of its input from coal, the
  remainder being from gas
  * 10% of vehicle fuel is derived from biomass.

2030B: Scenarios: key assumptions

2030Bi: Emissions abatement through energy efficiency.
Relative to 1987:

Domestic sector
  * Building standards, including retrofits, combined with
  climate warming result in space heating loads of 20GJ per

Table 4.2. Principal results of UK scenarios (Mtoe)

Scenario	1987	2000A	2000B	2030Ai	2030Aii	2030Bi	2030Bii
Coal	67	78	58	97	36	36	16
Oil	70	74	63	97	70	41	22
Gas	50	61	52	90	142	40	53
NF elec[1]	6	6.0	6.1	4.1	13.5	2.1	12
NF non-elec[2]	0.07	1.4	0.8	3.6	12.5	5.9	12.5
TPER	193	220	180	292	274	125	116
Carbon, MtC	161	184	147	241	185	97	68
Elec, TWh	304	358	295	436	431	220	245
CO_2 emissions by sector, %							
Domestic	30	27	27	25	24	26	24
Industry	33	33	32	26	27	30	32
Services	15	15	14	21	20	15	12
Transport	22	25	26	28	30	28	32

[1] Non-fossil electricity, output basis (nuclear, renewables, electricity imports, displacing 2-3 times as much fossil fuel input).
[2] Non-fossil non-electric sources, output basis (heat gains, biomass burning, biomass liquid fuels, displacing an equal quantity primarily of oil).

As a result of these developments, the primary energy requirements grow by 14% as compared with the base year,[15] and carbon emissions grow in proportion to primary energy, with continuing moves away from oil towards both coal and gas except for transport.

The 2000B scenario - emission abatement policies - reflects a situation in which many measures are pursued to encourage the adoption of existing more efficient technologies and practices. As a result space heating, lighting, and refrigeration efficiency increases much more rapidly than in 2000A. There is some structural shift away from metals to less energy intensive materials, and more rapid increase in industrial energy efficiency. Transport growth is somewhat moderated and vehicle efficiency increases more rapidly.

In all cases, the efficiencies achieved by 2000 are much less than could be obtained from full use of the current best technologies identified in Chapter 2, because of the inevitable persistence of old stock and wasteful practices and other aspects of inertia in the energy system, including consumer attitudes. Despite this and the general economic growth, primary energy consumption is reduced by 7% as compared with the base year. Carbon emissions fall by a greater amount - 9% - because of the disproportionate reduction in coal and oil use, with gas use increasing faster and a small rise in non-fossil power.

Longer-term scenarios

In the longer term, the options and uncertainties are much wider. End-use energy scenarios are developed, notionally for the year 2030, to highlight some of the opportunities which may arise in any longer-term attempt to limit emissions of greenhouse gases. In all the scenarios, population is taken as 60m, with GDP at more than double the base level. The proportion of industry relative to services declines slightly, to 35% of total GDP. There is a continuing growth in the number of domestic dwellings and floor area of the industrial and commercial sectors, though the latter indicators are slightly lower in the efficiency scenarios in response to higher energy and transport prices. Since oil reserves are

[15] The base year of 1987 was determined by the availability of sufficient data for estimating the demand structure. However, the scenarios reflect the possible impact of changes fromthe early 1990s; the rate of changes implied by statistics relative to the base year need to be interpreted in this light. In fact, the data available at the time of completing this text (to 1989) shows little evidence of resumed growth despite the price falls, so demand in the 2000 scenarios is likely to err on the high side.

narkedly less than gas reserves at all levels (national, regional and global), there is a continuing retreat from oil for heating - to coal, gas, and/or other sources according to the scenarios.

Most existing power plant will have had to be replaced by the year 2030. Consequently, the efficiency of generation is much higher. One option which does not feature significantly in the shorter term is the possibility of large-scale combined heat and power (CHP) schemes, combining electricity generation with district heating, as used widely in some other European countries. One of the major justifications for large-scale CHP could be as a means for coal to remain competitive against gas under strong environmental constraints, and it is assumed that any city-scale CHP generation is derived from coal; small-scale CHP is mostly gas-fired. Again, the key assumptions are summarized in the boxes.

There are two scenarios in which no particular measures are taken to improve the efficiency of using energy, and energy prices do not rise substantially. There is some improvement in building performance owing to new stock and continuing insulation improvement, and lighting and refrigeration efficiencies improve as efficient technologies gradually work into the system, replacing old stock. But overall, consumers remain largely indifferent to energy consumption in their choices of appliances and transport, and there is a very large growth in energy use for air conditioning and in general appliances, and for transport, with more modest growth in other sectors. As a result of these conditions, the total primary energy requirement by 2030 is 50% above the level of the late 1980s.

In 2030Ai, there are no attempts to support non-fossil power, or alter utility regulation to encourage use of renewable electricity sources; the non-fossil input actually declines with the retirement of nuclear plant. Gas also forms a relatively small part of power generation, reflecting a relatively pessimistic view on resources and government attempts to minimise gas imports in favour of coal. The scenario is thus almost a worst of all worlds' concerning carbon emissions, which grow in direct proportion to energy demand.

In scenario 2030Aii there are again no particular measures to increase energy efficiency and all intensities remain as in 2030Ai, but substantial changes in the fuel mix occur to reduce carbon emissions. In response to strong government measures supporting the growth of CHP and non-fossil electricity production, and allowing or encouraging gas into power generation, these sources grow substantially (as summarized in the box) and coal use is more than halved. Overall carbon emissions are well below those of 2030Ai, at about 15% above those of the late 1980s.

The 2030B scenarios explore what might be achieved with much greater energy efficiency. The changes are those which might occur under substantially higher energy prices and strong government intervention to promote efficiency. The efficiencies are still all within the range of what can be achieved with the best of current technology. Unlike the 2000B scenario, however, there is nearly complete adoption of the best technologies (on a 'BATNEEC'[16] basis), including substantial building retrofits, though with some allowance for degradation and the circumstances of practical use reducing efficiencies below the ideal performances noted in Chapter 2.

In some areas where there is a recognized large technical potential for savings, such as space heating, refrigeration and lighting, there are consequently major reductions in energy demand. Other end uses respond to a much lesser extent. Overall, the impact of the changes is to reduce primary energy consumption to under half of the 2030A value, at just 61% of the base year, despite the much greater GDP and other activity levels. The carbon intensity of the fuel mix remains much like that of the late 1980s, so that carbon emissions change in line with total primary energy requirement.

In scenario 2030Bii the gains of scenario 2030Bi are combined with a strong shift in the fuel mix aimed at reducing carbon emissions. As in 2030Aii there is a large proportionate growth in gas, primary electricity, and CHP, and much reduced coal demand. This case represents the strongest long-term combination of changes for reducing carbon emissions based on current understanding. The primary energy requirement is lower than in 2030Bi because of the reduced use of (and hence losses from) thermal power generation, and carbon emissions are reduced to 42% of the late 1980s levels.

4.5 Interpreting the end-use scenarios

All the scenarios inevitably reflect assumptions which contain substantial subjective elements; they reflect the author's best judgements

---

[16] 'Best Available Technology Not Entailing Excessive Cost' - a common criterion in pollution abatement.

of what is likely under different criteria, given the baseline assumptions. The most radical case is extreme by standards of conventional energy studies (though more modest than some projections), and this and other high efficiency scenarios raise a host of serious policy and institutional questions. These issues are discussed in the country chapters. Nevertheless, despite the inevitable uncertainties it is possible to draw a number of quite firm conclusions from this end-use analysis.

First, it is clear that *there is a wide possible range of future carbon emissions*. Even 10 years ahead, CO_2 emissions in the two scenarios differ by over 20%; taken out to 2030, the scenarios span a range of more than a factor of three. Given that the scenarios are all based on the same GDP and population growth rates, and given the implicit assumption that there are no major unforeseeable technical breakthroughs affecting the pattern of energy demand, the actual range of possible outcomes could be wider still.

A second general result is that the *forecasts of resumed rapid energy growth in developed economies produced by some top-down economic models do not appear to be feasible*, because of saturation of the major end uses which drove energy growth in the earlier stages of industrial and societal development. The example of domestic space heating has already been given but similar remarks apply to much heavy infrastructure, domestic and commercial cooking and in many cases lighting, and some other uses - even transport must saturate eventually. The scenarios all reflect assumed growth in activity levels and additional increases in comfort levels, but these trends are to an extent offset by saturation and the steady uptake of more efficient practices even in the business-as-usual cases. The 'A' scenarios, with an implied growth in energy demand of about 1%/yr from the 1987 baseline, represent what seems from the end-use perspective something close to the highest conceivable case.

In the industrial sector, restructuring and a continuing decline in energy intensities, as value-added continues its shift towards more refined and less material and energy intensive products, similarly limits the conceivable growth in energy demand (it should be emphasized that modelling of the industrial sector is by far the weakest component of this analysis, being a highly aggregated and subjective reflection of the trends discussed in Volume 1, section 6.4). The only non-transport sectors where strong long-term growth seems possible are air conditioning and miscellaneous categories, for example computers and entertainments. Miscellaneous uses involve processes of such a low energy intensity that it is hard to see how they can make much impact on demand, (a possible exception being the potential impact of air conditioning if the UK climate does warm substantially). In economic terms, this is equivalent to saying that energy and GDP progressively decouple as the economy gets richer; throughout the economy the GDP and price elasticities of demand decline; and the rate of autonomous efficiency improvement rises. Many top-down models assume constant values.

Third, *at least in the short term it is difficult to generate the scale of savings which some advocates of efficiency claim as possible because of the inertia involved in changing or retrofitting capital stock;* this to a significant extent is judgemental, but is refined by analysis in the following section.

A fourth observation is that, in the long term, *both energy efficiency and fuel switching are of great importance in reducing carbon emissions.* The efficiencies in the 2030B scenarios, relative to current perspective at least, are very radical. Yet even if such savings were repeated throughout industrialized countries, and neglecting growth in developing countries, the carbon emissions are still well above the level which would be needed to approach atmospheric stabilization. Unless there are fundamental breakthroughs in technologies for energy efficiency in a number of areas, fuel switching also appears to be crucial in approaching such levels.

This necessarily involves both non-fossil sources and gas, because in the UK the main non-fossil energy sources - nuclear and renewables - primarily produce electricity. Apart from some direct heat supplies, natural gas, used as efficiently as possible, is the main option for limiting emissions for non-electric applications.

A fifth broad conclusion is a more generalized version of the above. As illustrated by the 2030Bii scenario, *achieving major reductions requires an extraordinarily wide combination of measures.* Table 4.3 shows the percentage reductions in carbon emissions (from the 2030Ai baseline) which the measures outlined for 2030Bii would bring if taken individually. Only one individual category - non-fossil electricity - gives a greater than 10% reduction from the projected baseline. Major switching towards gas generation, and across-the-board efficiency improvements in space heating, industrial performance, and road

Table 4.3 Contribution of different measures to reducing long-term (2030) CO_2 emissions in UK scenarios

Measure[*]	Principal policy tools
Non-fossil electricity (12% reduction in C emissions)	Utility regulation; price (C-tax); subsidies; quotas; R&D; 'infrastructure'funding
Other large individual impacts (6-8% savings):	
Gas-fired generation	Utility regulation; price (C-tax)
Private road transport efficiency and	Standards or cost transfer incentives; road pricing to increase load factor
Improved building performance (domestic & services heating &fuels)	Building regulations (including retrofits; boiler standards; price
General industrial efficiency	Price; information & demonstration.
Moderate individual impacts (3-6% savings):	
Lighting, cooking, air conditioning	Price; standards; information performance in services
Domestic elec appliances efficiency	Standards; labelling
Industrial sector composition	Price; R&D
Public transport	Infrastructure use; subsidies; road pricing
Generating system efficiency	Prices; R&D; utility regulation
Alternative vehicle fuels	R&D; price; government coordination
Smaller individual impacts (<3% savings):	
Non-electric energy conversion	Price
Domestic sector CHP	Utility regulation; infrastructure funding (large schemes)
Increased gas heating	Price (C-tax); regulations (utility or partial electric ban)
Industrial sector CHP	Utility regulation; pricing; information
Air transport efficiency	Price; R&D
'Other' services efficiency	Information/labelling

* Note: the percentage reductions refer to the reductions in total carbon emissions from the 2030Ai scenario, if the measure (applied to the extent cited for 2030Bii) is applied in isolation from other measures. The savings are not additive. For measures which affect electricity consumption, the average carbon-intensity of electricity in 2030A is retained.

transport, might each contribute 6-8% savings; all other steps individually contribute 5% or less, but in total the myriad smaller measures are more important than any of the single major steps. The policy requirements for these measures are equally diverse. Price - notably carbon taxes - is a common theme in many, but nearly all could involve other more directed policy steps in addition; the form of utility regulation also features strongly. In many these more specific measures might be at least as important as price alone.

Finally, *technically the most difficult sectors for limiting long-term carbon emissions appear to be first transport, and second industry;* including indirect emissions from electricity generation, each accounts for about a third of emissions in the 2030Bii scenario, compared with 22% and 33% respectively in 1987, and the transport figure is only kept this low by the important contribution of biomass-based fuels, and some electric/hydrogen vehicles.

The scenarios cast further light on the role of electricity, as the most flexible of sources in both end use and production, and the impact of CHP in increasing the overall efficiency of electricity supplies and heating. As illustrated in Table 4.4, the scenarios all depict a surprising degree of consistency in the proportion of end use served by electricity (the electricity intensity), at slightly above 1987 levels. This reflects two opposing factors. Electricity is an option with large opportunities for savings, notably through improved appliance efficiency and by moving away from electric space heating, but this is more than offset by continued growth in new applications. Electricity is an attractive source; clean, convenient, and flexible, and the only option for many modern products, from home appliances and entertainment to computing and advanced industrial processes, where it often displaces less efficient fossil applications. Electricity thus remains a major component however large the end-use efficiency improvements, and this makes the efficiency of production, and - given the relatively high carbon emissions from even advanced coal plant - gas and especially non-fossil power a crucial factor in achieving substantial reductions of greenhouse gases.

The impact of increasing production efficiency and low carbon sources is apparent from Table 4.4. Despite a slight increase in end-use intensity, increased conversion efficiency and non-fossil sources (counted on an output basis) reduces the proportion of primary energy input to electricity. Despite this, in all but 2030Bii, electricity on average remains

Table 4.4 Electricity system intensities in UK scenarios

	1987	2000A	2000B	2030Ai	2030Aii	2030Bi	2030Bii
End-use intensities (Energy delivered/Total final consumption), %							
Electricity	15.5	17.3	17.5	17.3	17.4	17.8	19.4
Elec+Heat	16.4	18.3	18.6	18.3	19.9	23.0	25.7
Input intensities (Inputs to electricity/TPER), %							
	35.8	34.7	33.0	32.2	29.7	34.9	32.4
Carbon intensities (gC/kWh delivered; direct coal combustion=91)							
Electricity	220	215	191	188	116	170	81
Elec+Heat	207	203	179	178	101	132	61

the most carbon intensive energy supply. Furthermore, because the main resource constraints are liable to be on oil and non-fossil sources, and possibly gas, the marginal source - that used to meet any increase in total demand in the long term - may well be coal. Consequently the emissions associated with further electrification are those of coal plant. Increasing electrification there only helps emissions if (a) the waste heat can be used in place of other fuels, or (b) the end-use efficiency exceeds that of alternatives to a degree which offsets the power station losses.

Finally, encompassing the whole energy system in such an analysis reveals both synergisms and competition between different measures. High energy efficiency makes the contribution from non-fossil sources relatively more important still in the longer term; the non-fossil component alone reduces emissions from the 2030Bi scenario by nearly a quarter. Higher efficiency also makes greater use of gas in both electricity and transport relatively more effective and feasible in resource terms. Conversely, high heating efficiency considerably reduces the scope for CHP.[17] The savings from different measures, especially those aimed at limiting demand in the same sector, cannot simply be added.

Overall, an end-use analysis of the full energy system such as that presented here reveals the importance of understanding the structure of energy demand and supply in the country concerned, and comparing the activity levels and efficiencies against values they could assume in the future. This is an important component in assessing the likely potential for growth and the opportunities for limiting emissions. However, such analysis as it stands is limited for the reasons discussed above, and in the current context two weaknesses stand out. First, the implied rates of change are based on subjective estimates of the opportunities afforded by stock turnover. Second, the study reflects technical changes, not policy ones, and so gives little indication of what might be required to achieve the projected savings. The following section addresses these weaknesses.

4.6 Modelling policies for closing the efficiency gap: a case study

Modelling of energy supply competition and the impact of price changes is well established, though not without continuing debates and uncertainties. General end-use analysis has been addressed above. The remaining vacuum concerns the analysis of policy measures designed to 'close the efficiency gap' by regulatory changes which encourage the take-up of more efficient technologies which may well be cost effective, but which would be adopted only slowly (or not at all) in the 'business-as-usual' market. Volume 1 emphasized that many of the most cost-effective responses may hinge on this, and the 'B' scenarios above implicitly assume that such opportunities are heavily exploited.

In a bid to help fill this gap with a case study of stock turnover and policy modelling, the author approached the UK's Building Research Establishment (BRE) to examine the possibilities for more explicit

---

[17] An additional factor, not directly incorporated in the main scenario analysis but reflected in the studies in the following section (4.6), is that improving the efficiency of lights and appliances reduces the free heat gains from them; this is however a second order effect which has little impact on overall results.

[18] L.Shorrock and G.Henderson, Building Research Establishment, Garston, Watford, UK. Their work, a fuller write-up of which will appear separately, is gratefully acknowledged.

policy modelling of the UK domestic sector.[18] The importance of the domestic sector in the UK has already been noted. It is also the sector where traditional macroeconomic analysis, driven by prices, is least appropriate; the many market imperfections listed in Volume 1, section 4.1, apply most strongly to the domestic sector, and the evidence suggests that regulatory mechanisms could have far more long-term impact even than substantial price rises, as well as probably being politically more feasible. Some, notably building standards, have already been adopted to some degree in many countries for this reason.

The BRE has developed a detailed model of the UK housing stock, including its energy performance. The model includes detail of the different kinds of dwellings and, since it models houses as complete systems, it accounts for the various secondary effects such as free heat gains from appliances, etc, which are often held to invalidate simpler end-use energy studies that simply add up different contributions. The associated data includes trends and projections. To investigate the possible impact of policies for improving efficiency, the BRE compared a 'trends' case against one in which various measures, summarized in the box, come into force on 1 January 1993. The policy instruments modelled are mostly simple standards, which as discussed in Volume 1, Chapter 4, are amongst the crudest instruments. Other policies may be more effective, more acceptable, or both, for many applications. But simple standards can be among the most appropriate for many areas of domestic demand, and their impact is relatively simple to model. The rest of this section summarises the results, and compares them against the full UK scenarios.

Figure 4.2 shows how the energy demand and carbon emissions vary in the different cases, with results aggregated into two components for simplicity of presentation. The results suggest that significant impacts can be obtained from a combination of strong policy measures designed to exploit the 'efficiency gap', without incurring additional economic costs: the total resources devoted to meeting domestic energy needs would clearly be reduced, since almost all the technologies adopted as a result of the policies have a higher rate of return than investment in new energy supply even at the low energy prices of the late 1980s. In all, total domestic energy demand falls by about 1.3%/yr in the first decade (over 1%/yr faster than in the baseline, which projects slow decline), and by about 0.7%/yr over the second decade. Associated carbon emissions

Policy measures modelled in BRE policy scenario

To investigate the possible impact of policies for improving efficiency in the UK domestic sector, the UK's Building Research Establishment examined the impact of the following measures.

Time-of-sale insulation standards. When a house is sold, the finance company or other agent must ensure that certain minimum standards are met: if there is less than 100mm of loft insulation, this must be increased to 150mm; cavity walls must be insulated if possible (about 80% of cavity wall stock); and draft-proofing must be installed for all single-glazed windows if it is not already present. All of these steps are estimated to pay back in less than ten years nearly all buildings, and often in less than five. Mandatory double glazing, and further insulation for single walled buildings, were excluded as being more costly options (there is already a strong market for double glazing anyway because of its other attractions).

Domestic heating equipment. In the course of natural replacement of old stock, or construction of new, condensing boilers must be used (these are typically 15% more efficient than conventional gas boilers, and their extra cost is usually repaid in 3-6 years), and heating systems should be gas-fired where possible (ie. all but a few per cent of replacements, which retain the existing fuel for high-rise buildings or where there is no gas mains).

Appliance standards. The energy consumption of new appliances, per unit of service (volume, load, etc), must meet a standard corresponding to the best products on the market in 1988. Appliances were divided into: fridges; freezers; fridge-freezers; washing machines; clothes driers; dishwashers; and all others. As discussed in Chapter 2, variations in appliance efficiency often appear to have little or no impact on appliance costs, and in all cases these changes give an implicit payback of less than ten years.

Lighting. This is more difficult to treat in terms of specific policies, because the difference of cost and performance between high-efficiency and standard bulbs is very large; it was simply assumed that subsidies and promotional campaigns are developed sufficient to ensure a 50% take-up of fluorescent bulbs by 2000, and a 95% take-up by 2030. Lighting overall is a relatively small fraction of domestic demand so this is not a central feature.

Figure 4.2 Results of BRE policy scenarios

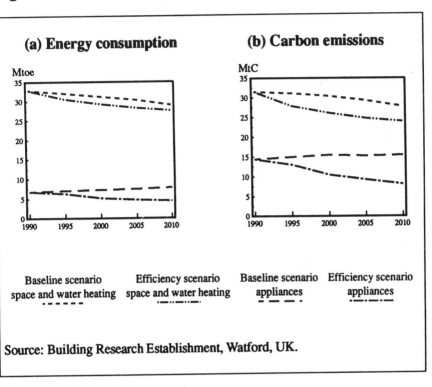

(a) Energy consumption

Mtoe

(b) Carbon emissions

MtC

| Baseline scenario | Efficiency scenario | Baseline scenario | Efficiency scenario |
| space and water heating | space and water heating | appliances | appliances |

Source: Building Research Establishment, Watford, UK.

decline substantially faster, both because the policies favour gas over electric heating, and because savings from electricity are achieved faster than in other fuels, because of the rapid impact of appliance efficiency improvements. The exact savings depend upon assumptions about changes in electricity production, but if combined with the supply developments projected in the full UK scenarios, would correspond to domestic sector CO_2 reductions of about 2%/yr in the first decade, and 1.3%/yr in the second.

The analysis illustrates the relative importance of and constraints on different policies. Policies for improving building efficiency are important, but the study also highlights the constraints on the rate at which this can occur, and the equal or greater importance for carbon emissions of *appliance* efficiency standards and of discouraging electric heating. Overall, the potential savings estimated in the UK 2000B scenario do appear to be within reach of stringent policies, not necessarily involving price increases (though these would help - and might be an important part of achieving changes in other sectors). This does not imply that the steps modelled would be politically easy.

When projected to the longer term, policy-driven improvements in the BRE scenarios level off, and indeed the business-as-usual trend begins to converge back towards it as many of the more efficient technologies are slowly taken up. This contrasts with the UK 2030B scenarios developed above, in which rapid efficiency improvements continue. Though there are many differences of detail, the biggest difference concerns space heating demand. In UK 2030B, the average dwelling demand has been more than halved. In the BRE scenarios, heating demand levels off towards 70% of the 1990 values, rather than continuing to decline, and space heating continues to dominate domestic energy requirements.

This points in part to the importance of old building stock, especially single-walled buildings where major improvements would be relatively expensive; these account for an increasingly important part of total energy demand as other buildings are improved. It is far from certain just much of this stock will be in use in 40 years time, and what opportunities might arise either for improvements during major renovations, or for novel techniques of retrofitting old stock (there are also strong social grounds for improving this stock using government finance, because it is old people living in these dwellings who account for the great majority of hypothermia cases in the UK). However, the nature of this stock could be an important constraint, and substantial costs might be incurred in bringing it towards the average performance levels implied in the UK 2030B scenarios unless radically new techniques were developed. The overall economics would depend upon the price trajectory and discount rate used.

This points to the inherent limitations of any long-term projections. Detailed engineering modelling is by its nature limited to currently familiar techniques. There are various possibilities which BRE could not model within the framework of established, short-term payback measures, for example: advanced control systems for managing light and heating requirements; selective or highly insulating windows; house-scale/estate CHP, which might greatly reduce the overall emissions from household heat and electricity demand; efficient heat pumps; heat exchangers to capture some of the energy in waste hot water.

The 2030B scenarios assume, by implication, that new building standards are tightened well beyond the 1990 levels, and additional measures are applied to make a substantial impact on the energy use in old buildings as well. It is impossible to know the extent to which this may be correct. Rather, the value of comparing the different approaches in the longer term is to identify the key issues, and to confirm that longer-term gains, unlike shorter-term ones, will probably require more than the currently identified set of policy instruments and/or technologies, if large costs are to be avoided.

4.7 Generalizing the results: carbon trends and policy impacts

Various general lessons may be drawn from this analysis. Detailed modelling of the impact of regulatory instruments is possible, and it can yield valuable insights into the rate at which various improvements might be achieved: in the UK domestic sector, carbon emissions reductions of more than 1%/yr below an already declining trend can be obtained at low cost, within the constraints set by stock turnover. However, to be convincing such analysis requires both very sophisticated techniques - in this case, complete models of building stock including thermal performance and appliance purchases and use - and correspondingly extensive data. This is only likely to be achievable via established research centres devoted to understanding overall sectors, not by short-term projects seeking quick results related to energy in isolation from the sectorial background.

Despite the limitations noted, the domestic sector in the UK is a sector for which unusually extensive data and advanced modelling capabilities are available. To obtain overall emissions projections, all sectors need to be combined. Each is likely to require a different approach: not only do the data in terms of technical possibilities and stock turnover vary, but in some (notably some industrial sectors) price and overall economic performance and structure may be of overwhelming importance, while others (such as most aspects of domestic demand and the use of dispersed renewables and cogeneration) may be much more affected by regulatory conditions. Sectorial information then needs to be combined in an overall model of the energy system (even if at the level of the simple spreadsheet analysis presented in this chapter) with information on bulk energy conversion, especially for electricity and heat, before a coherent picture can be developed.

To the author's knowledge, such analysis has never been conducted for a whole country, though some of the recent studies for the Dutch and Danish national strategies contain many of the elements.[19] However, many relevant observations can be drawn on the basis of these and the various studies reported in this volume and elsewhere. Detailed modelling of the UK transport sector suggested that a combination of measures directed both at improving vehicle efficiency and traffic management, against the background of official growth projections, might reduce carbon emissions from that sector by about 1%/yr - though a more realistic target may be to achieve improvements sufficient to stabilise emissions.[20] Neither services nor the industrial sector have been studied in this way, and in the UK it may not be possible given the limited data. Services in particular contain some elements in common with the domestic sector, and a substantial 'efficiency gap' even within industry has been noted in Chapter 2. Also, these sectors are relatively electricity-intensive, and as discussed in this book, the carbon intensity of electricity production can be expected to reduce with developments in generating technologies, and it is often the easiest route for fuel-switching measures. The UK scenarios reflect this in suggesting that if natural gas combined cycle plant develop as expected, the carbon intensity of electricity supply may fall by over 1%/yr for many years, and if non-fossil sources are supported, this rate might be extended and even accelerated in the longer term, though probably at some cost.

As suggested by the scenarios, if strong policies to improve efficiency can roughly stabilise total energy demand in service and industrial sectors, the implication is that overall CO_2 emissions could be reduced by around 1%/yr for at least a decade or two at little or no additional cost, and quite possibly net savings. Implicit in this, and particularly in the extrapolation of such trends further into the future, is that prices would also rise sufficiently to deter careless waste or growth in new and trivial energy applications, and in the longer term to encourage non-fossil

[19] Ministry of Housing, Physical Planning and Environment, *New Environmental Policy Plan Plus*, The Netherlands, 1990; *Nota Energie Besparing* (Memordandum on Energy Conservation), Ministry of Economic Affairs, The Netherlands, 1990; Danish Ministry of Energy, *Energy 2000*, Danish Energy Agency, Copenhagen, Denmark, April 1990.
[20] M.Fergusson and C.Holman, *Atmospheric Emissions from the Use of Transport in the United Kingdom, Volume 2: The Effect of Alternative Transport Policies*, WWF/Earth Resources Research, London, June 1990.

sources. Other detailed studies of UK emissions prospects complement this view, and span this estimate of feasible rates of abatement, as discussed in the UK/EC case study (section 5.3).

It is interesting to compare this with analysis conducted in some other countries. The policy scenarios prepared by the Danish Ministry of Energy suggest broadly similar rates of abatement.[21] The Dutch target, also based on detailed modelling, projects slightly slower decline, leading to a 3-5% reduction from 1990 emissions by 2000, primarily because of transport growth. The German target of 25% CO_2 reductions by 2005 is obviously much faster, but the analysis of how this might be done, and at what cost, is more preliminary.[22] The US and Japanese studies below report independent end-use studies which claim comparable rates of abatement, though these in general are grounded in technical appraisals rather than policy modelling. On a wider scale, the Energy for a Sustainable World study (outlined in Volume 1, Chapter 7) argued that technical options exist to reduce energy consumption in the OECD by nearly 50% over 30 years; though this is a highly optimistic assessment of what might be achieved in reality, a more modest interpretation combined with corresponding supply-side developments would again point to potential CO_2 savings on the order of at least 1%/yr.

While it is dangerous to generalise from such limited data, the detailed policy modelling studies and more general results discussed do suggest that the technical potentials discussed earlier in this book for cost-effective changes which improve end-use efficiency (Chapter 2) or otherwise limit carbon emissions (Chapter 3) can be translated into possible impacts of abatement policies. If appropriate policies are adopted, the studies suggest that reductions in CO_2 emissions roughly of the order of 1%/yr from many developed economies might be obtained at little if any net economic cost on the basis of known technologies implemented against a background of extrapolated rising activity levels, constrained by the inherent trends towards saturation as discussed in Volume 1, Chapter 6.

---

[21] Danish Ministry of Energy, *Energy 2000*, op cit.
[22] The German Parliamentary Commission on this issue established to their satisfaction that the German target is technically feasible, at modest costs, and detailed various policy instruments which could contribute to it. The weaknesses concerned assessment of policy implementation and impacts. For a summary see E.Jochem, 'Reducing CO_2 emissions - the West German plan', *Energy Policy*, 19(2), March 1991.

Naturally there would be substantial variations between countries, even among OECD countries. Population growth, as in Japan and the US, adds to demand, though to the extent that this is reflected in new homes and expanded production and services, the pressure could be limited significantly by ensuring that such growth uses the most efficient options available.[23] Lower levels of relative development, overall (as in some southern European countries) or in particular sectors (as in Japan) also add pressures for growth. Conversely, for countries which have static or declining population and access to abundant natural gas and/or renewable sources, such as many northern European countries, reductions exceeding 1%/yr may be quite feasible. In each case, of course, achievable rates of change will also be affected by the starting point in terms of existing efficiency and use of lower carbon resources, while many social and political factors will determine the extent to which policy instruments are effectively focused, as examined in the case studies below. Yet overall, it appears plausible that aggregate reductions from the developed world of up to 1%/yr could be achieved at very modest costs, if the opportunities offered by more efficient energy technologies for both supply and demand are exploited, and particularly if such measures are combined with the exploitation of gas and low-cost pockets of non-fossil sources.

This more detailed model and technology-based perspective underpins the discussion of Volume 1, Chapter 7. As emphasized there, such projections are permeated by uncertainties (particularly concerning trends in new energy technologies and uses) which multiply as the level of generalization broadens, and the further ahead projections are taken. These uncertainties become all the greater when the analysis turns to the 'transition' economies and developing countries. Yet the potential scale of impacts are readily apparent.

Finally, it should be emphasized that the focus on microeconomic policies and analysis of the 'efficiency gap' in this chapter should not detract from the importance of energy price. Rather, it reflects an attempt to help address a notable weakness in mainstream energy policy research and modelling, which has focused almost exclusively on the macroeconomic perspective of energy price and supply issues. As

---

[23] Thus, a given absolute target is bound to be more difficult if population is growing, but a given per-capita target will generally be easier because it is easier to enhance efficiency in new facilities.

emphasized by the discussion in Volume 1, Chapter 3, energy prices are both important and complex. Other work has highlighted the fact that policies targeted on improving energy efficiency have rarely succeeded while energy prices remain low, both because of the predictable macroeconomic responses and the broader psychological and political difficulties of pursuing policy efforts which seek to treat as valuable something which is very cheap to the consumer.[24] The key analytical challenge is to understand both the price and non-price dimensions of the issue; and the key political challenge, if emissions are to be seriously curtailed, will be to implement both in concert.

---

[24] L.Schipper, 'Improving energy efficiency in the industrialized countries', *Energy Policy*, 19(2), March 1991.

PART II: COUNTRY STUDIES

Chapter 5 Greenhouse Responses in the United Kingdom and European Community: Will Britannia Waive the Rules?

Michael Grubb
Research Fellow, Royal Institute of International Affairs
and Peter Brackley
Associate Fellow, RIIA, 1987-90

The authors are grateful to all the Programme staff for assistance in preparing this chapter, and give special thanks to Dieter Helm and Mike Parker for carefully reading the text and offering valuable comments and information.

Greenhouse Responses in the United Kingdom and European
Community: Will Britannia Waive the Rules?

*After more than two decades of broadly stable CO_2 emissions, UK
emissions may start to rise slowly in the absence of measures to
counteract this. Major options for limiting emissions exist, notably
cost-effective improvements in the efficiency of heating and appliances
in buildings, other varied efficiency improvements, and expansion of gas
and non-fossil electricity sources. Rapid growth in gas use for power
seems probable, but nuclear expansion will be extremely difficult given
the legacy of electricity privatisation; French imports are more likely.
Various renewables, particularly wind energy and wastes, may offer
better prospects but are likewise uncertain because of probable public
objections and the degree of government support required for some.
Scenarios suggest a very wide range of possible future emissions,
ranging from a 55% cut to a 50% increase from 1990 levels by 2030.*

*Current UK emissions and the mix of fuels are close to the EC average,
but the UK is unique in being the only member country to produce more
energy than it consumes, and in having substantial reserves of all fossil
fuels. Other variations within the Community include the differing stages
of energy and economic development in some southern EC countries, the
dominance of nuclear electricity in France and Belgium, and the
dominance of gas in the Netherlands. Abatement options also differ
considerably, though efficiency improvements in appliances and
vehicles, and the diversion of surplus subsidised agricultural land to
biomass energy, offer widespread opportunities. The differing trends and
circumstances will make uniform targets and responses impractical.*

Exploiting the technical opportunities for abatement would require widespread policy changes. In the UK these include reform of regulatory distortions which increase CO_2 emissions (VAT allocation, the form of utility price regulation, and company car allowances); standards of various forms especially for the building sector, and broad changes in transport policies including efficiency incentives or standards for vehicles. However, the role of UK government in energy supply has declined, and there is great reluctance to intervene in consumer markets. Letting markets work, in the sense of non-intervention, precludes many significant abatement options; these would require attempts to make markets work better, using both regulatory and price-based measures designed to overcome market imperfections and to accelerate the take-up of efficient and new technologies. Many such policies would face considerable resistance.

Many other European countries are less averse to regulatory measures for encouraging efficiency and renewables. Most depend heavily on fossil fuel imports, and many have strong cultural and political inclinations to environmental concerns; some already display policies which incidentally limit CO_2 emissions. Also France is seeking increased nuclear exports. The EC thus may take a forward role in negotiations, but the extent and form of responses is likely to be highly contentious, and may depend strongly on the UK's position.

The UK has traditionally been reluctant to apply the 'precautionary principle' to environmental concerns, has substantial domestic fossil fuel industries, and often follows US leads on major international issues. But Mrs Thatcher's high-profile warnings about the greenhouse effect, and the role of the UK as leader of the science working group of the IPCC, has established considerable official concern. Combined with the reluctance to intervene, UK policy thus exhibits a fundamental tension. The key uncertainty is whether concerns about the greenhouse effect and pressures from continental Europe will be sufficient to make the UK government waive the traditional rules which have determined energy policy.

Figure 5.1 UK energy consumption and CO_2 emissions, 1965-89

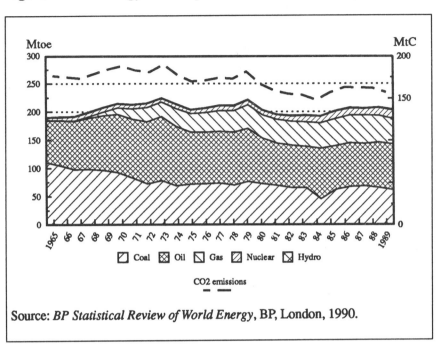

Source: *BP Statistical Review of World Energy*, BP, London, 1990.

This chapter examines the implications and policy issues raised by attempts to limit and reduce CO_2 emissions from the energy system in the UK and, in more general terms, the European Community (EC). Because of the role and importance of the EC, the chapter places UK issues in the European context, and considers the extent to which conclusions might be generalized on the European level.

5.1 Trends in UK energy consumption

The development of primary energy consumption in the UK, illustrated in Figure 5.1, shows clearly the major upheavals of the last two decades: the fall in total energy consumption following the oil crises of 1973 and 1979 and the replacement of coal by oil in 1984 during the year-long miner's strike. Overall, since 1973 consumption has been fairly steady, despite a substantial growth in GDP.[1]

---

[1] Figure 5.1 is produced from BP data. More detailed statistics, unless otherwise stated, are taken from the *UK Digest of Energy Statistics*, HMSO, 1990.

For more than two centuries, coal has been seen as the heart of Britain's energy industry, although steady decline during the 1950s and 1960s removed its dominance in numerical terms. The decline halted in the early 1970s and for nearly two decades coal demand has been roughly constant, at 35% of total energy, with a steady fall in the use of coal for direct heat being offset by its growth for electricity production. This constancy in output conceals a major restructuring of the industry, with a steady replacement of many small pits by large and automated 'superpits', and large labour and cost changes especially since the year-long miners' strike of 1984.[2]

Oil's share of the energy market declined from nearly half in 1973 to under one third in 1986, with a slight recovery in the late 1980s. The price rises during the 1970s stimulated further exploration and development of the newly discovered North Sea reserves, and within the space of five years Britain went from almost total dependence on oil imports to being a net exporter, with oil taxes generating several percent of government revenues.[3]

The fall in oil use up to 1986 was compensated by a doubling of both natural gas (from 12% to 25% of primary supply), and of nuclear power (from 3% to 6.5%, input equivalent). Gas growth has followed aggressive marketing, concentrating on the convenience and cleanliness as well as the cheapness of the product, and strong competition between gas and electricity has been a feature in all sectors, except transport, throughout the 1970s and 80s.

The UK was the first country in the world to generate electricity from a large-scale nuclear power station, at Calder Hall in 1956, but nuclear power has had a troubled history. The original Magnox reactors were considered too expensive to be used for a large-scale programme. Britain pursued the Advanced Gas-Cooled Reactor design, but this proved to be

---

[2] In the six years following the miners' strike, the workforce more than halved (from 221,000 to 78,000), labour productivity more than doubled, and production costs fell by some 40% (*Annual Report for 1989/1990*, British Coal, London).

[3] Tax revenues from UK oil and gas fields totalled about £65bn over 1980-89 (historic prices; *Development of the Oil and Gas Resources of the UK*, HMSO, London 1990). Total tax revenues in the UK were £133bn in fiscal year 1988/9, of which about half came from income taxes (Central Statistical Offie, Statistics September 1989, London, Table 3.12)

a technical and financial disaster.[4] In 1979 the government finally turned to Pressurized Water Reactor (PWR) technology developed in the US, still hoping for a rapid expansion of the nuclear industry. Planning delays, due in part to extensive opposition at public enquiries, meant that by 1989 the Sizewell B reactor was still the only PWR under construction. With privatization of the electricity industry at the end of the decade, nuclear power finally met a force stronger than itself - money. The new commercial groundrules combined with assessments of increasing reprocessing charges, rising costs for Sizewell, and a growing shadow of decommissioning costs for the Magnox reactors, and City financiers proved unwilling to bear the financial risks involved.[5] Nuclear power had to be withdrawn from the sale, and government plans for further PWR reactors were shelved, though work on the Sizewell reactor continues and a review of the future for the industry is due in 1994.

The trend of final demand by fuel and sector is shown in Figure 5.2. The most striking feature has been the rapid decline in industrial use, focused exclusively on coal and oil. This has offset the very slow increase in residential and services demand, and the more rapid upward trend in transport. Electricity demand in the UK was roughly constant over the decade following 1973, but began to rise again from the mid-1980s. From 1973 to 1986 the oil component in generation fell from 26% to 9%, with the balance being made up by coal (63% to 71%) and nuclear (9% to 18%). The completion of a cross-channel link in 1986 led to steady

---

[4] The House of Commons Select Committee on Energy reported an estimated average cost from the AGR reactors of 7.5p/kWh, 2-3 times the cost of coal stations (Fourth Report, *The Cost of Nuclear Power*, HMSO, June 1990, Volume 1 p.xiv.).

[5] The Select Committee Inquiry into the nuclear privatisation debacle examined 'why it was only when faced with the commercial discipline of life in the private sector that nuclear power (from both existing and proposed reactors) suddenly became an expensive form of generation', and concluded: 'we are convinced that there has been a systematic bias in ... costings in favour of nuclear power, both in ignoring risk and failing to provide adequately for contingencies, and, in respect of investment, in putting forward 'best expectations' rather than more cautious estimates ... the transfer of risks from utilities to the consumer or the Government has constituted an unacknowledged and major subsidy over the years to nuclear power ... the Department of Energy apparently made no attempt to obtain realistic costings .. until it was seeking to privatise nuclear power' (House of Commons Select Committee on Energy, Fourth Report, *The Cost of Nuclear Power*, HMSO, June 1990, Volume 1).

Figure 5.2 UK final energy consumption trends 1970-88

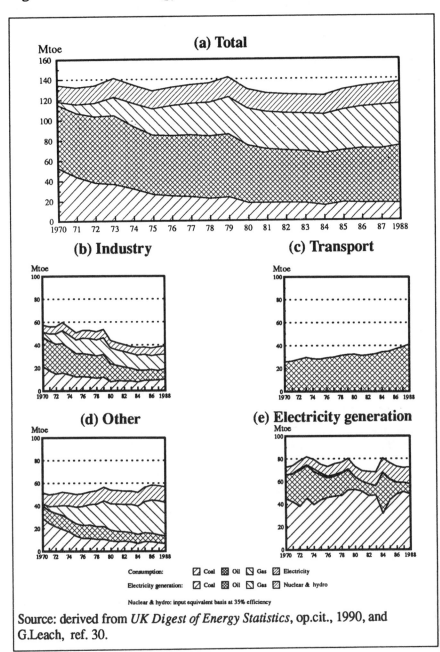

Source: derived from *UK Digest of Energy Statistics*, op.cit., 1990, and
G.Leach, ref. 30.

electricity imports from France, which by 1989 amounted to 4.3% of the UK's total supply.

National energy productivity (the ratio of GDP to energy use) improved by 40% over 1973-88 at an average rate of over 2%/year. This has come about partly through efficiency improvements in response to prices and government exhortation, and partly through major structural changes, in particular the loss of much antiquated heavy industry. The rate of improvement compares favourably with most countries and the absolute value in 1989 was roughly at the European and IEA average.[6] Combined with the levelling of demand, the growth in gas and nuclear power at the expense of first coal and then oil have progressively reduced CO_2 emissions from the peak of 1973, and in 1989 they were still below the levels twenty-five years previously.

Comparison with EC member countries

Comparative statistics of the EC-12 member countries are shown in Table 5.1. National energy productivities in the EC display considerable variation, from Italy and Denmark at 3.1 to Portugal and Greece at around 1.7 ($1000/toe at conventional exchange rates). Rates of improvement over past decades have varied widely; some countries have increased their fuel use relative to GDP. There is also much diversity in the mix of primary fuels. The four member states with the lowest total energy demand (Italy, Greece, Eire and Denmark; Luxembourg is considered together with Belgium) are almost wholly dependent upon coal and oil. The Netherlands stands out for high gas consumption, France and Belgium are distinguished by the high nuclear contribution. West Germany and the UK are not too dissimilar from the EC average, difficult though this is to define.

The proportion of primary energy used for electricity is similar across Europe, excepting the lower figure in the Netherlands, but the fuels differ greatly. In particular, France now generates over 75% of its electricity from nuclear power; nuclear expansion over 1980-88 resulted in a 70% drop in CO_2 emissions from the power sector. Belgium has also steadily increased its nuclear component to provide the bulk of electrical demand.

Whilst the UK figure for *energy* use per unit of GDP is similar to the EC and OECD average, *UK CO_2 emissions* per unit of GNP are somewhat higher due partly to the relatively small non-fossil input. UK

[6] IEA, *Energy Policies and Programmes of IEA Countries 1989 Review*, IEA/OECD, Paris, 1990.

Table 5.1 European Community-12 key statistics

	B+L[a]	Denmark	Eire	France	FRG[e]	Greece	Italy	Neth	Port	Spain	UK	Total
General indicators												
Area 1000 sq km[b]	33.1	43.1	70.3	547	357	131.9	301.2	40.8	92.1	504.8	244	2365
Population (m)	10.2	5	3.6	55.2	77.7	9.9	57.1	14.5	10.2	38.6	56.6	339
GDP (ECU bn)[e]	113	62	14	541	842	38	304	147	22	168	353	2604
PPP ratio[c]	1.11	1.37	1.03	1.16	-	0.75	1.07	1.10	0.62	0.92	1.02	-
1989 Energy consumption, Mtoe[d]												
Solid (coal)	9.4	5.6	0.1	18.7	142.2	7.9	14.3	8.2	2.9	19.2	61.4	290
Oil	23.1	9.1	4	88.4	123.4	13.6	94.3	34.3	9.3	46.6	81.2	527
Gas	9.3	1.7	1.4	24.4	21.6	0.1	37	30.8	0	4.5	44.9	176
Nuclear	9.1	0	0	59.9	37.6	0	0	1	0	12.5	15	135
Hydro	0.1	0	0.2	10	3.7	0.5	9.4	0	1	3.8	1.4	30
Total	51.0	16.4	5.7	201.4	328.5	22.1	155.0	74.3	13.2	86.6	203.9	1158.0
Fossil carbon emissions												
Total fossil carbon, MtC	35	15	4	108	269	20	116	56	11	62	161	856
Carbon/capita, tC/cap	3.4	2.9	1.2	2.0	3.5	2.0	2.0	3.9	1.1	1.6	2.8	2.5
Carbon/GDP, standard	308	237	298	199	320	527	380	382	481	369	457	329
Carbon/GDP, PPP basis	342	325	307	231	-	395	407	418	297	338	464	-

[a]B+L = Belgium and Luxembourg; [b]Central Intelligence Agency, *The World Factbook 1990*; [c] Ratio of purchasing power parity estimates to conventional exchange rates. Derived from OECD IEA Statistics, Second Quarter, 1990; [d]*BP Statistical Review of World Energy*, June 1990. Nuclear and hydro, input equivalents at 35% efficiency; [e]*United Nations Population Prospects* (data from 1985); [f]Figures for FRG include those for the former German Democratic Republic (GDR) which was incorporated into the FRG in October 1990. GDR consumption data from *Planecon Long Term Energy Outlook, 1990*.

per-capita CO_2 emissions are above the EC average, which itself is barely half the OECD average. Within the EC, France now has the lowest emissions per GDP, though Spain and Portugal have lower per capita emissions. Because the current situation, past trends and practices are very different, allocating any targets for CO_2 emissions, either on target criteria (eg. per-GDP), or on percentage reductions, would be extremely difficult; if the latter were attempted, the different trends means that the base year chosen would be important.

5.2 Energy resources and production

Fossil and nuclear resources

The UK lacks indigenous uranium resources, though large stockpiles have been built up, but is well placed for indigenous fossil energy resources. Various measures of these are illustrated in Figure 5.3.

Coal resources are very large. Though estimates vary widely, accessible reserves amount to at least many decades, and probably several hundreds of years, of production at the level of the 1980s. The fraction of this which could be extracted from low-cost superpits is unclear, and it may not be possible to re-open mines closed for economic reasons, but resource concerns have certainly not impeded the trend towards superpits.[7]

Despite steady domestic cost reductions, international traded coal in the late 1980s was still cheaper than most UK coal, and only agreements with the electricity utility have kept imports, currently about 10Mt/yr, from displacing more domestic production. The requirement to limit sulphur emissions is adding pressure for additional imports of low sulphur coal, as a way of avoiding the costs of Flue Gas Desulphurization. However, large imports would require considerable

[7] British Coal's *Annual Report for 1989/90* gives some idea of the quantities and complexities, in stating that: 'Technically recoverable reserves (that is, coal in known coalfields which could be extracted with existing technology) are estimated by the Corporation at 45Bt. The amount of these reserves that would actually be workable would, of course, depend on economic circumstances at the time. Recoverable reserves from existing mines and certain new mine projects, including the extractable and saleable coal which is sufficiently proved, of adequate thickness and quality and is in a suitable environment to support current mining plans, are currently assessed at between 3 and 5Bt'. Current total production is around 100Mt/yr.

Figure 5.3 Measures of indigenous fossil fuel resources

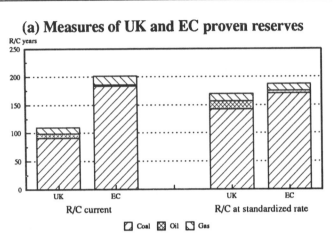

(a) Measures of UK and EC proven reserves

R/C current = ratio of resouces/reserves to current consumption of fuel (years)
R/C at standardized rate = ratio of resources/reserves to consumption at rate of
1kW/capita = 0.7toe/yr/capita

(b) Measures of UK fossil reserves and resources

p+e = proven and estimated reserves; p in p = proven resources in place;
est in p = estimated resources in place.
Sources: *BP Statistical Review of World Energy 1990*, BP, London, 1990;
World Energy Conference, *1989 Survey of Energy Resources*, WEC, London,
1989; Department of Energy, *Development of Oil and Gas Resources of the
UK*, HMSO, London, 1990.

expansion of port capacity, which would take substantial investment and time, and the overall economic outlook remains in dispute.[8]

The discovery of oil and gas on the UK continental shelf (UKCS) in the late 1960s transformed prospects for the UK energy economy, and exploitation was rapid. Oil production peaked in 1985 at 127Mt; a disaster at the Piper Alpha oil rig in 1988[9] helped to reduce 1989 production to about 100Mt, of which about a fifth was exported. Small amounts of refined oil products were imported.

Although the proven reserves of oil as of 1989 equalled only five years' production at existing rates, and gas reserves amounted to about fifteen years, the industry is confident that new finds and enhanced extraction techniques from existing fields will extend production for many years. The UK Offshore Operators Association suggests that UKCS oil production will decline by just 10% over the 1990s, with half the supply coming from new fields. The ultimate oil potential of the UKCS is estimated to be in the range 13-45 years of 1990 production, though the upper reaches of this are very uncertain and would require massive further investment in exploration, development and production.[10] Onshore oil is economically attractive but very limited.

Gas production, at around 40Mtoe/yr by the late 1980s, is set to grow. Originally concentrated in the Southern Basin of the North Sea, half of UK gas supplies now come from other areas, principally the associated gas from oil fields in the Northern Basin. Proven and probable UKCS reserves amount to 30 years at current production levels and this might well be extended with new discoveries; government statistics suggest a possible range of 21-70 years of supply at 1988 levels, but again, the upper levels are speculative and might require massive investment. Imports from Norway are currently being phased out, but a rapid growth in gas demand for power generation will almost certainly require new

---

[8] Some analysts argue that the practical import capabilities had been overstated, and likely international coal prices underestimated. For example, 'Unless and until power stations are built where the coal is landed, the economic case for steam coal imports for the power stations remains open' (B.W.Gladstone, 'UK steam coal Imports: Prospects and Constraints', *Energy Policy*, 19(2), March 1991).

[9] Many other rigs had to be closed temporarily for better safety measures to be installed, reducing production and increasing prices (Financial Times Energy Economist, 'The Price of Offshore Oil: the Consequence of Piper A', FTEE, July 1988).

[10] Department of Energy, *Development of the Oil and Gas Resources of the UK*, HMSO, London, 1989.

imports. Pipeline connections to Continental European networks - providing a link to Norwegian, Soviet and Algerian gas fields - are an issue of growing debate.

Renewable and geothermal energy resources
The UK is unusual in terms of renewable energy resources, estimates of which are shown in Table 5.2. *Hydro* resources are limited and concentrated in northern Scotland, where the best large sites have already been exploited. Further development of large schemes would be politically very difficult, though there is some potential for smaller schemes. Britain is too far north for *solar power* to offer good prospects, though moderate contributions to space heating would be possible; the average annual radiation density is about half that of tropical deserts and five-sixths of this comes in the summer months, whereas energy demand peaks strongly in the winter.[11] Nor does Britain have any significant resource of *geothermal aquifiers*;[12] a small scheme is being developed in Southampton but this is an exception.

Yet what the UK lacks in the more conventional renewable sources is made up by an abundance of less familiar types. Britain has the best *wind energy* resources in Europe, and probably some of the best in the world; winds average typically 7-8m/s (metres per second at 30m above ground level) in a broad band all along the west coast, and there are thought to be spots with higher windspeeds still, though in the absence of any national resource survey (as opposed to desk estimates) the estimates are uncertain. More than two-thirds of Britain, representing perhaps 80% of the energy resource, is classified in the top two windspeed categories of the European Wind Resource Atlas,[13] as indicated in the map of Figure 5.4. The size of the resource naturally depends upon siting assumptions, but on a rough approximation, for every 10% of current electricity demand to be derived from wind energy, windfarms would have to be

[11] K.Newton, 'Resource size estimates for the solar heating technologies', ETSU Note N-5/81, Energy Technology Support Unit, 1981; J.C.McVeigh, 'Solar Thermal Technologies and Photovoltaics' in M. Laughton, ed, *Renewable Energy Sources*, Watt Committee/Elsevier, London, 1990. The longer heating season in northern areas can increase the importance of 'passive solar design' of buildings.
[12] R.A.Downing and D.A.Gray (eds), 'Geothermal Energy: The Potential in the United Kingdom', *British Geological Survey*, HMSO, London, 1986.
[13] E.L.Peterson, I.Troen, N.G.Mortensen, 'The European Wind Energy Resources', *Proc. Euroforum New Energy Congress*, Saarbrucken, FRG, October 1988 (CEC/H.S.Stephens).

Figure 5.4 UK and European wind energy resources

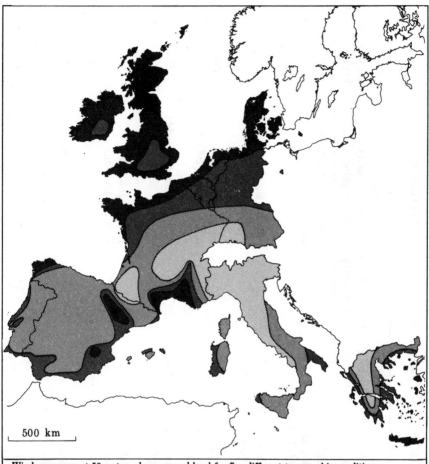

Wind resources at 50 metres above ground level for five different topographic conditions

| Sheltered terrain | | Open plain | | At a sea coast | | Open sea | | Hills and ridges | |
ms⁻¹	Wm⁻²	ms⁻¹	Wm⁻²	ms⁻¹	Wm⁻²	ms⁻¹	Wm⁻²	ms⁻¹	Wm⁻²
> 6.0	> 250	> 7.5	> 500	> 8.5	> 700	> 9.0	> 800	> 11.5	> 1800
5.0-6.0	150-250	6.5-7.5	300-500	7.0-8.5	400-700	8.0-9.0	600-800	10.0-11.5	1200-1800
4.5-5.0	100-150	5.5-6.5	200-300	6.0-7.0	250-400	7.0-8.0	400-600	8.5-10.0	700-1200
3.5-4.5	50-100	4.5-5.5	100-200	5.0-6.0	150-250	5.5-7.0	200-400	7.0-8.5	400-700
< 3.5	< 50	< 4.5	< 100	< 5.0	< 150	< 5.5	< 200	< 7.0	< 400

Source: I.Troen and E.L.Petersen, European Wind Atlas, Riso National
Laboratory, Roskilde, Denmark, 1989.

Table 5.2 Estimated UK renewable energy resources

Source	Resource (lower bound) Assumption	Elec output (TWh/year)	Non-elec (mostly heat) (Mtce/year)	Resource (higher bound) Assumption	Elec output TWh/yr	Non-elec (mostly heat) (Mtce/yr)
Large-scale hydro	Little additional potential owing to environmental objections	8		Extensive exploitation of remaining sites	15	
Micro-hydro	Head >3m, above 25kW Head <3m, above 25kW	1.2 0.8		Smaller sites also exploited	4	
Wind-onshore	Average 8x30m turbines every 100km^2	10		Average 25x60m turbines every 100km^2	200	
Wind-offshore	Min 5km from coast Max 30m depth	100		Deeper water accessible	250	
Domestic and industrial wastes	20Mt degradable @ 12GJ/t most landfill recovery 30%	6		30Mt degradable Half incineration: Half landfill:	18 2	7.5
Wave	30MW/km, x500km x 15% average efficiency	20		45MW/km, x100km x35% efficiency	130	
Agricultural wastes	20Mt @ 14GJ/t 50% recovered	11	5.0*	25 Mt, 90% recovered	44	11.3*

Forestry	5% land: waste collection @2t/Ha/yr	2.3	1.0*	10% land: waste collection @3t/Ha/yr	10	2.6*
	5% land: rotation forestry @7t/Ha/yr	8.4	3.6*	15% land: rotation forestry @13t/Ha/yr	82	21*
Tidal	Severn and Mersey, Morecambe Bay and Solway Firth[k]	35		Extended schemes and improved performance	50	
Geothermal hot dry rock (extracted to 7km depth at costs over 100 yrs)	ETSU estimate of resource below 48kWh (speculative)	20		Guesstimate of potential over wider regions at higher cost cut off	100	
Passive solar space heating	15% contribution, in 40% building stock, 1987 heating levels	5	3.9	30% contribution in 60% of building stock, 50% more efficient		5.5
Active solar water heating	40% contribution in 80% of building stock	5		60% contribution in 95% of building stock		30
Photovoltaics (PV, solar cells)	100km^2 at 8% annual efficiency	9		750km^2 at 12% annual efficiency		100

*Non-electricity figure is total energy content of recovered biomass, which could be used for various applications. Electricity figures show the total electricity potential of this (30% efficiency, lower limit; 50% efficiency, upper limit). Thus the heat and electricity figures cannot be added, though some heat recovery from generation would be possible.
For notes, references and discussion see source: M.J.Grubb, 'The Cinderalla options', *Energy Policy*, July/August 1990.

sited on 120-240km^2 - some 0.5-1% of UK land area.[14] Most of the land could still be used for farming, but the visual impact and other concerns have made the practicality and desirability of large-scale wind energy a subject of growing debate.

Britain is similarly endowed with large *tidal energy* resources. Most attention has focused on the Severn Barrage, a funnel-shaped estuary with tides of over 10m; the favoured 20km long 'inner line' could meet about 6% of electricity demand at a cost estimated to be 3.5-8p/kWh (depending largely on the discount rate chosen), with a capital cost of some £8000m and a 10-year construction time.[15] Two other large schemes along the west coast, at 10-40% higher costs, boost the tidal resource to about 15% of current electricity demand; numerous other smaller schemes, at similar energy costs but on a much less daunting scale, could provide further small contributions.[16] Other smaller and intermediate sites could be exploited at somewhat greater costs. However, strong environmental and other objections have already been raised to the Severn scheme, partly because of fears that it would interfere with the bird population on the mud-flats of the estuary, which is one of the major sanctuaries for wading birds in Europe. Environmental studies have proved inconclusive; the area of mud flats would be reduced but it is thought that the population density and species variety might increase as the silt loading in the water reduces.[17] Environmental groups are split over the consequences of the Severn and other tidal schemes.

As in other countries, *waste products* form a significant energy resource. Britain is beginning to exploit landfill gas, with a projected contribution of 0.7Mtoe by the mid 1990s and an estimated potential over 3Mtoe[18], but has few plans for waste incineration at present. There is growing interest in the possibilities for short rotation forestry, possibly

[14] M.J.Grubb, 'A resource and siting analysis for wind energy in Britain', *European Wind Energy Conference*, Glasgow, June 1989; M.J.Grubb, 'The potential for wind energy in Britain', *Energy Policy*, December 1988.

[15] Department of Energy, *The Severn Barrage Project: General Report*, Energy Paper No.57, HMSO, London, 1989.

[16] See notes to Table 5.1

[17] Department of Energy, *The Severn Barrage Project: General Report*, op.cit Chapter 3

[18] Converted from estimates of 1Mtce and 5Mtce respectively in K.M.Richards *Landfill gas exploitation in the UK - an update*, Energy Technology Support Unit ETSU-L-25, Harwell, UK, June 1988.

encouraged as a subsidized solution to the excess land in conventional agricultural use throughout the European Community.

Greater technical uncertainties surround other options. The seas surrounding Britain could provide *offshore wind energy and wave energy*. The exploitable offshore wind resource is estimated to be on the same scale as total electricity demand. With extensive deployment off the North-West and South-West coasts, wave energy might provide up to 20-40% of current electricity demand. A number of unresolved engineering issues and the lack of any experience in deployment means that the costs and performance of offshore wind and wave are very uncertain; desk studies place wind in the region 3-10p/kWh and wave at -15p/kWh.[19] Wave power cost and resource estimates in particular have been hotly disputed since the closure of the government's research programme in 1982.[20]

Returning onshore, the UK is a world leader in *geothermal hot dry rock* technology. Areas of relatively high heat flow have attracted interest, but these are poor compared with geographically active regions, and lie around areas of outstanding natural beauty. Government estimates of costs and feasibility have varied widely; a revised assessment in 1990 ed to curtailment of the research programme.[21]

Comparison with the EC

The UK is the only member of the European Community to produce more energy than it consumes, and the only one to have substantial reserves of all three fossil fuels. As indicated in Table 5.3, only Germany has more coal and the Netherlands more gas. Most other Community members, and the Community as a whole, are heavily dependent upon imports, particularly of oil. Coal resources in the EC (especially in

19] 1985 prices at 5% discount rate. Energy Technology Support Unit, *Background papers relevant to the 1986 Appraisal of UK Energy R,D&D*, (ETSU R-43), HMSO, London, 1987. This compares with around 3p/kWh for coal stations and less for modern gas plants when compared on the some basis.

20] The House of Lords Select Committee on the European Communities, 'Alternative Energy Sources', 1988, HMSO, reported 'a serious conflict of evidence which only an independent review could resolve'. In April 1990 it was recognised that earlier very high cost estimates had contained important errors (*New Scientist*, 14 April 1990, p.22).

21] R.Shock, *An Economic Assessment of Hot Dry Rocks as an Energy Source for the UK*, Energy Technology Support Unit, ETSU-R-34, Harwell, UK, provided an encouraging assessment of costs, but further research revealed problems which raised serious doubts about the feasibility of commercial schemes in the UK (ETSU, Harwell, UK, forthcoming 1991).

Table 5.3 Major European fossil energy reserves and 1989 production, Mtoe

	Coal		Oil		Gas	
	Reserves	**Prodn**	**Reserves**	**Prodn**	**Reserves**	**Prodn**
France	160	8.2	26	3.6	31	2.6
FRG	34300	138.5	36	3.8	330	13.6
Greece	970	6.3	3	0	4	-
Italy	22	0.2	90	4.5	270	15.3
Netherlands	330	-	26	0	1600	52.9
Spain	347	17.9	4	0	13	-
UK	6000	60.8	700	92	540	37.9
Norway	0	-	1500	75	2500	28.8
Poland	22700	112	0	0	100	-
Other Europe	13000	111	220	35	500	45
Totals	**78000**	**455**	**2600**	**214**	**6000**	**196**

Notes: European total including Turkey. Former GDR incoporated in FRG data

Source: Production:*BP Statistical Review of World Energy*, 1990. Reserves; WEC. Reserve statistics converted to Mtoe:1 Mtoe = 1.5Mt bituminous coal; 3.0Mt brown coal/lignite; 1.11BCM natural gas.

Germany) are mostly high cost, with continuing pressures to reduce total production. Outside the EC, Norway has the major European gas and oil reserves, and integration with Eastern Europe would give better access to coal in Poland and some oil in Romania. Beyond these lie the massive resources of the Soviet Union. Eastern Europe is wholly dependent upon Soviet supplies, and Western European dependence is an issue of long-standing debate.[22]

In terms of renewable resources, the Community spans an equally wide range. Solar water heating is already fairly common in southern Europe; photovoltaics could also be attractive in this area if the lower cost predictions are realized. The prospects for solar, other than for space heat contributions, decline as one moves north, though the Netherlands is

[22] J.Stern, *International Gas Trade in Europe*, Heinemann, London, 1984.

funding photovoltaics research as a possible response to environmental concerns. There are pockets of geothermal aquifer resources around the Italian Alps and the Paris basin; other areas may exist. There are good wind resources all along the Atlantic and North Sea coasts, and in the mountainous regions (Figure 5.4). The Atlantic coast brings in strong waves which could in principle provide significant power.[23]

Denmark is by far the most advanced country in terms of exploiting renewable resources; current projections envisage obtaining 10% of energy from renewables by 2000, with wind energy and straw being the largest contributors.[24] One of the biggest issues surrounding renewable energy resources is the use of agricultural and other waste products, and the use of agricultural surpluses and the land which would be released if these were removed from traditional agriculture. Ethanol production does not appear as promising as direct combustion for heat or electricity but could prove quite attractive if current agricultural supports were shifted to energy production. Biomass in Europe currently provides 20-40Mtoe/yr; the potential, without extending the area of cultivation, is estimated to exceed 100Mtoe/yr.[25]

5.3 Scenario resumé and policy background

Projections for UK energy vary widely. Forecasts from the IEA[26] show energy demand in 2000 up by about 11% over 1988, with 60% of the increase being met by coal for electricity generation, which would increase CO_2 emissions by some 11%. Projections by the UK

[23] A report for the European Commission reports an estimated theoretical resource of over 500TWh/yr from the Atlantic coast, plus around 200TWh/yr from the weaker Mediterranean waves (T.Lewis, *Wave Energy: Evaluation for the CEC*, Graham and Trotman, 1985). Practical constraints are hard to estimate, and would depend upon the technology developed.
[24] Danish Ministry of Energy, *Energy 2000*, Danish Energy Agency, Copenhagen, April 1990.
[25] D.O.Hall and F.Fossilo-Calle, 'Biomass, Bioenergy and Agriculture in Europe', *7th Canadian Bioenergy Research and Development Seminar*, Ottawa, Canada, April 1989. An EC report states that 'biomass in its totality - that is including waste and the use of agricultural products for non-food purposes - could cover in theory 5-10% of Community energy consumption before the year 2000' (Commission Communication to the Council on Energy and Environment, COM(89) 369 Final, Brussels, 1989).
[26] IEA, *Energy Policies and Programmes of IEA Countries 1989 Review*, IEA/OECD, Paris, 1990.

Department of Energy prepared for the Intergovernmental Panel on Climate Change (IPCC),[27] show primary energy demand growing from 201Mtoe in 1985 to about 290Mtoe in 2005 on a central GDP projection, with growth in all fossil fuels and a 37% rise in CO_2 emissions; the central projections to 2020 show a further rise of both primary energy and CO_2 emissions to more than 70% above 1985 levels. Skea's analysis[28] suggests that these projections are unrealistic, primarily with respect to the industrial sector, but concludes that CO_2 emissions would rise slowly in the absence of abatement policies, and that reducing emissions by more than about 1%/yr would be extremely difficult. In contrast, the Association for the Conservation of Energy estimate that a 20% cut in CO_2 emissions can be achieved by 2005 with policies directed at energy conservation,[29] a view broadly supported by Leach's analysis.[30]

Only Leach provides a detailed breakdown of energy end uses and efficiency trends. Consequently it is difficult to assess the real reasons for the differences in these outlooks, and the policy issues which might arise from them. Instead, this chapter works from the detailed end-use scenarios presented in Chapter 4, which reflect six main situations as summarized in the box. Results in terms of primary energy and emissions are summarized in Figure 5.5. This section sets the policy background in terms of resources and sensitivities; later sections discuss the explicit policy issues.

Resource impacts and fuel switching opportunities

There is little doubt that most of the demand in the shorter-term scenarios can be met from indigenous resources, though some may be imported as

[27] Department of Energy projections for IPCC Working Group III, November 1989, Published as *An Evaluation of Energy-Related Greenhouse Gas Emissions and Measures to Alleviate Them*, Energy Paper Number 58, HMSO, London, 1990. The study presented a range of scenarios with the average annual growth in energy demand to 2020 ranging from 0.9%/yr to 2.1%/yr. The report included extensive discussion of abatement technologies and their costs, especially concerning renewable sources, but these were not integrated in the scenario projections.
[28] Jim Skea, 'A case study of the potential for reducing carbon dioxide emissions in the UK', *Science Policy Research Unit Special Report*, University of Sussex, June 1990. The 1%/yr figure is the authors' interpretation of Skea's scenarios and discussion.
[29] Association for the Conservation of Energy, *Solving the Greenhouse Dilemma - a Strategy for the UK*, ACE/WWF, London, 1989.
[30] G.Leach and Z.Nowak, *Cutting Carbon Dioxide Emissions from Poland and the United Kingdom*, Stockholm Enviroment Institute, Stockholm/London, 1990.

UK Scenarios: main themes.

Short term - 2000. 25% GDP growth in the decade to 2000. No additional electricity imports or nuclear power, other than Sizewell. Fuel mix mainly follows the trends of the late 1980s. Two scenarios:

2000A: Business-as-usual. An absence of efficiency policies and of price increases leads to almost stagnant efficiency, with a modest revival in energy growth and CO_2 emissions.

2000B: Emissions abatement. Policy-driven efficiency improvements, including discouragement of electric space heating, lead to a decline in energy consumption and CO_2 emissions.

Long term - 2030. GDP roughly doubles from 1987 value, with continued growth for energy especially in the transport and commercial sector. Four scenarios:

2030Ai: Business-as-usual. Modest efficiency improvements and saturation of some end uses dampen but do not offset resumed demand growth. Non-fossil power and imports are negligible, and gas power generation is discouraged. CO_2 emissions are 50% above 1987 levels.

2030Aii: Emissions abatement through fuel switching. Demand as in 2030A(i), with extensive promotion of gas generation and in transport, and non-fossil and/or imports of electricity.

2030Bi: Emissions abatement through energy efficiency. Strong policies, including price rises, lead to efficiency levels approaching the technical potential as recognised in the late 1980s. This yields a steady decline in demand and emissions.

2030Bii: Efficiency plus fuel switching. The efficiency measures of 2030B(i) combined with fuel switching measures as in 2030A(ii) lead to a more rapid decline in CO_2 emissions (to about 45% of 1987 values).

For details of assumptions and methodology see Chapter 4, section 4.4.

Figure 5.5 Scenarios for UK energy consumption and CO_2 emissions 1988-2030

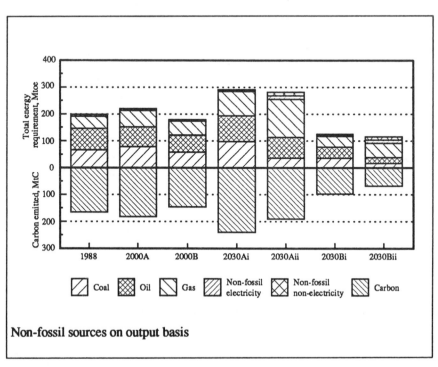

Non-fossil sources on output basis

a matter of economic choice. Oil production may not be sufficient to meet demand in the 2000A scenario, and the loss of foreign exchange, given the decline in the balance of trade, may add significantly to balance-of-payments problems.

The short-term scenarios do not explicitly consider fuel-switching measures. The main area of choice in end use is in heating. Given the implicit scenario assumption that people do not move away from gas central heating once installed, probably the only significant area for fuel switching in end uses is in the 30% (domestic) and 50% (service) of heating currently supplied by sources other than gas. These might convert to almost any fuel, probably with an increase in demand if this is concurrent with installation of central heating. Such fuel switching might make a difference of -1% to +10% to emissions in the 2000B scenario, with the large increase arising from switches into electricity instead of gas.[31] Limited fuel switching within industry might be possible on this timescale, but the other main possibility would be in electricity generation. The 2000A scenario has a nearly 20% increase in electricity output, which might come from either gas combined cycle or coal steam plant, possibly with some wind energy and smaller tidal stations. This choice could in theory reduce UK emissions by nearly 4% of the 2000A projection,[32] though the practical range of variation is probably lower. The potential for abatement from fuel switching is less in the efficiency scenario, because with no increase in electricity consumption there is likely to be much less construction of new plant. These variations therefore tend to confirm that, given the existing trends towards gas, efficiency is by far the most important area for policy aimed at achieving additional short-term carbon limitations, though discouraging growth in electric space heating is also important.

In the longer-term, as projected in the 2030Ai scenario, demand for coal and oil increases by 40-50%, and that for gas by nearly 70%, from 1987 levels. Almost all the oil would have to be imported, unless it were derived from coal liquefaction (which would only be economic if the oil price were very high, and would result in much higher carbon emissions). Most of the gas would have to be imported. It is unclear whether this level of coal consumption could be sustained from low-cost domestic resources, so there might be large coal imports as well.

Fuel switching to reduce emissions further exacerbates the import problem. Though oil demand is slightly reduced, gas demand in the 2030Aii scenario is nearly three times the 1987 levels. It seems doubtful whether such a pattern could be sustained at this level of demand at least if repeated throughout Europe, quite apart from the risks entailed by being so heavily dependent upon one or two major resource areas.

Some countries have grown familiar with being heavily dependent upon energy imports, though few have been very comfortable with this. The UK has grown used to self-sufficiency. Barring extensive

---

[31] About 25% of UK homes did not yet have central heating, and over 25% relied on solids or oil; all figures are higher for the commercial sector. The figures cited assume that a maximum of 20% overall can be switched between electricity and gas by the year 2000 and reflect the fact that most buildings within reach of gas will use it in the business-as-usual case.

[32] Assuming a least emissions case with an *extra* 10TWh of non-fossil electricity and imports and 30TWh of gas (corresponding to about 5GW of plant operating at baseload), both displacing coal.

discoveries of deep gas within Europe, or the economic feasibility of large scale in-place coal gasification, this scenario would almost certainly be politically unacceptable even it were economically feasible. Even the outcomes projected in 2030Ai would induce considerable political uneasiness, quite apart from the balance-of-payments impacts.

A rather different picture emerges from the high efficiency scenarios. In 2030Bi, fossil fuels are used in much the same proportion as in 1987 (though with some relative growth in gas and substantial sectorial shifts, oil being confined to transport and petrochemical uses) at about 2/3 of the 1987 level. The oil would almost certainly have to be imported, but gas requirements might be met from domestic resources if much more were discovered, and if not the import requirements would be modest. The coal demand could probably be met from relatively low-cost domestic resources.

The combination of fuel switching and efficiency in 2030Bii reduces oil demand in transport by some switching towards gas, electricity or hydrogen, and biomass fuels, and gas largely displaces coal in the other sectors. Despite this, gas demand is little above the 1987 levels. The UK would probably have to be integrated through the European grid, but if such a situation were repeated throughout Europe it would probably not unduly strain Soviet and other gas resources.[33] Attempting to reduce CO_2 emissions by fuel switching in this way would probably increase total fossil fuel imports only slightly, since the major shifts are from oil to gas and from coal to non-fossil electricity sources. The impact on overall import dependence would depend upon the nature of the non-fossil/import contribution.

The non-fossil/import contribution is taken as 160TWh in 2030Aii and 140TWh in 2030Bii; the total and rate of deployment in the latter case is slightly constrained by the low total demand and the reduced need for new plant. If a successful nuclear programme were started in the 1990s and sustained, these and higher levels would clearly be technically possible with nuclear power - France developed double this generating

---

[33] It should be noted that for such gas switching to have a large impact on greenhouse gas emissions, the European transport system would have to be very efficient and leak-proof; otherwise the end-use benefits could be offset by energy uses within the system and methane leakages (though these would have to be set against leakages from other sources, such as methane from coal mines, which at present are estimated to exceed leakages from gas production in the UK - See Appendix 2).

capability within the space of barely fifteen years. The economic and political uncertainties surrounding this are to an extent mirrored by those concerning renewable energy. As depicted in Table 5.2, if renewables can be successfully developed and deployed at the higher siting densities considered - which might in large part reflect public acceptance of widespread siting of renewable energy systems relative to the alternatives - over 140TWh could be met from the 'confident' renewable energy technologies of onshore wind, hydro, biomass and tidal energy. Such developments would require political commitment to overcome probably strong environmental objections but there should not be serious technical difficulties in reaching these levels by 2030. If only the lower densities can be achieved, the total resource of confident technologies amounts to 60-70TWh, even including the large tidal schemes.[34] To reach 140TWh at least half the contribution would have to come from more speculative renewables (offshore wind and wave, geothermal, and - for the UK - photovoltaics (PV)). Quite apart from the economic uncertainties involved, it is questionable whether obtaining such contributions from these technologies would be feasible even on a timescale of 40 years. With the exception of PV, all would involve extensive development and trial programmes before large-scale deployment could proceed.

Consequently, if constraints on renewable deployment tended towards the lower siting densities, then in the absence of nuclear power, the only option would be to import large amounts of electricity. The source of this would probably be French nuclear, though much might in principle also be derived from Icelandic geothermal and hydro stations,[35] and on a timescale of 40 years it could conceivably include PV electricity exports from Mediterranean countries. These options would of course still increase import dependence.

---

[34] The Department of Energy estimated a maximum contribution from renewable sources by 2025 of up 70TWh/yr of electricity, and 20Mtoe/yr from non-electric sources (Department of Energy, *Renewable Energy in the UK - The Way Forward*, Department of Energy Paper No.55, HMSO, London, 1988).
[35] A recent summary of proposals to transmit Icelandic hydro and geothermal electricity to the UK via undersea cable is given in 'Icelandic Power Could Cost Less', IEE Review, Institution of Electrical Engineers, London, February 1991. The economics to the point of landing the electricity in Scotland appeared to be promising, with cost estimates of 1.6-2.9p/kWh at the point of landing. Uncertainties include transmission of electricity through the system thereafter.

5.4 Policy options and constraints

Free markets and market measures

The UK government has traditionally been reluctant to intervene extensively in company activities, particularly at the level of consumer demand. This has been a major theme of successive Conservative governments since 1979 but even the Labour government before this was reluctant to use microeconomic instruments (eg. product standards) and macroeconomic measures were limited by the terms of an IMF loan in 1976. The political context is discussed further in section 5.6, but one consequence has been an interest in market mechanisms for achieving environmental goals.

Especially given the extent of road congestion the case for some form of road pricing seems compelling, but it faces strong political obstacles. A carbon tax is even more problematic, given strong political opposition and a widespread belief that it would harm the UK's competitive position unless applied throughout industrial countries (an assumption examined in Volume 1, sections 3.4 and 3.5). The 1990 Environment White Paper clearly stated that prices would have to rise in the long term to meet environmental goals, while disavowing any short term commitment (see box).

Before embarking on a carbon tax there are certain anomalies which could be removed. Value Added Tax is not applied to domestic energy supplies, on the grounds that it is an essential and not a luxury good, but it is charged on conservation materials. However, the principle of applying VAT only on luxury items has grown weaker as the tax has been applied to a wider range of goods, and VAT on energy - or its removal from conservation materials - would help to 'level the playing field'.

The fact that energy is an essential good does, however, highlight a specific problem with price-based measures for control. Britain still has some housing, often inhabited by the elderly, with thermal quality so low that occupants cannot, or feel they cannot afford to, keep themselves warm in cold winter spells. Every cold winter brings stories of old people dying from hypothermia, and total excess deaths in winter amount to an estimated 30,000-60,000 people each year.[36] Talk of taxation as a means of reducing energy use and emissions will, understandably, raise

[36] B.Boardman, 'Seasonal Mortality and Cold Homes', *Proc Conf on Unhealthy Houses: a Diagnosis*, Legal Research Institute, University of Warwick, December 1986.

Stated position of the UK government on global warming 1990

'The Government believes that countries must act together to respond to this challenge ... if other countries take similar action, Britain is prepared to set itself the demanding target of reversing the upward trend of CO2 emissions and returning them to their 1990 levels by 2005. When our action on all greenhouse gases is taken into account, the global warming potential of Britain's emissions should then be 20% less than in 1990.

The Government will take first those measures which save energy or are otherwise worthwhile in their own right. In the long term, action will inevitably have to include increases, achieved by taxation or other means,in the relative prices of energy and fuel. But the Government will not introduce measures which directly raise real energy prices in the next few years outside the transport sector.

Concerning energy efficiency, the Government will: encourage greater energy efficiency and step up the work of the Energy Efficiency Office ..; promote combined heat and power schemes; monitor the toughened energy efficiency standard for new buildings to see how they might be further strengthened; encourage energy labelling of houses, and of appliances ..; promote the use of energy efficient lighting; and press for minimum efficiency standards across Europe.'

Source: 'This Common Inheritance,' Summary of White Paper on the Environment, HMSO, 1990. The paper also stated intentions to review and encourage renewable sources, 'maintain the nuclear option', improve transport, and encourage tree planting.

an outcry until this problem is satisfactorily addressed, as discussed further below; and this is but part of broader distributional concerns.[37]

The effectiveness of price-based measures depends upon how well the market reacts to price signals. Figure 5.6 illustrates eight carefully costed efficiency measures in the UK which could total to nearly 10% of current demand. The cost of each, amortized over 15 years at an 8% discount rate, is much lower than current UK energy prices, so by most definitions they are cost effective, but at present they are not pursued. The widespread existence of such options points to areas of large-scale market failure which cannot be addressed by price changes alone. A parliamentary investigation concluded:

> The most striking feature of our enquiry has been the extent to which improvements in energy efficiency - across all sectors of the economy - are almost universally seen as the most obvious and most effective response to the greenhouse effect ... the evidence received overwhelmingly endorses the view that, for a variety of reasons, serious market imperfections persist ... widespread opportunities to invest profitably in cost-effective measures ... are being ignored.[38]

This is the 'efficiency gap' discussed in Volume 1; and as discussed there, measures other than price alone would be needed to address it. These are best examined by sector.

Demand-side measures for promoting energy efficiency

Domestic sector. A study by the Building Research Establishment[39] concluded that half the total UK CO_2 emissions come from energy use in buildings, with 60% of this from domestic dwellings. The study estimated that emissions from the domestic sector could be reduced by 35% using proven technologies, with over 2/3 of these measures being

---

[37] 'The area where environmental policy is likely to raise the most important distribution conflicts is in the pricing of domestic energy ... Policies aiming to encourage insulation and thermal efficiency, especially in poorer households, would then appear a necessary adjunct' (P.Johnson, S.McKay and S.Smith, *The Distributional Consequences of Environmental Taxes*, Commentary No.23, Institute of Fiscal Studies, London, 1990)

[38] UK House of Commons Energy Committee, *Energy Policy Implications of the Greenhouse Effect*, Vol.1, July 1989 (paras 102 and 107).

[39] L.D.Shorrock and G.Henderson, 'Energy use in Buildings and CO_2 Emissions', Building Research Establishment Report Cl/SfB (L7)(R3), BRE, Garston, Watford, 1990.

Figure 5.6 Costs of eight major UK carbon reduction measures

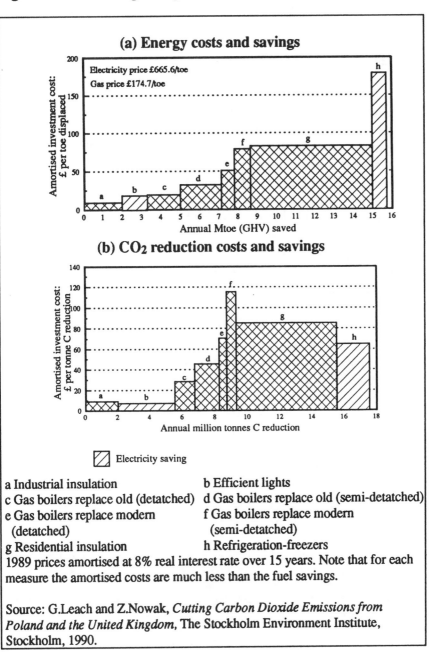

(a) Energy costs and savings

Electricity price £665.6/toe
Gas price £174.7/toe

Amortised investment cost: £ per toe displaced

Annual Mtoe (GHV) saved

(b) CO₂ reduction costs and savings

Amortised investment cost: £ per tonne C reduction

Annual million tonnes C reduction

Electricity saving

a Industrial insulation
b Efficient lights
c Gas boilers replace old (detatched)
d Gas boilers replace old (semi-detatched)
e Gas boilers replace modern (detatched)
f Gas boilers replace modern (semi-detatched)
g Residential insulation
h Refrigeration-freezers

1989 prices amortised at 8% real interest rate over 15 years. Note that for each measure the amortised costs are much less than the fuel savings.

Source: G.Leach and Z.Nowak, *Cutting Carbon Dioxide Emissions from Poland and the United Kingdom,* The Stockholm Environment Institute, Stockholm, 1990.

cost-effective. The UK scenarios suggest that the domestic sector is the area with the single greatest potential for savings, which are dominated by increases in the efficiency of space heating and consumer appliances; the former is more important in terms of energy demand, but appliances feature strongly in terms of carbon emissions.

Several researchers have noted large savings available on short payback periods in the domestic sector,[40] a fact which points to a pervasive failure of market incentives to efficiency. This occurs for many reasons, many of which seem hard to remove. There is no easy solution to the tenant/landlord division, nor to the fact that people often do not intend stay in a house long enough to take an interest in conservation measures, or other reasons for the short-term view of investments; and house prices and purchases rarely reflect running costs. To date, government action has been limited, and the building stock remains poor. In a review of OECD policies, Schipper noted:

> In Britain, *policies* were always very weak, comfort levels the lowest in Northern Europe, and homes the least efficient...the ironies of the record are still apparent in 1987, where the double glazing retrofit market is booming even as most homes are still built with leaky single windows and inadequate insulation! [Emphasis as in original][41]

Improved insulation standards for new buildings were approved in 1990, though environmental groups have claimed derisively that these still do not bring the UK standards to the level adopted in Sweden in the 1930s.[42] Given that the basic principles of standards have been accepted, they could be tougher - the incremental costs, up to levels significantly higher than those adopted in 1990, are small compared with the savings in the first few years of operation even at current fuel prices (Chapter 2). With the increasing greening of society and within the architectural professions it is unlikely that objections about the 'freedom of design' will carry much weight.

However, new construction adds less than 1% to the stock each year so even very tough standards would have only a slow impact. Also, as noted

[40] See for example ibid, tables in G. Leach, 1990 op. cit., and J. Skea, 1990 op. cit.
[41] Lee Schipper, 'Energy Conservation Policies in the OECD: Did they Make a Difference?', *Energy Policy*, December 1987.
[42] D.Olivier and M.Flood, 'Report on electricity congress, Gotenburg, Sweden', FoE/Greenpeace International, June 1989. There are reasons for these differences, in terms of climate and the dominant building materials and designs, but even allowing for such factors the requirements appear modest by north European standards.

above, improving the worst of the building stock would for social reasons be a necessary adjunct to energy taxes. The key issue is therefore retrofitting of existing stock. Those most seriously affected by poor buildings generally have little capital with which to pay for insulation, and/or often rent the accommodation, so government grants or other financial supports are necessary;[43] grants for insulation in low-income homes were reinstated in 1990. To encourage more rapid and broader improvements, however, grants would have to be substantial and not restricted by income, and the total cost to the Exchequer could then run to billions, raising considerable Treasury opposition.

Various local initiatives have played a significant, though varied role in improving buildings.[44] Compulsory energy surveys at the time of sale, or a legal requirement for a certificate of energy standards, might make an impact, at lower cost to government than grants. However, it would impose an additional cost on every sale, and running costs are usually the last thing on the mind of potential purchasers. Realizing much of the potential for household savings would require other measures.

An effective alternative, of no direct cost to the Treasury, would simply be to require existing buildings to meet certain standards before they could be sold. The most practical way of administering and financing the measures would be to put the legal onus on the estate agents. The costs of correcting substandard accommodation would be shared between seller, new purchaser, and estate agents. This approach would appear to solve the major logistical problems and would ensure that house prices reflect the standards demanded on economic, social and environmental grounds. The analysis in Chapter 4, section 4.6, illustrates the possible impact of such a policy focused on lower cost insulation measures.

Heating energy demand can also be lowered by improving the efficiency of new boilers as they replace old ones on a typical turnover of 20 years. Condensing boilers, giving a 10-15% efficiency improvement, are currently rare in the UK in contrast to some European countries. With a payback of 3 to 5 years at 1990 gas prices, a phased-in ban on non-condensing boilers could be justified as long as quality was

---

[43] Detailed policy options are discussed in B. Boardman, 'Energy Efficiency Policy and Low Income Households', in D. Reay and A. Wright (eds), *Innovation for Energy Efficiency*, Pergamon Press, 1988.
[44] B.Sheldrick and S.Margill, 'Local Energy Conservation Initiatives in the UK: their Nature and Achievements', *Energy Policy*, December 1988.

not compromised, but unless subsidized, the forced addition of £200-£300 in capital costs would be controversial. A substantial direct grant for condensing boilers, as applied in France and Holland, would be simpler though it would meet Treasury opposition.[45]

The scenarios emphasize the importance of appliance efficiency for reducing CO_2 emissions from electricity consumption. Currently there is a serious information problem: it is often very difficult to find out the energy consumption of appliances in the UK, and EC proposals on appliance labelling have been applied only haphazardly. Mandatory labelling would give some improvement, but as discussed in Volume 1 section 4.3, the problems run much deeper than this, and only some form of efficiency standards are likely to realize the economic and environmental potential from deploying the better technologies. The figures in 2000B assume that effective EC standards on refrigeration and some other appliances are introduced by 1993.

In the political climate of the early 1990s, mandatory standards for house sales seem most unlikely. The Conservative government has also been opposed to mandatory appliance standards on the grounds that they interfere with free-market forces, but there are strong and growing pressures for these within the EC, and the UK's 1990 Environment White Paper appeared to mark a shift of position, with its stated support for minimum efficiency standards in Europe (see box, p.211).

In addition to government measures, the domestic sector is the area in which 'green consumerism' could be most important. The impact of government measures will be greatly reduced if consumers still leave thermostats on high and open windows to cool houses, leave hot taps running, and boil two pints of water for each cup of tea, for example. Developing, through information and education, a culture which treats energy as a resource to be husbanded may be as important, and as difficult, as any of the measures noted above.

Service sector. Many of the same issues arise in the service sector as in the domestic, though the balance is somewhat different. Heating dominates demand and potential savings to a similar degree, but lighting (often used in daytime) and other appliances are relatively much more important. The size of many service sector buildings opens new technical

---

[45] The total additional cost of replacing old boilers with new condensing ones would be about £1bn (Leach, 1990, op. cit.). Grants totalling about 10% of this should be sufficient to equalize the capital costs compared with conventional boilers.

opportunities, principal among which are building management systems and small CHP units.

In policy terms the public sector (schools, hospitals, government offices etc.) can be very different from commercial operations. A major obstacle to energy efficiency is often that running expenses - including energy - can usually be claimed as unavoidable costs, whilst capital expenditure - such as insulation - is usually competing with strict budget limitations. This has resulted in absurd wastes; for example, a survey of hospitals revealed that many energy-saving opportunities which would pay back in under a year were not being pursued because of restrictions on capital expenditure.[46] Greater financial independence for public sector activities, as promoted during the 1980s, might well ease this problem where it does not conflict with other objectives. Where there are clear reasons for centralized budgets, the controlling agencies would need either to make special allowances for efficiency programmes, or manage them centrally. The scale of operations should enable especially attractive deals with energy service companies.

A central approach could also (and in some cases does) apply to large companies with many outlets. In general, however, the commercial sector is probably the most obvious target for the activities of energy service companies or utility-sponsored programmes, as discussed in Volume 1, section 4.5. Legislation affecting these activities and related factors (eg. electricity buy-back rates) would be the main issue and there is probably a relatively small direct role for legislation in the commercial service sector, though building standards could be applied to business premises as for domestic housing.

Industry. Industry is perhaps the sector with the most scope for price-based measures and the least for other approaches. The energy-intensive industries are relatively aware of energy costs and opportunities for savings in their processes, and government attempts to set standards in manufacturing processes would incur great risks of bureaucratic misjudgment. This is less true when energy is an incidental cost, a few per cent at most of total turnover. The culture of 'energy management' in UK industry has never been strong, and has grown much weaker since 1986: the attitude of industry towards incidental costs often has more in common with the 'don't know and don't care' behaviour of

[46] J.Chesshire, 'An Energy-Efficient Future: a Strategy for the UK', *Energy Policy*, October 1986.

some commercial and domestic consumers than the concern directed at energy-intensive processes. In addition to heating and lighting, this means that the large potential savings from more efficient electric motors are likely to go unrealized. The range of motor size and application is so wide, and poor performance so often tied to poor maintenance, that standards would be extremely difficult to develop or enforce. Probably the only practical specific approach would be targeted information campaigns.

Energy price increases would obviously encourage efficiency, and this would be one of the main mechanisms for encouraging a structural shift towards less energy-intensive industries. Industrial price rises would not incur the same social problems as for domestic prices, but they would create the dislocations associated with any industrial shift, and raise strong opposition from the energy intensive industries.

Transport sector. Transport is one of the most complex areas for policy analysis - and projections. Traffic forecasts in the 1980s, when energy use grew at 3-4% annually, systematically underestimated growth. Transport energy demand exceeded that of industry for the first time in 1986[47], and if the refinery losses incurred in producing transport fuels are included, transport accounts for over 70% of oil use. Traffic congestion in south-east England, especially, is severe and during the 1980s became a subject of major political sensitivity.

The Department of Transport forecasts project traffic volume growing by 80-140% by the year 2025.[48] In terms of recent experience these projections are conservative. From the opposite perspective, it is hard to believe that even the lower bounds will in fact occur; there must be a limit to how much time people want to spend in their vehicles. In 1990 the government announced a £12bn road scheme to try to alleviate congestion, but this has met with scepticism (as well as local opposition) because of the growing conviction that the problem is simply too many cars in too small a region, and that more roads may do little more than move congestion from one point to another. The pressures to limit growth

[47] Department of Transport, *Transport Statistics Great Britain 1977-87*, HMSO, London, 1989; M. Fergusen et al, *Atmospheric Emissions from the Use of Transport in the United Kingdom (Vol.1)*, World Wide Fund for Nature/Earth Resources Research, London, 1989.
[48] Department of Transport, *National Road Traffic Forecasts (Great Britain) 1989*, HMSO, London, 1989.

in urban traffic especially, rather than to try and accommodate it, is growing rapidly, and environmental concerns will be a minor component of this. The measures available are well known, and include: charging for the use of roads, or access to city areas; encouraging more people per car (eg. barring single passenger vehicles from some lanes); restricting parking; car pooling schemes; and rationing of vehicle use or access to given areas. All of these have been tried elsewhere, with mixed success. Some measures are likely in the UK during the 1990s. (A pilot road pricing scheme is due to be introduced in Cambridge in the early 1990s.)

One special feature in the UK is that of 'company cars'. Tax relief on cars given to employees by companies was originally conceived for those who needed a car in the course of work. It was extended as a perk to senior management during pay restraint in the 1970s, and by the mid-1980s more than half of all new cars in the UK were being sold as company cars. The car industry is largely geared to the company market, which associates status with style and engine power. Mileage allowances can also encourage employees to use their car even when they would prefer other transport. Revisions since the mid-1980s have moved to reduce this perverse incentive. Further steps would be to reflect more of the full cost of transport - including capital expenditures on roads and other factors - in the variable cost of driving (eg. through increased tax on petrol) rather than its partial inclusion in the fixed licence fee.

These and other measures could be unpopular, and will at best take time. The obvious surrogate is to subsidise alternatives, principally public transport. Though large subsidies for rail and cycle schemes have been anathema to the Conservative government, the political opposition would be much less deeply rooted than to a massive petroleum tax. Support for developing an advanced rail network, which many argue will be important for UK business in the Single European Market, would also help limit short-haul flights.

The greenhouse effect spotlights two other road issues, namely vehicle efficiency and alternative transport fuels. Currently there are no particular incentives to realize the various opportunities for efficiency discussed in Chapter 2, indeed since 1986 efficiency has dropped from the list of items considered by the industry as 'selling points'. To promote efficiency in the absence of very large petrol price increases - and road pricing of course would not help - will require vehicle standards, such as the CAFE programme in the US (see US study), or explicit tax incentives. Tax discrimination against cars in general would be bitterly opposed by the car lobby but a revenue neutral 'guzzler to sipper' transfer on the capital cost - making efficient cars cheaper and inefficient ones more expensive - could be more acceptable and equally effective.

With the large UK natural gas resources, natural gas cars (see Chapter 2) are also a possibility for the UK, and similar measures could be used to promote them, concentrating first on fleet vehicles. Electric cars are attracting more attention; they might not reduce carbon emissions given the current generating mix (as noted in Chapter 2, comparisons are still uncertain), but would if associated with a large expansion of gas or non-fossil power generation.

Supply-side policy options

Until the 1980s, UK energy was managed by separate national corporations charged with meeting demands for their product as efficiently as possible. There was no incentive to stimulate efficiency in end use, or to provide other services (such as direct heat from power stations). In practice, backed by government finance, the companies pursued very large-scale investments to maximise supply-side efficiency and company size.

A major feature of the 1980s was privatization of these national corporations, and by 1991 only coal remained under government ownership. This has changed company objectives and behaviour, for example by reducing the timescales of planning and shifting interest towards smaller, cheaper and less financially risky investments. Privatized utilities have however retained substantial monopoly power and the government has adopted price regulation based on a simple 'RPI-X+Y' formulation - prices follow the Retail Price Index (RPI), minus a fixed 'X' percentage annually to encourage unit cost reductions, plus a production cost factor 'Y'.[49]

For electricity, this pricing formula allows distribution companies to pass electricity purchase costs on to consumers, but does not allow for any conservation expenditure. Thus, although the costs of the distribution companies are almost entirely fixed, they raise nearly all their revenue from electricity sales, creating a strong pressure to promote sales to the maximum extent possible. Distribution companies have the most contact with customers and are well placed to promote, or to discourage,

[49] See for example T.G.Weyman-Jones, 'RPI-X price cap regulation: the price controls used in UK electricity', *Utilities Policy*, Vol.1 No.1, October 1990.

improved efficiency. Unless reformed, the arrangement adopted under electricity privatization will create a major obstacle to end-use efficiency gains.

Many possible pricing regulations for such utilities have been suggested, but few have considered this aspect, or given further thought to the possibilities for promoting investment in conservation in the UK. Legislation which genuinely established a system in which energy conservation is treated on the same financial basis as supply would be of revolutionary significance for UK energy. As discussed in Volume 1, section 4.6, a system to achieve this completely is probably impossible, especially for electricity because of the institutional division between generators and distributors. But revision of the pricing formula could at least make distributors less averse to conservation, and allow related measures which directly promote efficiency. To date, neither industry, reflecting a culture of large-scale engineering and sales growth, nor government, have shown any enthusiasm for such an orientation.[50] But such changes could make a large impact. The regulatory formulae and contracts established for electricity privatization all expire on 31st March 1993; a great deal will hinge on the nature of regulation which replaces it.

The area in which government supply-side policy could most clearly affect emissions is in fuel switching. Special taxes, investment support, and direct intervention all affect the relative standing and expansion of the different fuels. Price and regulatory measures can affect the end-use mix of fuels, but the main focus for more explicit intervention is bound to be in electricity production.

UK electricity policy over the last decade and more has had the twin planks of support for nuclear power and protection of the coal industry against imports. In the mêlée of privatization these twin aims survived in the form of a government-negotiated contract for the use of British coal, and a specified quota of 'non-fossil' power. This quota was intended as a guarantee on nuclear expansion; a separate renewable energy tranche (set at 600MW by the year 2000) was created later. With the collapse of

---

[50] Attempts to amend electricity privatisation legislation to force the privatised companies to adopt balanced supply/demand investment (a form of 'least cost planning') measures were rejected by the government on the grounds that they were unworkable, but it was made plain that the government was reluctant to consider such measures.

the nuclear programme, the non-fossil quota will still be employed to ensure a market for the output of remaining nuclear stations, operated by a public company.

As discussed in Chapter 3, natural gas in advanced gas turbine systems can provide low-cost power with about half the CO_2 emissions of coal steam plant. With low capital costs as well, they are likely to figure prominently in the more commercial generating market of the 1990s. An EC regulation preventing gas generation, designed to preserve gas as a 'premium fuel', has been withdrawn in the light of resource developments.

The government and industry have expressed hopes for nuclear expansion, from 'about 1994' - when the first round of licences expire, the uncertainties of privatization have died down, and capacity shortages are expected to loom. In lieu of environmental taxes some government support for non-fossil sources can be justified, depending upon assessments of the environmental and other risks of nuclear power itself. However, the objections of the City to nuclear power were not just to overall costs, but to the enormous financial risk revealed by the nuclear experience in the UK. Given this experience it is improbable that the privatized industry will invest in nuclear power without government guarantees against capital and fuel-processing cost overruns, decommissioning costs, and accident insurance. Any further nuclear plants would almost certainly have to join the existing ones in the public sector, where such guarantees are implicit and less visible. Yet when such effort has been devoted to privatizing the system, with the declared aim of ensuring competitive generation, this would be politically very difficult even if public distrust of nuclear technology dissipated - which it shows little sign of doing.

With privatization forcing full commercial assessment of nuclear power, a revival seems implausible until certain criteria are met: a rise in fossil fuel prices (eg. due to a carbon tax); an end to reprocessing of fuel (which has been the main source both of nuclear fuel cost escalation and of radiation scares in the UK); development of a broadly accepted method of handling waste; and, probably, successful development and demonstration of modular, 'passively safe' reactors. This implies a very long time span, and there is little evidence that the industry is thinking along these lines. Despite continued pronouncements of official support, nuclear expansion is probably a closed chapter for a long time. Any additional nuclear-generated electricity will probably come from France. If there is a genuinely open European electricity market, this will be hard to resist, but it could be a controversial issue. There could be a limit to how much the UK would be willing to rely on this and, possibly, a limit to the willingness of the French public to bear the responsibility, especially if there were an accident. The implications of the Single European Market in 1992 in this context remain unclear.

All this brings traditionally 'alternative' sources to the fore as the main non-fossil option, at least for domestic production. As noted earlier, renewable sources might make a large contribution depending upon siting constraints and technical developments, and there were widespread hopes that the twin reforms of 1990 - reform of the business rates system (which made independent generation financially non-viable), and electricity privatization - would give renewables their chance. In the event, privatization has not proved favourable: the price offered to new generators is low, because of the capital written off on existing plants and because of the provisions for protecting coal and nuclear; the high rate of return demanded by private financiers is unfavourable to capital-intensive sources; the market remains dominated by two big, centralized generating companies; and contracts for the non-fossil quotas have been set to a maximum of eight years by EC intervention, a period much too short to recoup costs. The 600MW renewables quota was greatly over-subscribed soon after announcement, but as the terms became clear the enthusiasm dissipated.[51]

The non-fossil quotas are an implicit subsidy by a government which recognizes the need for them, but which cannot bear to make them explicit. Explicit subsidies - if not prevented by EC intervention - combined with machine certification to prevent profiteering, would probably be a more effective tool. If applied together with more flexible variations of current arrangements for protecting existing nuclear and coal markets, which would enable renewables to sell into the system whenever power is available, a rapid growth of the market-based renewable sources could be possible.

---

[51] 'The Working Group do not believe that privatisation will work to the unmixed benefit of renewable resource development. New institutional and financial factors would seem positively to harm the prospects ..' (M.Laughton, ed, *Renewable Energy Sources*, Watt Committee/Elsevier, London, 1990, p.9)

The full potential for renewable sources cannot be realized from private efforts, however. Geothermal HDR, offshore wind and wave all require large-scale development programmes, which given the large uncertainties and timescales will not be borne by private industry alone. In 1990, the budget for all renewable energy R&D was around £18m, and this was projected to decrease as renewables are either commercialized, or dropped as unpromising.[52] Adequate development and demonstration of these 'big unknown' technologies, however, might require a several-fold increase in the renewable energy research budget, though the levels may still be small in comparison with the potential benefits, and in comparison with nuclear spending: about £90m/yr will be saved from the run-down of Fast Breeder Reactor research, while the total losses from completing and operating the Sizewell B reactor may total several billion pounds.[53]

Politically the most difficult source is large-scale tidal power. No combination of fossil fuel taxes and incentives could make the largest schemes commercially attractive because the timescales are too long and the schemes too large for private finance. As noted above there are also environmental concerns. Yet the benefits, in terms of providing large volumes of low-cost, pollution-free power for many decades, could be very high. Treated as a long-term development of national infrastructure, the large tidal schemes would be hard to beat, and they could be an essential component of attempts to reduce long-run CO_2 emissions; but as a commercial decision for short-term payback they are not viable. Major government commitment would be required, but as yet there is no sign of a government with the philosophy and courage required to take such a decision.

5.5 Political themes

Much is known about energy use in the UK. The 1979 study *A Low Energy Strategy for the UK*[54] prompted further analysis, resulting in extensive surveys and projections by the Department of Energy's Energy Efficiency Office of how energy is used, data which has in turn been

[52] Department of Energy, *Renewable Energy in the UK - The Way Forward*, op cit.
[53] For discussion see House of Commons Energy Committee, *The Costs of Nuclear Power*, Volume 1, 1990 (p.xv and p.xxxv).
[54] G.Leach, *A Low Energy Strategy for the United Kingdom*, Science Reviews Limited, London, 1979.

applied in several independent studies of the opportunities for energy saving (including this one). However, such knowledge has had little or no impact on policies. Explicit policies aimed at improving energy efficiency have amounted to some insulation grants (withdrawn in the mid-1980s, with some reinstated in 1990), some capital grants for encouraging industry to invest in new equipment, and sporadic information and advertizing campaigns. Even after the 1990 revisions, building standards are amongst the lowest in northern Europe, and the UK has consistently opposed EC attempts to develop appliance efficiency standards. The rapid improvement in the energy/GDP ratio from the mid-1970s was largely a consequence of the collapse of heavy industry, followed by industrial growth with newer equipment, combined with the general responses to the oil price shocks. The role of explicit efficiency policies may have been marginal.

The prime reason for this has been the deep faith of the British government in the desirability of 'free' markets and a consequent reluctance to pass legislation interfering with company or consumer activities. In 1982, the Department of Energy defined its role as:

> To remove market distortions where possible or otherwise seek to ensure that the energy market operates as nearly as possible as a free market.[55]

In assessing the implications of this a great deal hinges on what is considered as a 'market distortion'. The main obstacle to energy efficiency discussed above consists of market failures in the economic sense that they result in a non-optimum use of resources - but they reflect the natural consequence of consumer attitudes and institutions compared with those of producers, and highly interventionist measures would be required to correct this. *Making* the market work may be compatible with many of the measures required; *letting* the market work certainly is not.[56] In practice the government has interpreted its objective in the laissez-faire sense of non-intervention, especially on the demand side. If the UK is to limit emissions substantially, at least this interpretation will have to be reversed. This would be a major change, and much at odds with the traditional perception of the proper business of a free market

---

[55] Department of Energy, *Energy Projections* 1982, Evidence to the Sizewell B Public Inquiry, 1982.
[56] See Volume 1, sections 3.8 and 4.8, for further discussion of the economic principles involved.

government - though in response to environmental concerns, some have argued that it is quite compatible.[57]

In a speech to the Royal Society in 1988, and subsequently, Mrs Thatcher placed her stamp firmly upon concerns about 'humanity's massive experiment with the system of this planet itself' resulting from greenhouse gas emissions.[58] The UK Meteorological Office led the IPCC Science Working Group, drawing upon the internationally-recognized UK expertise in climate analysis, which endorsed concerns with what to many was unexpected firmness and clarity.

The result has been fundamental schizophrenia in UK attitudes. In declarations, and in the language of general principle, the UK has been firmly behind action. At the level of domestic policy, no significant steps have been taken, and even the much-heralded 1990 White Paper on the Environment (see box, p.211), despite devoting a chapter to global warming, did not put forward specific, substantive policy proposals. Perhaps the clearest sign of the UK's schizophrenia has been the UK's CO_2 target, presented as part of Mrs Thatcher's attempts to lead the world on the issue while in reality being the weakest of all targets set by European countries, and the only one made conditional on action in other countries.

At the time of writing the position of Prime Minister John Major is unclear, but it would not be easy to back down on previous statements given the concern of UK scientists and the Department of the Environment. Quite how long such inconsistency can be maintained is a matter of conjecture, but it seems clear that if the UK is to be at the forefront of the international effort, and attain anything remotely approaching the 2000B and 2030B scenarios, there would have to be radical departures in energy policy. At present there seem few clear reasons for expecting this.

---

[57] 'Free market does not mean "free for all". It never has. It is an essential part of the free market philosophy that regulation by government is necessary to secure the public interest in environmental protection.' Nicholas Ridley, *Policies Against Pollution: the Conservative Record - and Principles*, Policy Studies No.107, Centre for Policy Studies, London, 1989.

[58] Speech to the Royal Society, London, 27 September 1988. A Parliamentary Report also echoed strong concerns, concluding that 'action does need to be taken now' (House of Commons Select Committee on Energy, 'Energy Policy Implications of the Greenhouse Effect', HMSO, London, July 1989).

The Labour opposition may be more ready to intervene to improve energy efficiency, but is also more committed to protecting the coal industry.[59] Although its political strength has been broken since the 1984 strike, the coal industry still arouses strong emotions. Rapid decline would be painful, and perhaps costly given the large investments made in new pit facilities. However the threats to UK coal come not just from greenhouse pressures but from low-cost, low-sulphur imports; the sustainable level of deep-mined production if faced with unrestricted coal imports and gas has been estimated at barely half the current (1990) levels of around 80Mt/yr. A strategy focused on steady abatement and restricted imports might be no worse for UK coal than the current outlook. Indeed, efficiency improvements which limited electricity growth could deter the growth of gas-fired generation, and give more time for R&D on more efficient coal technologies to bear fruit. The government was reluctant to support such R&D during the 1980s,[60] but this may be reversed.

Irrespective of all this, any government which wanted to embark on strong abatement policies would have to overcome departmental reluctance with strong political commitment and sophistication, which has not yet been demonstrated. For abatement would raise major questions of institutions as well as ideology. Whitehall departments, like most civil services are deeply divided by discipline. The Department of Energy has traditionally seen its primary role as ensuring energy security and supporting the UK energy industries, and seems unlikely ever to find real enthusiasm for measures aimed directly at reducing their markets. The Department of Transport's main vision is the promotion of a national transport network which can meet all demands for personal and industrial

---

[59] The Labour Party 1990 policy statement included a commitment to 'change building regulations so that all new homes meet the highest insulation standards and help existing homes to meet the same standards. We will introduce energy labelling of appliances ... energy utilities will be required to promote and invest in energy saving ... Labour will act to secure the long-term future of the coal industry and reverse the current, unnecessary growth in coal imports ... ' (Labour Party, Looking to the Future, The Labour Party, London, 1990).

[60] 'This aspect of coal-based energy [R&D] appears to have been placed in a no-win situation: if it could obtain substantial industrial contributions the Department would not fund it because it would be undertaken anyway, whereas if it cannot obtain significant industrial contributions the Department will not put any money in' (House of Commons Energy Committee, The Department of Energy's Spending Plans, 1990-91, HMSO, London, 1990, p.vii).

mobility, and among the multi-billion pound road schemes is unlikely to focus on cycle lanes and public transport subsidies. The Department of Environment has traditionally had no business in either. Greenhouse gas emissions seem unlikely to be tackled seriously as long as this situation persists. In addition, it is apparent that other institutions are inappropriate for a major shift in policy; new bodies to match or replace the now bereft UK Atomic Energy Authority, but focused upon efficiency (including heat supplies) and renewable energy would be required.[61]

Responsibility does not just lie with governments, however. Consumer behaviour is a major source of waste. In limiting emissions, comfortable habits may not need to change but careless ones will. In spite of 'green warnings' little has changed, and global warming is perceived as an issue for governments, but not as something which individuals can do anything about. NGOs and the media will have a major part to play in changing this, though it will also be affected by perceptions of how seriously governments take the problem.

The historic role of environmental NGOs in the UK has been to criticize the government of the day. If there is a major change in government attitudes, then lobbying on behalf of government to facilitate unpopular decisions - such as carbon taxes or measures to tackle transport growth - could become just as important. That is a change which may not come easily. Also, an ambivalent or flatly contrary public attitude to renewable energy sources in practice - as opposed to the theoretical support - could greatly inhibit their development, since many rely on deployment at a large number of small scale sites.

5.6 An EC perspective

How do these various observations stand in the context of the European Community? As noted, the UK is uniquely well-endowed with energy resources within the Community, and has put a great deal of investment into infrastructure for exploiting those resources. Consequently the UK will be more reluctant than many EC countries to pursue measures to reduce demand, but is in a better position regarding fuel-switching measures, particularly if the renewable resources begin to be tapped or if the nuclear option is somehow revived. With its excess nuclear

[61] This is proposed for example, in a broader discussion of such institutional issues in D.Toke, *Green Energy - a non-nuclear response to the greenhouse effect*, Merlin Press, London, 1990.

capacity, the attitude of France (and to a lesser extent Belgium) is likely to be similar, though for different reasons.

A striking feature of the EC lineup is that the countries which have expressed the most concern about environmental matters - the Netherlands, Germany and Denmark - seem amongst the worst placed technically to limit CO_2 emissions, with relatively high efficiency already and relatively poor low-carbon resources. But traditionally these countries are also more comfortable with interventionist measures: Denmark, particularly, is already well embarked upon the road of efficiency in housing and elsewhere, use of natural gas, CHP, and exploitation of its renewable resource base. The Southern European countries are similarly heavily dependent upon imports, but most have larger non-fossil resources including potential for various forms of solar energy. There is therefore a potential for a long-run division in terms of policy priorities, with the north-west European countries inclining towards price-based and other measures to promote fuel switching, and the north-east focusing more upon microeconomic measures for improving end-use efficiency and supporting renewables. The southern European countries may occupy an ambiguous middle ground.

Calls for 'everything' may find little sympathy. Carbon taxes will exacerbate problems of the German coal industry, especially, in its attempts to defend itself against imports of French nuclear electricity and Soviet gas. Some governments might also oppose them on grounds of distributional impact. A major interventionist drive to limit electricity consumption could seriously hinder French attempts to recover the costs of, and ultimately reap the potential profits from, its immense nuclear commitment. Such divisions could become still deeper and more complex if the EC membership widens, particularly if the highly inefficient eastern European countries join.

Perhaps in view of these difficulties the Eurepean Commission has shown interest in more disaggregated incentives, such as tradeable emission permits. However, any national policy measures developed in response to such incentives would be set against the patchwork of the Single European Market. An enduring theme could be debate over the validity of national policy measures, such as efficiency standards and support for renewable energy, which could impinge upon free trading. It is clear that some kinds of unilateral standards will be possible,[62] but where the line is drawn is very much open to question.[63]

Irrespective of how these conflicts are resolved, the Commission could play a major role in responding to the greenhouse effect. Commission investigations in the field of electricity efficiency have had an impact and may yet lead at least to mandatory labelling of appliances throughout Europe. Such activities may well be extended into other areas.[64] EC support for renewable energy development is also stronger than many national governments, though far greater resources still flow into nuclear (especially fusion) programmes. Funding of R&D is not the only arena for EC action on renewables: the future of biomass energy and forestry will be inextricably bound up with policy towards surplus EC agricultural land. Overall the EC seems likely to act as a spur for most countries, though it may retard the 'leaders'. With Qualified Majority voting on many environmental issues it will be difficult for countries to block measures which carry an environmental label, and the dynamics of the European process are such that there is likely to be no shortage of proposals brought forward. The response of the whole may well be greater than would be the sum of the parts if separated.

5.7 International aspects

The impacts of climate change on the UK and other EC countries are highly uncertain. Popular reactions are mixed, and strongly correlated with those on other environmental attitudes. Professional climatologists for the most part, acknowledge the possibility of gains but are much more concerned about the possible costs, especially if the change is rapid.

---

[62] An EC test-case ruling of 1987 allowed Denmark to insist upon returnable bottle on environmental grounds. There were moves to take the Netherlands to the Europear court over unilateral incentives for cars with catalytic convertors, but the case was no pursued and eventually resulted in an agreement to require these units throughou Europe - something of a 'highest denominator' solution to the conflict.

[63] The implications of the Single European Act for environmental policy are examine in detail in N.Haigh and D.Baldock, *Environmental Policy and 1992*, Institute fo European Environmental Policy, London, 1989. A survey of the possible implication for the energy industries, and energy-related policy, is presented in Royal Institute o International Affairs/Science Policy Research Unit, *'A Single European Market i Energy'*, RIIA, London, 1989.

[64] European Commission, 'Proposal for a Council Decision Concerning Promotior of Energy Efficiency', COM(90)365 Final, 1990.

At international negotiations on limiting CFCs, the EC negotiated on behalf of member countries, after members agreed on a common position. This is far from easy with the greenhouse effect, but the leverage of member countries is greatly increased if they negotiate as a block. As a major net importer of fossil fuels, especially oil, and beset by the demands of an increasingly environmentally-sensitive public, the prospect of alleviating fossil fuel use is one the Community as a whole is likely to welcome despite the regional political difficulties it could cause. There is a good chance of the EC being at the forefront of international negotiations on limiting emissions.

These same factors mean that an international agreement may not be an important factor in the short-term response. The pressures for action on energy efficiency, expansion of gas use, etc, do not just arise from greenhouse concerns. Many measures, essentially cost-effective in their own right, may be taken irrespective of a global agreement. Despite having lower per-capita and per-GDP emissions than the US or USSR, the EC may be more willing than they to act irrespective of broader international developments.

5.8 Conclusions

After two decades of broadly stable CO_2 emissions, UK emissions may start to rise slowly in the absence of measures to counteract this. The most striking and cost-effective options for limiting emissions lie in improving the efficiency of both heating and appliances in buildings, but there are numerous other technical possibilities, including supply-side expansion of gas and renewables. The policies needed to realize these potentials span a wide range. They include:

* removal of existing legislative distortions (including VAT on conservation materials but not fuels, the form of utility price regulation, and company car allowances)

* energy price-based measures (notably an energy/carbon tax and additional road and petrol pricing)

* measures aimed at the consumer to help balance supply and demand-side investments (including grants, standards, and efficiency-dependent taxes/rebates on products)

* measures aimed at suppliers to promote investment in efficiency and low or non-carbon sources (eg. 'Least Cost Planning', support for market-ready renewable sources)

* government funding for tidal power and support for the development of the major undeveloped renewable sources of geothermal HDR and offshore wind and wave.

The scenarios developed suggest that a strong combination of such measures might reduce national CO_2 emissions at a rate averaging a little over 1%/yr, perhaps reaching levels half those of the late 1980s over a forty-year period, even on the basis of currently available technologies.

There is much to suggest that the costs incurred would be primarily political rather than economic. Achieving reductions of this magnitude would require extensive government intervention using many novel policy instruments, both of general energy/carbon taxes, and more focused micro-economic changes. It would imply rapidly declining markets for the oil and especially coal industries, which would have to diversify as broader energy service companies to avoid serious and painful contraction. The reductions could probably not be achieved without a concurrent change in consumer attitudes and the focus of NGO activities, acting more in concert with such government policies.

All this would imply major departures from traditional approaches to energy policy, and indeed from the broader and firmly established distrust of intervention especially in consumer markets. Reluctance would be reinforced by the impact on the UK's energy industries. Although perhaps not impossible, given Mrs Thatcher's strong expressions of concern and the role of the UK as leader of the IPCC science working group, combined with the relatively strong and centralized nature of the UK political process, the lower emission scenarios outlined can hardly be regarded as likely.

Other European countries share some of these themes, but many are less averse to intervention. The priorities and appropriate mechanisms may differ substantially between member countries, and deep divisions may develop concerning the extent and form of responses. Despite this, the EC is likely to play a major and forward role in policy development and in international negotiations if a common position can be developed.

Chapter 6 The Greenhouse Effect in the US: the Legacy of Energy Abundance

Steve Rayner
Deputy Director, Global Environmental Studies Center
Oak Ridge National Laboratory,Tennesse, US

Michael Grubb provided careful editorial advice and generous encouragement throughout the preparation of this paper. Nicola Steen of the RIIA and Mariann Huskey of ORNL provided invaluable technical help. Jae Edmonds, Bill Fulkerson, and Eric Hirst helped polish the argument with extensive reviews. The research on which this chapter is based was performed by a number of colleagues in the Energy Division at ORNL who have been generous in sharing their work with me and allowing me to plunder it shamelessly in assembling this chapter. Section 1 draws heavily on the labours of Bill Fulkerson and Bud Perry. Section 2 is built from components wrought principally by Ed Hillsman, Paul Leiby and John Reed for the US DOE Report to the Congress of the US. on which we collaborated, (A Compendium of Options for Government Policy to Encourage Private Sector Responses to Potential Climate Change, DOE/EH0102-0103, Washington DC, 1989). I thank them all. Section 3 reflects only my own views, which should not be construed as those of ORNL, Martin Marietta Energy Systems, Inc. or the US Department of Energy.

The Greenhouse Effect in the US: the Legacy of Energy Abundance

Like Caesar's Gaul, this study is divided into three parts. The first considers the present state of the US energy system, and presents illustrative scenarios which encompass a wide range of technical possibilities for the US energy sector. It is concluded that, although the prospects for CO_2 emissions reduction through energy efficiency are promising, socially acceptable alternatives to fossil energy are not sufficiently mature to provide US primary energy needs.

The second section considers the technical, institutional, and economic constraints for efficiency and fuel switching in the four major energy conversion sectors of the United States; electric utilities, transportation, manufacturing, and residential and commercial uses. Various opportunities exist for institutional and regulatory changes that could enhance the prospects for greenhouse gas reductions. However, major obstacles are raised by the complexity of decisionmaking procedures (especially in transport) and institutional inertia (especially in manufacturing and construction).

The final section examines the US political context and the prospects for greenhouse gas reduction policies throughout the energy system. The obstacles noted above are exacerbated by the confrontational nature of the global environmental debate in the US, occurring in an open political system that empowers dissenters to impede policy developments that may disadvantage them.

In the light of this, it is concluded that a realistic US contribution to global greenhouse gas reduction would consist of four elements:

* Aggressively pursue energy efficiency throughout all sectors

* Pursue an ambitious programme of energy R&D to provide practical alternatives to fossil fuels

* Develop an extensive technology transfer programme (perhaps linked to emissions permit trading) to save developing countries from reliance on fossil fuels in their economic development

* As new technologies are implemented in developing countries they should become economically more attractive in the US market to replace existing US fossil fuel infrastructure over the long term.

Many strategies for abatement aim to tackle the large present emitters of greenhouse gases first. The approach suggested here is directed initially at the areas of large growth in emissions (developing countries) and at relatively low-cost measures (energy efficiency, and development of renewable energy capacities of developing countries) rather than the very high costs of rapidly replacing existing US fossil fuel capacity.

6.1 The state of the US energy system

US energy flows and resources

The US energy system is a huge enterprise. Annual energy expenditures were about 8% of the US gross national product (GNP) in 1987, or about $376 billion; they were as high as 13.5% of GNP in 1980 and as low as 7.6% in 1972. Figure 6.1 illustrates energy flows in the United States for 1989.

A major portion of the energy supply is provided by large, costly physical facilities (eg. electric power plants and oil refineries) that are operated for decades. Many of these facilities are managed by large organizations which generally change slowly. Some end-use technologies (eg. automobiles) may change more rapidly but most (eg. buildings and industrial plants) have a long lifetime. Despite this, and despite being a net importer of energy, the US energy system has proved resilient over the past decade and a half in the face of the oil price shocks; in particular, the speed and extent of the adjustments in energy end-use patterns were largely unanticipated. For example, few would have predicted in 1974 that the United States would be using about the same amount of primary energy in 1987 as it did in 1973, although the economy grew 39% in real terms during that period.

The adjustments were institutional and technical. Significant institutional changes included: deregulation of oil and gas markets; development of the Strategic Petroleum Reserve (containing 550 million barrels by mid-1990); adoption of various efficiency standards, and utility involvement in energy efficiency. Energy research and development (R&D) was institutionalized with the formation of the Electric Power Research Institute (EPRI), the Gas Research Institute (GRI), and the Federal Energy Research and Development Administration, which later became the Department of Energy (DOE). Regulations, particularly concerning safety and the environment, were made more stringent. Fuel efficiency improved throughout the system, which also became more adept at fuel switching.

These and other adjustments in the energy system were not made easily, inexpensively, or smoothly. The oil price shocks caused or exacerbated two recessions and contributed to regional economic depressions. Additionally, the energy problems of the country probably worsened the impacts of the major restructuring that is occurring in US industry.

Figure 6.1 US total energy flow 1989 (Quadrillion Btu)

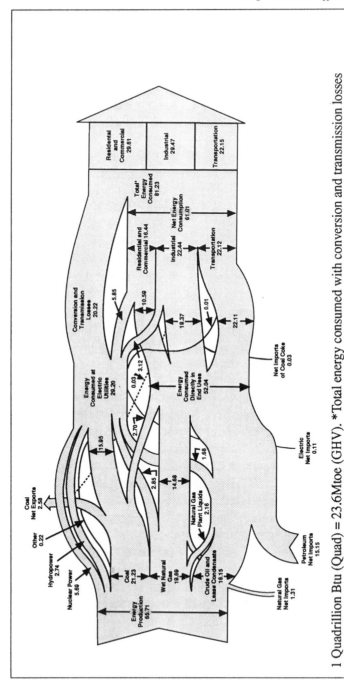

1 Quadrillion Btu (Quad) = 23.6Mtoe (GHV). *Total energy consumed with conversion and transmission losses allocated to end-use sectors in proportion to the sectors' use of electricity.

Source: US Department of Energy, *Annual Energy Review 1989*, DOE, Washington DC, 1990.

Figure 6.2 US energy consumption and CO2 emissions 1949-89

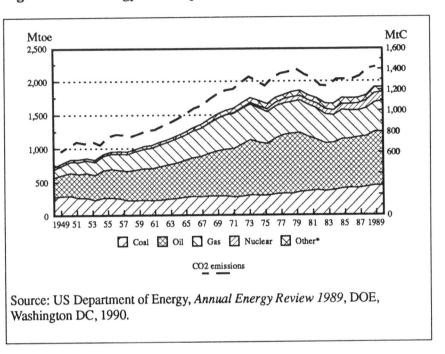

Source: US Department of Energy, *Annual Energy Review 1989*, DOE, Washington DC, 1990.

The components of the energy system have changed steadily. As illustrated in Figure 6.2, dominance of fossil fuels has declined a little (from 96% in 1973 to 89% in 1987) primarily because of the growth of nuclear energy to 6% of the total (input equivalent). Oil continues to play a major role in the US energy system, although not quite as much as 14 years earlier (43% compared with 47%). Indigenous US resources of coal (Figure 6.3) are enormous and should be sufficient to last much longer than 50 years, even with substantially increasing demand. However, there may be some regional shifts in coal supplies as clean air legislation forces further reductions in SO_x and NO_x emissions from power generation in Ohio, Indiana, Pennsylvania, Illinois, and Kentucky, which currently rely on high-sulphur indigenous coal. Oil and gas resources, though substantial, are more limited and the US has become steadily more dependent upon imports. Given the large land area of the US, its potential for renewable resources is great, but, so far, non-fossil sources other than hydro and wood (which together provide a little more energy than nuclear power) do not yet feature significantly.

Figure 6.3 US fuel reserves/consumption ratios 1987

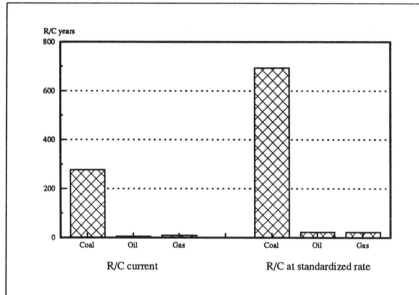

R/C current = ratio of proven reserves to current consumption of fuel (years)
R/C at standardized rate = ratio of proven reserves to consumption at rate of
1kW/capita = 0.7toe/yr/capita

Source: *BP Statistical Review of World Energy*, BP, London, 1990.

Both in its resource base and its energy infrastructure, the US clearly
has depended and continues to depend on fossil fuels for its energy needs.
Combined with its high demand, the US contributes the largest share
(22%) to the world's annual CO_2 emissions which, at 5 tonnes of carbon
per person, is (following the demise of East Germany) the highest
per-capita level in the world.

Prospects and scenarios

How much energy will people consume? In what form? The fact is that
nobody knows. Detailed projections range from at least 1% to +2%/year
average change in US energy use over the next few decades. This range
is not merely a matter of large uncertainties about a host of factors that

will shape the future use of energy; it reflects philosophical differences about how the country ought to develop.

There has been a fundamental disagreement between those who expect energy demand to rise and are chiefly concerned with ensuring an adequate supply, and those who believe that it is both possible and advantageous to reduce the ratio of energy to GNP (E/GNP) far enough and fast enough to support continued economic growth with little or no increase in energy consumption, and perhaps even a decrease, for at least several decades. These widely different expectations for the future result from different assessments of future population trends, growth in GNP, mix of goods and services, changes in living and working patterns, energy prices, and especially the prospects for reducing the energy intensity of activities in all sectors of the economy. Improved energy efficiency is partly a matter of technical possibilities, partly of government policies (including tax policies and regulatory standards) and partly of market choices.

Market choices alone, as projected in 'business-as-usual' studies, do not select a least cost mix, but they do take up a substantial degree of improvement. Carlsmith et al calculate primary energy consumption for 2010 on the basis of (a) 'frozen efficiency' at present levels 2,730Mtoe(115.4 quads)[1] (b) 'where we are headed' at the current pace of efficiency improvements without changes in government policy or instrument in R&D (2,406Mtoe) and (c) 'cost-effective efficiency' where decisions about energy are determined by life-cycle economic considerations (2,079Mtoe).[2] The cost-effective efficiency scenario saves 326Mtoe compared to 'where we are heading', or twice that compared to a period of technological and structural stagnation.

Within this range there are substantial uncertainties, even over as little as a decade. However, the opportunities for policy-driven changes by 2000 are very limited. Given the technical, political and institutional inertia of the US energy system, as discussed throughout this chapter, great changes cannot be expected on this timescale. The US Department of Energy (DOE) projections for the International Energy Agency (IEA)

---

[1] Units in the text are converted from quads (quadrillion British thermal units) which are a common unit in US energy literature. 1 quad = 23.65Mtoe.

[2] R.S.Carlsmith, W.N.Chandler, J.E.McMahon, and D.J.Santini, *Energy Efficiency: How Far Can We Go?* ORNL/TM-11441, Oak Ridge National Laboratory, Oak Ridge, Tenn., 1990.

Figure 6.4 Scenarios for US energy consumption and CO_2 emissions 1988-2030

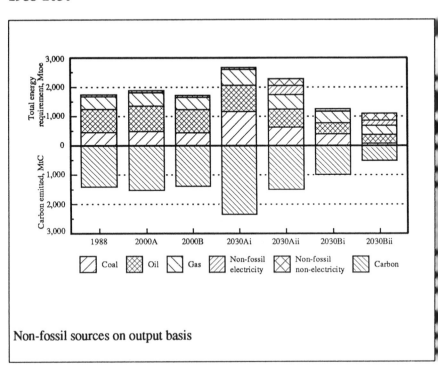

suggest US energy demand rising by about 13% over the decade 1990–2000, with coal rising faster than the average. Carbon emissions would rise proportionately. The best that could be expected of policies would be to prevent such growth. With the DOE projections taken as the business-as-usual scenario, the strong abatement scenario (2000B) shows CO_2 emissions a fraction below those of 1988 (Figure 6.4). Some analyses suggest that strong policies could deliver greater savings than illustrated in 2000B,[3] but these are not chosen for reasons discussed later in the text.

---

[3] William U.Chandler, Howard S.Geller, Marc R.Ledbetter, *Energy Efficiency: A New Agenda*, American Council for an Energy Efficient Economy, Washington, 1988.The high efficiency scenario developed for this study projected primary demand of 1,684Mtoe by 2000.

The uncertainties are much larger for the longer term. One major study is that of Edmonds and Reilly,[4] using an energy market equilibrium model for the world, with the United States modelled as one of nine disaggregated, interacting regions. The model establishes a detailed balance between energy demand and supply, the result depending on a large number of parameters characterizing supply and demand (eg. GNP, elasticities and technical-change indices). Each of the parameters is described by a range of values derived from different assumptions or sources. The base case is one run of the model using median values of all these parameters. In the base case, with the GNP growing at about 2.5%/yr, E/GNP declines at about 1.5%/yr, and primary energy use increases about 1%/year. This represents a reasonably central view of energy experts - insofar as any exists - as to future business-as-usual trends.

In contrast, Williams[5] concludes that technologies now available or in an advanced stage of development would permit roughly a fourfold reduction in E/GNP, and that such a reduction would be cost-effective at energy prices similar to those prevailing in the early to middle 1980s. Williams' analysis was not predicated on substantial lifestyle changes but did incorporate expected shifts in the composition of industrial output towards less energy-intensive products. The scenarios involved explicit technical assumptions for the energy intensiveness of specific activities, for example, miles per gallon for automobiles, kilowatt hours per lumen for lighting, and percentage efficiency gains in heavy industry. In his central scenario, with a GNP growth similar to that of the Edmonds-Reilly analysis, E/GNP declines at more than 3%/yr so that energy use decreases by about 1%/yr.

Fulkerson[6] summarized these studies, and analyzed cases with different supply mixes, including use of the Edmonds-Reilly (E-R) model, to explore trends extending to about 2050. The report presented scenarios based on the E-R base case, and the Williams high efficiency scenarios, for the years 2020 and 2040. These studies define a very broad

[4] J.Edmonds and J.Reilly, *The IEA/ORAU Long-Term Global Energy-CO$_2$ Model: Personal Computer Version A84PC*, ORNL/CDIC-16, CMP 002/PC, Oak Ridge National Laboratory, Oak Ridge, 1986.
[5] R.H.Williams, 'A Low Energy Future for the United States', *Energy*, Vol.12, Oct/Nov, 1987, p.929.
[6] W.Fulkerson et al, *Energy Technology R&D: What Could Make A Difference?* ORNL-6541/V1, Oak Ridge National Laboratory, Oak Ridge, 1989.

range of technically possible energy mixes and consequent carbon emissions. The 2030 scenarios in this chapter are drawn from this; interpolation of the baseline cases forms the 2030A scenarios, and the 2020 high-efficiency scenarios form the 2030B scenarios - achieving high efficiency, but ten years later than Williams' technical scenario. These are illustrated in Figure 6.4. The 2030Ai scenario is broadly comparable with the business-as-usual outlook of mainstream energy analysts, insofar any any consensus exists. The 2030B scenarios represent a very high degree of take-up of highly efficient technologies, with modest pressures from growth in the major energy-consuming activities.

Most of the technologies implied in 2030Bi are already available or in advanced development, and such an energy system would not necessarily be more costly than the 2030A scenarios; Williams and others argue that it would be cheaper. Far less technical confidence can be attached to the fuel switching scenarios. The principal non-fossil sources are projected to be biomass for liquid fuels (which if operated in a steady state gives no net carbon emissions), nuclear power, and hydro and other renewable electricity sources. In the Fulkerson fuel-switching scenarios for 2020, these contributions are projected to be respectively 473, 378 and 142Mtoe of primary energy on an input basis, or 236, 118, and 47Mtoe respectively on an output basis.[7] The estimates of biomass and other renewable sources assume the development of much more economic technologies. In all, Fulkerson finds that the non-fossil sources presently available to the US are just not good enough, including nuclear power; assessed as the only non-fossil source which could presently be mobilized in sufficient scale and reasonable cost to offset the growth of fossil fuels use. The nuclear contribution in the Fulkerson scenarios is assumed to be based on a second generation of reactors with passive safety features.

From this point of view, the US energy agenda is not adequate to meet the challenge of the greenhouse effect. A much greater effort is needed to develop and improve non-fossil sources and to improve the efficiency and economics of end-use technologies. Efficiency has the greatest potential to reduce the use of fossil fuels in the short to mid-term. Furthermore, the adoption of high-efficiency technology will provide

---

[7] The conversion efficiency of the biomass to liquids is taken to be 50%, and 33% is used as the average efficiency of displaced fossil power generation.

more time to develop the needed improved alternative sources. Achieving large reductions in carbon emissions requires a combination of much improved efficiency of fossil use and a greatly accelerated use of non-fossil sources. In the most extreme scenario (2030Bii) fossil carbon emissions are reduced to about one-third the 1987 value of 1.3GtC/yr. This optimistic estimate is based on the assumption that primary energy demand can be kept in the range of 1,420 to 2,129Mtoe and that non-fossil sources can supply 946 to 1,656Mtoe.

These scenarios focus on technical possibilities. They pay little, if any attention to the opportunities and constraints that institutions provide for the implementation of technological change. Also, technological scenarios tend to ignore the broader political and economic issues that shape their chances of realization. The remainder of this chapter examines these issues and proposes a strategy for the US energy sector to contribute to limiting global emissions of greenhouse gases.

6.2 Policy opportunities and constraints

The structure of energy demand in the US differs considerably from that in many other countries, as does the distribution of CO_2 emissions. As illustrated in Figure 6.5, transport and electricity production each account for about a third of US CO_2 emissions. The remainder consists of direct emissions from manufacturing (20%) and residential and commercial activities (13%); all sectors except transport are substantial electricity consumers. The following sections consider each sector in turn for the present composition of final demand and existing industrial processes. The intention is to identify current and short-term opportunities and constraints for change in each sector.

Change in the composition of final demand coupled with changes in the nature of materials and processes have the potential to exert a significance on future energy intensity.[8] However, there are significant political, institutional, and behavioural obstacles to implementing strategies to change the composition of demand. With few exceptions, US political culture prefers to leave demand for goods, services, and activities up to individuals and businesses, and does not consider public policies (or tax laws) explicitly formulated to influence demand to be legitimate. Thus, efforts to influence demand may require justification

---

[8] R.H.Williams and E.D.Larson, 'Materials, Affluence, and Industrial Energy Use', *Annual Review of Energy 1987*, Vol.12, 1988, pp.99–144.

Figure 6.5 Distribution of US CO₂ emissions by sector

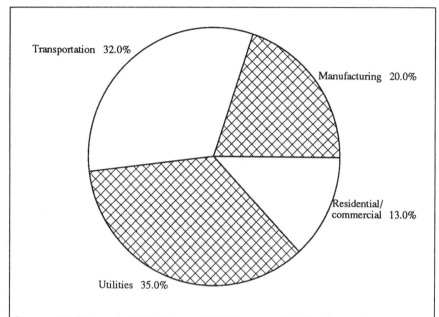

Source: J.A.Edmonds, W.B.Ashton, H.C.Chang and M.Steinburg, *A Preliminary Analysis of US CO₂ Reduction Potential from Energy Conservation and the Substitution of Natural Coal in the Period to 2010*, US Department of Energy, DOE/NBB-0085, Washington DC, 1989.

on other grounds. Some policies (such as waste reduction or land-use planning) would respond to public concern over solid waste disposal, housing costs, and traffic congestion. However, the US public does not yet appear to be concerned about other problems that would require reducing population growth or substituting leisure activities that require less energy as important parts of the solution.[9]

Because there is little public-sector experience of demand modification, it is likely that institutions would take some time to develop the expertise needed to be effective; during this time, their effectiveness

[9] E.L.Hillsman, G.Marland, and S.Rayner, 'Options for Technological Response to Climate Change', in M.S.MacCracken et al, *Energy and Climate Change*, Lewis Publishers, Chelsea, Mich., 1990.

probably would be offset, at least in part, by private-sector firms that have a stake in the activities to be discouraged (high-emissions materials, recreational travel). Hence each of the following sections adopts conservative assumptions about the prospects for rapid or early changes in the composition of demand.

Electricity generation

Most existing US generating plant burn coal. The continued role of coal as a fuel is demonstrated by the several billion dollars that have been invested in developing clean-coal technologies for the future. Given the abundance of this fuel we should expect that considerations of economics and national energy security will weigh heavily in favour of coal as the fuel of choice for meeting rising energy demands. Long-term trend analysis by the Department of Energy[10] projects a reference case in which electricity sales rise by 80% through 2010 on the assumption of recent economic growth rates eventually levelling off and that there are no major changes in environmental regulation. Electricity sales are expected to rise from 208Mtoe in 1987 to 343Mtoe in 2010. Coal used to generate electricity would become increasingly dominant, rising from 343Mtoe to 743Mtoe over the same period, consistent with, if not exceeding, the trends implied by the 2030A high demand scenarios. It is not necessary to accept these figures to appreciate that coal plant will continue to be the mainstay of the US utility industry for the foreseeable future.

Given the continued reliance on coal for US electricity production, an attractive possibility would be to recover CO_2 from fossil fuel combustion and sequester it in biomass reservoirs, the deep ocean or depleted oil and gas reservoirs. Various technologies exist for CO_2 collection.[11] Until very recently, the most optimistic cost estimates would roughly double (at least) the cost of electricity generated from coal.[12] However, researchers in the Netherlands calculate that oxygen-blown gasifiers can be used with the shift reaction and sulphur removal to produce largely hydrogen and CO_2, that can be separated and

[10] US Department of Energy, *Long Range Energy Projections to 2010*, DOE/PE-0082, Washington DC, 1988.
[11] Hillsman et al, 'Options for Technological Response to Climate Change', op.cit.
[12] M.Steinberg, H.C.Cheng, and F.Horn, *A Systems Study for the Removal, Recovery, and Disposal of Carbon Dioxide from Fossil Fuel Power Plants in the US*, DOE/CH/00016-2, US Department of Energy, Washington DC, 1984.

inexpensively sequestered in depleted gas wells 100 km distant for only a 30% increase in the cost of power.[13] The earlier US studies suggested the CO_2 removed would be injected into the deep ocean. Apart from the cost, the potential ecological impact of such a strategy has not been assessed and is likely to prove controversial in the US.

An alternative to stack removal is to use biomass to take up CO_2 from the atmosphere. However, while partial offsets are achievable, it has been calculated that to take up all US fossil fuel emissions would require new, fast-growing forest area the size of the entire eastern seaboard.[14]

In the long term, growing biomass to displace fossil fuels for energy, rather than as an offset, is likely to prove a more productive CO_2 control measure.[15] However, present investments in the necessary RD&D are wholly inadequate to bring such technologies to maturity in the short term and considerable changes in land-use patterns and practices will require decades to achieve.

Fuel switching is an alternative approach, but each option brings its own suite of problems. Present trends and knowledge of natural gas resources suggest that there may be a small substitution of natural gas for coal in the short-term. The outlook for substitution of natural gas for coal in the longer term will depend on the discovery and development of additional domestic reserves. Otherwise, a shift to natural gas in the power sector would require additional imports (with implications for energy security), or utility purchases would divert natural gas from the residential, commercial, and industrial sectors of the economy (possibly increasing emissions from these sectors).

Nuclear power remains the technology most nearly substitutable for coal, if its associated problems of cost and public acceptance can be

[13] C.A.Hendriks, K.Blok, and W.C.Turkenberg, 'Technology and Cost of Recovery and Storage of Carbon Dioxide from an Integrated Gasifier Combined Cycle Plant', *Applied Technology*, forthcoming.

[14] G.Marland, *The Prospect of Solving the CO_2 Problem through Global Reforestation*, DOE/NNB-0082, US Department of Energy, Washington, DC, 1988. High-intensity plantations absorbing 5tC/acre/yr would have to cover an area 267 million acres - the equivalent of all the eastern coastal states - to absorb US fossil fuel emissions. Conventional commercial forests, absorbing 1tC/acre/yr, would have to cover half the continental US to absorb as much.

[15] R.H.Williams, 'Biomass Gasifier/Gas Turbine Power and the Greenhouse Warming', in *Proceedings of an Expert Seminar, Paris 12–14 April 1989*, Vol.2, OECD, Paris, 1989.

solved. The barriers of public acceptance and investor confidence should not be dismissed lightly. New reactor designs with passive safety features will not be sufficient to turn around the opposition to nuclear energy that is firmly entrenched in the American public. Unless technical problems of uranium production and nuclear waste disposal are solved to public satisfaction and sweeping institutional changes are made in the management and regulation of nuclear technology, a US nuclear option can be discounted for the foreseeable future.

The US DOE projects the contribution of renewable energy to central station production to increase from the present 9% to 12% by the year 2000 and then to 14% by 2010.[16] Most of this growth is estimated to come from increased hydroelectric and geothermal capacity, with biomass making significant contributions to growth in dispersed generation. Other authors have suggested that the US, with its large land area, could derive much of its electricity from other renewables such as wind and solar, and these have indeed benefitted from utility reforms especially in California.[17] But further technical improvements would be required, and important institutional obstacles remain.[18]

Both the electric utility industry and its sources of greenhouse gas emissions are highly concentrated in comparison to the other sectors of the US economy. US fossil fuel generating capacity is accounted for by a little over 2,000 generating units operated by approximately 300 utilities.[19] Viewed as a decision-making system, the sector consists of the utilities themselves, the state public utility commissions (PUCs) and the federal regulatory agencies, the financial community, state and federal environmental regulators, equipment manufacturers, architectural and engineering firms, the ratepayers, and independent power producers. Thus, utility management must deal with many contending parties whose interests may be at odds with one another,

---

[16] US Department of Energy *A Compendium of Options for Government Policy to Encourage Private Sector Responses to Potential Climate Change*, Vol.2, DOE, Washington DC, 1989.

[17] C.J.Weinberg and R.H.Williams, 'Energy from the Sun', *Scientific American*, Vol.263 No.3 pp.146-155.

[18] S.H.Sawyer, 'Renewable Energy: Progress, Prospects', Association of American Geographers, Washington, 1986.

[19] S.L.Purucker and J.H.Reed, *Power Plant Life Extension and Pollution Emissions*, ORNL/TM-10942, Oak Ridge National Laboratory, Oak Ridge, 1989.

making a slow and uncertain decision process involving considerable compromise. The timeframes of the various parties differ, further complicating decision making.

Electric utilities are also the most capital-intensive sector in the US.[20] PUC rulings that some past investments were unwise, and hence cannot be passed through in rate increases, have made utilities reluctant to make major investments. Combined with other factors, this has led to utilities purchasing power from other utilities and independent power producers (IPPs). Current law requires utilities to accept such power. IPPs now own and operate only 25GW (about 4%) of the sector's generating capacity, but are projected to own as much as 12% by 2000.[21] Although high efficiency cogeneration potentially could help reduce greenhouse gas emissions, the current record of IPPs is mixed. Many have invested in using waste heat and renewables, helping to reduce greenhouse gas emissions. Others have built high-efficiency gas turbines specifically to sell power generation to utilities. To the extent that these displace coal and oil generation by the utilities they also help to reduce emissions. However, more than one-sixth of IPP production is from coal. Because IPPs are not subject to the same regulations as utilities, in some cases these plant are less environmentally friendly than the utility production that they displace. Furthermore, expanding the role of IPPs would increase the number of decision-makers responsible for emissions and may pose financial difficulties for utilities if the favourable terms established for IPPs are extended further.

Some utilities already are encouraging greater end-use efficiency to improve customer service, meet PUC requirements, enhance economic productivity and international competitiveness, reduce dependence upon imported fuels, and maintain their share of the end-use energy market. In addition, utilities are interested in some high-efficiency generating technologies, notably combined cycle, for reasons unrelated to greenhouse gas emissions.

The electricity generating industry is characterized by a slow capital-turnover rate. This is the single greatest constraint in reducing greenhouse gas emissions. Although the financial lifetime of plant often

[20] Edison Electric Institute (EEI), *Statistical Yearbook of the Electric Utility Industry, 1987*, EEI, Washington DC, 1988.
[21] *Electrical World*, 'Independent Power: How Big Will Be the Utility Share?', Vol.203, No.2, 1989, pp.12-15.

is assumed to be 30 years or less, with normal maintenance the lifetime of plant may exceed 40 years. With long-term maintenance and refurbishment the lifetime can be even longer. More than half of the fossil-fired capacity that was operating in 1949 was still operating 37 years later.[22] Fossil plant in use today will continue to be important for the foreseeable future. Coupled with this long lifetime is a lead time of 10–15 years to design, site, and build a large plant. A utility would require this much time to replace an existing plant with commercially available technology of this type if it made the decision to do so today. Such time horizons mean that many decades would be required to replace existing fossil plant with alternative generating technologies that eliminate or substantially reduce greenhouse gas emissions.

Existing policies and trends send contradictory signals to utility executives, state regulators, the financial community, and equipment manufacturers about what priority greenhouse gas reduction has in the United States. Mobilization of the utility industry to mitigate or reduce greenhouse gas emissions may require re-examination of all legislation and regulations related to electricity generation policy, with the objective of establishing an integrated, consistent utility policy for the nation.

The transport sector

American vehicles consumed 506Mtoe of energy in 1987,[23] nearly 28% of the primary energy consumed that year, and 63% of its petroleum consumption. Including energy used to manufacture transportation equipment, produce fuels, and build infrastructure, the sector consumes at least 30% of the nation's primary energy. These figures illustrate much greater use of cars and light trucks for personal transportation compared with other countries. Outside a few major metropolitan areas public transport is limited or non-existent. Furthermore, the use of rail for freight traffic is much more limited than, for example, in Europe where rail networks are better developed.

Transport patterns partly reflect the dispersal of population over a vast land area, and the pattern of development based on cheap domestic oil resources. Europeans visiting the US for the first time frequently are amazed at the travel times and distances to which suburban and rural Americans will submit themselves to shop, work, dine, and entertain

[22] Purucker and Reed, *Power Plant Life Extension and Pollution Emissions*, op.cit.
[23] Energy Information Administration (EIA), *Monthly Energy Review, November 1988*, DOE/EIA-0035(88/11), US Department of Energy, Washington DC, 1989.

themselves. US cultural values that emphasize the self-reliance of individuals lead Americans to prefer single family dwellings. Apartment living is much less common in America than in most of Europe, thus travel distances are increased. The value of self-reliance also promotes a preference for autonomy in transportation modes, which means individual use of automobiles rather than buses and ride sharing. The number of vehicle miles travelled in the US makes cheap petrol (gasoline) important to American consumers, who also are voters. Gasoline taxes in the US are a fraction of European levels and are not likely to be increased substantially in the current political climate of anti-taxation sentiment.

Despite these limitations, substantial opportunities exist to limit carbon emissions from transportation. Automobiles sold in 1986 averaged 28 miles per US gallon (mpg), 10mpg more than the average automobile in service that year.[24] Thus, as vehicles are replaced, if this trend continues, some reduction will occur in fuel consumption and CO_2 emissions. DOE has estimated that US vehicle manufacturers could improve the average fuel consumption of new cars to 34–40mpg over a 10-year period, using technology that would be cost-effective at gasoline prices of $1.50–$2.00 per gallon.[25] New models of heavy trucks use 15–10% less fuel per unit of service than previous ones,[26] and new commercial aircraft also are much more fuel-efficient than the fleet average. Similarly, the technology needed to build vehicles that run on fuels with lower greenhouse gas emissions has been proven and in some cases commercialized.[27]

Since 1950, the transport sector has accommodated more than a 65% increase in the nation's total population, and nearly a 200% increase in

[24] M.C.Holcomb, S.D.Floyd, and S.L.Cagle, *Transportation Energy Year Book: Edition 9*, ORNL-6325, Oak Ridge National Laboratory, Oak Ridge, 1987. One US gallon = 3.79 litres = 0.83 Imperial gallons.
[25] US Department of Energy, *Analysis of the Capabilities of Domestic Auto Manufacturers to Improve Corporate Average Fuel Economy*, DOE/RL/1830-H1, DOE, Washington DC, 1986.
[26] F.J.Stephenson Jr., *Transportation USA*, Addison-Wesley, Reading, Mass., 1987. D.L.Greene, D.Sperling, and B.McNutt, 'Transportation Energy to the Year 2020', in The Transportation Research Board, *A Look Ahead: The Year 2020*, National Research Council, Washington DC, 1988.
[27] D.Sperling, *New Transportation Fuels: A Strategic Approach to Technological Change*, University of California Press, Berkeley, 1988.

real GNP.[28] During the same period, commercial jet travel and interstate highway systems were put into place. Vehicle manufacturing and transportation service companies (airline, trucking, and railroad) have made rapid responses to major changes in competition and regulation. Such changes have not been painless, but they demonstrate significant potential to respond quickly to increased demand and changing regulatory circumstances. However, the structure of decision-making in the sector hinders rapid, major changes in basic technology. Furthermore, some of the options for limiting greenhouse gas emissions may be incompatible with current consumer preferences and economic trends.

Transportation affects three major public policy issues: economic competitiveness, energy security, and air quality. The sector consumes more petroleum than the US produces. Reducing petroleum consumption could reduce the nation's energy imports and help shrink the trade deficit. Although transportation energy is a relatively small fraction of transportation costs,[29] reducing the cost of transporting materials and distributing goods and services can make these goods and services more competitive in the domestic market and overseas. Reduced petroleum consumption also would improve national resilience to disruptions in world energy markets, such as those prompted by the Gulf crisis of 1990/91. Finally, in addition to greenhouse gas emissions, vehicles are major producers of several pollutants that affect human and environmental health more directly than CO_2. Although emission limits on stationary equipment and vehicles have been the main instruments for improving urban air quality, improvements in fuel economy can reduce emissions of all these pollutants.[30] Substitution of alternative fuels for petroleum fuels also can reduce these emissions.[31]

The opportunities for change in the transportation sector are offset somewhat by the fragmentation of decision-making among five constituencies. These are: government, which develops most infrastructure and regulates other activities; vehicle manufacturers, who

[28] Bureau of the Census, *Statistical Abstract of the United States 1988*, US Government Printing Office, Washington DC, 1989.
[29] Stephenson, *Transportation USA*, op.cit.
[30] D.L.Bleviss, *The New Oil Crisis and Fuel Economy Technologies*, Quorum Books, New York, 1988.
[31] Sperling, *New Transportation Fuels*, op.cit.

are highly concentrated; fuel suppliers, also presently concentrated; transport service companies, whose concentration varies with transport mode and who also may own and develop infrastructure; and consumers, including all individuals, businesses, and governments. Each group of decision-makers operates with the expectation that other groups will demand or supply goods that meet announced standards of performance. This decision-making structure permits incremental technological change, because technology standards and specifications are stated clearly and any firm able to meet them at an advantage will do so. On the other hand, the structure limits fundamental changes in transport technology, because it requires agreement among very diverse decision-makers to change the standards in unison. Fundamental changes in technology usually have come as new transport modes, not as major overhauls of existing ones, because with new modes there is less institutional inertia.

Another obstacle to fundamental change is the lead time, lifetime, and capital cost of infrastructure, fuel supply systems, vehicle production facilities, and many types of vehicles. Quick fixes can be introduced into vehicle production lines in 3–5 years, but fundamental changes usually require more than one product generation.[32] An innovation may require decades to saturate the market, and half of the vehicles sold in one year may remain in use 10 to 15 years later.[33] Infrastructure can last for many decades. The existing transportation system benefits substantially from economies of scale, and this places alternative fuels and new vehicle technologies at a disadvantage until and unless they develop or capture large markets.

Road transport is projected to double by 2020,[34] and air traffic is projected to increase by 60% by 2000.[35] If the projected demand materializes, fuel economy must improve at comparable rates to keep annual emissions from increasing, and at greater rates to reduce emissions from present levels. Unfortunately, many uncertainties remain about how people and businesses make decisions about travel behaviour,

[32] A.Altshuler, M.Anderson, D.Jones, R.Roos, and J.Womack, *The Future of the Automobile*, MIT Press, Cambridge, Mass., 1984.
[33] Holcomb et al, *Transportation Energy Data Book*, op.cit.
[34] Federal Highway Administration (FHWA), *America's Challenge for Highway Transportation in the 21st Century*, FHWA, Washington DC, 1988.
[35] C.P.Fotos, 'Heavy Debt Could Put Airlines at Risk if Traffic Growth Slows', *Aviation Week and Space Technology*, Vol.130, No.12, 1989, pp.203–206.

ind about how slow the projected rates of increase in demand. Americans clearly prefer the convenience, flexibility, speed, and comfort offered by high-emission modes such as trucks, commercial air travel, and the personal automobile. Federal policy supports these modes by taxing users and using the revenue to expand or improve the existing infrastructure, for example, through federal highway construction. Modes with lower emissions receive much less public support and use.

Perhaps the best indicator of the difficulty in changing the transport sector is the history of public policy to reduce petroleum consumption to improve energy security, an issue that hitherto has had a greater sense of immediacy than climate change. Fuel economy for new vehicles has nearly doubled since 1974, largely due to the Corporate Average Fuel Economy (CAFE) standards imposed by the federal government. However, the transportation sector overall consumed more petroleum and a greater share of the nation's energy in 1988 than in 1974. The nation's experience with attempting to reduce petroleum consumption is useful when considering options to reduce its greenhouse gas emissions.

The Detroit auto industry currently is pressing for repeal of the CAFE standards, arguing that a gasoline tax is an economically more efficient means to promote selection of cars with better mpg performance. However, research indicates that US gasoline prices would have to rise by about $1 per gallon to obtain a 10% increase in mpg.[36] The manufacturers and environmentalists know that such a high level of taxation would be politically untenable in the US, at least under present conditions. Environmental groups continue, therefore, to support a standards-based approach to improving vehicle efficiency. Such conflicts of economic interest and regulatory philosophy are typical of the obstacles in the way of a coherent US greenhouse gas policy.

Manufacturing industry

Manufacturing is responsible for around 20% of total US direct CO_2 emissions,[37] consumes much electricity, and serves as the source of all CFC-based products. Energy-intensive, heavy-industrial processes

[36] D.L.Greene, 'Cafe or Price: An Analysis of the Effects of Federal Fuel Economy Regulations and Gasoline Price on New Car MPG, 1978–89', *The Energy Journal*, Vol.11, No.3, 1990, pp.37-57.

[37] J.A.Edmonds, W.B.Ashton, H.C.Cheng, and M.Steinberg, *Preliminary Analysis of US CO2 Emissions Reduction Potential from Energy Conservation and the Substitution of Natural Gas for Coal in the Period to 2010*, DOE/NBB-0085, US Department of Energy, Washington DC, 1989.

are the dominant source of CO_2 emissions with fossil fuels for process heat and electricity for motive force.

Eight industries account for 65% of all fuel consumed in the manufacturing sector, and a concomitantly large share of CO_2 emissions. In order of total energy use (in 1985), they are: petroleum refining, chemicals, paper, steel, glass and stone, cement, transportation equipment, and aluminum. These eight industries depend to a surprising extent on natural gas (49% of fuel inputs), with purchased and self-generated electricity the next most important.[38] Coal and coke are most intensively used in the cement and the iron and steel industries. Fuel oil (distillate and residual) has declined to under 10% of energy expenditures in all industries except refining and paper. Use of coal and electricity has grown steadily since the mid-1970s; oil and natural gas use have declined. The concentration of emissions in a limited number of industries, mostly with uniform manufacturing processes across firms, may simplify abatement policies. The major exception is the chemical industry, which employs highly diverse manufacturing processes to produce over 2,000 products.

Many technical opportunities exist for reducing emissions. Improved efficiency is the most important, with large potential savings identified for the major uses of process heat (including waste heat recovery and process optimization), and a wide range of improvements available for electrical drives.[39] In addition, there are opportunities for greater use of non-fossil fuels especially in the pulp and paper industry, which already provides 52% of its own energy requirements by burning waste sulphate liquors and waste wood and bark.[40] Such producer fuel switching is especially valuable when processes or equipment are relatively rigid and the opportunities for technological change are small (as may be the case for cement calcination, for example).

---

[38] These percentages refer to the shares of identified fuels; coal, oil, electricity, or natural gas. Excluded are non-purchased or unspecified fuels, principally biomass and refinery gas.

[39] S.Baldwin, 'Efficient Motor Drives', in T.B.Johansson, B.Bodlund, and R.H.Williams (eds) *Electricity: Efficient End-Use and New Generation Technologies and their Planning Implications*, American Council for an Energy Efficient Economy, Washington DC, 1989.

[40] Electric Power Research Institute (EPRI), *The U.S.Pulp and Paper Industry 1984-2000 With Implications for Energy Demand*, EPRI, Palo Alto, 1984.

Manufacturers' ability to cope with fluctuations in energy supplies and prices by switching to alternative sources of energy plays a significant role in the nation's energy security. It also may indicate industry's capability for short-term greenhouse gas reduction. It is estimated that in 1985, 43% of residual fuel oil and almost 20% of distillate fuel oil consumption, totalling 92,000 barrels per day of fuel oil consumption (4.57Mtoe/yr), could have been switched to non-petroleum sources. Almost 30% of the 42.6Mtoe of coal and coke consumed by manufacturing were switchable.[41]

Materials recycling provides another opportunity for reduced energy use, particularly the recycling of aluminum, glass, and steel. Another opportunity for reduced energy use might lie in accelerating trends away from energy-intensive manufactured products.

Carbon taxes would decrease greenhouse gas emissions, but they also reduce international competitiveness for many energy-intensive industries - notably iron and steel, which has faced a four-fold increase in imports between 1963 and 1982, and remains in poor financial health.[42] Creating a disadvantage for these sectors of US industry could shift production overseas, resulting in US economic losses, with no net reduction in global emissions. To overcome concerns about international competitiveness, positive fiscal incentives (eg. tax breaks) for emissions reduction and energy conservation could be used, but they also may lower product price and increase product demand. The local and regional concentrations of many of these industries create further barriers. Such concentrated firms can bargain strongly against measures which would hurt them, using the threat of local economic dislocation to garner strong local support.

Without exception, the industries that are primary contributors to greenhouse gas emissions are capital intensive. As a result, adopting completely new equipment to meet new market or government policy imperatives is slow. A boiler, for instance, lasts 40 years. Some paper-making machines are 70 to 80 years old. Investment rates and technological change will be slowed further if demand for basic manufactured materials grows only gradually. This problem is

[41] Energy Information Administration (EIA), *Annual Energy Review, 1988*, DOE/EIA-0384(88), US Department of Energy (DOE), Washington DC, 1989.
[42] Steel Panel, *The Competitive Status of the US Steel Industry*, National Academy Press, Washington DC, 1985.

compounded by the low rate of R&D in certain basic manufacturing industries, notably pulp and paper, cement, and glass; chemicals is the biggest exception. These features reflect, in part, management attitudes and priorities more than any structural or economic aspect of the industry. However, retrofitting equipment can achieve much, and almost without exception, the industries under discussion met their voluntary energy savings targets set out during the Carter administration (albeit under the pressure of higher energy prices).

An additional factor which may create resistance to new environmental initiatives is manufacturers' experience of incurring high costs of environmental regulation under the 1970 Clean Air Act and the Water Pollution Control Act. The dramatic restructuring of the steel industry (including the closing of many plant and the shift to electric mini-mills) also is attributed partially to environmental costs.[43] Policies for reducing CO_2 emissions from manufacturing are unlikely to be either simple to design or uniformly appealing to all parties concerned. There are some clear opportunities, but the national concern of manufacturing firms to protect their own interests, if not properly recognized, may lead to continuing cycles of confrontation and policy destruction.

Residential and commercial energy demand

Housing and commercial services (including offices, warehouses, schools, hospitals, and eating facilities) are major energy consumers in the US, consuming about 210Mtoe and 144Mtoe respectively each year.[44] Factoring in the losses in producing the electricity consumed, these sectors account for about 19% and 15% of primary energy consumption; together they account for about 31% of CO_2 emissions, of which nearly two-thirds is due to electricity.

The most obvious opportunities to reduce greenhouse gas emissions through improvements in end-use efficiency are space heating, air conditioning, and lighting in the commercial sector and water heating in the residential sector.[45] Household energy use in the US declined by an average of 23.4% between 1970–1980 and by 11.2% between

[43] ibid.
[44] Energy Information Administration (EIA), *Energy Conservation Indicators, 1986,* DOE/EIA-0441(86), US Department of Energy, Washington DC, 1988.
[45] H.S.Geller, *Commercial Building Equipment Efficiency: A State of the Art Review,* and *Residential Building Equipment Efficiency: A State of the Art Review,* both published by the American Council for an Energy Efficient Economy, Washington DC, 1988.

1980–1985, but electricity use has continued to grow steadily. Natural gas is the dominant source which grew rapidly up to 1972, fell during the 1970s, and stabilized in the 1980s. Oil is less than 13% of the total residential heating market and coal is less than 1%.

In the commercial sector, natural gas and electricity each provides over 40% of the end-use energy consumed, while petroleum and coal account for 17% and 1.8%, respectively.[46] As in the residential sector, electricity use has been growing rapidly for many years, with an average annual growth rate of 3.4% between 1973 and 1983, and 5.6% between 1983 and 1986. The use of all other fuels, most of ll petroleum, has declined during since 1973.

Moderate population growth in the US (much of it from migration), combined with slower household formation and market saturation of various household uses, is likely to slow the growth in consumption. However, if slow growth combines with less capital turnover it may reduce opportunities for rapid penetration of new energy-efficient technologies. By contrast, the commercial sector is expected to be a major growth sector of the US economy. This need not necessarily lead to increased greenhouse gas emissions if energy-efficient technologies are chosen along with low-emitting fuels.

Although replacement of the current residential and commercial building stock with new energy-efficient structures would require many decades, the heating and cooling requirements of existing buildings can be reduced significantly by retrofitting a wide variety of weatherproofing measures. There already has been substantial retrofitting, especially in the North Central states with the encouragement of state governments and utilities. Conservation activity has been even greater in the commercial sector, where heating and cooling of buildings outside working hours has been reduced in about 85% of the buildings.[47]

A major factor constraining the market penetration of energy-efficient technologies is the fact many carry higher initial costs than traditional products.[48] Although the initial costs may be recouped over time,

---

[46] Energy Information Administration, *Energy Conservation Indicators 1986*, op.cit.
[47] ibid.
[48] E. Vine and J. Harris, *Planning for an Energy Efficient Future: The Experience with Implementing Energy Conservation Programs for New Residential and Commercial Buildings*, LBL-25525, 2 volumes, Lawrence Berkeley Laboratory, Berkeley, Calif., 1988.

consumer discount rates tend to be higher than market interest rates or the rates used by public policy-makers.[49] Hence the initial outlay inhibits builders and buyers as long as a lower-cost alternative is available.

The social organization of the residential and commercial sector, consisting of about 80 million dwellings and 4.15 million commercial buildings, imposes many constraints. Where there are relatively few barriers limiting information and decision-making opportunities (eg. in owner-occupied homes), market incentives (eg. changes in prices of fuels) can induce energy conservation behaviour. Consumers do seem to respond to prices.[50] The diversity of building uses and ownership arrangements limits the effectiveness of price alone. In many family establishments, consumption and investment decisions are not made by the same individual; other split incentives arise from the tenant-landlord and similar divisions. The energy needs of, for example, health care facilities differ from those of warehouses. The sectors are composed of many independent-decision makers who make innumerable choices which influence energy consumption but pay little attention to it.

Tax credits, subsidies, low-interest loans, and energy performance standards are among the opportunities available for inducing action without price rises. Tax incentives have been used to encourage the use of solar technologies and residential retrofits.[51] Favourable financing terms for energy efficient retrofits have been used successfully in combination with energy audits.[52] Mandatory conservation policies were found to reduce both operating and capital costs in simulation

[49] E.Hirst, J.Clinton, H.Geller, W.Kroner, and F.M.O'Hara, Jr, *Energy Efficiency in Buildings: Progress and Promise*, American Council for an Energy Efficient Economy, Washington DC, 1986.

[50] Shin documents responses to the average price perceived from the electricity bill. (J.Shin, 'Perception of Price when Price Information is Costly: Evidence from Residential Energy Demand', *The Review of Economical Statistics* Vol.67, 1985, pp.591-598) Research estimating price elasticities of demand for space-heating electricity and indoor temperature also suggests price responsiveness on the part of residential consumers. (J. Kushman and J. Anderson, 'A Model of Individual Household Temperature Demand and Energy-Related Welfare Changes Using Satiety', *Energy Economics* Vol.8, pp.147–154.)

[51] G.Sav, 'The Failure of Solar Tax Incentives: A Dynamic Analysis', *The Energy Journal*, Vol.7, 1986, pp.51-66.

[52] J.Laquatra, 'Energy Efficiency in Rental Housing', *Energy Policy*, Vol.15, 1987, pp.549-588.

udies of dwelling construction decisions performed by Dubin[53] and
tus may provide a valuable regulatory opportunity for the construction
f new homes.

The composition of the construction industry (typically small firms
)ecializing in discrete activities; contracting, architecture, engineering,
1aterials production, etc.) imposes additional constraints on the
:sidential and commercial sector. Builders are reluctant to make energy
fficiency improvements that will raise the initial costs which may make
1eir product less competitive on the market; many technologies may not
e widely available without a large established market. Also, because the
1dustry is largely craft-based and operates through unions which have
great deal of control over the acceptance of technological innovations,
1ere is a heavy reliance on existing ways of doing things and a general
:sistance to change. The result is a conservative social system that
:sists innovation.[54]

A variety of legal or regulatory constraints inhibit the adoption of
1easures to promote energy efficiency. For example, the setback
:quirements of zoning laws intended to prevent excessive visual
1trusion can preclude free-standing solar collectors, and height
:strictions may not allow the addition of solar panels on a building's
)of.[55] Efficiency standards for new construction, renovation, and for
:sidential appliances exist and strengthening them could be particularly
ffective in reducing energy use. These standards could be met with the
est of existing technology. Technological improvements to existing
ppliances are likely to improve efficiencies further by the mid-1990s.
'ommunity design standards also are likely to be important in
1couraging attention to albedo, which can influence cooling energy
onsumption significantly in urban areas. The widespread introduction
f trees and other plantings into the urban landscape may reduce energy
:quirements also. Since the residential and commercial sector is
haracterized by a very large number of dispersed and diverse

i3] J.Dubin, 'Will Mandatory Conservation Promote Energy Efficiency in the
election of Household Appliance Stocks?' *The Energy Journal*, Vol.7, 1986,
».99-118.
·4] R.Burby and M.Marsden, *Energy and Housing*, Oelgeschlager, Gunn, and Hain,
ambridge, Mass., 1980.
5] M.Schweitzer, *Review of Legal and Institutional Issues in the Use of Decentralized
)lar Energy Systems*, ORNL/TM-7078, Oak Ridge National Laboratory, Oak Ridge,
)80.

decision-makers, standards, although a relatively crude and ofter politically controversial instrument, would seem to offer the greates chance of success.

The potential costs of CO_2 reductions

Attempts to calculate the overall costs of emissions abatement have proved controversial. A study by Manne and Richels[56] presented scenarios for the cost of cutting US CO_2 emissions by 20% which ranged from US$0.8 trillion to $3.6 trillion (total cost to 2100, discounted a 5%). The high scenario entailed a marginal abatement cost of $250/t((expressed as a carbon tax level, more than quadrupling the cost of coal) and this estimate achieved great political prominence, especially after US official cited it at a major international conference in Bergen. The assumptions used in this estimate have been strongly attacked, both on grounds of technology costs and the fact that it assumed no 'autonomous improvements in energy efficiency, ie. no improvements due to technica developments or structural changes in the absence of energy price increases. Williams[57] argued that the costs could well be zero, and could not possibly be as high as in the Manne and Richels base case, view which Lave[58] suggested reflected 'technical optimism' i contrast to the 'technical pessimism' of the high scenario. Jorgensen and Hogan suggested that the costs could have been underestimated,[59 though Jorgensen later produced one of the lowest macroeconomi estimates of the carbon taxes required, at $15/tC.[60]

[56] A.S.Manne and R.G.Richels, 'CO_2 Emission Limits: An Economic Cost Analysi for the U.S.A.', *The Energy Journal*, Vol.11, No.2, 1990, pp.51–75.

[57] R.H.Williams, 'Low-Cost Strategies for Coping with CO_2 Emission Limits', *Th Energy Journal*, Vol.11, No.3, 1990, pp.35-59.

[58]'Manne and Richels emphasize the enormous costs the developed countries migr have to bear if they pursue stringent abatement of greenhouse gases. William emphasizes that the cost could be very low, if historical rates of innovation continu and if known technologies are disseminated. I agree with both. A $3.6 trillion price ta is worth a great deal of examination and discussion. At the same time there are man benefits to be gained from focusing on innovation to solve current and futur environmental problems.' L.B.Lave, 'Comment on R.H.Williams' Low-Cos Strategies..', *The Energy Journal*, Vol.11, No.4, 1990, pp.61-64.

[59] W.W.Hogan and D.W.Jorgenson, *Productivity Trends and the Cost of Reducin CO_2 Emissions*, Energy and Environmental Policy Center, John F.Kennedy School Government, Harvard University, Cambridge, Mass., 1990.

[60] D.Jorgenson and P.Wilcoxen, 'Global Change, energy prices and US Economi Growth', *GESL/CEPR Workshop on Economic/Energy/Environmental Modeling fc Climate Policy Analysis*, Washington, October 1990.

The abatement scenario 2030Bi results in an 30% cut in CO_2 emissions from 1988 levels, but as noted the author of this scenario argued that it would be substantially cheaper than long-term increased dependence on fossil fuels, though the costs of the more dramatic 60% reductions in 2030Bii are potentially high depending on developments in non-fossil sources. Some of the underlying reasons for such wide differences in cost estimates have been discussed by Grubb in Volume 1 (especially section 8.2). The public debate over abatement costs appears to show little sign of converging, and in the political sphere the view that the costs will be very high unquestionably dominates.

This debate is paralleled by one about the likely costs of global warming itself. Nordhaus[61] suggested a high damage function amounting to 2% loss of GNP, estimated to justify abatement up to a marginal cost level (carbon tax) of $30/tC, but his central and low estimates were well below this, implying that little abatement cost could be justified. Cline[62] pointed out that these estimates arbitrarily truncate the damage in time before the atmospheric concentrations reach levels where much higher damage might be expected; and also that the economic accounting approach used might seriously underestimate the costs of a given impact.[63] Also, the estimates made little allowance for possible surprises in global responses to greenhouse gas accumulation. Conversely, some have suggested that CO_2 accumulation might benefit the US.

It is not unnatural that protagonists in the debate select cost estimates as it suits their case. But, it is perhaps symptomatic of the debate in the US that estimates such as those of Nordhaus and the Manne and Richels high scenario, despite their obvious limitations and/or implausible assumptions, have assumed great political prominence, bolstering the reluctance of the US administration and of US industry to take action. Contrary studies such as those of Cline and Williams have remained largely invisible in the media and political debate, and there has been little public attempt to build consensus or common ground between

[61] W.D.Nordhaus, 'To Slow or Not to Slow: The Economics of the Greenhouse Effect', mimeo, Yale University, New Haven, 1990.
[62] W.R.Cline 'Economic Stakes of Global Warming in the Very Long Term', Institute for International Economics, Washington DC, November 1990.
[63] For example, agriculture is 2% of US GNP. Nordhaus op.cit., approach would therefore quantify the loss of all US agriculture as a 2% reduction in GNP.

contrasting views. This is no accident, for it reflects a deep characteristic of the US political process. To this political context we now turn.

6.3 The political context and prospects for greenhouse gas reduction policies

Rapid reductions of greenhouse gas emissions cannot be achieved through the actions of any single sector of the US economy nor be met through any single policy instrument. It will be a challenging technical and political task to select an appropriate mix of policies to achieve reduction goals at a cost tolerable to the private sector and consumers without unacceptably constraining other vital policy goals, such as international economic competitiveness and national energy security. The issues of costs, competitiveness, and energy security are linked closely to the US self-perception as the 'Saudi Arabia of coal'. It will require considerable effort to change that perception to recognition that all three goals can be as well served through energy efficiency with additional environmental benefits.

The selection of policy instruments is constrained by the larger socioeconomic framework and political culture of the United States, and by its position in world trade and affairs. The choices are complicated by various interactions. For example, political pressures may favour subsidies for low-carbon technologies over carbon taxes, but such subsidies may lower the prices of energy or energy-intensive products and encourage greater consumption.

Not all interactions and linkages are potentially disadvantageous. Many US manufacturers of basic materials also own energy resources. For example, firms in the paper and pulp industry frequently are vertically integrated to include forestry and forest-products. Although the costs of reducing greenhouse gas emissions from paper manufacture may be burdensome, incentives for silviculture intended as emissions offsets for utilities may be welcome. Similarly, many US railroads own coal reserves. Although these companies might be disadvantaged by a carbon tax on fossil fuels, they also might benefit from the tax if combined with other policies designed to shift freight from trucks to rail.

The social basis of policy choices

The Reagan decade signalled a preference for fiscal and informational instruments for a wide variety of government policies, in contrast to the aggressive regulatory approach of the Carter years. However, while environmentalists have begun to explore fiscal incentives to promote their goals, they remain concerned about regulatory capture and bureaucratic inertia. Most continue to favour regulations that allow little discretion to either the regulators or the regulated industry. Industrial and commercial interests are likely to favour fiscal incentives because of the high degree of discretion that remains with firms. An example of this tension is the current debate over the relative merits of a gasoline tax and the CAFE standards discussed above in section 6.2.

Responses to the more general question on how to respond to the threat of global warming can be divided into three characteristic positions: *prevention*, *adaptation*, and *sustainable development*. These divisions exist in all countries but they are particularly sharp in the US. Each of the approaches is supported by its own characteristic moral imperative and nature myth.[64]

In its extreme form, *prevention* ironically echoes the positions of the Reagan administration on drugs and of the American religious right on teenage pregnancy. All that is necessary to prevent the unwanted consequence is to persuade people to 'Just say "No"' and modify their behaviour accordingly. Proper choices are to be reinforced by regulation and legal sanctions. From this standpoint, discussion of adaptation to climate change is viewed with the same distaste that the religious right reserves for sex education in schools. Both are seen as ethical compromises that will in any case only encourage dangerous experimentation with the undesired behaviour. The *preventivists* include many of those who Lave would characterize as technological optimists.[65] The implications for the US of a complete preventivist response would be immense, implying a very rapid phasing out of fossil fuels.

The opposite of prevention, extreme *adaptation*, sees climate change as presenting new opportunities for human ingenuity that will be revealed through the workings of the market place. The adaptive approach to

[64] P.Timmerman, 'Mythology and Surprise in Sustainable Development of the Biosphere', in W.C.Clark and R.E.Munn (eds) *Sustainable Development of the Biosphere*, Cambridge University Press, New York, 1986.Schwarz, M.and M.Thompson, *Divided We Stand: Redefining Politics, Technology, and Social Choice*, Harvester Wheatsheaf, New York, 1990.
[65] L.B.Lave, 'Comment on R.H.Williams', op.cit.

climate change has its own implications for the US energy system. Its exponents tend to be technological pessimists.[66] *Adaptavists* tend to favour hard path energy strategies, including continuing reliance on coal through clean coal technologies, and greatly increased use of nuclear power. This clearly contains its own risks, even those to the energy system.

The dichotomy between prevention and adaptation reflects a long-standing division in US society, which parallels the continuing debate about the relative merits of preserving nature as humankind finds it as compared to treating it as a resource, to be protected only insofar as is necessary to protect its use for humans.[67] In response, has emerged a predictable synthesis, the extreme of which is the ideal of *sustainable development*. According to this third view, you can have your cake and eat it; it is possible to avoid global catastrophe by careful stewardship of the opportunities that nature provides for controlled growth.

Formally, sustainable development has been defined as 'development that meets the needs of the present without compromising the ability of future generations to meet their own needs'.[68] However, the concept seems to defy more rigorous definition.[69] The problem is that some see sustainability in any strategy that will get us through the next 70 years while others look forward to the next 700 or even 7,000 years. In many cases, the concept of sustainable development acts as a zone of *creative ambiguity* that allows adaptivist technological optimists and preventivist environmental pessimists to persist in their respective world views without acknowledging the conflict that is inherent between them. To the extent that sustainable development can be rendered as a coherent position in the American debate on climate policy, it implies a mixed energy strategy, probably of the sort that soft energy advocates such as Amory Lovins originally claimed was impossible.[70]

---

[66] ibid.

[67] D.H.Meadows, D.L.Meadows, J.Randers, and W.W.Behrens III, *The Limits to Growth*, Universe Books, New York, 1972.

[68] World Commission on Environment and Development, *Our Common Future*, Oxford University Press, New York, 1987.

[69] B.J.Brown, M.E.Hanson, D.M.Liverman, R.W.Merideth Jr, 'Global Sustainability: Toward Definition', *Environmental Management*, Vol.11, 1987, pp.713-719.

[70] A.B.Lovins, *Soft Energy Paths: Towards a Durable Peace*, Penguin Books, Harmondsworth, 1977.

Conflicts in US environmental policy

In developing US climate policy it is vital to recognize that the conflict between these views is not a superficial or transitory phenomenon, but a profound and persistent component of American culture and political life.[71] It is quite possible that broad support for action on climate change may fragment as the costs to various sectors of society become clear.

Even if the resulting opposition can be overcome, such conflict carries its own costs which must be considered part of the true social cost of a climate policy, just as emissions impacts must be considered part of the full cost of economic activities. Although these true social costs of conflict may appear trivial at first sight, the costs of conflict over nuclear power in the US, including the social opportunity costs of anti-nuclear campaigners as well as the costs to manufacturers and utilities, must run into billions of dollars.

The issues of global climate and the ozone layer already have demonstrated a dramatic broadening of the range of interest groups claiming legitimate roles as stakeholders in the decision-making process on both domestic US and international fronts.[72] In particular, the role of various types of non-governmental organizations has expanded markedly. Various environmental interest groups have been joined by scientific and technical associations, professional societies, industrial and trade associations, voluntary disaster-relief agencies, and non-profit organizations concerned with international development. Each of these types of organization is characterized by a particular world view and perceptions of self-interest and the common good. Currently, efforts to build coalitions are most discernable among organizations seeking prompt action in response to potential climate change. However, as more sectors of society become potentially affected, coalitions are likely to form to oppose policies and claim a role in decision-making.

Such claims are difficult to ignore in the US political arena. Past experience with hazardous waste and nuclear energy has demonstrated

---

[71] R.Nash, *Wilderness and the American Mind*, Yale University Press, New Haven, 1967. M.Douglas and A.Wildavsky, *Risk and Culture*, University of California Press, Berkeley, 1982.

[72] L.P.Gerlach, and S.Rayner, 'Managing Global Climate Change: A View from the Social and Decision Sciences', ORNL/6390, Oak Ridge National Laboratory, Oak Ridge, 1988.

that American society is ill-suited for excluding concerned groups from decision-making.[73] The democratic political and legal mechanisms that distinguish American society will ensure that determined stakeholders have their say. Policy actions selected through apparently rational procedures in legislative and executive arenas may be brought to an impasse by the actions of institutions and citizens that were not involved actively in the decision. Often, the objectors have been motivated as much by their sense of exclusion from the decision process as from any discomfort with the proposed technology.[74]

The greenhouse debate: status and prospects
Sound decision-making about climate-change policy may depend as much on the process used for the selection and implementation of policies and implementation instruments as upon the predicted outcomes of those policies. Success will not be guaranteed, but the probability of achieving desirable outcomes almost certainly will be enhanced if a broad range of parties are included in the process of negotiating responses. However, the difficulties are further compounded by the uncertainties surrounding the issue. In welcoming delegates from 17 governments to the 1990 White House Conference on Science and Economics Research Related to Global Change, President Bush claimed that political decision-makers are presently being asked to choose between 'two diametrically opposed schools of scientific thought' on the reality, severity, likelihood, and timing of global environmental change. He implied that politicians should resist the urge to meddle with the international energy system, industrial processes, and land use until the science of climate change and its impacts is more certain, a view advocated strongly by the White House Chief of Staff, John Sununu.

In reality these 'two schools' represent extremes of a broad range of scientific views. Most scientists support a view that the problems are real, but there is considerable uncertainty about timing and impacts. Most agree that there are some risks that should be minimized. In opposing

[73] E.Peelle, 'Beyond the Nimby Impasse II: Public Participation in an Age of Distrust', *Proceedings of Spectrum '88, International Meeting on Nuclear and Hazardous Waste Management, Richland, Washington, 11-15 September 1988*. L.P.Gerlach, 'Protest Movements and the Social Construction of Risk', in B.Johnson and V.Covello (eds) *The Social and Cultural Construction of Risk*, Reidel, Boston, 1987.
[74] S.L.Albrecht, 'Community Response to Large-Scale Federal Projects: The Case of the MX', in S.H.Murdock, F.L.Leistritz and R.R.Hamm (eds) *Nuclear Waste: Socioeconomic Dimensions of Long-Term Storage*, Westview Press, Boulder, 1983.

Sununu, the EPA Administrator William Reilly endorsed such a view and argued for abatement policies against the uncertain, but potentially disastrous, outcome of significant climate change. Essentially the debate is over rival concepts of prudence in the face of uncertainty.

Such differing attitudes to uncertainty make it difficult to envisage any sort of widespread agreement on what an optimal response would be. A further difficulty is that the impacts of climate change may be very unevenly distributed. Differing impacts has made hazardous facility siting in the United States extraordinarily difficult and controversial.[75] The optimal response is different for different stakeholders, and no amount of appeal to higher collective rationality about the general welfare of society is likely to sweep away concern for the welfare of individuals in a culture that derives so much of its strength and vigour from its recognition of the sovereignty of each citizen. In fact, this may suggest a second reason for acting while still very uncertain - to develop policy responses before the distribution of impacts is known, so that people perceive a more equal stake in preventing climate change.

In reality, the complexities and uncertainties, combined with the political constraints noted above, make it most unlikely that policies could be introduced quickly enough to achieve more than the stabilization illustrated by the 2000B scenario, and even this may be considered an optimistic case. Further ahead, if concerns about the greenhouse effect do grow, some hard-fought abatement efforts are likely. Indeed, growing recognition of the value of improving efficiency, combined with a change in attitudes towards the role of government in the energy sector, or greater state independence in pursuing efficiency policies, might conceivably bring about efficiency improvements tending towards the 2030Bi scenario. But adding fuel switching for further abatement to this, as in 2030Bii, implies much additional investment in energy sources which would directly displace existing fossil fuel industries already placed under strong pressure by declining demand. Given the political leverage which large industries have in the US political system when their position is seriously threatened, such a scenario is probably politically impossible irrespective of its technical feasibility. One final issue further complicates the process - namely the international perspective.

---

[75] R.E.Kasperson, (ed.) *Equity Issues in Radioactive Waste Management*, Oelgesschlager, Gunn and Hain, Cambridge, Mass., 1983.

The international perspective

The United States is the world's largest emitter of CO_2, with 22% of global fossil emissions. This fraction is barely half that of thirty years ago, owing largely to the rapid increase in the former centrally-planned economies. Nevertheless, US per-capita emissions are the world's highest, at five tonnes annually.

The scale of US carbon emissions is raised frequently by representatives of developing countries, particularly those who have been criticized by US representatives for destroying rain forests. Non-governmental organizations sometimes raise similar complaints. However, equity concerns about the relative size of US emissions are barely noticeable on the national political scene. US citizens are infinitely more aware of the federal budget deficit and more concerned about equity issues arising from the runaway collapse of savings-and-loan banks than they are about the national carbon budget. Despite public and professional political concern about the federal budget and the savings-and-loan crisis, public policy to address these issues has been conspicuously unsuccessful; a significant reminder of the overwhelming inertia of the US political system.

Such is the domestic context of the cautious approach that the US administration has taken in international negotiations on greenhouse gases. In the course of these negotiations, the administration has proposed what it terms the 'comprehensive approach' to greenhouse gas controls. This would require that the sources and sinks of all greenhouse gases be considered in accounting for each country's contribution to emissions controls.[76]

The comprehensive approach provides for a more economically efficient solution to greenhouse gas emissions controls than tackling CO_2 in isolation. It also permits US policy-makers to counter accusations of foot dragging on climate change by pointing to the US commitment to rapid phase-out of chlorofluorocarbons and the global warming benefits of the 1990 Clean Air Act. Because of its geography, the US also has greater potential to provide new biomass sinks for CO_2 than many countries. However, critics of the comprehensive approach have pointed to the immense difficulties in measuring all sources and sinks with

---

[76] Task Force on the Comprehensive Approach to Climate Change, *A Comprehensive Approach to Addressing Potential Climate Change*, US Department of Justice, Washington DC, February 1991.

sufficient accuracy to adopt realistic quantitative targets and view the comprehensive approach merely as a delaying tactic to stonewall agreement on CO_2 reductions.

Such a monolithic view of the administration is misguided. Once again, there appears to be at least two camps within the administration corresponding roughly to the adaptivist position and sustainable developmentalist views discussed above. The first of these is the hard-line position that essentially would prefer the US government not to intervene in the energy sector to achieve CO_2 emissions reductions and will continue acting to delay any agreement committing the US to emissions targets. However, there are many actors within the administration who would be willing to sign the US on to emissions targets provided that the mechanisms for achieving them could be shown to be economically efficient. In part this concern stems from the long experience of US government departments and agencies in dealing with the inefficiencies and inequities produced by a generation of cutting-edge, but piecemeal, domestic environmental legislation. For this constituency, the long-term benefits of establishing an efficient framework outweigh the additional short-term environmental costs of delaying agreement.

The challenge to those seeking rapid progress in international negotations is to detach those who would act on the assurance of economic efficiency from those who prefer not to act at all. One way might be to concede the comprehensive principle to the US, but proceed immediately on the basis only of those gases, sources, and sinks for which we do have reasonable measurement capabilities (for example, all CFCs, CO_2 from fossil fuels, and possibly methane from natural gas production and transportation). Although monitoring problems might be an obstacle, it is not even necessary that all countries reduce emissions of the same gases simultaneously. The point is that the comprehensive framework is what is important to those who are willing to act only on the basis of economic efficiency. Much flexibility exists within the framework for implementation, including early emphasis on CO_2. Once the comprehensive principle is conceded, hard-liners opposing any US government action could find themselves isolated within the administration.

The global effectiveness of any radical programme to curtail fossil fuel emissions in the US will depend on the paths taken by developing and newly industrialized countries. With four-fifths of the global population, and barely one-quarter of the fossil carbon emissions, the potential for growth in these countries is clearly enormous; deforestation adds further to their emissions. Consequently, efforts to cut emissions by the US and other developed countries would be rendered ineffective to prevent warming without a simultaneous effort to limit emissions in developing countries. This would almost certainly require transfer of alternatives to fossil technologies, at no more cost to the recipients than present fossil technologies.

Such an arrangement could be achieved with some degree of equity through an international system of tradeable CO_2 emissions permits.[77] Developed countries could buy part of the CO_2 allowance allocated to developing countries in order to avoid the costs of premature retirement of fossil plants. The payments to developing countries would be made in technology transfers that would aid these countries' development, with minimal greenhouse gas emissions.

There would be substantial political problems to be faced. Some adaptivists would resent paying any costs to developing countries. Many US citizens already have difficulty understanding why the Congress authorizes $20 billion a year in development assistance while the US budget deficit runs at over $220 billion. Others, particularly in developing countries but also domestically, could regard it as morally unacceptable or hypocritical for the US to continue its profligate use of fossil fuels while preaching restraint on using fossil energy to the developing countries.

The international situation thus adds further layers of complexity. Because of its very high per-capita and absolute emissions, many countries look to the US to be one of the first to act to reduce carbon emissions. Yet for reasons discussed in this chapter, it may be more practical, and a better use of resources, to make limiting the growth of emissions in other countries a higher priority. Indeed, unilateral action by the US, in the absence of action in other countries, would make a relatively small long-term contribution. But, as things stand at present, action in developing countries is unlikely without US action first. Given these complexities, and all the other issues discussed above, what would be a sensible approach for US policy on the greenhouse effect?

[77] M.Grubb, *The Greenhouse Effect: Negotiating Targets*, Royal Institute of International Affairs, London, 1990.

A flexible response strategy for the US energy system

The scientific and social constraints on decision-making may make it exceedingly difficult to produce a broad ranging and well mapped-out climate change policy for the US that would be acceptable across the spectrum of relevant stakeholders, such as might be feasible in Japan, for example. With continuing divisive debates, people and interest groups become firmly polarized and less amendable to persuasion by new information. One possible outcome, at least over extended periods of time, is policy gridlock, ie. the inability to take definitive action. A primary goal of any policy should be to encourage key sectors of the economy to develop their capacities for flexible responsiveness to changing circumstances and new information. Particularly given the considerable uncertainty about the urgency of responding, the technical options, and political and institutional reactions, a more flexible approach is needed offering the ability to learn from experience and to deal with surprises as they arise.

Policies can be developed to encourage the US energy system to engage in trial-and-error modifications to its activities, to enhance social learning about the greenhouse gas issue, and to develop the capability of various key players to respond flexibly to new information and changing circumstances as they arise. The purpose is to respond to the practical challenges of potential global warming, without generating unacceptable costs of conflict over policies. Such an approach might contain several elements.

A rational approach must include the reduction of uncertainty through scientific inquiry, such as the continuing diverse DOE Carbon Dioxide Research Program. In addition to studies concerning the fundamental science of the greenhouse effect, more information is needed about greenhouse gas emissions and the technical options available for abatement. Furthermore, there is a pressing need to improve our understanding of the institutional limitations to greenhouse gas reduction, and of the differing situations in and perspectives of other countries. Use of fiscal and informational instruments rather than command-and-control regulation will require that we improve our understanding of the types and distribution of decision-making across the energy sector. In particular, better understanding of the widely differing investment behaviour of consumers, utility managers and other decision-makers would help to target policies.

The sobering conclusion of the study conducted by Fulkerson[78] is that the US (and the world) has not yet developed practical, safe, and socially acceptable, energy technologies that could replace fossil fuels. A much-intensified R&D effort is required urgently to develop and improve renewable and other non-fossil sources of energy in all sectors if we are ever to consider sustained control of CO_2 emissions, and to develop technologies that will improve the efficient end use and conversion of all fossil fuels.

Such an energy R&D programme seems prudent from any realistic business perspective; it would be purchasing options for the future. In the private sector, options are considered to have a real economic value, even when they are not exercised. The price tag, estimated at $1bn/yr, seems to be modest for such an insurance policy. Furthermore, US leadership in stimulating the development of such technologies could place US manufacturers in the position of being major world suppliers. Some products could find immediate markets in developing countries independently of any interest by such countries in reducing greenhouse gas emissions.

For the reasons discussed, trying to reconfigure the US energy system in the short term would be extraordinarily expensive and probably politically impossible. However, unlike charity, the best place to start displacing coal as an energy fuel may not be at home. Many developing countries have yet to make such large capital commitments to energy infrastructure as the US. An extensive programme transferring advanced non-fossil energy technologies to developing countries appears to be another policy that it would be prudent to pursue aggressively, even for those who are sceptical of the dangers of climate change. This would bring other benefits to developing countries and the US would improve its competitive position as a world supplier of energy technology.

This does not mean that the US should do no more at home than conduct research for exportable technology. Despite the obstacles to change described in section 6.2 of this paper, the opportunities for end-use efficiency improvements in the US are vast. Lighting, appliance, vehicle and building efficiency standards combined with informational policies and actions to address market failures for efficiency (such as the split incentives problem in rented buildings) are obvious policies described in section 6.2 that will reduce US dependence on energy imports and

---

[78] Fulkerson et al, *Energy Technology R&D*, op.cit.

improve the competitive position of the US economy as well as environmental quality.

Energy efficiency is the most obvious example of a class of measures designed to reduce greenhouse gas emissions that make sense on their own merits and ought to be pursued regardless of potential climate change.[79] A policy package that takes advantage of the positive externalities produced by pursuing other goals would have much to commend it, especially if the goals are pursued independently and do not, therefore, provide the same opportunities for opposing coalitions to be formed as, has been argued above, is likely with a single over-arching climate policy package. These 'no-regret' policies are options that should be pursued aggressively without delay and will strengthen the resilience of the US energy system in any event. It does not seem viable at this time, for the US utility industry to be forced to replace its existing investments in fossil-fuelled electrical generation or for consumers to be faced immediately with the economic burdens of an effective carbon tax. But the US energy system needs to be given greater flexibility through R&D and improved efficiency so that displacing fossil fuels becomes more conceivable.

Should the international community, at some time, opt for an international tradeable emissions scheme on either a global or smaller multilateral basis, the ability of the US to trade-off domestic emissions against alternative technology transfer to developing countries would be a useful asset to have developed. There would be certain monitoring advantages in bartering non-fossil technology for emissions rights rather than paying for them in cash.

This flexible approach has the advantage that it permits a wide range of decision-makers to respond in the least-cost fashion to the challenges that affect their particular activities. It avoids the misleading implication that any given figure for greenhouse gas emissions represents an environmentally-stable equilibrium that can or ought to be achieved. Finally, it avoids the commitment of society to the expenditure of vast resources to achieve an emissions reduction goal for the US that would make little difference to the rate of climate change if the developing countries follow a fossil fuel dependent pattern of development.

---

[79] S.H.Schneider, 'The Greenhouse Effect: Science and Policy', *Science*, Vol.243, 1989, pp.771-781.

However, the need for flexibility has to be balanced against the need for a stable policy environment, particularly for industries that would benefit from long-term planning. These include utilities, petroleum refining and transportation, forestry, construction, automakers, and other manufacturers making R&D or other long-term investments. At present some of these industries - particularly refining and utilities - have a short-term focus, partly because of rapid regulatory changes which have created great uncertainty about the future business environment. Any policy designed to engage these industries in effective abatement policies requires both a stable regulatory environment and signalling to encourage planners to expand their horizons to include long-term environmental concerns, such as global warming.

Many policies of long-term usefulness may have to be initiated soon. For example, due to the long lead times required to develop some alternative technologies, medium- to long-term R&D should be initiated or stepped-up without delay. In other cases technologies are well-proven but the long lifetime of existing infrastructure and housing stocks requires immediate decisions if they are to have significant effect before the extended term. Bans and limits on carbon-emitting activities will have to be phased in, both to permit industry to win their political acceptance and to retool. Hence, decisions about these instruments are also needed well before they are required to operate. The need to implement some policies long before the phenomena they are designed to prevent become visible may present major difficulties in sustaining support for a policy; particularly in the face of a coalition that is aware of the costs of the policy but sceptical of its benefits.

It certainly makes sense to think strategically and not to isolate climate policy goals from other environmental and societal goals. However, calls for strategic thinking usually extend the military metaphor to advocate a full-frontal assault on greenhouse gas emissions and deforestation. It is worth considering whether the superior flexibility and sustainability of guerilla warfare does not provide a more appropriate metaphor for thinking about a climate policy for the US energy sector.

Conclusions

The threat of global climate change may result in disputes among nations concerning the use of fossil fuel and forest resources. Because of the geography of these resources, the actions of only a few nations are likely to be of paramount importance. Hence, what a few do may determine the fate of all.[80] The US is clearly one of those key nations. The major developing countries are also of great importance, but in very different ways, because of their immense potential for growth.

This study has focused upon the prospects for reducing emissions of greenhouse gases from the US energy sector. The review inexorably paints a challenging picture. The history of US energy demand and the existing resources, infrastructure and institutions make the US economy as dependent on fossil fuels as a heroin addict is on the needle. Analysis of future projections, the institutional obstacles, and the US political process suggest that achieving major changes to break the addiction would be a momentous political task.

Technologically, the situation is mixed. There are many opportunities to improve efficiency, but non-fossil alternatives are quite inadequate. Infrastructural constraints would make rapid deployment of non-fossil alternatives very costly, even if the technologies were better. Above all, even if these technological and infrastructural constraints were less severe, institutional and societal constraints are such as to limit the rate at which efficiency can be improved or non-fossil sources deployed.

The challenge facing the US and the world energy system is to steer a course between global environmental disaster and global energy crisis. Success depends on viewing the energy system as a global system. This is why a key component of US policy must be a programme of generous technology development, demonstration, and transfer to developing countries to help stave them off the dependence in the first place. The alternative to such assistance by the developed world is to risk non-cooperation in emissions limitations by developing countries that would easily negate the benefits of any domestic attempts at emissions controls.

In summary the most important contributions the US energy system can make in response to this challenge is to:

* pursue domestic efficiency now

* embark on aggressive R&D to develop technological options that can be implemented as need is justified economically and environmentally

[80] W.Fulkerson, R.M.Cushman, G.Marland, and S.Rayner, *International Impacts of Global Climate Change*, ORNL/TM-11184, Oak Ridge National Laboratory, Oak Ridge, 1989.

* engage in generous technology transfer to save developing countries from becoming dependant on fossil fuels for their development and as new technologies are implemented in developing countries they should become economically more attractive in the US market to replace existing US fossil fuel infrastructure over the long term.

The payoff to the US would be a more resilient energy system, improved economic competitiveness, and a range of environmental advantages.

Chapter 7 The Greenhouse Effect in Japan: Burden or Opportunity?

Akira Tanabe
Tokyo Electric Power Company,
Visiting Research Fellow, RIIA, 1989-1991
and Michael Grubb
Research Fellow, RIIA

We would like to thank all the people who gave us comments on our earlier drafts including the attendees at the study group held at Chatham House, London.

We would also like to thank all the people whom we visited in Japan in 1989, or whom we met at various seminars and conferences on the greenhouse effect issue. Their ideas and comments were very helpful.

We would also like to thank both the Tokyo Electric Power Company and the Royal Institute of International Affairs for the arrangement to second one of the authors from TEPCO to the RIIA to participate in this project, through which both the authors could meet and work together.

Finally, we would like to thank all the staff of the Energy and Environmental Programme of the RIIA for directing the research, editing the manuscripts and providing editorial assistance.

The Greenhouse Effect in Japan: Burden or Opportunity?

Japan's CO_2 emissions are among the lowest in the OECD both on a per capita and per GDP basis. As a major industrial country, energy consumption in the industrial sector is high compared to other OECD countries and there is pent-up demand for energy consumption in the residential, commercial and transport sectors. Because of this demand potential, CO_2 emissions constraints are perceived as a burden for Japan in its quest to meet growing consumer demand, and Japan takes a cautious attitude towards any commitment to international emissions agreements.

On the other hand, since Japan is a country with very scarce indigenous fossil fuel resources, reducing dependence on imported fossil fuel, especially the continuing high dependence on oil from the Middle East, forms a basic tenet of energy policy. Displacing oil by coal, LNG and nuclear power has featured strongly, together with the pursuit of energy conservation and promotion of renewable technologies. But the world-wide low oil price of the 1980s, enhanced by the strong yen have not reinforced these objectives. In this respect, CO_2 emissions constraints are perceived as an opportunity for Japan to revitalize energy conservation and other policies which are desirable in and of themselves. Future nuclear power development, another controversial issue for Japan, is a potential policy which could be implemented whether or not the potential for renewables and energy conservation is realized.

Japan has derived much of its success from technology development and application, and government and industry both focus on 'technological *breakthroughs' as the main means by which CO_2 emissions might be limited. There is less discussion of domestic energy policy issues, and a reluctance to consider legislation to limit CO_2 emissions. But the close relationship between government and industry, often working towards agreed national goals, has proved effective in the past in meeting the challenges of earlier environmental concerns and the oil price shocks. This, and Japan's growing consciousness about its international position and image, contrast with the natural conservatism of the country and the scepticism of many about the greenhouse effect. Much will depend on how the international process develops and on the extent to which the greenhouse effect is taken as a serious challenge.*

This chapter discusses possible policy implications for Japan in reducing CO_2 emissions by using a wide range of feasible energy balance scenarios and concludes that Japan has promising but as yet uncertain prospects for achieving such a solution.

Figure 7.1 Japan energy consumption and CO_2 emissions 1971-89

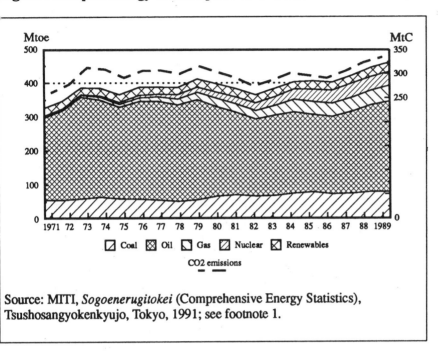

Source: MITI, *Sogoenerugitokei* (Comprehensive Energy Statistics), Tsushosangyokenkyujo, Tokyo, 1991; see footnote 1.

7.1 Development and trends in the energy balance

In Japan, as in other developed economies, the total primary energy requirement (TPER) hardly increased from 1973 until the middle of the 1980s. Although there were some fluctuations in direct response to the two oil crises in that period, TPER in general kept constant at the level of about 350-400Mtoe per annum[1] despite the steady growth of GDP (Figure 7.1).

[1] There are at least four different TPER statistics for Japan (UN Energy Statistics, OECD Energy Balances, BP Statistical Review and MITI Comprehensive Energy Statistics) and they differ substantially, mainly due to the different heat values (Gross or Net Heat Value) and conversion factors (from electricity to primary energy on whether input or output basis) used, and the different definitions which include or exclude items such as bunkers. For example, Japan's 1987 TPER were 319Mtoe (UN), 372Mtoe (OECD), 377Mtoe (BP) and 422Mtoe (MITI), respectively. This chapter uses the Ministry of International Trade and Industry (MITI) statistics unless otherwise stated because of their completeness and availability. All the studies referred to in this chapter attributed to MITI or commissioned by them are available on application to MITI.

In 1988, demand increased by 5.4% and exceeded for the second year running its past highest recorded level set in 1979; and, in 1989, demand increased again but by a smaller amount of 3.7%. Although this increase reflects a world-wide trend, Japan experienced much higher growth rates in its energy demand than other OECD countries.[2] These can be attributed to growing economic activity with domestic demand expansion, low and stable energy prices due to both the decline of oil prices and the strength of the yen, and the slowdown of energy conservation.

Since the first oil crisis in 1973, there have been energy conservation policies directed at all energy consuming sectors, but the majority of the improvements were achieved in the industrial sector (see Figure 7.2) through changes both in structure and energy conservation. Energy consumption in the residential/commercial and transportation sectors has continued to grow even during the period of response to the two oil crises. While this growth has been offset by reductions in industrial consumption, the share of the industrial sector in total final energy consumption (TFC) is still higher than in other OECD countries.

Oil still dominates energy supply. Although its share in TPER decreased from 77% (298Mtoe) in 1973 to 58% (267Mtoe) in 1989, it is still high compared to other OECD countries (average 43% in 1988). Virtually all oil is imported, and reducing dependency continues to be a major objective of Japan's energy policy. In the past, about half of the reduction was achieved by fuel switching in power generation, for which there is limited further scope.[3] Recognizing the need to secure its oil supply, the government has followed three main policies: oil stockpiling; diversification of sources of imported oil to reduce the heavy dependence on the Middle East; and extensive support for exploration and development of oil and gas resources, both domestically and overseas. In 1988, the import of oil from overseas exploration projects accounted

---

[2] *BP Statistical Review of World Energy 1990* shows that Japan increased TPER and oil consumption by 3.7% and 3.6% respectively in 1989, far exceeding the OECD average growth rate of 1.3% and 0.5%.

[3] About 10% of total electricity is generated by autoproducers in Japan for their own use mainly in the industrial sector. The sale of electricity by autoproducers to general customers is only permitted if that sale does not hinder the benefit of other customers supplied by electric power companies. Unless otherwise stated, figures for electricity generation are those for public electricity generation.

Figure 7.2 Japan final energy consumption trends 1971-89

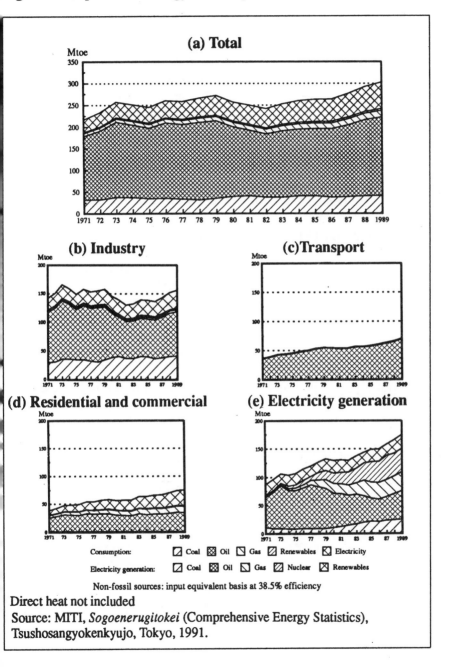

for 12% of total oil imports.[4] The proportion of oil in generation fell from two-thirds to under one-quarter over the period 1973-89 and, by 1989, it accounted for only 15% of total oil consumption.

Natural gas and nuclear have increased steadily from about 1% of TPER each in 1973 to 10% each in 1989. Most of the natural gas is imported as liquefied natural gas (LNG) and about three-quarters of the total is used to generate electricity. Despite strong concerns about cost and engineering, LNG was first introduced in 1969 from Alaska as a clean fuel for both electricity generation and city gas supply around Tokyo where urban air pollution was severe.[5] The trading of LNG is usually based upon a long-term contract (20-25 years) with a high 'take-or-pay' obligation on the customer. Although more flexible contracts are being sought for new LNG projects, this supply guarantee in return for the obligation to buy helps secure imported energy resources for the future. By 1989, 21% of electricity was generated by LNG.

The share of nuclear power in the supply rise is comparable with that of LNG and its contribution to total electricity output reached 26% in 1989. There is a rapidly growing anti-nuclear movement, but, on the premise of the safe management of both operation and radioactive wastes, nuclear power in Japan has been evaluated and supported by policymakers as an energy resource which is stably supplied, economical,[6] relatively clean, and which reduces import dependency.[7]

Coal used to be the major energy resource until the beginning of the 1960s. In 1960, 85% of coal was indigenous and this accounted for more than 40% of TPER. However, it was supplanted by cheap imported oil and declined to 13% of TPER by 1978. Following the two oil crises, this trend reversed mainly through the expanded import of less expensive

---

[4] Compared to 16.7% in 1973, the ratio has declined. *Nikkei Shimbun*, 25 May 1989.
[5] By 1987, Japan imported 39Mtoe of LNG (more than three quarters of the total world LNG trade) from Indonesia (52%), Malaysia (20%), Brunei (18%), Abu Dhabi (8%) and Alaska (3%).
[6] MITI produce annual figures which evaluate the costs of generating electricity from all sources, including nuclear. According to 1989 figures, average generating cost (operational life) is as follows: hydroelectric Y13/kWh, oil-fired Y11/kWh, coal-fired Y10/kWh, LNG-fired Y10/kWh, nuclear Y9/kWh.
[7] Although all the uranium is imported, nuclear power is considered to be quasi-indigenous because of its longer stock-piling capacity (more than two years) than imported fossil fuels (less than a hundred days).

coal.[8] Of the coal consumed in 1989, 90% was imported, about one-quarter was used to generate electricity and accounted for 10% of generation in 1989.

Hydroelectric power used to be the major electricity generating resource until the early 1960s (52% in 1960), but contributed 12% of generation in 1989. Most of the large-scale and economical hydroelectric power sites have already been developed and further expansion is expected mainly through the development of medium and micro-scale sites. Geothermal resources contributed 0.2% of electricity generation in 1989.

Electricity use increased steadily by 3.4%/yr from 1973 to 1989. Electricity demand in the residential/commercial sector is growing especially rapidly and now constitutes about the same amount as in the industrial sector.[9] To meet this growing demand, input to electricity generation, inclusive of autoproducers, has increased from 106Mtoe (27% of TPER) in 1973 to 175Mtoe (37% of TPER) in 1989, producing 466TWh and 791TWh respectively.

In 1989, autoproducers, mostly through cogeneration in the industrial sector, generated 12% of total electricity supply. Since the mid-1980s, the cogeneration system in the residential/commercial sector has grown rapidly, with a generating capacity that grew to 0.12GW in 1988.[10] This is still small compared with the total public generating capacity of 165GW in 1988, but is expected to grow by more than twenty times with the introduction of fuel cell cogeneration by the year 2000.[11]

Despite the expansion in coal use, with the increased use of LNG and nuclear power, and the decreased use of oil, emissions of CO_2 from Japan have kept at around 300MtC/yr since 1973, except for the late 1980s

---

[8] In 1987, Japan imported 68Mtoe of coal (the largest importer in the world, over four times larger than the second largest, which was Italy) from Australia (50%), Canada (19%), USA (11%), South Africa (7%), China (4%) and other countries (6%).

[9] Electricity demand growth rates from 1973 to 1989 were as follows: industrial sector (1.7%/yr), residential/commercial sector (6.1%/yr), transportation sector (2.3%/yr) and in total 3.4%/yr.

[10] Cogeneration by: gas turbine (0.009GW), diesel engine (0.08GW), gas engine (0.032GW), in total 0.12GW in 1988.

[11] Denki Jigyo Shingikai Jukyu Bukai (Electric Utility Council (for MITI) Supply-Demand Working Group), *Chukan Hokoku* (Summary of the Interim Report), 1990.

spurt leading to the record high of 1989 (335MtC/yr) (Figure 7.1).[12] Japan's per capita and per GDP CO_2 emission figures fall among the lowest among OECD countries. These figures illustrate the high level of energy efficiency achieved in Japan. This partly reflects the fact that residential and commercial demand are still at an early stage of development relative to many industrial countries,[13] but it is also evidence of a genuine efficiency in industry. Comparisons have demonstrated that the energy used per tonne of steel production, for example, have fallen by 8% since 1980 and is now the lowest in the world by a considerable margin.[14] This example is not atypical within industry. A high level of efficiency has been achieved by a combination of high energy prices and strong policies developed and implemented jointly between government and industry including both technical improvement and steps to minimize wastage. If the conditions of the 1980s persist with relatively low energy prices reflecting a state of relative abundance of energy worldwide, the extent to which Japan can or will maintain strong further increases in energy efficiency is far from certain.

Indigenous energy resource base

The overriding factor for Japan is the scarcity of indigenous reserves, with almost no oil or gas reserves, and most of the available coal reserves being difficult and expensive to extract. Consequently, Japan is more dependent on imported fossil fuels than any other major OECD country; in 1989, only 2% of fossil fuel consumption was produced indigenously.

---

[12] MITI's estimate of 1988 CO_2 emissions from Japan was 294MtC (Advisory Committee to MITI for Energy, Long-term Energy Prospects Subcommittee, *Chukan Torimatome* Interim Report, 1989), compared with this chapter's estimate, 324MtC. This may be due to different coefficients (from heat value to CO_2 emissions) used or treatments of feedstocks for chemical industry and non-energy use amounts. (See Appendix 2)

[13] Japan's TFC in residential & commercial sector per capita in 1987 was 0.4toe, much less than other developed countries; US 1.6Mtoe, former W.Germany 1.2Mtoe, France 0.9toe, UK 0.9toe, Italy 0.6toe, OECD average 1.0toe. Conversely, Japan's TFC in the industrial sector per capita (0.98toe) did not fall below the level of those countries except US and former West Germany and was comparable to OECD average (1.1toe). Derived from *OECD Energy Balances, 1987*, OECD, Paris, 1989.

[14] According to the Japan Steel and Iron Association, comparison of energy efficiency among major steel producing countries in 1987 was as follows: Japan=100 (energy consumption per unit weight of crude steel), US 141, Italy 120, UK 120, W.Germany 114, France 117, Brazil 124.

As a result, Japan is the largest coal and natural gas importing country and the second largest, next to the US, oil importing country in the world. Domestic projects are not expected to contribute in quantity, but are considered to be necessary in order to develop and maintain oil exploration technology.

Despite Japan's relative abundance of coal, estimated to be 562Mtoe (852 million tonnes) of proved reserves,[15] the domestic coal industry started to decline from the 1960s. The second coal policy plan of 1964 clearly specified that it was a national requirement to secure the production of domestic coal, and a target of 50 million tonnes of domestic production was set. Due to the increasing price difference (three-fold in 1987) between expensive domestic coal and less expensive imported coal (for both coking and steam coal), the current coal policy plan issued in 1986 set as a target for the future an annual production level of 10 million tonnes.

Indigenous renewable energy resources

In contrast to fossil fuel resources, indigenous renewable resources are abundant, and have the potential to become a major energy resource (see Table 7.1). Since the first oil crisis, the government has sponsored extensive R&D[16] in an effort to expand their use. To date their use has been limited since they are either not competitively priced or require further technological development for commercial use.

Being a mountainous country with much precipitation, Japan is blessed with extensive hydroelectric power resources. In total, hydroelectric power resources are estimated to be 134TWh/yr, of which 83TWh/yr have already been developed.[17] Most large-scale hydroelectric power sites are already in use, leaving only medium and small hydro power sites for future development. It is possible to reduce construction costs through the standardization of equipment for these smaller sites and thus encourage their development.

15] *BP Statistical Review of World Energy*, 1990.

16] MITI initiated the 'Sunshine Project' in 1974. This is a large-scale long-term national technology development project aimed at utilization of various oil-alternative new energy sources including solar energy, geothermal energy, gasification and liquefaction of coal, hydrogen energy and wind energy.

17] MITI, *The 5th Hydro Power Survey (1980-1985)*.

Table 7.1 Indigenous renewable energy resources

Source	Technical resources in lower density (per year)		Technical resources in higher density (per year)	
	Assumption	Estimate	Assumption	Estimate
Hydro	Half of potential surveyed[a] is developed	25TWh	Full potential surveyed[a] is developed	51TWh
Wind - onshore	2.9GW[b] (small size + remote islands) Capacity factor = 30%	8TWh	5.8GW[b] (small size + remote islands + grid) Capacity factor = 30%	15TWh
Wind - offshore	10% of higher potential	2TWh	Strong wind area: 78km^2 (continental shelf),1 unit/1ha	17TWh[c]
Solar water heating	Potential roof space,[d] 228km^2 (residential/commercial sector), 0.09kW/m^2 efficiency=50%	8Mtoe	Potential roof space,[d]395km^2 (residential/commercial & industry sector), 0.09kW/m^2, efficiency=50%	13Mtoe
Photo-voltaics	6.1GW[e] (public service & commercial use)	8TWh	48GW[e] (public service, commercial, residential & industry)	63TWh
Domestic & industrial waste	10% of higher potential	2Mtoe	Domestic 9Mtoe Industrial 10Mtoe	19Mtoe[f]
Agricultural waste	10 % of higher potential	1Mtoe		10Mtoe[f]

Source	Technical resources in lower density (per year)		Technical resources in higher density (per year)	
	Assumption	**Estimate**	**Assumption**	**Estimate**
Biomass crops	10% of higher potential	9Mtoe	60% of biomass from forest and urban greenery, bamboo grasses are utilised	91Mtoe[f]
Geothermal aquifiers	10% of higher potential	6Mtoe	<2,000m, 50 sites	56Mtoe[g]
Geothermal hot dry rock[h]		-----		-----
Wave-shoreline	20% of higher potential	1TWh	60km (1% of total shoreline)	5TWh[i]
Total		44TWh +26Mtoe		151TWh +189Mtoe

Sources: derived from

a. MITI, 5th Survey of Hydro-Power Resources (1980-1985). Potential hydro resources are estimated to be 134TWh/yr, with 83TWh/yr already developed.

b. MITI, *Shinenerugi Donyu Bijon* (New Energy Introduction Vision), 1985, Tsushosangyochosakai, Tokyo, p.130.

c. T. Honma, *Furyoku Enerugi Dokuhon* (Wind Energy Handbook), Ohumusha, Tokyo, 1979, p.151.

d. MITI, *Shinenerugi Donyu Bijon* (New Energy Introduction Vision), Tsushosangyochosakai, Tokyo, 1985, p.113.

e. MITI, *Shinenerugi Donyu Bijon* (New Energy Introduction Vision), Tsushosangyochosakai, Tokyo,1985, p.90.

f. A.Honda, *Baiomasuenerugi* (Biomass Energy), Shoenerugisenta, Tokyo, 1986, p.154.

g. NEDO, *Nyu Enaji* (New Energy), Denryokushinposha, Tokyo, 1989, p.74.

h. Research is being conducted by NEDO. Technical potential is estimated to be large.

i. *Enerugi Kanri Gijutsu, Netsukanrihen* (Energy Management Technology, Heat Management), Shoenerugisenta, Tokyo, 1989, p.19.

It is estimated that 5.8GW of wind power generating capacity[18] can be utilized in Japan, and assuming the capacity factor of 30%, they can generate 15TWh/yr. Offshore resources on the continental shelf are estimated to be 17TWh/yr.[19] Smaller-scale power generating technology (15-300kW) is now proven. More than 10 units are being used in Japan, and 400 units have already been exported.[20] Given the relative lack of strong winds, typical generation costs are currently estimated to be about twice as much as large thermal power stations. However, installed in areas such as remote islands, which are not connected to large electricity grids and have strong winds, wind power systems are thought to be an economical and feasible alternative to diesel power generation.[21]

With most of Japan lying below 40°N, the solar radiation density is about half that of Saudi Arabia.[22] Solar water heater equipment has been in use in Japan since the late 1940s. More than 2 million such water heaters are estimated to have been in use before the beginning of the first oil crisis,[23] but uptake has since been slow. In 1988, less than 1% of households were equipped with solar systems, and almost all of these were for hot water only. Despite fluctuations due to the decline in oil prices from 1986, their use is steadily becoming more widespread. A more advanced solar system technology for both heating and hot water, consisting of a heat storage unit and auxiliary heater in addition to a heat collector, has been available commercially for domestic use since the late 1970s. Solar system technology for industrial use is now being developed. The resource potential for solar heat for both the

[18] 2.5GW for smaller scale plants less than 100kW, 0.4GW for remote island use, and 2.9GW for larger-scale plants which could be connected to the national grid, see MITI, *Shinenerugi Donyu Bijon* (New Energy Introduction Vision), Tsushosangyochosakai, Tokyo, 1985, p.130.

[19] T.Honma, *Furyoku Enerugi Dokuhon* (Wind Energy Handbook), Ohmusha, Tokyo, 1979, p.151.

[20] Japanese government, *Contribution of Energy Technologies to Reduction of CO2 Emission*, MITI, 1989, p.26.

[21] MITI, *The Twenty-First Century Energy Vision*, 1986, p.132.

[22] According to Science and Technology Agency, *Saisei Kano Enerugi no Riyo Shisutemu ni Kansuru Chosa* (Renewable Energy Utilization System Survey), Tokyo, 1985, p.42, annual average solar radiation in Japan is 0.132-0.147kW/m^2 whereas in Saudi Arabia 0.238-0.289kW/m^2.

[23] Japan Solar Energy Society, *Taiyo Enerugi Dokuhon* (Solar Energy Handbook), Ohmusha, Tokyo, 1975, p.38.

esidential/commercial and industrial sectors is estimated to be 3Mtoe/yr. It is estimated that 48GW of photovoltaics could be utilized or public service, domestic and industrial use.[24] Assuming a capacity actor of 15%, they could generate 63TWh/yr.[25]

The energy content of domestic and industrial waste has been estimated t nearly 10Mtoe each per annum.[26] Currently, about 70% of domestic vaste is incinerated.[27] Although using steam for electricity generation ·n site expanded after the first oil shock, there is still a great margin for mprovement. Some incinerators generate electricity only for their own peration while others produce enough of a surplus to sell to electric tility companies.

Japan produces 282 million tonnes of biomass per year (with a calorific alue of 4,200kcal/kg) from forests which cover 70% of its total land nass. Assuming that about 60% of that biomass can be utilized, it onstitutes a possible biomass resource of 70Mtoe. Added to this, iomass from urban greenery and bamboo grasses, the potential is ·1Mtoe.[28]

Among the various types of agricultural wastes, rice hulls and rice traws are the most efficient energy resources because of their low water ontent (about 10%), relatively high calorific value (3,500kcal/kg), and he ease with which they can be collected and treated using large-scale ice threshing systems. Out of an estimated 10Mtoe, 7Mtoe derives from his rice-related waste but currently, only 0.2Mtoe is utilized.[29]

Japan is situated on the Pacific Rim volcanic belt and has 76 active ·olcanoes, although currently, geothermal energy is for the most part

24] MITI, *Shinenerugi Donyu Bijon* (New Energy Introduction Vision), op.cit., p.90.
25] MITI has estimated that by the year 2030 it may be possible to introduce 12Mtoe/yr about 60TWh/yr) through photovoltaic power. Japanese government, *Contribution of :nergy Technologies to Reduction of CO2 Emission*, op.cit., p.28.
26] A.Honda, *Baiomasuenerugi* (Biomass Energy), Shoenerugisenta, Tokyo, 1986, ·.151.
27] 72.6% in 1987. Environment Agency, *Kankyo Hakusho Kakuron* (White Paper on ne Environment, Details), Ohkurashoinsatsukyoku, Tokyo, 1990, p.150.
28] Honda, op.cit. p.154, and according to Hideo Iwaki, biomass energy potential in apan amounts to 160Mtoe but the utilizable amount would be 17Mtoe if the following actors are fully taken into consideration: competitive usage of lands, forest nanagement and ecological care. Hideo Iwaki, 'Baiomasu to Ekoroji (Biomass and :cology)' in *Enerugi to Miraishakai* (Energy and Future Society), Shoenerugisenta, okyo, 1990.
29] Honda, op.cit., p.156.

untapped and is used only for local power generation and heat supply. The technical potential for geothermal aquifiers to a depth of 2,000m is estimated to be 56Mtoe/yr. If deeper geothermal energy resources can be used, including techniques to extract energy from hot dry rocks (HDR), the available energy resources increase significantly.[30]

It is estimated that about 5TWh/yr of electricity could be generated through wave power using 1% of Japan's coast line. The potential for renewable energy from tidal sources does exist but the maximum tidal height is 4.9 metres at the Sea of Ariake, and is far from economic using currently considered techniques.

Table 7.1 shows estimates of resources at low and high densities of renewables exploitation and demonstrates that, at the higher density, the contribution of renewables could be about 60% of the 1989 fossil fuel requirement level.[31] There are, of course, many technical and economic and other uncertainties to be resolved in exploiting some of these resources.

7.2 Projections and options to the year 2000 and 2030

This section summarizes the main themes and assumptions of the scenarios which will be used to illustrate the possible range of future energy balances and CO_2 emissions, and the impact of policies. The detailed structure of demand for each scenario is tabulated in the Appendix to this chapter, and the main scenario results are illustrated in Figure 7.3 and summarized in Table 7.2.

2000A: Business-as-usual

As reviewed in section 7.1, the stabilization of TPER and the consequent effect on CO_2 emissions was achieved through energy conservation (mainly in the industrial sector) and the substitution of oil by gas and nuclear power, both of which have been the main objectives of Japan's current energy policy. However, because of changes in energy supply and demand, unless the current energy policy is greatly changed, both Japan's TPER and CO_2 emissions will grow strongly towards the year 2000. The steady growth of energy demand in both the residential/commercial and transportation sectors will no longer be offse

---

[30] NEDO, *Nyu Enaji* (New Energy), Denryokushinposha, Tokyo, 1989, p.74.
[31] 151TWh*860kcal/kWh/45%=29Mtoe, 29Mtoe+189Mtoe=218Mtoe (55% of th 1989 fossil fuel requirement level, which was 393Mtoe).

Figure 7.3 Scenarios for Japan energy consumption and CO₂ emissions 1988-2030

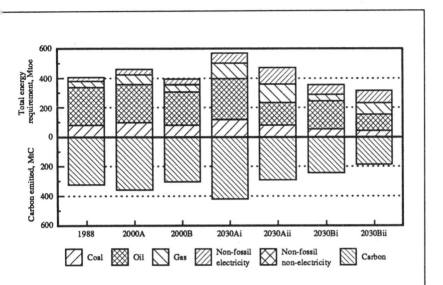

Note: Non-fossil sources on output basis. Non-fossil contributions therefore appear different from data in Figure 7.1, Table 7.2 and Appendix which use input equivalents (estimated fossil fuel displaced).

by a reduction of energy demand in the industrial sector. Moreover, natural gas and coal consumption will continue to grow and this increase is not likely to be offset by a decrease in oil consumption as in the past.

In constructing the 'business-as-usual' scenario for the year 2000, it is assumed that the following trends continue for each energy consuming sector (see also Table 7.2):

* The industrial structure continues to shift towards less energy-intensive industries with moderate energy conservation throughout industry. This offsets the growth in energy demand due to the overall expansion of industrial production.

* Although the population to the year 2000 shows a minor increase (4.6% from 1990 level), the total number of households as well as the

Table 7.2 Summary of assumptions for each scenario

	TFC Ind	Res/Com	Trans	Elec generation TWh	Nuclear GW	Nuclear %	TPER Coal	Oil	Gas	Renew	Nuclear	Total	CO₂ MtC
	<---- Mtoe ---->						<----------------- Mtoe ---------------->						
1973	166	48	44	401	2	2	60	298	6	19	2	385	313
1989	156	76	71	696	29	26	80	267	46	27	41	462	335
2000A	152	97	86	900	47 (29)	34	98	259	65	31	69	523	360 (385)
2000B	130	87	79	764	47 (29)	40	80	225	51	31	69	455	302 (327)
2030Ai	173	146	110	1464	77	35	118	278	105	56	97	654	422
2030Aii*	173	146	110	1270	107 (77)	55	79	154	126	115	135	609	290 (325)
2030Bi	115	107	91	860	77	59	54	191	44	52	91	432	243
2030Bii*	115	107	91	802	77	63	4	109	80	92	91	414	185

Notes:*Fuel switch options:TFC/Industry sector: 20% of coal and oil to gas; 30% of electricity to localized renewablesTFC/Residential and commercial sector: 30% of oil to gas; 30% of electricity to localised renewables TFC/Transport sector: 70% of oil to gas (20%), renewables (30%), elec (20%)

For detailed structure, see Appendix to this chapter.

( ) indicates different CO₂ emissions under higher nuclear capacity; see text

floor space per household continues to grow.[32] Energy consumption per household also continues to grow, reflecting the still low level of space heating, the growing demand for air conditioning, the increase in home automation and the use of larger or more sophisticated appliances.[33]

* Energy consumption relative to office space remains the same since the higher energy efficient air conditioning and lighting equipment offsets the increasing energy demand of office automation. However, the floor space per employee in the commercial sector grows steadily.

* Automobiles and trucks together, currently accounting for 83% of total energy consumption in the transportation sector (1987),[34] continue to be dominant. Car possession per capita, oil consumption for road transportation per capita and highway length per vehicle all continue to grow moderately.[35] The average fuel economy for all new automobiles in Japan, which is determined by the actual composition of different sized cars, continues to decrease. This is partly due to the consumer's increasing preference for more luxurious and less fuel-efficient cars, and offsets the improvement in fuel efficiency for cars of each size category. Road transport of goods continues to grow steadily in Japan due to the development of urbanization primarily around the Tokyo-Osaka Metropolitan area, the decentralization of industrial facilities, and the increase in the parcel delivery business. Energy consumption per unit amount of transportation remains the same since improvements in highway networks offset the expansion of small and individually-oriented commodity flow.

32] The floor space per household and per employee in Japan is still much less than in •ther developed countries, and demand for more space remains high.

33] For example, share of larger refrigerator in total sales increased from less than 10% n 1983 to more than 35% in 1988, and larger television set also increased from less han 5% to more than 20%. Advisory Committee (to MITI) for Energy, *Enerugi no Riyo Coritsuka ni Mukete* (For Improving Energy Utilization Efficiency), 1990.

34] Energy consumption for domestic transportation in 1987 was shared by; .utomobiles (40%), trucks (43%), buses (3%), rail (5%), navigation (6%) and air (3%). Ministry of Transport, *Unyu Hakusho* (White Paper on Transportation; 1989),)hkurashoinsatsnkyoku, Tokyo, 1990.

35] Car ownership per capita in Japan was 0.24 in 1987, lower than other developed :ountries: US 0.57, former W.Germany 0.46, France 0.39, UK 0.36, Italy 0.39. (Derived :rom Japan Automobile Manufacturers Association, *Shuyokoku Jidosha Tokei* Automobile Statistics of Major Countries), 1988).

* Electricity demand continues to grow steadily due mainly to the strong growth in the residential/commercial sector. Coal, gas and nuclear contribute an increasing proportion of electricity generation, whereas oil decreases slightly. Nuclear power accounts for 34% of total electricity output, with a capacity increase from 29GW in 1989 to 47GW in 2000. The average thermal power generation efficiency increases to 38.5% (GHV),[36] compared with 37.9% in 1988.

As a result of the above assumptions, TPER grows to 523Mtoe, 61Mtoe above the 1989 level. The resultant CO_2 emissions in the year 2000 would be 360MtC, 7% more than the 1989 level. This relatively small increase in CO_2 emissions compared with larger increase of TPER (13%) results from the expansion of nuclear power. If the nuclear capacity which has been commissioned is not on stream by 2000, then the CO_2 emissions will be 385MtC, 15% more than the 1989 level.

2000B: Emissions abatement

In this scenario the current energy conservation policy is assumed to be strengthened through such means as a national campaign, efficiency standard setting and financial incentives.

Under these assumptions demand in the industrial sector decreases to 130Mtoe from 156Mtoe in 1989, instead of remaining constant as in business-as-usual. This projected demand of 130Mtoe in the industrial sector is the same as in 1982, which was the lowest in the 1980s. Growing energy demand in both the residential/commercial and the transportation sectors is assumed to be suppressed, leading to a smaller increase from the 1989 level than in business-as-usual. Electricity output also grows at a slower pace and nuclear power accounts for 40% of the reduced electricity output (compared with 34% in business-as-usual), but with the same capacity increase from 1989. However, TPER reduces only slightly from the 1989 level.

Under this scenario, CO_2 emissions would be 302MtC in the year 2000 10% less than the 1989 level, achieved mainly through oil replacemen by natural gas and nuclear power. But again, if nuclear capacity does no increase from the 1989 level, then the CO_2 emissions will be 327MtC the same level as the 1989 emissions. In order to achieve this level o CO_2 reductions without increasing nuclear power, greater energy

[36] Gross Heat Value (GHV) generating efficiency figures are usually between 5% an 10% lower than Net Heat Value generating efficiency.

conservation or more use of renewables would be required; for reasons discussed in section 7.1, this would be difficult.

2030Ai: Business-as-usual

In Japan, energy projections for the 21st century were prepared by both the government and major energy industries in 1986. All of these project TPER in 2030 between 590Mtoe (by the petroleum industry)[37] and 800Mtoe (by the Ministry of International Trade and Industry (MITI), a high scenario).[38] The TPER level of 654Mtoe chosen for the business-as-usual scenario falls between these two projections which is a 25% increase from the year 2000 (see Table 7.2 and Figure 7.3).

Japan's population is projected to level off at about 129 million from 2000 to 2025, but a steadily expanding economy and rising consumer expectations are likely to lead to substantial increases in the services demanded in all sectors.[39] Suppression of energy demand through the diffusion of more energy efficient technologies will be offset by: the increasing output and sophistication in the industrial sector (higher quality products, replacing human labour by robots etc.); greater comfort, convenience and affluence in the residential/commercial sector; and greater mobility in the transportation sector, which are all sought by using more energy.

Nuclear power generating capacity is assumed to increase from 47GW at the year 2000 to 77GW by the year 2030, by a 1GW/yr increase and to contribute 35% of total electricity output. Electricity generation by renewable resources is assumed to be 150TWh/yr compared with 90TWh/yr in the year 2000. The average thermal power generation efficiency increases to 45% (GHV), compared with 38.5% at the year 2000.

Based on the above assumptions, CO_2 emissions would be 422MtC in 2030, a 26% increase from the 1989 level.

[37] The Committee for Energy Policy Promotion, *Enerugi Sangyo Choki Bijon* (Energy Industry Long-Term Vision), Tokyo, 1986, p.34.
[38] MITI, *The Twenty-First Century Energy Vision*, 1986, p.111.
[39] For assumptions of population growth and projections of space increases see MITI, *The Twenty-First Century Energy Vision*, 1986. It is projected (pp.6,88,99) that residential space per household will increase to 120m² by the year 2030 from 100m² at the year 2000, and office space per employee will more than double from 5m² in 1985 to 12m² by 2030.

2030Aii: Emissions abatement through fuel switching

This scenario assumes that in the industrial sector 20% of coal and oil are replaced by gas and 30% of electricity is replaced by renewable energy. In the residential/commercial sector 30% of oil is replaced by gas and also 30% of electricity is replaced by renewable energy. In the transportation sector 70% of oil use is replaced by gas (20%), renewables (30%) and electricity (20%) (see Table 7.2 and Figure 7.3).[40]

Based on these assumptions, CO_2 emissions would reduce to 325MtC, the same level as 1989 level. To further reduce CO_2 emissions, if nuclear power generation capacity is increased to 107GW instead of 77GW in the year 2030, then the CO_2 emissions would further decrease to 290MtC, and by 13% less than the 1989 level. In this scenario, oil use decreases by 40% from the 1989 level whereas gas use increases three-fold.

2030Bi: Emissions abatement through energy efficiency

This scenario assumes great improvement of energy utilization efficiency in all sectors through the diffusion of various technologies including cogeneration, heat pumps and a new transportation system.

This scenario incorporates the assumptions as summarized in Table 7.2. Demand in the industrial sector further decreases to 115Mtoe from 130Mtoe as a continuation of parallel policies adopted in the 2000 scenario, instead of increasing to 173Mtoe as in the business-as-usual. Demand in both residential/commercial and transportation sectors grows moderately to even a level slightly higher than in the 2000 business-as-usual. Electricity output also grows moderately and nuclear power (being assumed to be the same generating capacity of 77GW as in the business-as-usual case) accounts for 59% of the reduced electricity output. As a result, TPER reduces to 432Mtoe, about the same level as in 1989.

Based on these assumptions, CO_2 emissions would decrease to 243MtC, a 27% reduction on the 1989 level.

2030Bii: Emissions abatement through efficiency and switching

This scenario is based on the assumptions of fuel switching in the 2030Aii scenario with the lower level of demand in the 2030Bi scenario

---

[40] With vehicles powered by Compressed Natural Gas (CNG), photovoltaics and electric power.

and results in a decrease of CO_2 emissions to 185MtC, a 45% reduction from the 1989 level (see Table 7.2).

7.3 Policy options and constraints

Evaluation of the feasibility of reducing Japan's CO_2 emissions varies within the different branches of government. MITI is concerned that rapid CO_2 reduction may not only hinder economic growth but may also require the government to intervene extensively to control energy demand, a prospect it deems undesirable.[41] On the other hand, the Environment Agency view is that even the target of a 20% reduction in CO_2 emissions by the year 2005 is not impossible for Japan to achieve. In support, it points to the example of the strengthening of automobile emission standards which, in the long run, contributed to the improvement of productivity of the automobile industry and consequently to the reinforcement of the overall economy.[42]

MITI's report for the year 2000 and 2010, projects CO_2 emissions to increase by 16% by 2000 from the 1988 level and then stabilize at that level from 2000 to 2010.[43] Their underlying economic growth assumptions for this projection were 4% for the period between 1988 and 2000 and 3% afterwards (2000-2010). The same economic growth rate of 4% and stabilization of CO_2 emissions by 2000 were estimated to be achievable in the Environment Agency's case study, by adopting policy options at a cost of 3.6 trillion yen per year.[44]

Despite this difference in evaluation of the feasibility of CO_2 reduction between these two governmental organizations, a majority of the basic policy options each lists for consideration are common to both. MITI's policy options for the next two decades are summarized in the box (pp.302-303). Most of these were also considered by the Environment Agency in their case study; although assumptions for the quantitative

---

[41] Advisory Committee (to MITI) for Energy, Long-term Energy Prospects Subcommittee, *Chukan Torimatome* (Interim Report), 1989, and MITI, *The New Earth 21 - Action Program for the Twenty-First Century*, 1990.
[42] Environment Research Center, Japan, *Interim Report of the Study Group on Policy Options for Moderating Global Warming (Excerpts)*, Tokyo, 1990.
[43] MITI, *A Summary of the Long-Term Energy Supply-Demand Outlook*, 1990.
[44] Private capital investment : 2.0T yen/yr, private end-use investment: 0.8T yen/yr, public investment : 0.8T yen/yr, total 3.6T yen/yr. Environment Agency, Japan, *Case Study on Stabilization of Carbon Dioxide Emission (Draft-Material for Discussion)*, 1990.

MITI's energy conservation policy and energy supply policy options

Energy conservation policy

I. Promotion of energy conservation as a whole system

Utilization of unused urban and industrial energy [methods: public investment for energy infrastructure, organization, R&D]
* utilize unused energy by heat pump technology to meet increasing heat demand in residential/commercial sector
* promote district heating and cooling by utilizing temperature difference of sea water, river, sewage; waste heat from power plants; urban waste heat (waste incinerating plants, underground transportation facilities)
* utilize waste heat from industry sector for neighbouring demand in both industry and residential/commercial sector

Improvement of energy efficiency in supply and utilization system
* improve energy efficiency in housing and buildings by heat pumps
* improve energy efficiency in housing and buildings by automated system of energy consumption using sensors and AI technology
* promote of cogeneration by fuel cell, etc.

Social system
* utilize recycled paper, recycling of bottles and cans
* improve transportation system by introducing public transport, mitigation of road traffic congestion
* summer time system, five-day working week, long summer holiday

II. Promotion of energy conservation in the individual sector [methods: assistance for citizens' movements to stimulate energy conservation and resource recycling, strengthening of education]

* promote energy conserving process at production process [methods: strengthening of incentives by taxation and financial treatment]

* improve building efficiency by promoting insulation, decreasing air conditioning demand, diffusion of energy conserving design principle [methods: strengthening of financial assistance, information]
* promote diffusion and development of energy conserving equipment
* improve energy utilization efficiency for specific equipments
* improve fuel efficiency for passenger automobiles
* improve electricity generating efficiency by development and introduction of combined cycle generation, etc.

Energy supply policy

* promote solar and wind energy as much as possible [methods: R&D (to improve cost, efficiency, reliability), policy-induced creation of demand, expansion of institution]
* promote hydro and geothermal [methods: R&D (to improve cost), expand siting]
* promote nuclear [methods: strengthen safety, promote siting by incentives and public relations, achieve nuclear fuel cycle]
*promote natural gas [methods: flexibilize contract, improve economy, prepare background for expansion, secure supply by diversification of supply source and direct investment]
* retain certain level of coal [methods: R&D for higher efficiency in coal electricity generation and meld-reduction process for steel and iron production, expand direct development and import, promote commercialization of Coal Cartridge System and Coal Water Mixture, establish coal utilization flow]
* reduce oil dependency, secure supply [methods: promote deregulation of oil industry, strengthening of friendly and cooperative relations with oil exporters, promote development of own investment, strengthen stockpiling]

Source: derived from Advisory Committee (to MITI) for Energy, Long-term Energy Prospects Subcommittee, *Chukan Hokoku* (The Interim Report), 1990.

effect of each option differ. All are listed as necessary measures to achieve a CO_2 reduction target which the government set in October 1990 after almost year-long inter-ministerial negotiations (mainly between MITI and the Environment Agency).[45] The policy options, with no attempt at ranking are in the areas of: urban and regional structure, transport systems, production structure, energy supply structure, and realization of life style.

The scenarios in this study with the lower levels of CO_2 emissions assumed that those common policy options were put into practice. Some of the policy options may require thorough macroeconomic analysis before they receive full governmental support. But most of them could be initiated relatively easily, if the political will were there, as they are desirable in and of themselves.

The wide difference in CO_2 emissions under the different scenarios, which the authors estimated as feasible variations for Japan, suggests that Japan does have a potential to reduce CO_2 emissions through various policy options. The critical questions concern the acceptability of the required policy, as well as the appropriateness of assumptions about the trends and impacts. Whether the lower level of CO_2 emissions can be achieved depends on the successful overall restructuring of the current energy conservation policy which, up to now, has been effective in constraining demand since the first oil shock.

The study group for the 21st Century Energy Conservation Policy which was coordinated by the Energy Conservation Center of Japan under the auspices of MITI in 1989 clearly admitted that although conservation technologies are already at an advanced stage of development, they are not as yet in widespread use in Japan.[46] In addition to advocating thorough diffusion of those technologies as well as continuous R&D efforts towards more advanced technologies, the group pointed out the importance of (1) the promotion of an energy conservation consciousness which makes a moral appeal for people to

---

[45] The government of Japan, *Action Program to Arrest Global Warming*, 23 October 1990. Two stabilization targets, per capita CO_2 emissions and the total amount of CO_2 emissions (through progress in the development of innovative technologies) in the year 2000 and beyond at the level as in 1990, were set in Japan and expressed at the Second World Climate Conference in Geneva, in October 1990.
[46] Energy Conservation Center of Japan, *21 Seiki ni muketeno Shoenerugi Seisaku no Arikata ni tsuite* (What Should the Energy Conservation Policy be Towards the 21st Century), Tokyo, 1989.

reduce consumption further by stopping unnecessary waste, in practise requiring little real sacrifice, (2) expansion of rational utilization of energy not only designed within each energy-consuming equipment or sector, but also designed to be effectively incorporated as social systems (see box p.306).

While energy efficiency in the industrial sector is one of the highest levels in the world, this does not mean that no further energy conservation is technically possible. Even the steel or cement industries which have achieved very high levels of energy efficiency internationally, still waste a substantial amount of energy,[47] partly because recovery is not economical at current prices. Further energy conservation is achievable for most of the industry if, instead of trying to reduce energy consumption by adding auxiliary equipment such as waste recovery equipment to currently existing production processes, the production processes are themselves replaced by ones that are more efficient. In addition, at small and medium-sized factories, the level of energy conservation is not yet very high; approximately 70% of those factories are judged to still have margin for sufficiently cost-effective energy conservation measures.[48] Further promotion of energy conservation would be possible if additional policy support were given which provides private firms with incentives by either strengthening existing financial arrangements (eg. capital recovery allowances or financial aid), or by increasing energy taxes. Careful consideration should be given to this kind of governmental support from the fair trade perspective. Strictly financial measures may not be sufficient for companies for whom energy is a minor cost. To realize the potential from efficient motor drives, for example, targeted information and incentive campaigns as well as standard setting may be required.

Changes in industrial structure from more energy-intensive industries to less energy-consuming industries also has an effect of reducing energy consumption. Increasing the share of manufactured products within total imports will contribute to reducing energy consumption in this sector, as would transferring domestic manufacturing capacity abroad through direct investment. Therefore, in order to effectively reduce CO_2 emissions in the industrial sector, trade and industrial policy as well as

---

[47] 35% and 20% of total input energy is still wasted in the steel and cement industries in Japan. Energy Conservation Centre of Japan, op.cit., p.9.
[48] op.cit., p.9.

Recommendation for the 21st Century Energy Conservation Policy by the study group set at the Energy Conservation Center of Japan (1989)

Promotion of energy conservation consciousness

 * appealing to people's sense of duty but not requiring real sacrifice

Expansion of rational utilization of energy as a social system

 * social utilization of waste energy from factories and cities
 * efficient energy supply and utilization system, eg: cogeneration, heat pump system
 * cut off peak of electricity demand curve
 * total energy management system utilizing information and communication technology
 * creation of new energy conservation equipment and system
 * energy conservation evaluation by life cycle cost
 * social institutional approach for energy conservation, eg: summer time system'[+] five-day working week, long summer holiday[++]
 * recycling of resources

[+]Summer time system is now applied in OECD countries except Iceland and Japan. Although the Japanese government examined the feasibility of summer time system following the second oil shock, the adoption was suspended.
[++]According to data published by the ILO, Japan had 2192 working hours per year per employee in the manufacturing sector (1985), which was 30% above the average for the 15 Western countries. JETRO, *Business Facts & Figures Nippon, Tokyo*, 1988.

conventional energy conservation policy should be considered. Steps should be taken to make sure that only the best available energy conserving technology is transferred; transferring inferior technology might reduce domestic emissions but would increase the global total.

The spread of the new technology for higher generating efficiency will continue as older facilities are replaced. Promoting the scrapping of such facilities could be one policy option to accelerate this trend. For example, the average thermal power generation efficiency of Japan was 37.9% in 1988 with a high of 42.4% (LNG combined cycle power plant constructed in 1986). If the average efficiency is increased by 3 points from 37.9% to 40.9%, this would reduce fossil fuel consumption in the electricity generation sector by 7%.

Demand for the more efficient utilization of secondary energy through such means as cogeneration, fuel cell and heat pumps is increasing. With the ongoing deregulation of the energy market, cogeneration by the gas and oil industries is rapidly increasing, in competition with the heat pump systems of the electric power industry.[49] This competition is expected to contribute to improving total national energy efficiency in the residential and commercial sectors, and thus, to reducing CO_2 emissions. Fuel cell technology is also expected to expand significantly from the 1990s both as dispersed power plants and on-site cogeneration.

In Japan, most existing old buildings are neither insulated (less than 15% of the total stock are estimated to be insulated) nor centrally heated. Portable kerosene or gas stoves emitting fumes which require that windows be opened every couple of hours during the cold winter, are still widely used. Increasingly, newly constructed buildings in Japan are insulated.[50] However, the energy saved by replacing existing less energy efficient buildings is offset not only by the increasing floor space per household, but also by the increased quest for amenities such as central heating for comfortable and clean indoor environments. Until

---

[49] Heat pump systems were promoted only by the electricity industry, but now gas and oil heat pumps are also entering the competition.

[50] Currently, the standards for judging the energy efficiency of buildings are set by the government under the Rational Use of Energy Law. Insulation standards in this law are much less strict than the Swedish standards or American guidelines. Therefore, the strengthening as well as the enforcement of existing building guidelines would be an effective means of limiting the demand for energy. See H.Nakagami, 'Energy Conservation in Japanese Homes and Buildings', *Environmental Research Quarterly*, No.77, January 1990.

Japan reaches some saturation point in terms of the average space per household, which is many years and probably decades away, demand for amenities will remain strong.

For non-heating demand such as for lighting, appliances and air conditioning, which is small at present but growing rapidly, substantial opportunities for more efficient technologies exist, and the latter are gradually spreading in the market. But again, due to the increasing size of each appliance or the growing floor space per household, these new technologies do not contribute significantly to the reduction of total demand. Minimizing the rate of growth of demand, or possibly reducing non-heating demand may require explicit legal (standard) or informational (campaign) support by the government in order to continuously improve the efficiency. A prime example would be extensive promotion of solar systems for water and space heating. The utilization of waste heat from incinerators, underground transportation, sewage systems, underground transmission lines and buildings is now technically possible and is gradually expanding through the use of heat pumps at urban redevelopment projects or where individual buildings are being replaced. Policy support including administrative guidance would be effective in promoting these systems.

By 1985, the fuel economy for cars of each size category achieved levels set by the government. This achievement, however, disguises the current trend towards increasing preference for more luxurious and less fuel-efficient cars which is compounded by the disincentive caused by the consumption tax introduced in Japan in 1989. The former commodity tax which was much higher for larger cars was abolished making larger cars more accessible.

Reflecting the growing concern about the global warming, the automobile industry of Japan has expressed its determination to continue to develop more energy-efficient engines. Among these, one major automobile company's decision in 1989 not to enter the luxury car market,[51] and a solar cell manufacturer's project on solar commuter cars initiated in 1990,[52] are examples of the industry's positive reaction as well as their expectation of new business opportunities.

---

[51] The president of Honda said that business in luxury automobiles with low fuel efficiency is like going against the times, *Asahi Shimbun*, 14 November 1989.

[52] *Asahi Shimbun*, 13 January 1990.

Government interference in personal decisions such as automobile purchases is controversial. However, depending upon how seriously the public views the greenhouse effect issue, policies such as fuel efficiency standards and taxation on luxury automobiles might be more easily accepted.

The price of automobile fuels almost doubled from 1978 to 1982 and the consumption of fuel almost stabilized during this period. In order to suppress energy demand in this sector, still larger increases in price would be required. In 1988, fuel prices for automobiles were as low as the level prior to the second oil shock, and to gradually increase taxes could be one option.[53] However, tax burdens (including fuel taxes, commodity taxes, annual automobile taxes, etc.) for owning an automobile in Japan are comparably high and further increases would meet strong opposition from car-owners, the car-manufacturing industry and the petroleum industry.

Despite the scarcity of indigenous resources, a wasteful and extravagant way of life is now prevalent in Japan. It is now recognized that changes are needed as a result not only of the gradual increase in environmental consciousness but also because of the recognition of the scarcity of waste deposit sitings within the small archipelago. Increasing recycling prior to incineration is considered as a promising option in order to reduce the final amount of waste for dumping but some radical changes to alter life-styles based upon mass production and mass consumption even at the cost of reducing GNP are now being discussed.

Excessive packaging at department stores, the custom of semi-annual courtesy gift sending, floods of direct mails, automatic vending machines for drinks requiring energy to keep the temperature cold during summer and warm in winter, twenty-four hour convenience stores which receive delivery of inventories more than twice per day to keep stocks fresh, all are contributing to the expansion of domestic demand and convenience as well as to the increase in waste, pollutants and energy demand.

Industries argue that they have to meet the demands of consumers otherwise they cannot survive under competitive commercialization. Consumers argue that they are tempted by the unnecessary supply of

[53] The tax component of gasoline in Japan was 47% in 1988, the third lowest among OECD countries, but the price itself was the fifth highest. International Energy Agency, *Energy Prices and Taxes*, IEA/OECD, Paris, 1989.

goods and services from industry. Resources are wasted without contributing to the improvement of the quality of life.

The loss of interest among urban consumers to save in order to buy their own houses due to extremely high prices of properties associated with an ineffective land policy is said to push up their consumption level for ephemeral satisfaction. The huge level of corporate business expenses amounting to almost 10% of governmental annual expenditure is often criticized as not only jeopardizing fair business competition but also as contributing to the increase of irrational and wasteful consumption of resources. All these are highlighted as issues related to a greenhouse house effect response. Governmental intervention through its legislative authority would be effective in altering these trends but, to the extent that this could interfere with individual life style, it would be controversial. Less interventionist, but still effective policies to bring about changes through reforms in land policy and the restriction of corporate business expenses require strong public support. However, once an idea takes root among Japanese, it is quick to spread. If new life-styles using less resources and political consciousness to support social renovation can become a fashion especially among young people, the contribution to reducing CO_2 emissions could be rapid and huge.

Feasibility of emissions abatement scenario
Over the six years after the second oil shock, Japan reduced energy consumption in the industrial sector by 28Mtoe at an annual reduction rate of 3.2% per year. In terms of annual growth rate, scenario 2000B assumes less severe demand suppression than those experienced following the second oil shock, to be continued over the period of 11 years (1989-2000). Demand suppression in the residential/commercial and transportation sectors is assumed to continue throughout the period but at about the similarly moderate growth rate Japan experienced over the several years following the second oil shock.

Achieving this scenario target would require a strong level of commitment from government, industry and the public at least as much as was devoted to tackle the past oil crises. Strong policy initiatives including taxation and/or financial arrangements would be required in the absence of high energy prices. If the gradually growing public concern about the environment is used to lead the Japanese public to review their wasteful, affluent way of living, and to change their consumption pattern, this might contribute to a further reduction of CO_2

emissions. Thorough analyses of the impact of this target on the economy and society may vary between analysts. Some may say it involves too much optimism without realistic and responsible consideration, others may say it involves too much conservatism without a driving will. The authors believe that this target, more ambitious than the government's stabilization target set in 1990, is not infeasible for Japan and that it should not be excluded from consideration along with other possible future targets.

Feasibility of fuel switching

In all the 2030 energy projections gas will gain markets in place of oil. The petroleum industry now asserts that a reduction of burdens on the industry, such as higher taxes or obligation to stockpiling, is necessary for fair competition. While the gas industry could supply even the highest demand scenario,[54] fuel switch options require a firm energy policy because it takes a long time for project development, the construction of infrastructure and R&D for new utilization and marketing. In the last two decades, fuel switching has been promoted in order to reduce oil dependency and thus secure energy supply as well as to reduce the overall national energy cost. If reducing CO_2 emissions could be perceived as important as energy security and the reduction of energy costs, then the necessary momentum could be initiated regardless of conflicts among the energy industries.

Both the 2000 and 2030 business-as-usual cases assume the steady expansion of nuclear power forecast by the government and the electric power industry. Nuclear power is expected to generate one-third of total public electricity at both the year 2000 and 2030 with a capacity increase from 29GW in 1989 to 47GW in 2000 and 77GW in 2030.[55] The 'fuel switch' scenario for the year 2030 assumes that nuclear capacity increase to 107GW, providing 55% of public electricity. The relative reliance on nuclear power in reducing CO_2 is high in 2000 and much higher in 2030.

[54] The 2030 gas supply projection by the gas industry is 90Mtoe and the 2030 petroleum supply projection by the petroleum industry is 265Mtoe, both falling within the range adoped in this chapter's 2030 scenarios for gas (44-126Mtoe) and oil (109-278Mtoe).The Committee for Energy Policy Promotion, *Enerugi Sangyo Choki Bijon* (Energy Industry Long-Term Vision), Tokyo, 1986.
[55] According to MITI's projection prepared in 1990, Japan's nuclear capacity is expected to be 50GW (2000) and 72GW (2010), generating 330TWh (35%) and 470TWh (43%) respectively. *Denki Jigyo Shingikai Jukyubukai* (Electric Utility Council (for MITI) Supply-Demand Working Group) *Chukan Hokoku*, (Summary of the Interim Report), 1990.

However, considering the growth of the anti-nuclear movement and the possibilities of electoral change towards the Japan Socialist Party which is against new nuclear power plants and is seeking a non-nuclear future, it is possible that Japan's nuclear power development may have to be altered. If so, and if Japan is to reduce CO_2 emissions, efficiency measures alone would not be enough, and Japan would have to rely extensively on renewable sources.

Although the government initiated steps to develop renewable energy soon after the first oil shock with such measures as the launching of the Sunshine Project in 1974 and the establishment of NEDO (New Energy Development Organization) in 1980, renewable energy resources so far are not expected to supply a substantial amount of energy, at least not in the next couple of decades. On an optimistic assessment, a significant amount of renewable resources could be developed as seen in Table 7.1. However, if only the lower density exploitation can be developed, or major renewable technologies prove impractical, their contribution to reducing CO_2 emission would be small. Immediate policy actions are required both to strengthen the existing R&D projects to reduce some of these uncertainties and to accelerate the commercial use of the results. Also, since the utilization of renewables will be more easily accepted as local energy, national land policy might have to be changed to achieve a more locally-activated, decentralized system rather than the current centrally-activated, metropolitan system.

Feasibility of reduced demand for fossil fuels

The fact that Japan imports almost all its fossil fuels has the advantage of giving Japan greater flexibility in determining its energy supply mix than countries with ample amounts of specific indigenous fuels. Up to now, the conversion of fuel sources from coal to oil and oil to natural gas, took place in response to external changes in the energy supply situation in combination with local environmental concern.

The potential for further conversion from coal and oil to natural gas exists for all the energy consuming sectors. A large potential exists for the residential and commercial sectors through cogeneration of heat and power (CHP) or air conditioning by gas. Cogeneration by gas is currently being rapidly introduced in urban areas in competition with cogeneration by oil and electricity or gas heat pump systems. Policy support can accelerate gas cogeneration. However, the kind of government intervention required would also reduce the benefits of recent increased competition among energy industries in Japan.

The same applies to the recent enactment of strict NOx emission controls by local governmental authorities for gas turbines, gas engines, and diesel engines. Although cogeneration can have a higher level of efficiency, the plant also emit large amounts of NOx which in turn cause local air pollution[56] as well as contribute to the greenhouse effect by forming ozone, another greenhouse gas, through photochemical reaction. Currently, instead of using direct policy intervention to determine which energy-efficient system shall be used, local authorities are allowed to set NOx emission standards. Both the gas and oil industries are actively trying to improve their technology to meet those standards.

Because electricity demand is projected to grow steadily, CO_2 emissions from the electric power industry are expected to grow unless generation from nuclear and/or renewables is increased significantly, more than is currently projected. Fuel cell cogeneration is expected to contribute to reducing CO_2 emissions if heat supply from cogeneration replaces electricity demand for heat. The demand side management approach is gaining attention among both industry and regulators as a promising option to further promote energy conservation. The introduction of real-time pricing is also expected to increase system efficiency and reduce CO_2 emissions.[57] The electricity industry is currently concerned about the application of pro rata reduction regulations for each industry, should Japan agree to a unilateral international CO_2 reduction target.

The renewable industry sector, which still plays a very minor part, has been putting forward ambitious projections for future development if oil prices should stabilize at a higher level. Policy support could take a strong role in encouraging these industries to grow or in encouraging other

---

[56] The Environment Agency stated that attention should be paid to protection of the local environment when introducing cogeneration in urban areas with high nitrogen dioxide concentrations. Environment Agency of Japan, *Kankyo Hakusho Sosetsu* (White Paper on the Environment, General Remarks), Ohkurashoinsatsukyoku, Tokyo, 1990.

[57] See Chapter 2, section 2.2. Application to large industrial users is considered feasible now. Extension to the domestic sector would require expansion of home automation connecting to electricity companies. Considering the Japanese public's tendency to quickly expand use of new technologies once commercially available (eg. faximile, personal computer), real-time pricing is a promising option.

major industries to shift their business to the renewable energy technologies.

Feasibility of 2030 efficiency and fuel switching scenarios

The fuel switching considered in 2030 may be quite modest considering the trend of future technological development. Expansion of gas use would be determined by supply conditions and costs, whereas nuclear expansion by public acceptance. The projected level of renewables expansion is in all cases below the higher density exploitation level.

Projections requiring tripling of natural gas exceed the level projected for the year 2030 by the gas industry itself. This would require substantial expansion of gas (LNG) receiving and utilizing infrastructure throughout the country and congestion of LNG transporting ships at narrow sea routes may become a safety problem. The expected amount of renewables in the highest use is at a level higher than the lower density exploitation level summarized in Table 7.1 and would need government incentives to produce to this level as discussed above. The highest projection of nuclear capacity (107GW) at the year 2030, is almost equivalent to per capita nuclear capacity already achieved in France in 1988, but considering the growing anti-nuclear movement and the size of Japan's land mass, this target would require extensive efforts to promote both nuclear plant and reprocessing facility siting and nuclear waste disposal.

Reductions of coal by 50% in the high efficiency scenario would also require reduced use in steel production, through increase of steel technology using less coking coal and/or transferring steel-producing capacity to developing countries.

Constraints

Japan has derived much of its success from the development and application of technology, and government and industry both focus on 'technological breakthroughs' as the main means by which CO_2 emissions might be limited. There is less discussion of domestic energy policy issues, and a reluctance to consider legislation to limit carbon emissions. This springs from: their belief that a response to this issue just by limiting emissions through direct legislation may hinder economic growth and in the long run lead to a delay in reaching a global solution; their expectation to make the most of this opportunity to free themselves from various energy resources-related restrictions; and characteristics of

Japan's institutional structure such as dominance of MITI over the Environment Agency.

Such obstacles exist in many countries, but pressure from environmental groups may counter them. In Japan, although there is a new wave of public discussion on the greenhouse effect issue mainly triggered by the mass media, well-organized environmental groups similar to those in other developed countries which produce comprehensive and influential policy proposals, do not exist.

Japan is a conservative country, and many are sceptical about the rationale for taking measures to combat the greenhouse effect issue at present. Unless there are major changes in perception, from a purely domestic perspective action is unlikely. A possible impetus to action, however, will come from the international situation. The first step came with the decision of the government in October 1990 to stabilize Japan's CO_2 emissions by the year 2000 at their 1990 level. This was a major change during a one-year period from their cautious attitude against committing themselves to any specific reduction target at the Noordwijk conference of November 1989. Domestically, the decision was received as a surprise even among experts working closely with the government since the inter-ministerial negotiation process was kept strictly closed to the public. Many of those experts, including some from industry, believe that this target is a costly commitment for Japan. Its organizational capability to achieve set goals, and its commitment to honour its international objections, suggests Japan is likely to achieve this target despite the scepticism of experts.

7.4 International aspects

There is a general domestic recognition that Japan should seek to contribute to the global warming issue not only as a major economic country with technological potential but also as a major natural resource-importing country. One indication of this intention was the government's decision to increase the amount of Official Development Assistance in the environmental protection field from 60 billion yen per year (1986-88) to 100 billion yen per year (1989-1992).[58]

Japan did not take the initiative in formulating the international agreement on CFCs and as a result was criticized by other countries for

---

[58]Environment Agency of Japan, *Kankyo Hakusho Sosetsu* (White Paper on the Environment, General Remarks), op.cit.

its negative attitude. There is a strong concern within government that Japan should not make the same mistake in tackling the CO_2 issue.

Ways of contributing to the solution of the greenhouse effect issue currently discussed in Japan in addition to efficiency and switching as previously discussed include technology transfer and reforestation.

Three factors are combined in forming Japan's attitude towards this issue at international negotiations. One is to seek equity in international agreements based upon the belief that a relatively higher level of energy efficiency has already been achieved, a higher level of fuel switching has already taken place, and the quest for comfort is still unsatisfied.

The second is to seek to fulfil their responsibility, recognizing that while CO_2 emissions per capita are lower than OECD average they are still twice as large as world average, and to seek for leadership in the environmental field. This intention is also supported by the recognition that Japan's economy is highly dependent on significant amounts of imported natural resources. The government believes in making a contribution to the solution not only for the sake of fulfilling its obligations as one of the major economic countries, but also as a necessity in order to take responsibility for its past and present exploitation of natural resources.

The third is recognition that not only Japan but other developed countries also have specific needs which should be considered in attempts to reduce CO_2 emissions. These include energy consumption due to military commitments, geographical situation (eg. transportation requirements), climatic situation (longer winter requiring more energy for heating, etc.). Despite having a strong desire to seek equity in international CO_2 reduction target-setting, Japan would not hesitate to agree to an unilateral target if other OECD countries, especially France or former West Germany join the agreement. These countries could make the same assertion as Japan in seeking equity against other countries with still higher levels of energy consumption per capita, but if they do not do so, then Japan's logic would be weakened in negotiation.

Japan's approach to the greenhouse effect issue attracts attention from both developed and developing countries because of several characteristics of the country. First, the relatively high energy efficiency of the country. If Japan agrees to the CO_2 emissions target by further improving energy efficiency or whatever other measures, that would have some impact on other developed countries in considering their potential.

Second, Japan has become a developed country during the past three decades, achieving a rapid economic growth, and is the only G7 country from Asia. Developing countries show interest in applying processes used in Japan to their own national economic planning.

Third, Japan has successfully developed nuclear power in the past fifteen years and is one of the few OECD countries which still maintains a steady expansion programme. All the nuclear power countries are now interested in the future development of nuclear power in Japan.

The government and industry both believe that a 'technological breakthrough' is the primary means through which Japan can contribute to tackling the CO_2 issue. This can take place through the transfer and export of the new technology. One effective means of reducing domestic CO_2 is to transfer energy-consuming industries to developing countries.[59] In this way, Japan can reduce its own CO_2 emissions and developing countries can enjoy economic growth without leading to an overall increase in CO_2 emissions. Direct investment abroad for the purpose of transforming Japan's industrial structure so as to make it more compatible internationally was one of the central proposals of the Maekawa Report.[60]

7.5 Conclusions

In the past, to achieve successful economic development under the scarcity of indigenous energy resources, Japan had to clear two hurdles. One was to address environmental issues throughout the country in the 1960s and early 1970s due to the exclusive focus on economic growth. In those days, Japan was considered one of the world's most environmentally-polluted countries. However, through extensive efforts by both the government and industry, Japan was able to establish various legal and social structures as well as to develop technologies for environmental protection. The second hurdle consisted of the two oil shocks. As a result of concerted effort, Japan was able to improve various energy utilization technologies to one of the highest efficiency levels in

[59] Yasuhiro Murota, *Nikkei Shimbun*, 24 September 1989.
[60] Proposals of the Maekawa Report (Adjustment of the economic structure for the sake of international harmony), presented to the then Japanese Prime Minister Nakasone, 1986.

the world, which in the long run, contributed to the overall economy of Japan. In clearing these two hurdles, Japan was able to conceive of them not as constraints but as challenges which could be met.

The CO_2 challenge is not as easy to meet as the first two. It may take more time to solve and may require more international agreements to initiate action. Because CO_2 is emitted not only from industry but also from the residential/commercial and transportation sectors, a different approach is required from the one used to successfully curb the SOx emissions whose main source is industry. However, this issue also provides industry, consumers and policy makers with a great opportunity to carry out social renovations which are at the same time desirable in themselves and necessary for future generations, especially for a country like Japan with no abundant fossil fuel resources.

Industry and the government have already begun to tackle this issue in various ways, giving increasing support to accelerate the development of technology and the implementation of policy. The scenario evaluations and policy discussion clearly suggest that once set on a target and once momentum is built up, Japan can develop and maintain a strong positive momentum for the achievement of a goal. With economic and technological potential, commitment within industry and government to the idea of a 'third industrial revolution' or paradigm shift concerning the global warming issue, Japan has promising but as yet unquantifiable prospects for achieving a solution to reducing CO_2 emissions.

Appendix: Energy balances and CO_2 emissions in different scenarios

		Coal	Oil	Gas	Other	Nuc	Elec	Total	CO_2
1973									
TPER	Mtoe	60	298	6	19	2		385	
Electricity generation(public)	Mtoe	-8	-66	-2	-15	-2	35		64
	TWh	<--- 326 --->			65	10	401		
	GW								
Electricity generation(auto)	Mtoe	-2	-10	0	-2	0	6		10
Other losses	Mtoe	-13	-49	4	0	0			52
TFC:Industry	Mtoe	36	101	2	2		24	166	124
TFC:Residential & commercial	Mtoe	1	30	5	0		11	48	29
TFC:Transport	Mtoe	0	42	0	0		1	44	35
CO_2 emissions	MtC	65	245	4					313
1989									
TPER	Mtoe	80	267	46	27	41		462	
Electricity generation(public)	Mtoe	-20	-41	-33	-20	-41	60		77
	TWh	<--- 424 --->			90	182	696		
	GW					29			
Electricity generation(auto)	Mtoe	-5	-9	0	-4	0	8		13
Other losses	Mtoe	-13	-36	2	2	0			42
TFC:Industry	Mtoe	41	77	4	3		31	156	111
TFC:Residential & commercial	Mtoe	1	34	11	1		28	76	36
TFC:Transport	Mtoe	0	70	0	0		2	71	57
CO_2 emissions	MtC	87	219	29					335

		Coal	Oil	Gas	Other	Nuc	Elec	Total	CO₂
2000A(Business-as-usual)									
TPER	Mtoe	98	259	65	31	69		523	
Electricity generation(public)	Mtoe	-34	-34	-45	-20	-69	77		92
	TWh	< --- 502 --->			90	308	900		
	GW					47			
Electricity generation(auto)	Mtoe	-5	-10	0	-5	0	9		13
Other losses	Mtoe	-18	-31	3	2	0			43
TFC:Industry	Mtoe	41	69	5	3		33	152	105
TFC:Residential & commercial	Mtoe	1	36	15	3		42	97	40
TFC:Transport	Mtoe	0	80	2	2		2	86	67
CO₂ emissions	MtC	107	21	40					360
2000B(Emissions abatement)									
TPER	Mtoe	80	225	51	31	69		455	
Electricity generation(public)	Mtoe	-24	-24	-33	-20	-69	66		67
	TWh	< --- 365 --- >			90	308	764		
	GW					47			
Electricity generation(auto)	Mtoe	-4	-8	0	-4		7		11
Other losses	Mtoe	-14	-27	3	2	0			36
TFC:Industry	Mtoe	36	60	5	3		26	130	91
TFC:Residential & commercial	Mtoe	1	32	14	3		37	87	35
TFC:Transport	Mtoe	0	74	2	2		2	79	62
CO₂ emissions	MtC	87	184	31					302

		Coal	Oil	Gas	Other	Nuc	Elec	Total	CO2
2030Ai (Business-as-usual)									
TPER	Mtoe	118	278	105	56	97		654	
Electricity generation(public)	Mtoe	-46	-46	-62	-29	-97	126		127
	TWh	< ---808 --- >			150	505	1464		
	GW					77			
Electricity generation(auto)	Mtoe	-8	-15	0	-8	0	14		21
Other losses	Mtoe	-20	-25	3	3	0			40
TFC:Industry	Mtoe	44	59	13	6		52	173	104
TFC:Residential & commercial	Mtoe	0	39	28	13		66	146	50
TFC:Transport	Mtoe	0	93	5	5		8	110	79
CO2 emissions	MtC	128	228	65					422
2030Aii (Fuel switching)									
TPER	Mtoe	79	154	126	115	135		609	
Electricity generation(public)	Mtoe	-24	-24	-32	-29	-134	109		65
	TWh	< --- 417 --->			150	702	1270		
	GW					107			
Electricity generation(auto)	Mtoe	-7	-13	0	-7	0		12	
Other losses	Mtoe	-13	-14	3	6	0			18
TFC:Industry	Mtoe	35	48	34	21		36	173	98
TFC:Residential & commercial	Mtoe	0	27	40	32		46	146	47
TFC:Transport	Mtoe	0	28	23	33		26	110	37
CO2 emissions	MtC	86	126	78					290

		Coal	Oil	Gas	Other	Nuc	Elec	Total	CO$_2$
2030Bi (Energy efficiency)									
TPER	Mtoe	54	191	44	52	91		432	
Electricity generation(public)	Mtoe	-11	-11	-15	-27	-91	74		30
	TWh	< ---204 --->			150	505	860		
	GW					77			
Electricity generation(auto)	Mtoe	-5	-9	0	-5	0	8		12
Other losses	Mtoe	-9	-17	3	3	0			22
TFC:Industry	Mtoe	29	48	9	6		22	115	77
TFC:Residential & commercial	Mtoe	0	32	18	13		44	107	38
TFC:Transport	Mtoe	0	74	5	5		8	91	63
CO$_2$ emissions	MtC	59	157	27					243
2030Bii (Energy efficiency plus fuel switching)									
TPER	Mtoe	43	109	80	92	91		414	
Electricity generation(public)	Mtoe	-8	-8	-10	-27	-91	69		21
	TWh	< --- 146 --- >			150	505	802		
	GW					77			
Electricity generation(auto)	Mtoe	-4	-8	0	-4	0	8		
Other losses	Mtoe	-7	-10	3	5	0			11
TFC:Industry	Mtoe	23	39	25	13		16	115	72
TFC:Residential & commercial	Mtoe	0	22	28	26		30	107	36
TFC:Transport	Mtoe	0	22	20	27		22	91	30
CO$_2$ emissions	MtC	47	89	49					185

Notes to Appendix:
1. Sources for 1973 and 1989 figures: MITI, *Sogo Enerugi Tokei* (Comprehensive Energy Statistics),1990.
2. Conversion factors to CO_2 emissions(MtC) from fossil fuel consumption(Mtoe): Coal, 1.09; Oil, 0.82; Gas, 0.61. Unit: MtC/Mtoe
3. Conversion factors from electricity (Mtoe) of renewables and nuclear output to input equivalent primary energy(Mtoe):

1973, 1988	1/0.381
2000A, 2000B	1/0.385
2030Ai, 2030Aii, 2030Bi, 2030Bii	1/0.450

4. The column 'Other' includes hydro, geothermal and solar.
5. Nuclear: (1)generating capacity in the year 2000, 47GW was based upon the industry's 1990 projection; (2)generating capacity in the year 2030, 77GW for 2030Ai, 2030Bi, 2030Bii and 107GW for 2030Aii were the author's assumptions; (3)capacity factor was assumed to be 75%.
6. Fossil fuel: the share of coal, oil and gas to total fossil fuel consumption in public electricity generation was assumed to be 30%, 30% and 40% respectively for both 2000 and 2030 scenarios.
7. Electricity generation by autoproducers was assumed to be 12% of total electricity generation for both 2000 and 2030.

Chapter 8 Soviet CO$_2$ Emissions: Not a Burning Issue?

Jeremy Russell
Shell UK Ltd, London
Visiting Research Fellow, RIIA

My sincere thanks to Matthew J Sagers and R Caron Cooper for agreeing to be 'readers' of this chapter and for their most helpful and constructive comments. I would also like to thank David Wilson, I Amerov and A V Tolokonnikov and members of the Chatham House Study Group who made time to read the early manuscript and to send me their comments. I am most grateful to Michael Grubb and Jonathan Stern for their constant wise counsel and vigorous questioning throughout the project.
I am particularly glad to acknowledge the sterling efforts of Nicola Steen and Rosina Pullman of the Energy and Environmental Programme at the Royal Institute of International Affairs who respectively prepared all the graphic materials and edited the final text, and Cindy Canham and her colleagues who initially captured it on the word processor. Finally, I am grateful to Shell UK Ltd for lending me to Chatham House so that I could undertake the necessary study and acquire enlightenment.

Soviet CO$_2$ Emissions: Not a Burning Issue?

The Soviet Union has abundant resources of all fossil fuels, and Soviet central planning has emphasised production targets and a price structure independent of costs of production or world energy prices. As a result the Soviet Union has, until recently, paid less attention to the conservation of energy than have other industrialised countries. Combined with rapid industrialisation focused on heavy industry, this has resulted in energy consumption and carbon emissions growing prodigiously. Little or no specific response to the global energy price rises of the 1970s can be detected in Soviet energy consumption or interfuel substitution, and the Soviet Union uses up to twice as much energy to produce a unit of GDP as some OECD countries.

The potential for energy conservation is therefore considerable. A major issue under debate is whether the traditionally supply-oriented investment policy should or indeed can be continued, or whether a substantially greater proportion of investment should be switched to energy conservation and, if so, how best to do this. Given the scale of resources now devoted to Soviet energy infrastructure, economic growth may come to depend pivotally upon success in energy conservation.

There are three main groups of reasons why so much energy is used in the Soviet economy: energy infrastructure and distribution; end-use equipment and practices, (reflecting age and design of the existing capital stock); and the traditional economic and social attitudes to energy as a cheap and readily available resource, which have greatly undervalued it relative to other economic inputs. Change seems inevitable as a result of perestroika, and Soviet energy planners are beginning to approach Soviet problems from perspectives more familiar to Western energy analysts. The energy industries cannot remain immune from perestroika and must play a key role in it.

The Soviet Union was, by the end of 1989, releasing over 1 billion tonnes of fossil carbon combustion annually into the atmosphere, or 17% of the global total. A combination of efficiency measures and fuel switching, with an increased role for hydroelectricity and nuclear could mean long-term carbon emissions significantly below 1990 levels. This would be feasible only if major and radical structural, technological and economic changes were introduced at the earliest opportunity. The direct involvement in the Soviet economy of foreign companies possessing advanced energy-saving technologies would have to be actively sought. Public support would have to be secured by direct appeal, riding on the wave of environmental concerns. A major move in this direction would have to be made, before any reaction to the current shake-up in Soviet society sets in, and changes in energy demand structures and investment in renewable resource opportunities initiated rapidly. In practice, it is more likely that more natural gas and coal and less nuclear electricity will in fact be used, and reform will be slower and less dramatic.

The Soviet Union, largely because of decisions to exploit fully its massive natural gas resources and potential for generating primary electricity, may already be said to be embarked upon an emissions-abatement course, although it could be a long time before CO$_2$ emission-abatement per se will become other than a coincidental of economic reform. While energy-saving will be one of the primary outcomes of modernisation it will need to be promoted specifically, and with increasing purposefulness. The long-term potential for emissions abatement is very large indeed. However, the Soviet attitude internationally is likely to be a mixture of support at the academic and 'megaphone' levels, but, at least initially, a rather slow and muddled practical response.

8.1 The Soviet energy system

Two factors combine to make the Soviet energy system radically different from those in most industrial countries. Firstly, it not only has abundant natural energy resources but is also the largest producer of oil and natural gas in the world, the third largest producer of coal and has substantial reserves of uranium ore and a major potential for hydroelectricity production. Secondly, since 1917 the system of central planning has emphasised production targets and a price structure independent of costs of production or world energy prices. As a result the Soviet Union has, until recently, paid less attention to the conservation of energy than have other industrialized countries. Little or no specific response to the global energy price rises of the 1970s can be detected in Soviet energy consumption statistics, in growth rates, or interfuel substitution.[1] Furthermore, energy prices remained unchanged throughout the 1980s although a proposal by the Ministry of Finance to increase the price of oil by 130%, gas by 100% and coal by 90% in 1990, had been under discussion for almost two years. It should be stressed however that there are systemic problems in all centrally-planned economies in using prices as an economic lever.

Since the bulk of its annual energy production is consumed domestically, it is clear that the USSR must feature prominently in any discussion on carbon emissions to the atmosphere and the associated complex of issues concerning global warming. Total consumption of all fuels has risen from a total of 781 million tonnes of oil equivalent (Mtoe) in 1971 to 1,418Mtoe in 1989. The Soviet Union was, by the end of 1989, releasing over 1 billion tonnes of carbon from fossil fuel combustion annually into the atmosphere, or 17% of the global total, and was exceeded in this respect only by the United States.

Energy supply-side problems perpetually threaten but the government has been prepared to allocate additional investment funds and because there are abundant reserves of the three main fossil energy sources the country as a whole has never gone short of energy. Logistical shortcomings have resulted in shortages of electricity and of certain types of oil products and grades of coal.[2] Until recently they have been

[1] A.Hewett, (ed.) *Energy Economics and Foreign Policy in the Soviet Union*, Chapter 3, The Brookings Institution, Washington DC, 1984.
[2] David Wilson, 'Soviet Energy to 2000', *The Economist Intelligence Unit Special Report No.231*, EIU, London 1986.

short-lived and localized but there are signs of a more serious and persistent situation developing which will be exacerbated if the nuclear electricity programme is curtailed for environmental or safety reasons.

It seems quite possible that the political and economic developments of 1989 and 1990 herald a major discontinuity in the relationships between the energy supply industries, energy demand growth and economic growth rates. It may, indeed, become less satisfactory to adopt the traditional 'top-down' approach to the analysis of energy and environmental issues in the Soviet Union;[3] analyses of regional inter-relationships may become increasingly valid. However, while future socio-economic and political uncertainties proliferate, a deeper understanding of the existing energy supply and demand situation, and its development over recent decades, remains crucial in understanding the problem areas and the possibilities for (and constraints on) change in environmentally more desirable directions.

8.2 Development of Soviet energy consumption

Figure 8.1 shows the trend in primary energy consumption since 1971, and illustrates the rise in the contribution of natural gas and the corresponding fall in that of oil and coal. This pattern is repeated in the changing contribution towards electricity generation, with significant implications for carbon emissions reductions. These two decades saw a much slower but significant growth in primary electricity consumption as first hydroelectric and then nuclear generation increased as a result of substantial investment.

The Soviet Union uses up to twice as much energy to produce a unit of GDP as some OECD countries,[4] and the potential for energy conservation is therefore considerable.[5]

---

[3] See Chapter 4, this volume, and Volume 1, section 7.1 for a detailed discussion of analytical techniques. Briefly, 'top-down' projects general trends in demand and judges the macroeconomic influences upon it.

[4] A chronic problem exists in relating GDP statistics as understood in OECD terms with comparable Soviet statistics. The Soviet Union uses the measure of 'National Income Produced', and Western analysts refer to NMP (Net Material Product) to show that the Soviet measure does not include depreciation or services which do not contribute directly to material input. Growth rates of NMP appear some 2.4% higher than GNP on average. See Dr Mikhail B. Korchemkin, *Energy Aspects of The Perestroika*, EURICES Paper No 89/2, Centre for International Energy Studies, Rotterdam, April 1989.

Figure 8.1 Soviet energy consumption and CO_2 emissions 1971-89

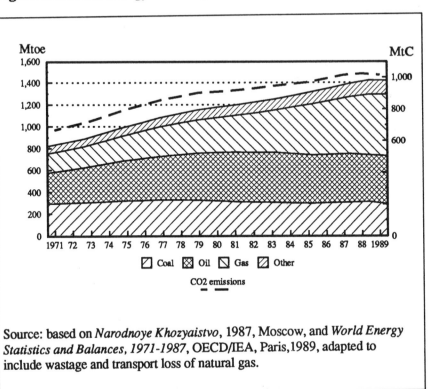

Source: based on *Narodnoye Khozyaistvo*, 1987, Moscow, and *World Energy Statistics and Balances, 1971-1987*, OECD/IEA, Paris,1989, adapted to include wastage and transport loss of natural gas.

Since the 1960s, significant energy efficiency improvements have been achieved, but primarily in the supply industries in certain centrally-controlled sectors of the economy, particularly in electricity generation. This has been largely through economies of scale, the introduction of advanced engineering technology and a drive to capture potentially wasted heat for cogeneration.[6] Elsewhere, in more diffuse and smaller-scale industries, and in the domestic and commercial sectors,

[5] A.V.Tolokonnikov, 'Strategies for Reducing Energy Pollution in the USSR', (preliminary draft), Commission of the USSR Academy of Sciences on Productive Forces and Natural Resources, November 1989.
[6] Albina Tretyakova and Barry Kostinsky, 'Fuel Use and Conservation in the Soviet Union', study papers submitted to the Joint Economic Committee of the United States Congress, November 1987.

no such control has existed. Large-scale district heating schemes in many Soviet cities clearly enhance efficiency, but their effectiveness is impaired by the virtual absence of metering devices and by poor temperature-control provisions in both individual apartments and in communal buildings.

Throughout the 1970s and 1980s sectoral demand patterns for fuel have remained fairly constant, with the most significant changes in the increased use in the transport and chemical feedstock sectors. Increases in the transport sector reflect expanding vehicle fleets and the growing volume of natural gas reflects increases to fuel compressor stations in the steadily expanding gas pipeline network. The breakdown of energy consumption by economic sector is shown in Table 8.1. Industry, construction and agriculture together account for 64% of end-use energy consumption. By comparison, the 13 million cars in the USSR consume less than 1% of total energy.

Aggregate apparent energy consumption in the Soviet Union increased by 2.2% in 1988 compared with an average annual growth during 1984-7 of 3.1%,[7] and since 1981 of 2.6%. GDP growth averaged 2.2% over the same period. It is estimated that in 1989 energy consumption declined marginally as a result of economic and political difficulties rather than for reasons of efficiency. A similar pattern is likely to have emerged in 1990.

Carbon emissions from Soviet energy consumption increased by 55% from 670MtC in 1971 to over 1 billion tonnes (GtC) in 1989, despite the rapid increase in the shares of natural gas and primary electricity in the energy balance (see Figure 8.1). Actual carbon emissions are likely to be higher than depicted since the figures on which this is based do not include flared associated gas, fuelwood or natural gas leakage.[8] The relative decline in carbon emissions *per unit of energy* consumed is set to continue whether or not specific emission-abatement measures are introduced, provided that natural gas consumption continues to displace oil and coal.

---

[7] *PlanEcon Report*, Vol.V, No.4, January 1989.

[8] Leakage from the distribution network is estimated at 2% of production or 16BCM. See A.A.Makarov and I.A.Bashmakov, et al, 'USSR: A Strategy of Energy Development with Minimum Emission of Greenhouse Gases', *Carbon Emissions Control Strategies: Case Studies in International Cooperation*, Battelle Memorial Institute, Washington DC, 1990, p.18. For a general discussion see Appendix 2.

Table 8.1 USSR fuel consumption - sectorial breakdown 1970 and 1987(%)

	1970 %	1987 %
Electric power	27.2	30.4
Industry	32.8	26.3
Housing and municipal	14.5	11.4
Transport (including pipelines)	10.8	14.3
Non-fuel use	4.7	8.3
Agriculture	5.7	5.1

Source: PlanEcon, *Long Term Energy Outlook*, Fall 1988.

8.3 The Soviet energy resource base and production

Despite vast reserves (see Figure 8.2) there is a fundamental and growing mismatch between the location of many of the natural energy resources and the centres of industrialization where the demand for energy is greatest. Most of the major currently exploited and undeveloped energy resources lie thousands of miles to the east, where the population is sparse and where geographical and climatic factors are much harsher. Escalating investment costs for the industry as a whole reached 45 billion roubles in 1988 - over 24% of total centralized investment - up from 11.7% in 1980.[9] The share of new investment seriously threatens to deprive other sectors of funds.

[9] Matthew J. Sagers (ed.), *Soviet Geography*, 1989, pp.306-52, and *Narodnoye Khozyaistvo*, 1987.

Figure 8.2 Soviet fuel reserves/consumption ratios

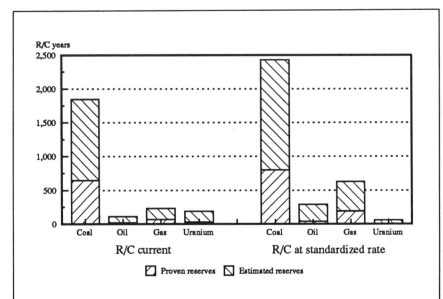

R/C current = ratio of resources/reserves to current consumption of fuel (years)
R/C standardized = ratio of resources/reserves to consumption at rate of
1kW/capita = 0.7toe/year/capita

Source: World Energy Council, *1989 Survey of Energy Resources*, WEC,
London, 1989.

The gas industry has been the star performer of the Soviet economy
during the 1980s[10] with average growth rates in excess of 6.5%.[11]
In 1988, 45TCM were classified as proven, representing some 40% of
global proven reserves.

[10] For an analysis of the prospects for the Soviet gas industry see Jonathan P. Stern,
European Gas Markets: Challenge and Opportunity in the 1990s, Dartmouth/Gower,
Aldershot, 1990.
[11] Soviet gas production statistics are for gross volumes measured at 20 °C, but these
have to be corrected for temperature and pressure to arrive at the net usable volume,
usually some 6-7% less. See Korchemkin, op.cit.

Criticism of the environmental impacts of gas production and distribution operations particularly on the Yamal Peninsular is beginning to be openly expressed.[12] Annually 15BCM of associated gas (mostly methane) are flared or vented owing to shortage of treatment and collection facilities.[13]

There seems to be a measure of agreement on a lower limit to Soviet proven oil reserves of 8 billion tonnes, with a less confident estimate of an upper limit between 12 and 14 billion tonnes.[14] Reserve estimates have increased over time, and the proven reserves to production ratio has remained at around 13 years for nearly two decades despite growing production.[15] There are substantial deposits of oil shale but commercial exploitation is so far negligible. Gas condensate (some 35 million tonnes in 1988) is included in the total oil production statistics.

Soviet experts have always been more sanguine about their oil industry's ability to deliver than have Western analysts but there are unmistakable signs that the production plateau maintained at around the 600 million tonnes per annum level for over a decade may at last be turning down. The capital investment required per tonne of new oil capacity has soared from 46 roubles in 1970 to 88 roubles in 1985 and the figure for 1990 could turn out to have been nearer 129 roubles.[16]

Coal is by far the Soviet Union's largest energy resource but much of it is located far to the south and east. Proven reserves are currently put at just over 287 billion tonnes[17] and with production of 770 million tonnes in 1988 the reserves-to-production ratio was over 370:1. The industry is experiencing considerable problems with outdated equipment, unsatisfactory working conditions, depletion of the better

---

[12] Korchemkin, op.cit.

[13] It has been estimated that 12% annually, currently some 95BCM, of increased natural gas production up to the end of this century will be spent simply on transporting the gas from Western Siberia to end-users in the West. See David Wilson, *The Demand For Energy in the Soviet Union*, Croom Helm, London, 1983.

[14] World Energy Council, *1989 Survey of Energy Resources*, WEC, London, 1989; and A.S.Tischenko suggests that by the year 2000 Soviet proven reserves of oil are 'expected to be about 31-32 billion tonnes' although exact definition of the categories involved is not given, 'Soviet Oil and East-West Trade', *Petroleum Review*, January 1989.

[15] In 1974 proven reserves were estimated at 5.7 billion tonnes, see J.L.Russell, *Energy as a Factor in Soviet Foreign Policy*, D.C.Heath, Hants, 1976.

[16] Sagers, op.cit.

[17] WEC, *1989 Survey of Energy Resources* op.cit.

coal seams and saturation of the rail system. Coal quality is declining, and average calorific content went down from 4,854kcal/kg in 1970 to 4,236kcal/kg in 1988,[18] largely due to the eastward shift in extraction to regions with lower quality coal such as Ekibastuz and Kansk-Achinsk. The environmental impacts of such massive open-cast mining operations as those undertaken in Siberia and Kazakhstan, are giving rise to official concern.[19] Substantial research within the USSR is being directed into processing and combustion techniques which will minimise environmental impacts but seem unlikely to affect CO$_2$ emissions except in so far as they increase end-use efficiency.

The Soviet Union has substantial uranium resources, and an exploitable hydroelectricity capability estimated at nearly 4,000TWh/yr.[20] Of the total 1,705TWh of electricity generated in 1988, nuclear accounted for 12.6% (215TWh) and hydroelectric for 13.5% (230TWh).[21] Efforts to increase these shares in the electricity balance may encounter considerable problems. For example, combined production increased by 4.2% in 1988 to 97Mtoe, a considerable shortfall on plan targets, partly accounted for by dry weather and partly by the Chernobyl accident. In 1989, overall Soviet electric power production increased by only 1% to 1,722TWh.[22]

There are reportedly 16 civilian nuclear power stations in operation in the Soviet Union with a combined capacity of some 35,000MW. The Soviet nuclear programme has clearly fallen well behind its rather ambitious targets to bring total capacity to 69,000MW by 1990.[23] A

---

[18] Korchemkin, op.cit.

[19] See Fred Singleton, Lynne Rienner (eds), *Environmental Problems in the Soviet Union and Eastern Europe*, Chapter 3, London 1987.

[20] WEC, *1989 Survey of Energy Resources* op.cit.

[21] For converting primary electricity to Mtoe a conversion factor of 1TWh = 0.24Mtoe is used.

[22] *PlanEcon Report*, Vol. VI, Nos.9-10, March 1990.

[23] Soviet uranium reserves have long remained unpublished. However, at a conference organised by IAEA in Czechoslovakia in the autumn of 1989 a set of figures was given by Soviet sources for all the East European CPEs and the Soviet Union itself, relating to 'known resources of elemental uranium at a price of up to $130 per kilogram or above, and broken down into "proven" and "additional"'. For the Soviet Union the figures in the two categories were 160,000 and 800,000 tonnes respectively. It is not clear to what extent these figures represent new data and a manifestation of glasnost or simply a Soviet reworking of Western estimates. 1 tonne of uranium is equivalent to between 8,000 and 16,000 tonnes of oil equivalent depending on the type of plant in which it is used.

number of proposed new plant or expansions to existing plant have been
reported cancelled or postponed or converted to natural gas in the wake
of the Chernobyl accident, and stricter norms for the siting of new plant
are being introduced, particularly where there is any risk of seismic
activity, for example in the southern Republics.[24] If no account is taken
of environmental factors, nuclear electricity costs twice as much to
produce as electricity from coal, and three times as much as that from
natural gas.[25] While there is no indication at present that the Soviet
nuclear electricity programme might be abandoned, it is likely to grow
more slowly than previously planned.

Hydroelectric resource potential is estimated at nearly 4,000TWh/yr or
18 times current production and equivalent to 940Mtoe.[26] The load
factor of many of the major hydroelectric projects in the Soviet Union is
well below design capability,[27] largely because insufficient demand
for electricity exists in those relatively under-developed parts of the
country where these projects are located. It is planned to increase
hydroelectricity generation to over 350TWh (84Mtoe) by the year 2000.
Projects are beginning to encounter considerable opposition from
economists and environmentalists at both local and national levels.

Little effort has so far been made to develop other renewable resources
such as tidal, solar, wind power or geothermal power on any significant
scale and their current contribution is negligible. The Soviet long term
energy plan does envisage that by the year 2000 renewable energy, most
of it solar, biomass and geothermal, will be contributing between 15 and
30Mtoe per annum or around 1% of demand. Biomass is currently used
in local Combined Heat and Power (CHP) units to the limited extent of
approximately 1.4Mtoe/yr. The biomass potential, both from agriculture
and forestry (62 million tonnes of fuelwood and charcoal were produced
in 1987) must be substantial, while the wind resource is estimated at
2,000TWh/yr, or 480Mtoe. There is immense scope for solar energy in
the dry southern areas, and while the existing 50,000 square meters of
solar collectors provide the heat equivalent of burning approximately

[24] Ian Smart, 'Energy and Politics', *Oxford Analytica*, Oxford, 1989.
[25] Tolokonnikov, op.cit.
[26] WEC, *1989 Survey of Energy Resources* op.cit.
[27] Sagers, op.cit.

5000 tons of standard fuel there are plans to increase substantially the share of solar heating.[28]

8.4 Projections and options to the year 2000

Detailed disaggregated Soviet energy demand statistics are not available in published form. Furthermore, in view of the insulation of the Soviet energy system from world prices and international competitive forces, the application of criteria and analytical techniques appropriate to the analysis of market economies to the Soviet system should be approached with extreme caution. Change in the quality and quantity of statistical information seems inevitable as a result of the process of perestroika and Soviet energy planners are beginning to approach Soviet problems from perspectives more familiar to Western energy analysts. The energy industries cannot remain immune from perestroika and must play a key role in it.[29]

There are currently few clear signposts to the way in which future Soviet energy demand will develop to the end of the century except that the increased use of natural gas will be promoted wherever possible, with Soviet planners referring to a 'Gas Wave' in coming decades. A major issue under debate is that of whether the essentially supply-oriented investment policy traditionally pursued by Soviet energy planners should or indeed can be continued, or whether a substantially greater proportion of investment should be switched to energy conservation and, if so, how best to do this. Difficulties in securing sufficient imports of technology and machinery which would significantly contribute to higher energy efficiency and to the success of the plans to modernise and renovate the country's capital stock may occur, and economic growth unconstrained by energy under-supply may therefore come to depend pivotally upon success in energy conservation.[30]

[28] Vyacheslav Batenin, 'Alterntive Power Sources in Use in the USSR', *AMBIO*, Vol 19, No.4, July 1990.
[29] See Grubb, Volume 1 for an analysis of the underlying assumptions in the country case studies. pp.48-51.
[30] A.A.Arbatov, 'Energetics and Perestroika', Committee for Productive Forces and Natural Resources, USSR Academy of Sciences, Moscow, 1989.

Figure 8.3 Scenarios for Soviet energy consumption and CO2 emissions 1988-2030

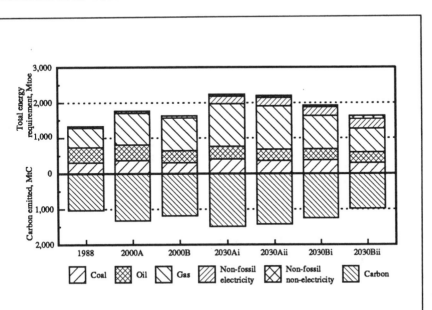

Source: Non-fossil sources on output basis

2000A: Business-as-usual

In the absence, at the time of writing of any annual, let alone any longer term, economic plan, a 'business-as-usual' supply-driven scenario, which notes but does not attempt to predict the outcome of political and economic turmoil in the country, would have to assume GDP growth and energy production and consumption trends similar to the average achieved over the past decade. The average has been 2.2% per annum for GDP growth, 2.7% per annum for production and 2.5% for consumption (see Figure 8.3). In view of the problems encountered by the economy generally and by the oil, coal and nuclear energy industries in particular in 1989 and 1990, 'business-as-usual' is scarcely a realistic scenario, but takes existing Soviet longer-term energy plans into account. New energy plans are thought to be imminent and could significantly alter the supply and demand relationships, but it seems clear that the long-predicted descent from the oil production volume plateau has finally begun.

For the purposes of this scenario it is assumed that 620 million tonnes of crude oil and condensate is available in 2000. A sustained 1% per annum growth in mined coal production would result in some gross 990 million tonnes in 2000, equivalent at best to 395Mtoe. A growth trend continuation at 3% per annum would raise the contribution from hydroelectricity to 80Mtoe by 2000. Gas production may be limited to 1,180BCM (990Mtoe) in 2000.[31] For nuclear electricity, an average annual growth in excess of 6% could see production at some 105Mtoe in 2000. Non-hydro renewables and others could contribute a further 35Mtoe. The key uncertainty in this scenario would be the extent to which the Soviet economy could stand the strain of an ever-increasing investment share being allocated to the energy supply sector.[32] Carbon emissions would be some 25% higher than the level in 1990.

2000B: Emissions abatement

This scenario recognizes a 'discontinuity' in Soviet economic affairs and sees a smaller overall growth in energy demand as stricter and more specific energy conservation measures directed towards the coal and oil-using industries are eventually introduced and reinforced by attitudinal changes and an official shift towards demand-side investment. There is greater investment in domestic and imported energy-saving technologies and the impact of substantial energy price rises in the early 1990s is felt by end-users.[33] Reduction in oil and coal use would be compensated by increased production and use of natural gas, and primary electricity consumption growth as investment in this sector is seen as economically and environmentally preferable. A consequence is reduction in the rate of carbon emissions.

In this scenario, with economic growth held at 2.2% on average, energy demand grows on average at slightly under 2% per annum, to a 2000 total of 1,780Mtoe, implying a sustained decline in energy intensity of over 0.2% per annum from the mid-1990s. Contributing to this decline

[31] *Eastern Bloc Energy*, Vol.11, No.3, Energy Economics Research Ltd., Reading, 1989.

[32] Thane Gustafson, *Crisis Amid Plenty: The Politics of Soviet Energy under Brezhnev and Gorbachev*, Princeton University Press, New Jersey, 1989.

[33] R.H.Williams, 'Decoupling Energy and Economic Growth in the Soviet Union', (draft), Centre for Energy and Environmental Studies, Princeton University, November 1989.

in energy intensity would be the gradual restructuring of the economy away from heavy industry and towards the service sectors, but the full impact of the changes would not be felt until late in the decade.

Natural gas production would be pushed to 1,220BCM, (equivalent to 1,010Mtoe) with demand reaching 920Mtoe, (a massive 51% of the energy balance) leaving 90Mtoe available for export. Oil is further displaced by natural gas in industry and power generation, and oil production is allowed to decline to an economically more sustainable level around 550 million tonnes. Pressure for hard currency earnings requires the maintenance of export levels approaching 200 million tonnes. Domestic demand falls to 340 million tonnes, just 19% of total energy requirements, and this will require a substantial increase in the depth of refining.

The coal industry receives reduced investment, but improved technology permits more economic electricity transmission over long distances. Gross production increases by 0.5%/yr to 850 million tonnes; the contribution to the energy balance is only 17.5% or 310Mtoe. Improved combustion technology allows coal to be used more efficiently and reduces SO_2 (but not CO_2) emissions. Primary electricity production is boosted. Modifications to some of the more environmentally-contentious hydroelectric schemes reduces local opposition, and combined hydro and nuclear electricity production increases to 830TWh, equivalent to 11% of primary energy or 200Mtoe.

Key uncertainties in this scenario would be the inertia of the system; the timing of the introduction and implementation of the changes; the future course of global oil prices which could influence attitudes of Soviet energy supply planners; the ability or desire of both West and East European gas markets to absorb larger volumes of Soviet gas; the determination of the leadership to enforce energy saving measures to a hitherto unprecedented degree; the political consequences of reducing investment in the coal industry so severely; and the strength of the 'green democracy' wave. Carbon emissions could be only some 10% higher than 1990 levels.

8.5 Projections and options to 2030

If Soviet energy demand and production were to continue at the rate of growth implied in the 2000A scenario, they would nearly triple. However, given growing environmental and economic difficulties such

Energy efficiency in the USSR: potential and practice

The Institute of Energy Research of the Soviet Academy of Sciences has listed selected energy efficiency measures which might be applied over the next fifteen years, the total capital cost of which is estimated at 50 billion roubles, and the potential saving achieved by 2005 amounting to some 350 Mtoe (25% of current demand). The savings to the Soviet economy are difficult to quantify, but if these savings freed an equivilent amount of oil for export at US$20/barrel, this would equate to US$50bn. The list, *in descending order of Mtoe saved,* includes:

- Regulated electric drive - efficient lighting - gas turbine and combined cycle power plants - low capacity (multi-fired) automated boilers (using solid or liquid or gaseous fuels) - centralised mass production of improved efficiency fuel ovens - improved insulation in centralised heat supply networks - control and measurement in energy use - switching small boilers from low-grade to high-grade fuels - shutting down low-efficiency ovens - switching to large boilers in areas with high heat consumption density - improving gas compressors in pipeline pumping stations - transition from harvesters to on-site threshing of grain - advanced technologies for reinforced concrete, electrical heating and heating by waste combustion gases - scrap recycling in the steel industry - insulation of cattle breeding stations - reduction of electricity transmission losses - automation of central and individual heating stations - replacing wet cement clinker production by the dry method - improved brick production.

Other suggestions discussed in Soviet magazines and journals include closing down factories and plants for whose goods there is no demand, and the introduction of a completely new type of long-term energy programme akin to 'least cost planning' including end-use efficiency improvements. Compared with the current system these would be radical changes. By implication few such measures are included in the scenarios discussed here.

developments are clearly implausible and overall energy production options are limited. Soviet economic growth could, in various regions, be adversely affected by chronic electricity supply shortages unless much greater use is made of coal. Ever-growing Soviet energy exports may no longer be counted on by either Eastern or Western customers. They could in due course decline well below current levels, particularly if the Soviet economy can develop alternative exports, and logistics might indeed necessitate increased oil imports. Soviet borrowing from the West could initially increase substantially in order specifically to finance those imports required to embark upon any concerted emissions-abatement programme.

While the Soviet Union today accounts for about 12% of world economic output, its higher energy intensity results in a relatively higher (17%) share of world CO_2 emissions. Electricity demand growth is outstripping non-electric energy demand and will require 30% or more of total fuel used in 2030 compared to some 26% today. While considerable scope for energy saving in the residential and commercial sector undoubtedly exists, much of it is likely to be offset by increases in per-capita floor space, which at present is well below levels in OECD countries.[34] Reduction in energy demand by the industrial sector offers the best prospects for decreasing growth in overall energy demand.[35] A heavy programme of construction will be involved in perestroika, not least in the residential sector.[36]

2030Ai: Business-as-usual

Using a demand base in 2000 of 1,910Mtoe and gradually declining annual growth rates of 2% to 2005, 1.5% to 2010, 1% to 2020 and 0.5% to 2030, total Soviet energy demand in 2030 would be 2,635Mtoe. This assumes both a gradual decline in GDP growth and a reduction in energy-GDP ratios to well below 1.

[34] Lee Schipper and R.Caron Cooper 'Energy Conversation in the USSR: Prospects for More Efficient Energy Use', *International Energy Studies*, Lawrence Berkeley Laboratory, University of California, January 1990.
[35] Professor Yuri Sinyak, 'USSR Energy Efficiency and Prospects', paper presented at IIASA Workshop, Laxenberg, Austria, January 1990.
[36] Schipper and Cooper, op.cit., and a useful analysis of the sectoral composition of Soviet energy consumption is contained in an article by Albina Tretyakova and Matthew J.Sagers entitled 'Trends in Fuel and Energy Use and Programmes for Energy Conservation by Economic Sector in the USSR', *Energy Policy*, Vol.18, No.1, February 1990.

Under this scenario the upper limit on gas production now being contemplated (1.25TCM) is raised to 1.5TCM, equivalent to 1,335Mtoe. Domestic consumption has risen to 1,200Mtoe, equivalent to 46% of the energy balance, leaving 135Mtoe for export. Coal production reaches a plateau around 1.2 billion tonnes, but declining quality limits its calorific contribution to 400Mtoe, of which 15Mtoe is exported. Oil production declines to 460 million tonnes and, with exports held to 100 million tonnes, domestic demand falls to 360 million tonnes, under 14% of the total. Renewable energy, particularly biomass, solar and geothermal contributes 50Mtoe, and 'others' 25Mtoe. Primary electricity contributes 615Mtoe, requiring average annual increases of around 4% between 2000 and 2030, subject to improved environmental and safety management. Carbon emissions are some 40% above 1988 levels.

2030Aii: Emissions abatement through fuel switching

Some 1,225Mtoe of natural gas would be consumed domestically, leaving only 110Mtoe for export. Oil production is lower at 400 million tonnes and demand would be reduced to 320 million tonnes, down to 11% of the total, still leaving 80 million tonnes for export. Coal consumption is down to 340Mtoe, and with non-hydro renewables, especially biomass, solar and wind, rising to 50Mtoe (the resource bases would be adequate but the economics and geographical locations would be constraints) and 'others' at 25Mtoe, the balance of 695Mtoe is contributed by primary electricity. Carbon emissions are some 35% above 1988 levels.

2030Bi: Emissions abatement through improved energy efficiency

This scenario would see a substantially lower total energy demand, at 2,375Mtoe, with annual increases falling below 0.5% between 2010 and 2015, ceasing altogether but permitting GDP growth to average 2% by the end of the period. To achieve this lower demand total while maintaining reasonable economic growth there must in the next two decades be substantial investment in energy-saving technology, the adoption of more effective economic and industrial management techniques and the scrapping of older, less efficient industrial plant and equipment. Sustained increases in energy prices in the 1990s and in the early years of next century would have affected demand in all sectors of the economy. Industrial enterprises would be permitted to increase hard currency imports in line with the energy savings they could achieve.

Energy exports could rise during the early years of this scenario, to pay for some 'pump-priming' energy efficient technology and equipment imports, but would fall during the later years as non-energy exports increased and domestic production of energy efficient equipment was able to satisfy domestic demand.

Production of natural gas would be maximized with a peak of 1.25TCM (1,045Mtoe) being reached in 2005, and maintained until 2030. Gas exports decline to 100Mtoe. Consumption of natural gas would fall to 945Mtoe, or 40% of the fuels energy balance. Oil production, with the aid of offshore and arctic discoveries, is maintained at 400 million tonnes but exports would be down to 90 million tonnes, and demand at 310 million tonnes, just under 12% of the total, would be almost exclusively for the transportation, petrochemical and agricultural sectors. Coal consumption, with the aid of emission-reduction technology, would be 355Mtoe, and with non-hydro renewables and others contributing 75Mtoe the balance which would have to be met by primary electricity would amount to 715Mtoe. Carbon emissions would be 20% above 1988 levels.

2030Bii: Emissions abatement through efficiency and switching

In addition to a nationwide campaign to encourage and enforce energy conservation, a strenuous and sustained effort to reduce carbon emissions significantly below current levels is instituted in the near future. Demand would be lower, at 2,130Mtoe, assuming a successful balancing of increased requirements by increased conservation as a result of changes in investment allocations in the early years of next century and demand growth ceasing after 2015. Production would be substantially lower. A change in the later years of this scenario would be some switching out of natural gas. A massive increase in primary electricity use would be necessary along with the adoption throughout society of an energy-conservation ethic. The shares of heavy industry and the service sectors are reversed from the current levels of 70% and 30% respectively, by the end of the period.

Limited further switching out of oil might be achieved, and heavy investment in renewables might see their contribution exceed 100Mtoe. By far the largest share, over 35% of the fuels energy balance, would be contributed by primary electricity, to which investment would be diverted at a very early stage from other energy sectors. Combined-cycle gas turbine CHP technology would be introduced on a large scale. Oil exports would be no higher than 100Mtoe, and domestic demand would fall to 300 million tonnes, largely for the transportation, petrochemical and agricultural sectors. Coal utilization, would be down to 300Mtoe, largely for electricity generation and the metallurgy industries, while soaring primary electricity production would contribute 785Mtoe. Of this, hydroelectricity might supply 255Mtoe leaving 530Mtoe to come from nuclear, which would necessitate average annual growth rates of between 5.5% and 6.0%. Carbon emissions could be significantly below 1990 levels.

This scenario would be feasible if major and radical structural, technological and economic changes were introduced at the earliest opportunity. The direct involvement in the Soviet economy of foreign companies possessing advanced energy-saving technologies would be actively sought. Public support for this sort of scenario would have to be secured by a direct appeal, riding on the wave of global concern about environmental issues. But a major move in this direction would have to be made very soon, before any reaction to the current shake-up in Soviet society sets in, and research into energy demand structures and renewable resource opportunities initiated immediately. In practice, it is more likely that greater quantities of natural gas and coal and less nuclear electricity will in fact be used.

8.6 Policy options and constraints

More than two-thirds of Soviet carbon emissions are produced by the industrial and energy supply sectors in which power plant are the principal source. The Soviet Union, largely because of decisions to exploit fully its massive natural gas resources and potential for generating primary electricity, may already be said to be embarked upon an emissions-abatement course, although for socioeconomic, logistic, infrastructural and technological reasons, rather than any expressed intention to reduce greenhouse gas emissions. There will also continue to be a reduction in the energy demand/GDP ratio in coming decades.

The Soviet energy situation has traditionally been dominated by supply-side considerations, so much so that it is in danger of becoming locked into the vicious circle according to which increasing supply-side investment is required to maintain or slowly increase production surpluses which can be exported to secure hard currency imports. There could be immense advantages for the Soviet economy in switching to a virtuous circle according to which investment in energy demand-reduction would not only permit a reasonable level of energy exports but would enable investment funds to be directed from the energy production to other, less energy-intensive, sectors of the economy and the generation of exports based on them (see Figure 8.4). Substantial price rises for energy would assist in this development but additional, more systemic incentives would be necessary, involving widespread decentralization of economic responsibility and the opening up of the Soviet economy to international competition and other global economic forces.

The repercussions of such a fundamental change as the introduction of a realistic pricing system upon inflation and upon the input costs in those industrial sectors using energy-intensive raw materials, would be dramatic. Furthermore, the rouble is being progressively devalued, and these two measures should go some way to oblige enterprises to take energy conservation much more seriously. Whether future measures will include, for example, integrating energy conservation targets with quantitative production targets at the enterprise level, or gearing energy production targets to serve the actual, optimum energy-demand requirements of consumers, perhaps on a regional as opposed to a nation-wide basis, will be reflected in the outcome of internal political and economic restructuring.

Demand-side sectoral considerations and potential for energy savings

Changing the energy supply/demand balance in favour of energy conservation and demand reduction will be comparable to changing course in a supertanker. Yet by the early part of next century, considerable reductions in energy demand growth could be achieved if the system is changed, particularly if the unquantified but obviously substantial energy requirements associated with maintaining the massive Soviet military sector can be reduced following improvements in the international political climate. Also there is no particular reason why the Soviet Union could not bring about reductions in energy intensity, similar to those achieved by other industrial countries, once the management of the Soviet economy follows the market forces-related procedures familiar in the West, but one should not underestimate the timescale in which such a radical change could be brought about and produce the desired effects.

Figure 8.4 USSR energy balance: a strategic vision

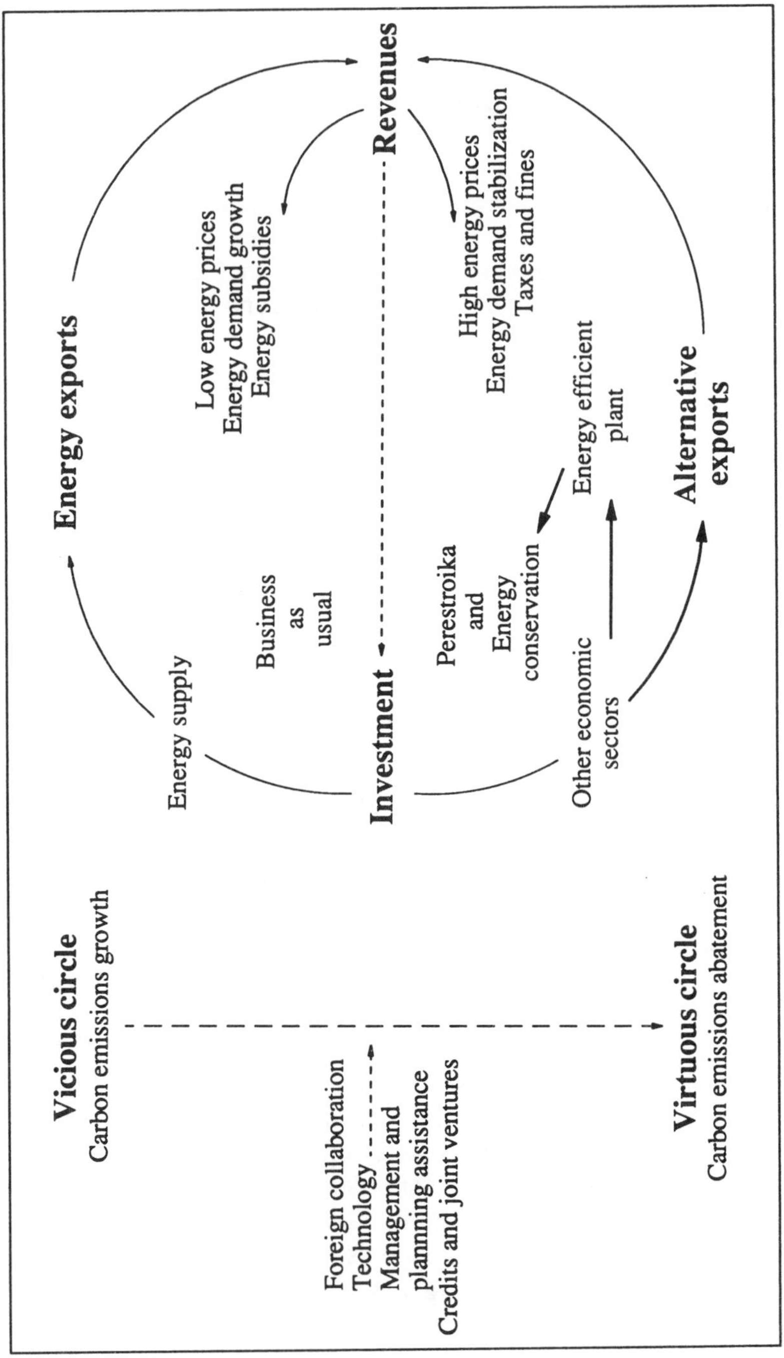

It has been suggested by Soviet analysts that up to 30% of the available annual energy resource is being wasted, either by not being used, as in the case of associated gas and gas liquids or through leakage and other transmission losses, or by radiation and insulation losses to the atmosphere.[37] There are three main groups of reasons why so much energy is not being harvested for the Soviet economy.

Energy infrastructure and distribution. These reflect not only the enormous distances over which energy must currently be transmitted from production to consumption centres, but also the condition (age and state of repair) of transmission systems, especially in the gas industry. They reflect the inadequacy of collection and processing facilities, and the steadily growing consumption of energy by the energy production industries themselves. While much saving can be achieved through improved maintenance and the provision of adequate and up-to-date equipment, energy losses due to the 'penalty of distance' will endure.

End-use equipment and practices. These reflect, throughout the economy, the age and design of the existing capital stock and the failure to use it in ways which conserve energy. They are particularly apparent in the transport sector in general and the vehicle sector in particular where there is a need not only to reduce the age of the truck and car pools but also to improve maintenance, the quality of the road system, the location of refuelling stations, the scheduling of commercial journeys and the mix of fuels more in favour of diesel. Changes under perestroika aimed at renovating the country's capital stock will bring about significant improvements in the industrial sector, and improved availability and quality of consumer durables will similarly enhance energy conservation in the domestic sector.

Economic and social. Traditional attitudes to energy as a cheap and readily available resource have greatly undervalued it relative to other economic inputs. Low prices and subsidies combined with inadequate metering have resulted in widespread over-use of energy, and there has hitherto been no clear-cut focus of responsibility for energy conservation and only half-hearted enforcement of such conservation measures and targets as have been belatedly introduced over the last 20 years. A major structural reason for high energy consumption is the predominance of heavy industry, and this is exacerbated by the high proportion of

[37] Tolokonnikov, op.cit.

energy-intensive raw materials used throughout the economy, particularly in the construction sector and in the military sector. Motivation, currently lacking, to value energy more highly and conserve its use will develop as more enterprises become cost-accountable (khozraschot) and as long-anticipated energy price rises are introduced. However, while under perestroika prices of many goods and services will increasingly be determined by the market place, indications are that, for strategic and security reasons, energy prices will continue for the time being to be determined by the State. Furthermore, price rises may initially only be made at the enterprise level, and while this will benefit the energy producers, who will be able to reinvest more profit, it is not yet clear to what extent enterprises will be permitted, or able, to pass the rises on to other end-users and the general public for whom energy is heavily subsidised.

There would probably be a wide measure of public support for any environmentally-slanted marketing of necessary energy conservation measures given the widespread and growing concern now beginning to be expressed openly about all aspects of environmental pollution and conservation, but the exploitation of the country's energy resources will need to be changed by pricing discipline and concerted educational effort from the schoolroom upwards. While non-fossil electricity will clearly have to play a major role in any emission-abatement scenarios, some of the safety and environmental problems associated with hydro and nuclear electricity which will have to be overcome seem daunting. Primary electricity will have to be packaged on a 'lesser of two evils' basis and much will need to be done to convince people on the safety and relocation aspects. If this cannot be achieved, electricity supply problems will become acute and greater quantities of fossil fuel will have to be consumed in domestic power stations, adversely affecting carbon emissions.

In a country as large as the Soviet Union, in which immense areas are sparsely populated, the aesthetic impacts of wind, geothermal and solar power-generating installations should not give rise to much opposition. The systematic utilization of the huge biomass resource should be perfectly feasible provided the necessary technology can be made available on a large enough scale and can be made to operate in wilderness areas remote from the basic infrastructures. A fundamental economic problem with many of these renewable opportunities is similar to that already faced by the hydroelectricity industry, namely the absence of population and industry concentrations nearby which can both help develop the infrastructure and utilize the energy produced. Distribution losses will be large unless substantial advances in long distance high-voltage electricity transmission are made, and the analysis of opportunity for regional least-cost energy planning, currently being jointly undertaken by US and Soviet researchers, could produce encouraging pointers in this context. However, it should be noted that Soviet energy economists currently consider capital costs of non-hydro renewable energy developments are likely to remain highly uneconomic, given the abundance of conventional energy resources.[38]

Under the programme of economic restructuring President Gorbachev intends that Soviet industry will mainly be re-equipped through increases in domestic capital equipment manufacture particularly of energy-efficient technology and equipment. Reduced need for expenditure in the military sector is seen as making a key contribution in this connection.[39] The energy industries may be obliged to become more efficient, invest more of their profits and attract more foreign participation. The demand for investment generally is growing more rapidly than the planned supply of investment goods, and this implies increased imports from both Eastern Europe and the West. Assuming that political developments in the Soviet Union do not render cooperation too difficult, an extension of Western credit, perhaps conditional upon expenditure on energy conservation measures, will probably be an important consideration in the success of the Gorbachev initiative. As a corollary there would seem to be compelling logic in favour of selectively curtailing the least cost-effective parts of the coal, oil and even gas production efforts and restructuring, retraining, relocating and technologically upgrading those operations which remain, so that they would be economically self-sustaining and providers of profit instead of absorbers of subsidy. Investment funds diverted from the energy production industries could go towards the manufacture or import of energy-efficient equipment and technology.[40]

For the immediate future, unless economic growth rates and thus energy demand, are severely curtailed by prolonged socio-political

---

[38] Makarov and Bashmakov op.cit.
[39] ibid.
[40] See Arbatov, op.cit.

troubles, carbon emissions will continue to grow, albeit at a declining rate. The current period of readjustment will be a long one, and while energy-saving will be one of the primary outcomes of modernization it will need to be promoted specifically, and with increasing purposefulness. However, it could be a long time before CO$_2$ emission-abatement per se will become other than a coincidental of economic reform in the Soviet Union. The Soviet bureaucratic and technological infrastructure, let alone the individual and management style, is just not ready for 'a federal case' on greenhouse gases at the moment. Nevertheless, increased attention to greenhouse gas issues in the Soviet Union is something that could enhance the prospects for cooperation in other areas, for example the extension of loans on favourable terms and accelerated technology transfer.

The long-term potential for improvement in emissions-abatement in the Soviet Union is very large indeed. While the government is currently concentrating upon SO$_2$ and NO$_X$, general economic restructuring leading to energy demand growth reduction will contribute to CO$_2$ emission abatement goals.

What if...?

By December 1990, there had been no firm indication that any radical change in the Soviet energy system was contemplated, officially, in the near future. Energy prices had not been raised and no new Long Term Energy Programme or Economic Plan had been published. However, should the Council of Ministers decide to make those radical changes which Soviet energy researchers and academics are now advocating, the following are the measures which could be put in place: energy prices double, or more than double - energy subsidies to the end-users get phased out - all industrial enterprises adopt khozraschot (self-accounting) - energy conservation targets to be strictly enforced, using 'sticks and carrots' - energy-saving technology to be mass-produced by Soviet industry - some equipment and technology to be purchased from abroad, perhaps on 'conditional' loans - a massive information/educational campaign covering management options, technological fixes and all practical means of saving energy to be launched - foreign corporations specialising in energy conservation to be encouraged to enter into joint ventures with Soviet enterprises - those losing their jobs in the energy supply industries to be retrained and relocated - the energy supply industries to have investment funds stabilized or reduced in real terms over a period of years - the economy to be progressively be restructured away from heavy, energy-intensive industries towards the service and consumer goods sector.

Under these conditions, there could be a dramatic and progressive reduction in Soviet energy intensity and in overall energy demand growth with substantial benefits to the natural environment, gathering pace towards the turn of the century and achieving, first, stabilization of energy demand and, by 2030, even a possible decline. Economic growth rates might initially need to be somewhat lower than currently anticipated, but should be able to rise later in the period as the burden of investment in the energy supply side is eased.

Irrespective of theoretical benefits, all this may be taken to indicate the enormous scale of changes which would be required to realise the efficiency potential. Few, if any, analysts really consider such changes likely to come about in the near future.

8.7 International aspects

Energy and particularly oil sales have provided an essential and indeed dominant component of the range of exportable goods, as a means both of earning hard currency in the West and of maintaining a degree of economic hegemony within the Council for Mutual Economic Assistance (CMEA). The weakening of political and ideological ties within the former CMEA heralds a lessening of economic ties with the countries of central and eastern Europe. Whereas priority in the allocation of energy exports has clearly been given to the requirements of its CMEA allies until recently, a fundamental change can be expected in respect of export allocations, particularly of oil, during the next few years, especially when transactions cease to be in transferable roubles.

A degree of East-West energy interdependence in Europe has been established over recent decades in which the Soviet Union has been seen by Western energy importers as a valued supplier and Western energy markets have been seen as essential for the bulk of hard currency earnings. Moreover, economic self-interest has dictated that some West European countries for more than a decade, have risked being connected by an 'umbilical' gas line to the Soviet Union's vast reserves and, indeed have supplied large diameter steel pipe and related equipment and technology destined for the Soviet gas industry. From the Soviet side, imports from the hard-currency area are to at least some degree necessary to enable their economy to produce replacements for energy exports. If production growth is halted (or reduced) in favour of a shift to energy conservation, the need for international technical and financial cooperation could grow substantially.

The questions raised by such interdependence have implications for emission-abatement scenarios but more immediately for terms of trade. It may well be that importers from both East and West requiring access to Soviet energy resources may ultimately be obliged to negotiate joint ventures to assist in their extraction and to contribute not only hardware and labour but also technology and expertise. Joint-venture, other trading conditions and a management approach more compatible with established practices elsewhere in the world would need to be fully adopted by the Soviet Union, and while there are indeed clear indications that the Ministry of Foreign Economic Relations is addressing the challenge. There were only some thirty joint ventures fully in operation in the energy industries by the end of 1990, largely in the upstream sectors. Indeed, in future, joint ventures to develop energy resources may increasingly be arranged between individual republics and foreign companies, with a reduced involvement by the central authorities in Moscow, although the latter will almost certainly vigorously resist any such trend.

Turning now to international environmental and energy matters in general and atmospheric warming in particular, the Soviet Union has clearly expressed itself in favour of the establishment both of a code of international environmental conduct and a global environmental fund. No doubt increasingly conscious of its high profile on CO_2 emissions, it has taken part in international conferences concerning the greenhouse effect, and is collaborating with scientific establishments in the United States and elsewhere.

The greenhouse effect will impact both positively and negatively upon direct Soviet interests. Some industrial activity in parts of the Arctic, Baltic and Black Sea coasts would be vulnerable to sea-level rises brought about by atmospheric warming. Extraction of oil and gas from the tundra and permafrost regions depends to a considerable extent upon the land and water surface being well frozen for extended periods to permit the transportation of hardware for drilling and the construction of energy distribution infrastructures. Here, any significant shortening of the freezing period would undoubtedly hamper the production effort. It is not clear to what extent atmospheric warming would release significant quantities of methane from frozen hydrates which would intensify the emissions problem. Soviet agricultural production is likely to be affected by climatic change, and while the northern limit for the growing of, for example, grain crops might be extended, the possibility arises of the intensification of desert conditions in southern and central regions, where extensive irrigation is already giving rise to salt encroachment problems. Climatic changes would be likely to affect rainfall distribution and this could exacerbate water shortage problems already being encountered by existing hydroelectricity production schemes. On the positive side, climatic warming would be likely to extend the period for which northern rivers would remain navigable and also benefit marine transportation along the Soviet arctic coast. Warmer winters would reduce demand for heating fuels. The rate at which any climatic changes occurred would be crucial, and given the enormous distances involved and the huge areas likely to be affected, together with the relatively inflexible nature of the Soviet physical and bureaucratic infrastructure, any adaptive response might well be initially too slow either to capitalize on the beneficial aspects or to avoid the more adverse repercussions.

The Soviet attitude towards international limitations on carbon emissions is likely to be a mixture of enthusiastic support at the academic and 'megaphone' levels, but, at least initially, a rather slow and muddled practical response. The Soviet Union is currently considering the implications of a carbon tax, and is reasonably well placed to fulfil any agreements on equal reductions of emission growth rates, but while per-GDP or Net Material Product (NMP) targets could be favoured, with an economy likely to move gradually away from heavy industry towards the service sector, there could be great difficulties in agreeing the true starting point. At this stage it is possible either that the Soviet Union will pay lip service to whatever may be agreed internationally while developing its own approach to the problem of emission-abatement, or that it will warmly embrace international cooperation as a way of justifying the implementation of unpopular domestic measures.

8.8 Conclusions

The Soviet Union is relatively well placed to play its part in any international coordination of efforts to reduce the rate at which anthropogenic carbon emissions are produced. However, with so much uncertainty surrounding Soviet economic and political developments it is far from clear whether and to what extent the Soviet Union will be able to concentrate resources upon issues related to global warming. Problems on the energy supply front resulting from the logistics and escalating costs of their mobilization and from environmental issues, are already dominating much of the economic debate. Major question marks overhang the future of the Soviet nuclear energy and hydroelectricity programme; which could play a key role in reducing carbon emissions.

Reducing greenhouse gas emissions at a rate faster than that which would be determined by basic domestic economic considerations may be seriously addressed only if there are seen to be tangible gains in, for example, the country's international standing, or if other countries make it economically and technologically advantageous. Otherwise, it could be argued that the Soviet leadership will have problems enough trying to match economic growth and growth in energy demand with the likely availability of domestic supply at growth rates which will not impose unsustainable burdens upon the rest of the economy. In the absence of any firm proof that the enhanced greenhouse effect is both of largely anthropogenic origin and disadvantageous, the Soviet Union could claim that it was already, by changing the fuel mix in favour of natural gas, contributing to the good of the global ecosystem and would moreover continue to do so over the next few decades as restructuring resulted in a substantial reduction in the GDP/energy use ratio.

On the other hand, the Soviet leadership may in spite of all the other problems, decide strongly to support any global initiative to reduce greenhouse gas emissions, for example because green issues can provide useful moral support for good husbandry and other energy conservation initiatives it is seeking to promote. It is not immediately apparent, however, that unaided it will in practice be able to do a great deal more than stringent energy conservation programmes would in any case cause it to do. The Soviet Union's constructive involvement in the formulation and institution of any international code or agreement relating to a carbon tax or permit or equal per-capita entitlement to carbon emissions is at least possible since it has acknowledged that carbon emission ceilings must be established. It will be enlightening to see where it will stand in the debate at the interface between industrialized and developing countries on the future use of carbon-based fuels.

Chapter 9 China: the Continuing Dominance of Coal

Michèle Ledic
Birkbeck College, London

would like to thank Alyson Bailes, Stan Calder, Michael Grubb, onathan Stern, Bruce Vernor and Mao Yu-Shi for their valuable comments. Also Rosina Pullman and Nicola Steen for their detailed care hat they put into editing the text and figures, and into preparing the paper or publication.

China: the Continuing Dominance of Coal

China with its vast land area, and its natural resources, is striving for faster development of its energy industry, to suit the needs of its fast growing economy and population, which is now estimated to be around 1,110 million people.

China ranks third in the world both as a fuel producer and consumer. Though there are some reserves of other fuels, coal dominates Chinese energy resources, and in both production and consumption coal accounts for more than 70% of total commercial energy. This, combined with the fact that China is a very inefficient energy consumer (its energy intensity is more than double that of India, for example), makes China one of the major contributors to carbon emissions in the world. Emissions rose by nearly two-and-a-half times between 1970 and 1988, at an average rate of almost 5% annually, to reach 720 million tonnes of carbon/yr. However, although per capita energy consumption is well above the level of the other major low-income developing countries, it is far below that of industrialised countries, at about 10% of the level in the United States.

Serious ecological problems on a large scale are now facing many parts of China. Apart from air pollution in both urban and rural areas, there is soil erosion and deforestation, as well as water pollution and water shortage.[1] Energy is recognised as one of the major sources of environmental degradation but the greenhouse effect is not regarded as

---

[1] For a full account of China's ecological problems see: V.Smil, *The Bad Earth - Environmental Degradation in China*, M.E.Sharpe, Inc., New York, 1984.

one of the important issues, and policies focus on trying to clean up coal rather than curtail its expansion.

With some exceptions, energy prices have been kept at well below world prices. The price structure for energy gives the wrong incentives, and distorts the pattern of energy production and investment. This has reduced the incentive for energy conservation, particularly in the use of coal, crude and heavy oil. Price reform is difficult, particularly given the political trends since 1989. Energy efficiency is expected to increase substantially, but in general, Chinese energy developments focus on securing adequate supplies and managing the constraints of the transport system for delivering coal.

Supply-side options for limiting emissions might include devoting more resources to gas exploration and infrastructure; greater development of China's large hydro resources; and improving biomass supply and utilisation. However, greater regionalisation might improve efficiency and encourage more use of local renewable sources. These options are constrained by the lack of capital and hard currency with which to obtain modern technology. The need for export earnings also increases pressures to maximise oil and coal production.

Commercial energy consumption is projected to increase by some 60% by the year 2000, with carbon emissions growing in step. Abatement policies are likely to yield only a modest reduction in this. In all the feasible scenarios for 2030 per capita carbon emissions in China will still be well below those of advanced countries, reflecting its comparatively low living standards. Despite this, China's energy needs for continued economic development, together with its great reliance on coal, make it inevitable that its greenhouse gas emissions will continue to increase, for as far ahead as can be seen.

.1 The economic context

⁷or three decades following the formation of the People's Republic of China in 1949, China's economy was centrally planned and directed, with successive five-year plans setting production targets for industry. Some 90% of enterprises are state-owned and managed. They are given production and labour utilization targets, and also pollution targets. Prices for all commodities were set and remained unchanged for many years. In 1978 China embarked on major economic reforms and the 'open door' policy. Domestically, the main objective was to quadruple the Gross Value of Industrial and Agricultural Output (GVIAO) between 980 and the year 2000. As part of this aim, China was seeking to increase energy supplies by 100%, and also to increase efficiency with which energy is used by the same percentage.

Reforms first introduced in agriculture were proved to be effective at the time, and in 1984 they were introduced into the industrial and urban sectors. A two-tier price system was introduced, under which output above the planned quota was allowed to be sold freely, at market prices. Links with the rest of the world economy were intensified and liberalized at the same time. There were however problems. The policies led to greater regionalism, inequalities and tensions between different interest groups, and extensive corruption. The trade balance deteriorated dramatically. In addition, the pace of inflation quickened. The authorities reacted by imposing greater controls on foreign trade in 1986, and in the autumn of 1988 introduced a stabilization programme to damp down the growth of the economy and to try to rectify growing economic imbalances, while not abandoning the economic reforms as such.

The events in Tiananmen Square of June 1989 led to further moves towards re-centralization, curbs on imports, and a retreat from market mechanisms, partly in an attempt to bring down inflation and partly to reimpose central power. But this apparent reversal in policy was to a considerable extent a continuation of trends that had already begun in 986, and had brought with them much unpopularity for the Chinese leadership.

Even before the economic reforms of the 1970s, legislation was enacted on pollution targets.[2] The most clearly defined outcome has been the

---

2] In 1973 the State Planning Commission promulgated the Directive 'Some Regulations on Protecting and Improving the Environment', which was the first formal environmental regulation in China. An Environment Protection Office was set up in

development of standards for environmental quality. Othe
consequences have been an emissions fee system and the imposition o
fines to compensate for environmental damage.[3]

However, where pollution infringements occur, as for example in th
case of effluent causing water pollution, standards are often not strongl'
enforced. Nor are fines high enough to induce enterprises to reduc
pollution. It has also been reported that it is standard practice for a
enterprise to pay the fee at the beginning of the year (based on th
previous year's emissions) and then pollute at will for the rest of th
year.[4] A further disincentive for the prevention of pollution occurs i
an enterprise which is liable to pay pollution charges is running at a los
since the subsidy to the firm may be increased to offset the charge.

Another relevant factor is that input prices for raw materials may bea
little relation to their costs of production, while prices for final product
may be set independently of costs. Where, therefore, an enterprise ha
to bear a pollution charge, this may not be passed on in final prices, thu
removing from consumers any incentive to economize on the product
concerned. Particularly relevant to the inefficient use of energy is the fac
that, with some exceptions, energy prices have been kept at levels we.
below world prices.[5] This has reduced the incentive for energ
conservation, particularly in the use of coal, crude oil and heavy o

---

1974. The Law of Environmental Protection was issued in 1979 and the Environmer
Protection Commission (EPC) established. The National Environmental Protectic
Agency (NEPA), the EPC's executive arm, together with regional Environment.
Protection Bureaus (EPBs) were created to formulate and carry out environment:
regulations.

[3] Mao Yu-Shi, 'Environmental Charges and the Price System: The Chines
Perspective', presented at a conference on 'Economic Incentives as a Means
Environmental Policy', Free University of Berlin, November, 1989, pp. 31; 'Saving tl
Ozone Layer', *China-Britain Trade Review*, April 1989, p.6; A. Krupnick an
I.Sebastian, 'China: Case Study of Air Pollution in Beijing', The World Ban'
Environment Department, 1989, (mimeo), pp.32.

[4] See Mao Yu-Shi, op. cit., pp.4-8.

[5] A comparison of Chinese retail prices with international energy prices, using offici
exchange rates shows the price for coal was 30% and of fuel oil between 16% and 30'
of the international level. See National Institute for Research Advancement (NIRA
The Present State and Future of China's Energy Problem, Tokyo, 1986, p.37; *Chin.
Long Term Issues and Options; Annex C: Energy*, The World Bank, Washington, 198
p.76. International price comparisons are difficult to interpret, particularly with respe
to CPEs. See M.Grubb, *The Greenhouse Effect: Negotiating Targets*, RIIA, 198
Appendix 1 and Figure 5, p.18.

Petroleum prices were at the world level, but diesel prices were 20% and coal prices 60% below the world level. Energy prices for industrial use were similarly distorted.

This price structure for energy not only gives the wrong incentives, as regards energy saving, but it has effects on production. The long-term marginal cost of coal is estimated to be nearly twice as much as the price at the state-owned mines, so that on a true calculation new mines cannot cover the costs of exploiting the resource.[6] On average, coal subsidies are said to amount to 20% of the price. Refineries are encouraged by relative prices to produce gasoline rather than diesel oil, even though the latter gives higher fuel efficiency. The railway tariff for coal transportation is estimated to be only two-thirds of long-term marginal costs, thus further distorting true economic costs of energy and encouraging long hauls and the uneconomic use of coal at coastal sites far from the coalfields. In contrast the price of natural gas is the lowest in terms of heating value. This discourages producers from gas exploration. It also causes demand by consumers to outstrip supply, and encourages the inefficient use of gas.

Another consequence of low energy prices is that there is little incentive to renew or improve inefficient energy consuming devices. Much old equipment is in use, and one important consequence is that the percentage coal consumption in power generation is higher than in more developed countries.[7] Energy saving technology is introduced only slowly. This is due also to a shortage of resources for investment, a lack of awareness within many levels of government of the importance of greater energy efficiency, and an absence of effective competition between electricity producers. As has been mentioned, the economic reform programme brought the gradual adoption of the two-tier price system, as a first step towards market pricing. This rather partial programme gave rise to anomalies and much discontent. Since September 1988, and especially since June 1989, there has been a turning away from the price reform process on the part of government planners.

[6] *The Study of China's Energy Utilization and Policies for Comparison with India*, Institute of Nuclear Energy Technology (INET) & Institute for Techno-Economics and Energy System Analysis (ITEESA), Beijing, 1987, p.234; The World Bank, op. cit., p.75.
[7] Coal consumption in power supply in 1985 in China was 431tce/GWh, in comparison with 328tce/GWh in the USSR, 377tce/GWh in the USA and 383tce/GWh in the UK; INET, op.cit., p.125.

The wrong signals will therefore continue to be given and energy efficiency through use of the price mechanism will continue to be discouraged.

9.2 Developments and trends in the energy balance

Coal dominates energy production and consumption. There are large reserves of coal, and the bulk of investment in energy has been until recently concentrated in the coal sector. Investment in oil exploration was largely neglected before the 1970s, and investment in natural gas exploration has been on even a smaller scale. This is one of the reasons for such a high dominance of coal in China's energy mix (see Figure 9.1).

Table 9.1 illustrates China's energy balance in 1987.[8] Little coal was exported in that year, but about 25% of oil production was exported, in spite of a severe shortage of oil at home. The structure of primary energy consumption changed during the period 1970-89, mainly due to large investment in the oil industry and in hydro-electric power generation. Coal was the dominant fuel throughout. In 1987, coal accounted for 55% of total energy consumption and over 79% of primary commercial energy consumption[9] (compared with an average across industrialized countries of about 30%). Biomass fuels, used mainly in rural households, are the second most important energy source. Their share in total energy consumption in 1970 appears to have been as great as that of coal, but by the end of the 1980s they accounted for some 30% of total consumption.[10] Oil increased its share to 16.8%, while natural gas and hydroelectricity together increased their share to the still very low figure of 3.6%.[11] The highest percentage rates of increase in the production

[8] Energy consumption in 1987, excluding biomass, was some 479Mtoe in all, or 0.44 toe per capita. This was just over one-third of the world per capita average and one-sixth of the level of all European countries taken together. But it was at the same level as in Brazil, and two and half times as high as in India.

[9] The usage in this chapter is that total energy consumption *includes* biomass and use in power generation, unless otherwise stated, and primary commercial energy excludes biomass.

[10] For the purpose of this study, of the many estimates of biomass consumption, the one by the Ministry of Energy, for 1987, has been adopted (*Energy in China 1989*, p.87). As a first approximation, the population growth rate has been applied to that estimate to obtain the estimates for previous years.

[11] Primary energy consumption is calculated on the basis of: production - exports + imports. The shares of fuels in energy consumption, calculated in this way, differ from those in Chinese data.

Figure 9.1 China energy consumption and CO_2 emissions, 1970-89

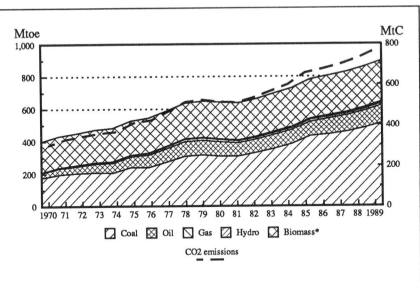

Note: Primary energy consumption is calculated on the basis of: production
-exports + imports; Biomass data is author's estimate.

Source: *Statistical Yearbook of China 1984 and 1986*, State Statistical Bureau,
Beijing, 1985 and 1987; *Energy in China*, Ministry of Energy, Beijing, 1989.

and consumption of natural gas and hydroelectricity were seen during
this period. Oil and coal consumption grew less rapidly, but their growth
was much greater in absolute terms.

Electricity production rose by approximately five times, and in 1989
accounted for 8% of delivered energy. Thermal and hydroelectric power
generation grew by similar amounts.[12] Power generated from thermal
and hydroelectric power plants accounted for 80% and 20% respectively,
of total electricity production. Coal's share of total thermal generation
had risen from 70% to over 80%. This was the result of government

[12] In Chinese statistics the percentage of hydroelectric power is higher, and that for
coal lower, than shown in this study. This is because Chinese statistics for hydroelectric
power are in terms of the indigenous coal that would be needed to generate this amount
of electricity.

Table 9.1 China: energy balances 1987 (Mtoe)

| | Production | | | | Demand | | |
	Mtoe	%share commercial energy	%share total energy		Mtoe	%share commercial energy	%share total energy
Coal	464	75	54		457	79	55
Oil	134	22	16		102	18	12
Gas	13	2	2		13	2	2
Hydro-elec	9	1	1		9	1	1
Total commercial	620	100	72		581	100	70
Biomass	247		28		247		30
Total	867		100		828		100

| | Final Consumption | | | Sectoral share (%) | | | | |
	Mtoe	%share commercial energy	%share total energy	Agri	Ind	Trans	Res	Other
Coal	347	72	48	5	60	4	31	0
Oil	87	18	12	13	59	17	3	8
Gas	8	2	1	-	96	-	4	0
Elec	37	8	5	10	79	2	6	3
Total commercial	479	100	66	7	62	6	23	2
Biomass	247		34		6		94	
Total	726		100					

Sources: *World Energy Statistics and Balances 1971-81*, OECD/IEA, Paris, 1989.
Energy in China, Ministry of Energy, Beijing, 1989.

policy of replacing oil by coal in power generation, in order to release much needed oil into the economy, and also to make more oil available for export.

Industry is by far the largest user of commercial energy, followed by residential/commercial use. In particular, it uses some 80% of total electricity generated. In the industrial sector, 80% of total energy was used by heavy industry and 20% by light industry. Three heavy industrial sectors, metallurgy, chemicals and building materials, accounted for 50% of that use. Light industry, however, produced almost half of industrial output in value terms.[13]

The residential/commercial sector used about a quarter of total commercial energy, but only 6% of electricity. Most of this consumption was in urban areas and in the service sectors. In the rural areas of China, where 80% of the population lives, electricity in household use accounts for just over 1% of total rural energy consumption. The proportion of commercial energy used in transport, at only 6%, is remarkably low, and illustrates the underdeveloped state of China's transport system. Also it is a reminder of the complexities of China's modernization programme, in a country where transportation of coal occupies 40% of the total freight volume.[14]

Carbon emissions have followed energy use closely (see Table 9.2). Total carbon emissions rose by two-and-a-half times between 1970 and 1989, at an average annual rate of almost 3.5%, to reach 766 million tonnes of carbon (MtC). Emissions from electricity production are high in relation to electricity output, because of the dominance of low efficiency coal-fired power plants.

China's energy balance was unaffected by the first oil price rise of 1973. At that time China was building up her oil production, insulated from world market trends. The reaction was different in 1979, however, when oil prices rose again. By that time domestic oil production had grown considerably, and at the same time the 'open door' policy was in progress. China took advantage of the high world price for oil by greatly stepping

[13] Wang Jiacheng, 'Energy Use in Chinese Industry', in *Proceedings of the Chinese-American Symposium on Energy Markets and the Future of Energy Demand*, Lawrence Berkeley Laboratory, University of California, November 1988, pp.201-206.
[14] Yang Hongnian, 'Energy and Transport in China', in *Chinese-American Symposium*, op.cit., pp.181-186.

Table 9.2 China: carbon emissions 1987 (MtC)

	Agri	Industry	Trans	Res	Other	Total	Share (%)
Coal	19	226	15	116	2	378	55
Oil	9	42	12	2	6	71	10
Gas	-	5	-	0	0	5	1
Electricity*	13	102	2	8	4	129	19
Biomass**	-	-	-	108	-	108	15
Total	41	375	29	234	12	691	100
Share (%)	6	54	4	34	2	100	

Carbon emission coefficients:coal 1.09MtC/Mtoe, oil 0.82MtC/Mtoe, gas 0.62MtC/Mtoe.
* Thermal power plant efficiency of 28%
** Fuelwood only, emission coefficient taken as for coal.

Source: see Table 9.1.

up its oil exports, and replacing oil with coal in power generation. Oil exports went on rising until the oil price collapse of 1986.[15]

One effect of this policy towards oil exports was that there was a fall in China's domestic oil consumption between 1978 and 1982. After that consumption rose, but it did not surpass the 1978 level until 1986, in the aftermath of the world oil price collapse and with China reaching an agreement with OPEC about its export quotas.

This policy of exporting oil for balance of payments purposes was a controversial one. Energy specialists have since argued that the economic damage from domestic restriction far outweighed the benefits

[15] M.Ledic, 'China: Energy Key to Economic Growth', *Petroleum Economist*, No.11, 1987, pp.405-9.

from the foreign exchange earned.[16] It is notable that during the period 1987 to 1989 China's net exports of energy fell from US$4.0 billion to US$2.6 billion, mainly due to a rise in the value of imports of oil and oil products, while the corresponding exports were reduced by 10%.

In recent years, China has admitted to annual energy shortages (estimates vary) in the region of 30 million tonnes of coal, 10 million tonnes of petroleum and 60-70 billion kWh of electricity. Energy shortages contribute towards China's claimed 30% under-utilization of its manufacturing capacity.[17] Despite these shortages, however, economic growth in recent years has been very rapid. In the period 1981-89, total industrial output grew in real terms by 14% per annum.

China has two major problems in the energy field which affect the balance between production and consumption. One is the serious regional imbalance. For example, two-thirds of China's coal production is in the North, North-East and East regions. There is a major need to transport coal from these production sources to the areas of high consumption, notably to the deficit areas of the south, and the southern coastal provinces.[18]

The other problem is the differing patterns and major structural divisions between urban and rural areas, as regards energy production and consumption. The 80% of the population located in rural areas consumes less than 40% of the total energy produced. Their consumption is largely from local sources, and less than 10% of their energy consumption is met by allocation from nationally-controlled sources. Of the total rural energy consumption in 1987, biomass accounted for just under 60%, and consumption of coal, electricity and oil products for just over 40%. About one-third of the total is used for production purposes in rural and township enterprises, and two-thirds in households (see Figure 9.2).[19]

[16] *The Sectoral Energy Demand Analysis in China - Utilization of Medee-s Model*, Energy Research Institute, State Planning Commission, Beijing, 1989.

[17] Renmin Ribao, Beijing, 17 June 1989, in *Summary of World Broadcasts (SWB)*, FE/W0084 A/3, 5 July 1989.

[18] See M.Ledic, 'The Energy Sector', in D.S.G.Goodman (ed.), *China's Regional Development*, Routledge, 1989, pp.94-112.

[19] For more detailed analysis of biomass in China see: *Energy in China 1989*, Ministry of Energy, Beijing, p.87; Zhu Liangdong, 'Present and Future Status of China's Energy', in *Chinese-American Symposium*, op.cit., pp.1-7; J.M.O.Scurlock & D.O.Hall, 'The Contribution of Biomass to Global Energy Use', *Biomass*, No.20, 1989, pp.1-7;

Figure 9.2 China rural energy consumption, 1987

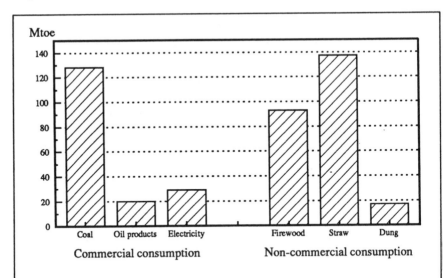

Sources: *Energy in China*, Ministry of Energy Beijing, 1989, p.87; *Survey of Energy Resources*, World Energy Council, London,1989; 'Present and Future Status of China's Energy', Proceedings of the *Chinese-American Symposium on Energy Markets and the Future of Energy Demand*, Lawrence Berkerley Laboratory, University of California, November 1988, pp.1-10; Wu Wen and Chen En-Jian, 'Our Views on the Resolution of China's Rural Energy Requirements', *Biomass*, No.3, 1983, pp.287-312.

Coal, as the main fuel, is at the same time the source of major air pollution in China. Low-quality coal is directly burned at low efficiency.[20] Only some 3% from State mines is washed. There are no figures for the proportion of non-State produced coal, which accounts for half of the total, put through washeries etc., but it is unlikely to be any greater and may indeed be very much less. Coal burning releases some 14.6 million tonnes of sulphur dioxide and 28 million tonnes of

World Energy Conference, *1989 Survey of Energy Resources*, WEC, London, 1989; Wu Wen & Chen En-Jian, 'Our Views on the Resolution of China's Rural Energy Requirements', *Biomass*, No.3, 1983, pp.287-312.
[20] The present efficiency of the direct combustion of coal in China is said to be 15-20% for household cooking; 40-50% for household heating, using cooking stove; 50-60% for industrial boilers and 28% for power generation.

dust into the air every year. Power stations account for at least 25% of the sulphur dioxide emissions and over 40% of the dust.[21] They also account for at least 25%of total carbon emissions while industrial boilers and furnaces account for around 40%. In many cities throughout China, the particle concentration often exceeds more than six times China's first class criterion (150mg/m^3) and more than ten times the World Health Organization optimal criterion of 90mg/m^3. In 1987 the amount of sulphur dioxide in urban areas was over 80% above the international standard.[22]

9.3 Indigenous energy resource base

China's proven reserves of coal total 770 billion tonnes (385Btoe)[23] according to the World Energy Council (the Ministry of Energy puts them at 860 billion tonnes). China's proven reserves of bituminous coal are over 45% of the world total - by far the largest in the world - and of lignite and sub-bituminous coals over 16% of the world total. These reserves amount to more than seven hundred years of consumption at the 1989 level (see Figure 9.3). China's reserves of lignite are surpassed only by those of the United States and the Soviet Union. State-run mines produce less than half of total coal output, and this share is planned to continue until the year 2000.[24] Almost all coal is deep-mined.

Geographically, coal reserves are spread from the North-East to the West, but are mainly concentrated in the North and North-West regions. Of the proven reserves 6% are in the East, 65% in Central China (Shanxi province) and 29% in the West. This uneven distribution results in a coal transportation pattern which puts a great strain on its transportation system, and is bound to cause additional problems with the increase in coal production envisaged in the next century.

The size of oil and natural gas reserves is much less certain. Proven oil and gas reserves are estimated at present to be much smaller than coal reserves. Looking first at natural gas: according to WEC, China has 870BCM of proved recoverable reserves of natural gas, accounting for

[21] Zhong Janmin, 'China's Energy Development and Environment Protection', Energy Research Institute, Beijing, 1989, (mimeo).
[22] ibid., p.3.
[23] This figure of 385Btoe uses a coefficient approximate to the relatively poor quality of Chinese coal.
[24] 'Plugging the Energy Gap', *China-Britain Trade Review*, Issue 293, February 1989, pp.1-5.

Figure 9.3 China fuel reserves/consumption ratios 1987

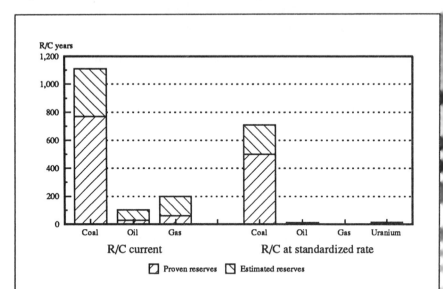

R/C current = ratio of resources/reserves to current consumption of fuel (years)
R/C at standardized rate = ratio of resources/reserves to consumption at rate of
1kW/capita = 0.7toe/yr/capita

Sources: *Energy in China*, Ministry of Energy, Beijing, 1989; World Energy
Conference, *1989 Survey of Energy Resources*, WEC, London, 1989; *BP
Statistical Review of World Energy*, BP, London, 1989; *World Resources
1988-89*, World Resources Institute, Washington DC, 1988; *The Petroleum
Resources in China*, Energy Information Administration, US Deaprtment of
Energy, Washington DC, 1987; J.P.Dorian and A.L.Clark, 'China's Energy
Resources', *Energy Policy*, February 1987, pp.73-90.

60 years of consumption at the 1989 level. These non-associated gas
reserves are nearly all concentrated in Sichuan province, while 'wet' gas
is associated with the oilfields of Daqing, Shengli, Liaohe, Dagang,
Huabei, Zhongyuan and Karamay.

There appears to be great potential for additional discoveries of oil,
because proven reserves are only 13% of estimated potential resources
and promising geological areas extend for some 5 million km^2. Estimates
of its oil reserves vary a great deal. WEC puts proven and estimated

recoverable reserves at 2.45 billion tonnes, or 2.1% of world reserves. At the 1989 level of consumption, this yields a reserve-consumption ratio of just under 26 years (see Figure 9.3). Proven oil reserves are mostly concentrated in North and North-East China. These are the 'traditional' oil-producing regions, and promising basins elsewhere in China have been largely ignored until recently. The discovery and delineation of additional reserves are now vital, as the traditional fields have all reached the mature stage. Production from them could be expected to decline in the next century, unless there are major imports of sophisticated technology for enhanced recovery.[25]

The China National Offshore Oil Corporation (CNOOC) was founded in 1982 to exploit China's offshore oil resources. Since then China has had three rounds of international tender invitations. Prospecting and exploration have continued steadily, with foreign cooperation a key element. However, exploration has not come up to expectations, and in 1988 offshore oil production represented only some 0.5% of total oil output.[26]

The level of exploration for natural gas is still very low, although after long years of official neglect the need to exploit more energy resources has driven the government to end the stagnation of the natural gas industry. Geologists argue, however, that its gas deposits are more difficult to find than oil deposits, because continental movements have left gas deposits fragmented and buried deep underground.

An increase in proved natural gas (and oil) reserves depends on the stepping-up of exploration. There are large areas of sedimentary basin, continental shelf in coastal areas, and the western districts (eg. Xinjiang and the Tarim basin), that are likely to have abundant oil and gas reserves. The area that has been explored up till now accounts for only a small part of these regions. The future of natural gas is hopeful, if enough investment and expertise are brought into the industry. Natural gas resources associated with coal could also be abundant. The more optimistic experts estimate that, at an average depth of 3,000m, there are dozens of TCM of natural gas to be exploited.

[25] B. Vernor, 'China's Sinking Surplus: Seeking New Sources to Meet the Burgeoning Demand for Petroleum', *China Business Review*, Vol.17, No.2, March-April 1990, pp.6-8,10-12.
[26] Han Baochen, 'Developments in China's Offshore Oil Industry', *Beijing Review*, 10 July 1989, pp.27-29.

China's uranium resources are concentrated in the Shanxi and Xinjiang provinces, and in some provinces in the south - Yunnan, Guangxi, Guangdong and Hunan. Economically exploitable reserves of uranium are estimated to be a minimum of 100,000tU, with total known reserves in excess of 800,000tU. The latter is approximately equivalent to Australia's total level of known reserves, which are the largest in the Western world. However, exact comparisons are difficult to make, because of a lack of information regarding China's system of classifying reserves. If speculative resources are added to total known reserves, the estimates reach 3MtU.[27] According to Chinese sources, China's uranium resources can meet its needs for short-term nuclear energy development, but not its long-term development plans.[28]

China's hydroelectric power potential is estimated to be the largest in the world with an estimated theoretical capacity of 676GW, of which up to 400GW can be economically exploited. By the end of 1989 less than 10% (with a capacity of 34.5GW) had been developed. The problem, as with reserves of coal and other fuels, is that the regions where the potential energy exists are far from those where there is the greatest demand. In addition, there is a shortage of investment funds for major hydroelectric power schemes.

The Chinese government has vacillated over the Three Gorges project on the Yangtze River, which was planned to have a total installed capacity of 17.7GW, with an annual power output of 84 billion kWh, equivalent to 40 million tonnes of coal. This controversial project would have caused the relocation of more than 1.4 million people and submerged 44,000 hectares of cultivable land, while the cost has been put at around US$20 billion, and 20 years to complete construction.[29] Early in 1990, Vice Premier Yao Yilin announced that the project would not go ahead in the next Five Year Plan (1991-95). In May 1990, a revised version of a 1959 plan for development of the Yangtze river, over a 40 year period, was submitted. The plan suggests that power stations with an annual power output of 117 billion kWh will be built. The river course will be

[27] J.P.Dorian and A.L.Clark, 'China's Energy Resources', *Energy Policy*, February 1987, pp.73-90; A.D.Owen & P.N.Neal, 'China's Potential as an Energy Exporter', *Energy Policy*, No.5, 1989, pp.485-500.
[28] Xinhua, 21 May 1990, in *SWB*, FE/W0130 A/6, 30 May 1990.
[29] Yao Jianguo, 'Experts Okay Three Gorges Project', Beijing Review, 12 December 1988, pp.5-6.

dredged to improve transportation, and the proportion of irrigated farmland in the area affected by the project will be increased to 85% by the year 2030.[30]

Renewable energy resources, especially biomass, have been an important part of life in China for generations. The area covered with forests accounts for nearly 13% of China's territory, or 128m hectares, with an estimated productive area of 119m hectares (see Table 9.3). But centuries of exploitation in the same areas has led to serious environmental degradation, such as deforestation and soil erosion. Many Chinese forests are not 'fully stocked' in comparison with forests in Scandinavia, for example. The process of industrialization has increased pressure on the forests, because of the demand for wood for construction and other purposes. In addition, the growing rural population has led to a demand for biomass which has contributed to relatively uncontrolled deforestation. This is particularly serious in China, which has a comparatively small forest area by international standards.[31] Other widely used biomass resources are straw and animal manure (see Table 9.3 and Figure 9.2).

It has been argued that biomass resources could be used more efficiently. Traditional stoves have a fuel efficiency of only 10-15% when biomass is used. The efficiency could be doubled by expanded use of more efficient stoves that the government is trying to promote. Even better results would be obtained by using biomass as a raw material in digesters to produce biogas. However, it is estimated that there are already more than 5 million biogas digesters being used by rural residents. Similarly, much of the manure which is applied directly as fertilizer could be put into biogas production, producing methane and leaving the effluent as a high-quality fertilizer. The Chinese authorities already actively encourage the production of biogas, but more could be done to educate rural communities as to its advantages.

Geothermal energy is spread throughout the country, and used in agriculture and aquaculture, to generate electricity, heat greenhouses,

[30] Xinhua, 29 May 1990, in *SWB*, FE/W0131 A/4, 6 June 1990.
[31] Over the years there have in fact been massive reforestation programmes, although shortages of funds have sometimes meant that only part of these programmes have been carried out. In addition, necessary conservation measures to maintain the new forests have not always been undertaken.

Table 9.3 China estimated renewable energy resources

Source	Gross capability	Exploitable capability	Production 1987	Comments
Hydro	6,000 TWh/yr	> 1MW 1,923TWh/yr < 1MW 245TWh/yr	100TWh	30,200MW present capacity Planned: 68,700MW
Wood	1.28m km^2 forest area	1.19m km^2 productive fire	230 Mtonnes firewood	
Other biomass straw dung	unknown unknown	unknown unknown	391.5Mtonnes 67.0Mtonnes	
Geothermal	unknown	unknown	395MW 216,000toe 'energy saving'	18MW present capacity 14MW under construction
Wind	unknown	160GW	unknown	8MW present capacity
Solar	unknown	unknown	unknown	
Tidal & oceanic	unknown	unknown	unknown	5MW present capacity

Source:World Energy Council, *1989 Survey of Energy Resources*, WEC, London, 1989; *Energy in China*, Ministry of Energy, Beijing, 1989.

and to dry crops etc. The direct use of geothermal energy is estimated to be equivalent to 395MW per annum.

China has more tidal schemes than the rest of the world put together, although they are comparatively small and present capacity is put at 5MW only.

In recent years, much progress has been made in utilizing solar energy. The scope of solar energy application has expanded to include heating water systems, solar energy stoves, solar desiccators and solar cells. Estimates suggest that there are in use about 130,000 solar energy stoves of different kinds, 400,000m^2 of heating water apparatus, and 200 solar houses, mostly in North and North-West China.[32] There are about 60 specialized factories over the country which produce solar energy water heating apparatus. One type of solar energy stove is mass produced and has been exported to the USA, Japan and elsewhere. Solar cells for space use have reached an advanced level, while those for ground use have been extensively applied for example to railway signals and automatic meteorological stations.

China boasts an abundance of wind energy with an average density of 100W/m^2. It has been estimated that 160 million kW of wind energy is exploitable. There are more than 30 factories annually producing over 30,000 wind-driven generators with capacities ranging from 50W to 200kW. The China Wind Energy Development Centre has developed a number of experimental aerogenerators and is working with Danish and British assistance to develop wind-diesel technology and the use of wind-farms to top up transmission losses on high voltage lines in remote areas.

Of these renewable sources, the use of solar energy appears to have the greatest potential after biomass. The Chinese government has secured US, Japanese and Australian expertise and finance, in order to foster research and investment in the exploitation of solar energy. There is no doubt that biomass will continue to be the dominant fuel in rural areas for the foreseeable future. But other renewables could make a substantial

---

[32] For solar, wind and other renewable sources see, Hu Chengchun, 'Development of new and renewable sources of energy in China', Energy Division, The State Science and Technology Commission, Beijing, 1990, (mimeo); 'A brief overview of China's energy', presented at *China Energy '89*, International Energy and Energy Conservation Equipment and Technology Exhibition, October 1989, Shanghai, (mimeo); David Nianguo Li, 'China's Renewable Energies', *The China Business Review*, July/August 1985, pp.32-35.

supplementary contribution to China's energy needs, especially in these areas. It seems likely moreover that some of them could be developed much more actively without the need for heavy investment.

9.4 Projections and options to the year 2000

China's long-term plans formulated in conjunction with the World Bank at the beginning of the 1980s were to quadruple the gross value of industrial and agricultural output (GVIAO) between 1980 and the year 2000, at the same time, seeking to double energy supplies, and energy efficiency.[33] Even with these forecasts, already proved optimistic, it has been estimated that by the year 2000 China would still encounter energy shortages in the region of some 200Mtoe per annum.[34]

The World Bank projected energy demand from 1980 to the year 2000, based on nine different combinations of three scenarios of economic growth, and three levels of energy demand, depending on various degrees of energy saving.[35] The three scenarios were Quadruple (6.6% per annum GDP growth), based on industrial growth, Moderate (5.4%), and Balance (6.65%), based on service industry growth. The analysis suggested that under the Quadruple plan an energy supply shortage may be inevitable. In order to balance energy supply and demand, economic growth targets would have to be lowered and measures for energy saving reinforced. In addition, exports of fuel oil would probably need to be restricted, in view of the domestic demand-supply balance.

2000A: Business-as-usual

The Ministry of Energy development targets for energy production in the year 2000 have been used as a basis for the 'business-as-usual' scenario.[36]

The assumptions under this scenario are that, compared with 1988, primary energy demand increases at an annual rate of 3.9%, coal

---

[33] The World Bank, *China, Long Term Issues*, op.cit.

[34] Ministry of Energy, op.cit. p.11.

[35] The World Bank, op.cit.

[36] See 'Plugging the Energy Gap', op.cit.; also the Address by Vice-Minister Lu Youmei, Ministry of Energy Resources, at UNDP seminar held on 15 December 1988, Beijing. They are as follows; the target for the year 2000 is 1.2-1.4bn tonnes of coal, 0.16-0.20bn tonnes of oil, 20-30BCM of gas, 50-60GW of hydroelectric power 4.5-6.0GW of nuclear power, with a total installed electricity capacity of 200-240GW and yearly power output of 1-1.2TWh.

Figure 9.4 Scenarios for China energy consumption and CO₂ emissions 1988-2030

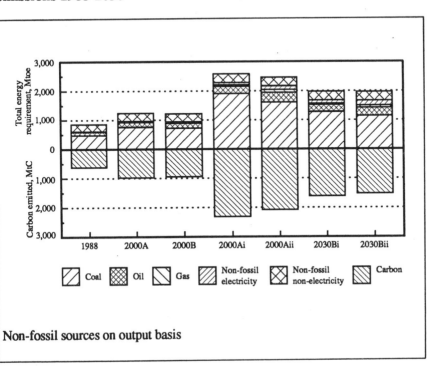

Non-fossil sources on output basis

production rises by nearly 60%, and oil by 45%. A rise of some 70% is foreseen for gas, and 80% for hydroelectricity (see Figure 9.4).

The planning authorities at present intend to continue to invest significant amounts in hydroelectricity. According to the Ministry of Energy, it will account for 35% of total new installed generating capacity but 45% of power investment throughout the period of the Eighth Five Year Plan (1991-95).

One-third of coal consumption, and just over a quarter of oil consumption, goes to thermal electricity generation. Thermal power in 1988 represented 80%, and in the year 2000 is put at 75-80%, of total power generated. Thermal power output is assumed to be more than double that of 1988 (see Figure 9.5). Efficiency in producing thermal electricity is expected to rise to 30%, from 28.5% in 1988 to the level it had been in the early 1980s.

Figure 9.5 Scenarios for China power generation 1988-2030

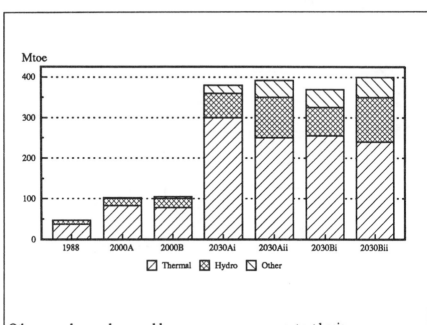

Other = nuclear and renewable energy resources, on output basis
(1kWh = 0.08kgoe)

There is a nuclear electricity output of 3Mtoe projected, to be produced by the Daya Bay nuclear power plant in Guangdong Province, which will have a generating capacity of 1,800MW, and by the Qinshan I nuclear power plant (now under construction) near Shanghai, which will have a generating capacity of 300MW. A further stage, Qinshan II, is to have 600MW, or possibly 2 x 600MW capacity.

Coal exports are projected to be 2% of production, but the significant energy exports are assumed to be those of oil, with some 20% exported in the year 2000. This is due to a continuation of the policy of replacing oil with coal in power generation, leaving oil available for exports, and for transport use.

Biomass consumption is projected to rise approximately in line with population, since supplies of electricity to the rural areas, from the existing seven regional grids, are not expected to increase their present share. Local supplies of electricity, from small hydroelectric plants, are expected to continue to be small. It is assumed that the policy of 'rural self-sufficiency' in energy will continue.

Carbon emissions under this scenario are some two-thirds above the comparable level (ie. excluding emissions from biomass) in 1988.[37]

Increases in energy efficiency are planned, even though energy prices may fail to give the appropriate signals in this direction. The projections from the Ministry of Energy imply that GDP more than trebles during the period, while energy consumption rises by two-thirds and energy intensity halves during the period: a formidable target for any country to achieve.

2000B: Emissions abatement

This scenario assumes that the improvement in carbon emissions is brought about partly by greater efficiency in the use of energy, and partly by some switching to non-carbon-emitting sources of power generation. Part of the improvement is brought about by a change in export strategy, away from oil towards coal. Coal production is stepped up accordingly. The proportion of oil used in thermal electricity production is increased, thus reducing carbon emissions (see Figure 9.4). Greater emphasis is given to developing renewable resources such as solar and wind power, but the total is still very small. Efficiency in producing thermal electricity is put at 32%.

The result of these changes is that total carbon emissions grow to 934MtC, an average annual increase of 3.5% from 1988. Investment requirements would necessarily seem to be largely concentrated in increasing coal production to a high level, partially to replace oil in exports, as well as investment in hydroelectricity and other renewable sources of energy. Increases in coal production and exports to the high levels postulated do not take into account the disruption of the world coal market that these exports might cause.

An important implication of this level of coal production by the year 2000 is that even greater pressure will be put on China's transportation resources, and especially on its railway system, which is already congested on account of large coal shipments. This is one of the reasons why the Chinese are at least considering very large minehead power plant

[37] In all the scenarios it is assumed that biomass consumption will give relatively very little, or no net carbon emissions. This is because crops burned each year are expected to be replanted to an equivalent extent. The same applies to firewood, thus making net emissions negligible.

and high voltage power transmission lines. This would do nothing for the greenhouse gases emissions, except in as much as it could reduce growth of demand on the railway system, which uses coal as a source of power. Such plant and transmission lines are likely to involve foreign technology and should therefore be more efficient than China's current average, or even China's current best, technology.

It is assumed that the economic structure of China will have begun to move in the direction of more developed countries. The share of GDP represented by agriculture is likely to fall, while those of transportation and other services are likely to rise. The total share of industry may fall somewhat below the present 50%, and the share of light industry will probably rise at the expense of heavy industry. Some economic incentives are expected to be introduced into the system, thus encouraging much-needed improvements in end-use energy efficiency. Also, increasing foreign participation, including that of international organizations, may be involved in coal exploration, and in introducing cost-effective energy conservation investment.

9.5 Projections and options to the year 2030

All projections for China assume that the population will go on increasing, partly on account of the age structure, although possibly at a relatively slower rate. The annual rate of increase between the years 1985 and 2000 is expected to be over 1%, but between 2000 and 2030 is expected to be below 0.5%. Similarly, all projections expect that the rapid GDP growth rates of the early 1980s will not be achieved in future years.

One study forecasts an increase in GDP per capita of some 6.7% per annum between 1985 and 2000, but of 4.1% per annum between 2000 and 2030.[38] The same study foresees energy consumption per capita continuing to rise, but again at a declining rate. Total energy demand rises by 4% per annum between 1985 and 2000, but by 2.5% per annum between 2000 and 2030. Energy intensity is expected to fall by much the same proportion in the thirty years following the year 2000 as in the fifteen years preceding it. The general framework of this study has been used as a guideline in building the following scenarios.

By the year 2030 total power generated is expected to be around eight-and-a-half times the 1988 level, when thermal power from fossil

[38] *Energy Demand Forecasting in China for the Year 2030*, INET & ITEESA, Beijing, 1989.

fuel was 80% of the total (see Figure 9.5). Thermal power from fossil fuel in 2030 accounts for between 60% and 80% of the total, depending on the assumptions made. Efficiency in producing thermal electricity is put at 35% at least. The relative fall in the importance of thermal power from fossil fuel, in three of the four cases, results partly from a large increase in hydroelectricity, and partly from a very large increase in other sources of power, mainly between the years 2000 and 2030. Nuclear energy is the largest source of this growth. Various provinces have announced plans to construct nuclear power plants. Among these are Lianong, Guangdong, Jiangsu, Fujian, Jiangsi and Heilongjiang (a possible joint-venture with Soviet Union). In the medium term, a rapid development of nuclear power will be restricted by a shortage of investment funds, by the need to explore for domestic sources of uranium, by technical problems and the need to develop infrastructure. In the longer term these problems will diminish, but public opposition,which is currently non-existent, may well become an obstacle.

Coal is expected to remain the dominant fuel well into the next century. There is likely to be much development in the production of gas, nuclear energy, hydroelectricity, and other renewables, but the considerable increase in energy demand expected will need large supplies of coal, of which ample reserves are available, as has been seen. It is difficult to envisage, even in the long term, under any scenario, any significant reduction in the importance of coal in the Chinese economy.

2030Ai: Business-as-usual

An increase in primary energy demand of 2.9% per annum, from the year 2000, rising to 2,259Mtoe is envisaged. This is a much lower growth rate than the 7.5% experienced by China over the decades 1960-1990. Coal remains predominant in demand with 83% of the total (excluding biomass), but the largest relative increases will be in hydroelectricity, nuclear power and renewable energy. Exports of coal of 6% of production, and 18% of oil production, are projected. Since greater cooperation between China and the Soviet Union is envisaged, gas production is augmented by imports from the Soviet Union, particularly into the North-East. Biomass use is expected to grow much more slowly compared with the period before the year 2000, partly because it is assumed that saturation is approaching as regards soil erosion and deforestation, and partly because a much larger proportion of the population is assumed to be living in the urban areas.

GDP per capita is estimated to reach US$3,500 (in 1980US$). The increased disposable income, combined with living in urban areas, would be expected to change the pattern of consumption, with higher demand for consumer goods and higher expectations of the transportation system, among other things. But taking into account the political dimension of Chinese society, and the fluctuations that can occur in economic policy, it will not necessarily be the case that the pattern of Chinese consumption will be dramatically changed, even in such a long period. It is therefore envisaged that the economy, and with it the energy sector, would still contain significant rigidities for another 30 years.

Carbon emissions rise in line with demand from 974MtC in 2000A to to some 2,300MtC, at an average annual rate of 2.9% from the year 2000, mainly because of the high proportion of coal used (see Figure 9.4).

2030Aii: Emissions abatement through fuel switching

Under this scenario production of primary energy would be achieved by large increases in gas and hydroelectricity production. Total consumption, as well as electricity production, are however similar to the previous scenario, on account of greatly reduced consumption of coal.

China is assumed to be a small net importer of oil, thus enabling it both to use oil for power generation and for much-needed transport and other purposes. This would be possible partly because the regions would become more independent of the centre, and would be allowed to pursue, to an extent, their own economic and energy policies. The oil-rich regions would not cease to export oil, but the oil-poor regions, such as the southern coastal regions, would now be free to import oil from other countries.

In the 30 years before 2030 there would have been considerable investment in gas exploration, resulting in substantial gas discoveries, not very far away from centres of demand. Imports of gas from the Soviet Union are also envisaged. Considerable investment would have been made in hydroelectric installations, and in the power transmission lines to distribute their output. Investment in nuclear power plants would have been heavy, including joint ventures with Hong Kong and the Soviet Union. One-third of the power generated would be exported to them.

Foreign investors would be called into China, in order to provide not just capital, but the technology and expertise needed to achieve these substantial investments. This assumes that the political climate in China is stabilized in a direction in which foreign investors are confident to make large, long-term commitments.

Carbon emissions from fossil fuels would be at a level of some 2,100MtC, some 10% below the previous scenario (see Figure 9.4). This comparatively small fall in carbon emissions illustrates that, in China's case at least, heavy investment in fuel switching may be needed to bring with it significant falls in carbon emissions.

2030Bi: Emissions abatement through energy efficiency

This scenario assumes coal will still dominate primary energy consumption with over 75% of the total (see Figure 9.4). Some 4% of output will be exported. The growth of oil production will slow down somewhat, but the policy of exporting oil will be maintained, at a level of some 10% of production. There will be no major gas discoveries, but there will be a major increase in nuclear capacity, to help offset the reduced use of coal. Renewable sources of energy will make a further advance, partly with less expensive technologies being developed, and partly with regions having to be more responsible for running their economies in a more efficient and competitive environment. Efficiency in producing thermal electricity is assumed to be 40%.

Considerable reductions in the use of coal, and some reduction in oil and gas are envisaged. This implies heavy investment in energy-saving technology, together with other economy measures, especially as regards coal. Another assumption is much greater reliance on market pricing, thus encouraging fuel efficiency. Realistic exchange rates would help rationalize energy prices and improve fuel allocation between domestic and export use.

The sectoral composition of production is assumed to change away from heavy industry, with its great reliance on coal, towards light industry, transport and services. In addition it would require the implementation of measures of energy conservation, mainly through installing modern equipment with much higher efficiency, in order that energy intensive manufacturing industry in China in 2030 should be able to reach the levels in the best advanced countries in the late 1980s. Rail transport would also turn away from coal to some extent, relying more on diesel and electric locomotives, although an expansion of the rail network would create a need for more energy. The growth of road transport, both trucks and cars, would also generate more energy demand, even with considerable improvements in fuel efficiency. Transport's share of energy consumption is likely to increase to well over 10%.

As far as the residential sector is concerned, it is estimated that some 45% of the population will be living in urban areas, compared with 20% today. They will have large demands for energy, for refrigerators, heating and other appliances. It is assumed that government policy will place great emphasis on energy-efficient appliances.

Total carbon emissions would be some 1,600MtC, 30% below the business-as-usual case.

2030Bii: Emissions abatement through efficiency and fuel switching
This scenario postulates similar assumptions to the fuel-switching model above in that major investments in exploration for natural gas would take place, so that there would be a switch from coal into natural gas, as well a switch to oil. Hydroelectric power would have a higher than ever share in primary energy demand with some 6% of the total, due to major progress on the Yangtze river schemes (see Figures 9.4 and 9.5).

Primary energy demand is increased by more than two-and-a-half times in relation to the year 1988, to reach 1,655Mtoe. Coal exports are put at 12% of production, while coal demand within China represents 64% of primary energy demand. Even though a considerable increase in renewable energy, other than biomass, is assumed, even under this scenario they are not expected to play a substantial role in the Chinese energy balance, amounting to only 1% of total primary energy supply. Energy intensity is assumed to have fallen to only 25% of the 1988 level.

Carbon emissions, based on very considerable coal savings, are 1,520MtC. They have still, however, grown at an average annual rate of 2.1% since 1988.

9.6 Policy options and constraints

The above scenarios show substantial increases in carbon emissions above the present level - to between 2.3 and 3.5 times. Yet, to achieve the GDP growth envisaged in these scenarios, while keeping emissions at the levels shown would require great determination and consistency by government. The business-as-usual scenarios already envisage large energy efficiency improvements, and although further improvements might ease some aspects of Chinese development, the fuel switching measures would add further to the already heavy investment requirements of expansion based on coal, with rapid implementation of technical advances.

It has been estimated that the percentage of carbon emissions attributable in China, compared to that of the world as a whole, has increased from 1.4% in 1950 to 10% in 1988. Under the scenarios this ratio is likely to increase greatly, especially if other major countries reduce their carbon emissions.[39]

The fundamental problem is that China's stage of economic development is still so low that the pressures to increase living standards are very strong. These exist no matter whether China reverts to greater central planning, or eventually introduces considerable elements of market freedom. Along with the pressure for higher living standards, there is a consequent need for greater use of energy. Severe supply constraints of coal, oil and electric power have all manifested themselves for many years. These constraints need to be overcome, while at the same time more energy needs to be made available for growth purposes and perhaps for export also. Given the state of China's energy reserves, it seems inevitable that the growth of coal production should be the main source of increased energy supplies.

As has been seen, China is an inefficient user of energy. This has partly been due to a policy of keeping energy prices low, so that there has been no economic disincentive to the use of energy. And since the system of State allocation of energy resources is still in place, with its emphasis on quantitative targets, there is, especially combined with subsidized prices, no incentive for energy conservation. Considerable progress was made as a result of government action during the 1980s. A policy of switching emphasis from energy-intensive heavy industry to light industry was adopted, partly to save energy and partly to increase the output of consumer goods. Energy conservation was encouraged, and a policy was adopted of moving industry nearer to the sources of primary energy. Nevertheless, the lack of a price mechanism reflecting true costs has hindered further progress. Since the end of 1989, emphasis has again been placed on the development of heavy industry, which is energy-intensive. On the other hand, rural industry (which employs 100

[39] Similar trends are envisaged in Wu Zongxin and Wei Zhihong, 'Energy Consumption and CO_2 Emission in China', INET, Beijing, 1989, (mimeo), p.17.

million people and produces nearly one-quarter of GDP) has been discouraged, among other things, for being too entrepreneurial. This sector has contributed largely to GDP growth but is wasteful in the use of energy, so that fuel savings may result from this decision. One consequence of the growth of rural industries had been demands for a larger share of nationally supplied electricity, with all the attendant problems of investment in generating plants and in power transmission lines. Government policy is to encourage rural demand to be satisfied by locally-produced electricity from mini hydroelectric power plants and small coal mines, but these are likely to continue to have low energy-efficiency.

The result of all these factors, along with the development of the Chinese economy, especially since 1979, has been a massive and growing pollution problem, which has been by no means confined to the emission of greenhouse gases. The Chinese government has officially taken action to reduce pollution since the 1970s. Limits have in theory been placed on polluting discharges, and effluent standards in relation to water pollution were introduced as long ago as 1979. Such improvements in these directions that have taken place, however, have been more than offset by increases in the sheer scale of energy use. It has been estimated that at least 640 billion yuan (US$173 billion) is needed to solve China's environmental problems by the year 2000.[40] This means that 2.4% of GDP annually needs to be spent on reducing pollution in China as compared to the current percentage of only 0.65% of GDP. Government agencies regard the figure of 2.4% as being too high, and suggest that a more realistic amount needed annually, to control further deterioration of the environment, is 1.0% of GDP.[41] These orders of magnitude can usefully be compared with those for investment in energy generally in China: investment in the state-owned coal, gas, oil and power sectors was about 1.7% of GDP in 1988. But in that year private investment in energy was put at 2.7% of GDP, making 4.4% in all; when estimated energy-related investments in coal transport and refineries are added, this increases the 4.4% to over 5% of GDP.

Massive investment resources are a pre-condition of GDP growth on the scale envisaged, but properly directed investment should also be in an energy-saving form. Investment in energy-efficiency, therefore, may

---

[40] 'Environmental protection urged', *China Daily*, 8 August 1989.
[41] *China Daily*, op.cit.

sometimes require a different sort of investment rather than more investment. For such developments to occur, however, large changes are also needed in the popular attitude to the wasteful use of energy, and in governmental attitudes. Given the scale of the problem, it is not surprising that the Chinese authorities have argued that China cannot be expected to make a significant contribution to the carbon emissions problem unless it receives very large international aid for this purpose. In any event, stabilization of emissions at present levels is considered impossible, since this is seen as preventing the development of the economy.[42] Even large international aid for energy conservation purposes is unlikely to have the required effect in the absence of a drastic reform of energy pricing, combined with the adoption of profit-maximizing objectives for enterprises. Heavier fines for polluting also need to be introduced. In the absence of such measures, there will be little incentive for enterprises and individuals to conserve energy, by seeking for ways of reducing fuel usage, and by using new equipment efficiently. The energy savings demonstrated in the scenarios given above will certainly not be achieved without such reforms.

There is likely to be international pressure on China to adopt stringent measures of this sort, especially as China's pollution has international repercussions - and not only where greenhouse gases are concerned. But at present the reduction of pollution and emission of greenhouse gases are not at the top of the Chinese government agenda. Even if changes in attitudes occur, there is the inescapable fact that China is bound to rely mainly on coal as a fuel for the foreseeable future. Renewable sources of energy can only be partial substitutes for coal. And in the rural areas, biomass will dominate energy consumption for the foreseeable future. The scope for fuel switching in China is necessarily small, due to limited proven reserves of other energy sources.

These considerations suggest that the emphasis in China must be on methods of using coal much more efficiently. The removal of subsidies and the use of market prices might well make the greatest contribution. In addition, taxes on the use of coal may be desirable. Tight standards for air pollution will also be needed. New technology will have to be implemented to enable the standards to be met. Even if such technology is available, however, this will not be easy to apply, given the multitude of coal mines in China, many of them privately operated, and small.

---

[42] 'Global Warming Action Plan in Autumn', *Financial Times*, 9 June 1990, p.3.

Inducements must also be implemented to reduce carbon emissions from biomass in rural areas by increasing its efficiency in use. Here technological means are perhaps the most promising. It may however prove to be a difficult task to get new technology accepted, given the very large number of people and the extensive areas of land involved. Other measures include subsidies for the adoption of efficient equipment, information campaigns, the encouragement of appropriate research and development, and the adoption of product standards. All these would reflect the high priority that needs to be given to limiting carbon emissions. Finally, a strengthening of present policies of afforestation would be an important method of improving the carbon balance in China. It may indeed prove to be the principal contribution that China can make towards reducing the global effects of her emission of greenhouse gases.[43]

9.7 International aspects

The warming of the atmosphere brought about by the greenhouse effect would be bound to impact upon so vast a country as China in many ways. The heavy flooding of its major river basins by summer rains could be increased, and crop irrigation would be adversely affected by the admixture of salt water that would occur with sea level rise in some coastal areas. China has a very long coast, with much industry based in coastal regions, which would certainly be affected if the sea level were to rise.

If global warming occurs large areas of the interior would be adversely affected by a 'drying-out': rainfall is barely enough now in the north to support crops and may become inadequate. However, since harsh winters generally restrict crop growing to the summer, it could be that the rainfall pattern in these areas may be affected by global warming in such a way as to benefit agriculture. In addition, parts of China are dry in winter, and the length of the winter determines whether or not the land can produce more than one crop a year. Shorter winters, on account of global warming, might therefore help to increase crop production in many areas.

Emissions abatement policies would have some global implications. Fuel switching away from coal might have effects on world trade in

[43] See T.A.Siddiqi, 'Implications of Climate Change for Energy Policies in Asia', prepared for 'Responding to the Threat of Global Warming: Options for the Pacific and Asia', East-West Center, Honolulu, Hawaii, 1989, (mimeo), p.27.

energy, if this policy were to result in a decline in oil exports and a need for greater coal exports. It might be the case, however, especially by the year 2030, that emissions policy throughout the world will have caused a retreat from coal that would greatly lessen potential demand for exports of Chinese coal.

Official Chinese attitudes towards environmental concerns, as reflected in their 1979 and 1984 legislation, appears to be positive, but they have been cautious in committing themselves on these issues when participating in international conferences. During 1990, however, the attitude of Chinese officials became more cooperative. One of the reasons for this appears to be that environmental awareness on the part of the Chinese government has been increased as a result of the activities of China's scientific community. The official view however is still sceptical about the scientific evidence for global warming. Nevertheless, at the IPCC in Geneva in late 1990, China was in favour of an international convention on global warming, but was not prepared to commit itself to an agreed level of CO_2 emissions by a particular date. It was stressed that any commitments would have to be accompanied by a transfer of relevant technologies on favourable terms.

In practice, even given environmental concerns in the government, efforts are being directed more towards economic growth than towards energy efficiency and the absence of environmental pollution. The authorities are aware of the substantial proportion of GDP required to be spent on increased energy production, and on improvements in infrastructure. At the same time, they know that their own carbon emissions, however high in relation to energy use, are as yet small, on a per capita basis, in comparison with those of the developed world. In these circumstances, the Chinese attitude towards the immense extra capital that would be needed, both to introduce modern technology in order to increase energy efficiency, and to further develop non-fossil sources of energy is that China is unable to bear the burden alone. Already there has been some international help. An important source of investment funds leading to reduced carbon emissions from the energy sector has been Hong Kong, which is to become part of China in 1997. The Daya Bay nuclear power station is a joint venture between the Hong Kong Nuclear Investment Company (a wholly owned subsidiary of China Light and Power - CLP) and the Guangdong Nuclear Investment

Company. Some 70% of the electricity generated is to be supplied to Hong Kong.

There are other forms of energy cooperation between China and Hong Kong. CLP's system was interconnected in 1979 with that of the Guangdong General Power Co. Under this agreement, coal is shipped from China to CLP in exchange for electricity, with the balance being paid in cash. In July 1985, CLP signed an agreement to supply electricity to the Shekou Industrial Zone. In addition, a number of joint venture energy negotiations are continuing between CLP and Chinese-owned companies. Agreements of this sort may involve the continued use of coal to produce electricity, but they do at least transfer power generation to Hong Kong, which is at present more energy efficient. CLP has also supplied consultancy and project management services to China. It is clear that these and other energy links between Hong Kong and China will continue to expand. Hong Kong finance in particular is likely to play a role of some importance in energy development in China, and this development is likely to be more energy-efficient.

Hong Kong alone can only make a limited contribution. The general view in China, in common with other countries with low per capita income, is that the developed countries can spare the necessary resources much more readily than they can, especially as they would share the benefit from a reduction in carbon emissions.

9.8 Conclusions

Environmental consciousness is still in its infancy in China, and there appears to be little popular support as yet, in so far as this can be judged, for 'green' policies. There seems to have been no link so far between political discontent and environmental concerns, although there have been some reported cases of peasants protesting against severe local cases of pollution. While the government is increasingly aware of pollution problems, it is doubtful whether, given the perceived need to raise China's low living standards, high priority will be given to pollution issues in the foreseeable future. In this context, it is worth considering the relationship between energy, the environment, and regional devolution in China. The last of these is generally associated with 'reformism' and is thus currently under a cloud. If it gains ground again in the future, it may have good environmental effects on account of greater local sensitivity to environmental problems. It does not however follow that improvements in one region of the country will necessarily be emulated elsewhere.

The fact that China has great needs for investment resources in energy exploration and exploitation will divert attention away from environmental investment. But on the other hand, anti-pollution planning could be worked into investment projects from the start. New investment in China is likely to be of much greater energy efficiency than in the past, simply because it will be designed to be more energy-efficient and hence more economical. The need both to exploit energy resources and to reduce pollution involves a very large scale of investment. The scale is far beyond anything an international aid programme could cope with, even in a favourable international climate. The bulk of the resources needed must therefore come from China itself. But foreign expertise, as well as foreign investment funds, can make a major contribution. For this reason, apart from any other, good relations between China and the rest of the world are very much in China's own interests.

Whatever happens in the way of international assistance, however, China's energy needs, together with its great reliance on coal, make it inevitable that its greenhouse gas emissions will continue to increase, for as far ahead as can be seen.

Chapter 10 The Greenhouse Effect in India: Vast Opportunities and Constraints

Ajay Mathur
Research Fellow
Tata Energy Research Institute, New Dehli

I would like to thank all those who have read this work and offered valuable comments, especially Dr Pachauri, and other staff at the Tata Energy Research Institute for all their help. I am also grateful to all those at the Energy and Environmental Programme for their assistance and for the stimulating opportunity to work on this project.

India is a large, poor, but rapidly developing country. Population is growing at about 2%/yr, and during the 1980s the economy and total energy consumption grew at roughly twice this rate. Most people still live in rural areas with little or no access to modern amenities or to affordable commercial fuels, so that non-commercial biomass fuels (wood, agricultural, and animal-wastes) play a central role. Reforestation has halted net forest loss, but the move towards commercial fossil fuels with increasing income represents a large pool of potential demand. Primary consumption of commercial energy grew at around 6%/yr during the 1980s, but 1989 fossil CO_2 emissions were nevertheless at about one twentieth of the average in developed economies.

Production of all fossil fuels is expanding rapidly, and 90% of energy consumption was met from domestic sources by 1988. Coal is plentiful but most is of poor quality and suited mainly to power generation, and is unevenly distributed. Oil and gas resources are more limited, though predicted reserves could meet growing demand for a few decades, the key constraints on gas especially being inadequate infrastructure. Nuclear power is unlikely to contribute much because of the high costs, long gestation period and poor performance of existing reactors, and because of growing public opposition. Total hydro resources are large, but their exploitation is constrained by regional divisions, the long planning and financing requirements, the problems of land submergence and population resettlement. Solar and wind resources are large but are not expected to play a significant role because of their capital cost and the weakness of the grid system.

There are many inefficiencies in the conversion and use of energy. System development is completely supply-oriented, and focused on very short timeframes in order to overcome perpetual (and growing) shortages. This promotes existing technologies (particularly coal and coal-based thermal power) at the cost of efficiency improvements, diversification, and demand management planning. Conservation policies exist but will have limited impact unless supplemented by extensive capital for renovation, refurbishment, and modernisation of equipment.

Policies are also needed to overcome informational, institutional, and financial barriers to technology development, including support for multi-party barter or swaps, norms and standards for various new processes and applications, together with performance incentives and R&D.

Evolution from current social and sectorial pricing towards integrated energy and transport pricing, reflecting the real costs of fuel extraction including depletion charges, with graded tariff structures, and regional variations to reflect delivery costs, would encourage conservation and promote fuel substitution including dispersed renewable sources. Rural development based on vigorous afforestation, transfer of afforested land to the rural landless, and development of agro-industries, would help ensure adequate biomass supply and purchasing power for efficient technologies. Incentives for more efficient vehicles and for para transport services, and more capital for public transport infrastructure would also be required to arrest explosive growth in transport.

The most probable scenario is that Indian energy consumption will continue with rapid growth based on commercial fossil fuels dominated by oil for transport and coal for power production, in which case carbon emissions can be expected to increase six-fold over the next forty years. Any move towards an efficient renewable-based economy would lag well behind that in developed economies unless accelerated by major reforms and large-scale financial assistance to overcome the financial and social obstacles created by capital constraints, and technology transfers to overcome the lack of hard currency and other barriers to disseminating advanced technology.

India is a vast, poor, but rapidly developing country. Population, growing at about 2%/yr, is expected to exceed 1 billion by the year 2000, and the economy is growing much faster. Despite such rapid growth, most of the population still lives in rural areas with little or no access to modern amenities or to affordable commercial fuels. Per-capita consumption of commercial fuels in India, and associated carbon emissions, are about one twentieth of the average among OECD countries. The pressures for growth in emissions are immense, but there are important technical opportunities for modifying projected growth, if ways can be found to exploit them in the course of development. This chapter examines the prospects for CO_2 growth and limitation in the world's largest democracy.

10.1 Development and trends in the energy balance

Primary energy consumption in India over 1971-88,[1] illustrated in Figure 10.1, rose from 131Mtoe to 245Mtoe, an average annual increase of 3.75%.[2] A notable feature of this consumption has been the large contribution of traditional energy sources (principally biomass). In 1970-71, biomass fuels accounted for around 70Mtoe, more than half the total primary energy consumption. The absolute level of biomass use has continued to grow, reaching about 95Mtoe in 1987-88, but not nearly as fast as commercial fuels, which grew from 61Mtoe to 151Mtoe over the same period. After allowing for conversion losses in commercial fuels (especially in electricity), in 1987-88 biomass still accounted for nearly half the final energy consumption.

Since net carbon emissions correspond only to net deforestation, biomass fuels are not of prime importance from the perspective of global warming as they contain carbon recently absorbed from the atmosphere. However, the shift away from biomass fuels in the Indian energy economy is of great significance as it indicates the potential demand for

[1] All references to years in this chapter are to Financial Years which run from 1 April to 31 March.
[2] The oil equivalents (in terms of calorific value) of various fuels used in India are taken such that 1 kg of oil equivalent (kgoe) equals: Coal/charcoal 0.5kg; Soft coke 0.56kg; Kerosene 1.07 litres; LPG 1.14kg; Natural gas 0.86 cubic meters; Fuelwood 0.46kg; Agricultural wastes 0.3kg; Animal dung 0.2kg. In accordance with the other studies, non-fossil electricity inputs in the diagram have been represented in terms of the fossil fuel they displace, at average generating efficiency of 25%; data in the text uses the output basis (1kgoe=0.08kWh) unless otherwise stated.

Figure 10.1 India energy consumption and CO_2 emissions 1971-88

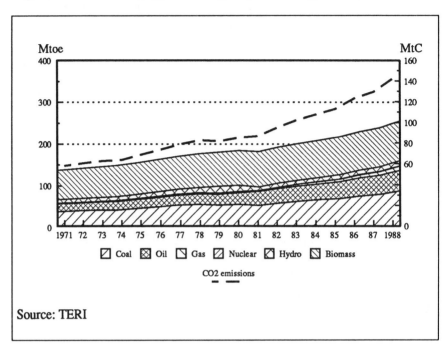

Source: TERI

fossil fuels as biomass fuels become relatively scarce. The move away from non-commercial fuels to commercial energy sources in rural India represents a large pool of potential demand for fossil fuels. However, the magnitude of this potential demand, and even the historical trends for biomass consumption, are only known very approximately. Statistics for commercial energy balances are much more precise. In view of this large difference in the levels of uncertainty associated with commercial and biomass fuels, and other wide differences, recent trends in their supply and consumption are discussed separately in the following sections.

Commercial energy supply and consumption

Total commercial energy supplies (net of changes of stocks) in India increased from about 92.3Mtoe in 1980-81 to 151Mtoe in 1987-88 at the rate of over 6% per annum.[3] During the same time period, indigenous production of commercial energy increased from about 72.6Mtoe to over

[3] Commercial energy supply/consumption data is from *TERI Energy Data Directory and Yearbook, 1989*, Tata Energy Research Institute, New Delhi, 1990.

133Mtoe, at the rate of over 7.8% per annum, and thus accounted for nearly 90% of supply by 1987-88.

Production of all fuels expanded. Opencast coal mining increased and new mining techniques were introduced. More and larger powered fuel equipment (shovels, draglines, dumpers, etc.) is now being deployed to permit opencast mining up to a depth of as much as 500 metres. However, with the increase in opencast mining, the average quality of mined coal has deteriorated. The increase in oil and gas production was due largely to the accelerated development of the Bombay High Offshore Basin. Crude oil production nearly trebled during the eight year time period, from about 10.5Mtoe in 1980-81 to over 30Mtoe in 1987-88. Similarly, gross natural gas production more than quadrupled from 2.02Mtoe in 1980-81 to 9.8Mtoe in 1987-88. However, a significant part of the natural gas produced continues to be flared, primarily because of delays in commissioning downstream gas infrastructure. There is apparently little flexibility in reducing the production of associated gases, which will be possible only if oil production is also limited - but which may lead to a higher oil import bill. It is possible to limit the production of gas only from fields which have non-associated gas reserves (eg. South Bassein): the production rate from such fields may be adjusted to the extent gas can be utilized purposefully downstream. Gas flaring has increased from 0.66Mtoe in 1980-81 to 2.93Mtoe in 1987-88.

Nuclear power generation also increased marginally after 1980-81, as 3x235MW of new nuclear capacity came on stream. Primary nuclear power generation doubled from then to produce about 2.4TWh by 1987-88. Hydroelectric capacity increased to about 17,000MW by 1987-88. Given typical fossil generating efficiencies of about 25%, these sources displaced a total about 13Mtoe of fossil fuel in 1987-88.

India continues to be a net energy importer, net crude oil and petroleum product imports in 1987-88 being 21.5Mtoe, a slight reduction from the beginning of the decade. However, imports of superior grade coal doubled to 1.45Mtoe in 1987-88. As a percentage of foreign exchange earnings through commodity exports, India's net oil imports declined from about 78% in 1980-81 to about 22% in 1987-88. This is due largely to: a rapid increase in indigenous crude production, at least until 1984-85, when nearly 29Mtoe were produced; and generally soft oil prices in the international market, particularly after 1986. However, the outlook for a further rapid increase in indigenous crude production, as during 1980-81

Table 10.1 Commercial energy supply and conversion in India (Mtoe)

	Coal	Oil	Gas	Hydro	Nuc	Elec	Total
1980-81							
Production	53.6	33.0	2.0	2.1	0.1	9.6	91
Input to elec	21.6	2.3	0.4	2.1	0.1	-	27
Elec output	6.6	0.7	0.1	2.1	0.1	9.6	10
Final consumption	32	28.4	0.8	-	-	7	68
Losses	15.0	3.9	1.1	-	-	2.6	23
1987-88							
Production	88.2	48.9	9.8	3.1	0.2	18.7	150
Input to elec	45	2.7	3	3.1	0.2	-	54
Elec output	13.7	0.8	0.9	3.1	0.2	18.7	19
Final consumption	43.1	43.7	3.2	-	-	13.3	103
Losses	31.4	4.4	5.7	-	-	5.4	47

Note: Electricity output from thermal fuels estimated from average thermal losses. All non-fossil electricity on output basis

Source: TERI.

to 1984-85 period, is not likely - in fact, crude oil production has more or less stabilized at about 30Mtoe/yr since 1984-85.

Table 10.1 lists the primary energy supply, conversions, and final energy consumption for various commercial energy fuels. This indicates that the net availability of commercial energy for final consumption increased from about 68Mtoe in 1980-81 to 103Mtoe in 1987-88, at the rate of 5.3% per annum, while energy lost in conversion processes (power generation, oil refining, soft-coke production, etc.) increased from about 24.1Mtoe to nearly 48Mtoe.[4]

Figure 10.2 shows how the sectorial pattern of final consumption has developed, based on various official statistical statements of the government of India. Although there may be significant shortcomings in the consumption data (such as the split between transport and agriculture sectors for diesel), they do highlight some important aspects. The industrial sector is the major commercial energy-consuming sector, accounting for just over 50% of commercial energy throughout the 1980s. Transport has however become a major oil consuming sector; diesel and petrol consumption increased from 12.13Mtoe in 1980-81 to 21.3Mtoe in 1987-88, reaching a share of over 46% of all oil consumed. Agricultural, residential and other sectors are not major commercial energy consumers. It is important to realize however, that if the roles of traditional fuels and draught animal power are also included, sectoral shares of total energy consumption are considerably different.

In terms of calorific content, direct use of coal (ie. excluding coal used for thermal power generation) still accounts for over 50% of total commercial energy consumption, and petroleum products for nearly 40%. However, despite a quadrupling of investment in real terms since 1974-75 in the coal, petroleum and electricity sectors, shortages still continue. The persistent shortages in coal and electricity supply during the past decade, coupled with the relative ease in the availability of oil have led to a rapid increase in the consumption of petroleum products. Diesel oils are used to mitigate the effects of electric power shortages, while fuel oils are used in industrial boilers in times of coal scarcity. Additionally, the pattern of growth of the transport sector, ie. an increasing share of road transport in freight movement, and the rapid increase in cars, two-wheelers (scooters and motorcycles) and motorized taxis (as opposed to the marginal growth rate of road-based public modes) has lead to a rapid increase in the percentage of petroleum in total energy consumption. Planners have responded to the shortage in power supply by preferring to invest in coal or gas-based thermal power

---

[4] Increased flaring of natural gas is the single most important reason for the increase in energy conversion losses, due to lack of transport and utilization infrastructure resulting from a policy debate on the relative merits of utilizing gas as an energy source or as a chemical feedstock. However, pipelines, gas-based combined cycle power plants, fertilizer plants and petrochemical complexes are nearing completion (January 1990).

Figure 10.2 India final commercial energy consumption 1971-88*

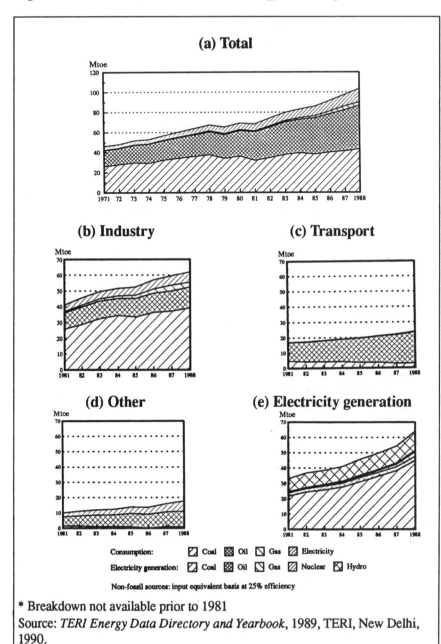

* Breakdown not available prior to 1981

Source: *TERI Energy Data Directory and Yearbook*, 1989, TERI, New Delhi, 1990.

Table 10.2 Biomass energy consumption, (Mtoe)

	Fuelwood	Agricultural waste	Animal dung	Total biomass energy consumption
1970-71	44.9	7.8	12.1	64.8
1975-76	49.1	8.5	13.3	70.9
1980-81	53.2	9.3	14.5	77
1985-86	57.4	9.9	15.5	82.8
1987-88	59.1	10.1	15.9	85.1

Source: see footnotes 4 and 5

stations whose gestation periods are usually less than that of hydroelectric and nuclear power stations. Consequently, the shares of hydro capacity and hydro generation have decreased gradually over the past decade as shown in Figure 10.2(e).

Traditional energy

Data related to biomass supply are normally estimated from secondary sources such as rate of deforestation (for fuelwood), production of foodgrains (for agricultural wastes), and livestock population (for animal dung). Various estimates of supply have been derived for each of the biomass energy sources; however these estimates vary with respect to year of estimation, methodology used, primary data source employed, etc. Recently, Kaul[5] has collated and analyzed all estimates developed earlier relating to forest biomass combustion, and derived an internally consistent data set for tree biomass, grass and litter burnt in Indian forests since 1953. The data set for fuelwood consumption is presented in Table 10.2. Consumption has doubled between 1953 and 1990; signifying an average increase of 1.9% per annum.

[5] O.N.Kaul, *Forest Biomass Burning in India*, TERI Discussion Paper, Tata Energy Research Institute, New Delhi, 1990.

Supply and consumption data for agricultural wastes and animal dung pertaining only to energy use are extremely difficult to estimate, especially on a year-on-year basis. It has been estimated that average annual per capita consumption of agricultural wastes and animal dung for energy purposes in rural areas is 17.6kgoe and 27.6kgoe, respectively.[6]

All biomass energy is used for cooking and heating in the domestic sector. While biomass energy consumption in India is large, typical stove efficiency is of the order of 8%, implying that biomass energy users get very little delivered energy.

10.2 Indigenous energy resource base

Fossil fuel resources

India is endowed with substantial fossil fuel resources; coal, largely of sub-bituminous grade, being the most abundant commercial energy source. The latest assessment, based on geological mapping, placed the total reserves located up to a depth of 1,200 metres (m) and in seams of thickness above 0.5m at 80,000Mtoe. Of this, 23,000Mtoe (29%) are proven reserves; indicated reserves are estimated at 33,000Mtoe (42%); the balance (29%) are inferred. The bulk of the reserves (64%) occur at depths up to 300m. Oil exploration near Kalol in Gujarat in western India led to the discovery of a large deep-seated (1,500m) lignite deposit, which is being considered for in situ gasification. The geographic distribution of coal reserves is uneven, with 53% located in Bihar and West Bengal in the eastern region, with the north-western, western and southern regions of India far from the coal bearing areas.

The quality of Indian coals is generally poor, characterized by high ash content, with most of the ash being finely ingrained. Reserves belonging to the coking variety are limited, estimated to be about 14,000Mtoe (17.5%), of which only 2,735Mtoe are of prime quality. The bulk (65,000Mtoe or 82.5%) is non-coking variety. Nearly 60% of non-coking coal reserves are of inferior grade with an ash content of 25-40% and a low sulphur content (0.2-0.4%). As the large reserves of poorer grade coal are not suitable for most uses, they are allocated primarily for power

---

[6] *Promoting Large-Scale Manufacturing and Commercialization of Decentralized Energy Systems in India*, Report prepared by IT Power, TERI and IDS for the government of India, November 1988.

generation, and they are seen as the key resource for fuelling India's electricity expansion.

Lignite deposits occur mostly in southern India, where the inferred reserves are about 1,320Mtoe of which about 800Mtoe are proven. Some smaller lignite deposits in west India are also being developed for power generation.

The total predicted reserves of crude oil and natural gas are estimated at about 17,000Mtoe. Approximately 10,200Mtoe are in Category I basins, while the rest are in Category II and III basins.[7] About 63% of total predicted reserves are in offshore areas, and about half of total theoretical reserves are expected to be in the form of natural gas. However, in 1987, the proven and indicated balance recoverable reserves of crude oil and natural gas were only 581Mtoe and 463Mtoe, respectively. These reserves are located mainly along the west coast between the Gulf of Cambay and Bombay, and in the north-east.

In addition, India possesses significant uranium resources. The Department of Atomic Energy estimates them to be about 70,000 tonnes, stated to be sufficient to sustain reactor equivalent of about 3Mtoe/yr. India also has thorium deposits, estimated at 360,000 tonnes, that can support a large nuclear programme based on breeder reactor technology. Thorium is seen as the single most important energy resource in the long term. However, their successful exploitation necessitates the development and deployment of Fast Breeder Reactors (to upgrade the thorium), followed by Thermal Reactors to utilize the processed thorium fuel. It is doubtful whether the thorium-route can be developed into a commercial success in India, though technological success is likely.

Two other factors influence the future growth of nuclear power in India. The first is the economics of nuclear power. The Nuclear Power Corporation of India Ltd (NPCIL) asserts that nuclear power is no more

---

[7] The Category classification of petroliferous basins is based on commercial exploitability, rather than geological exploration. Both Category I and II basins are proven reserves; the distinction is based on whether commercial production has commenced or not. Category III basins fall in both possible and prospective categories in which significant shows of hydrocarbons have not yet been found, but which, on general geological grounds, are considered prospective. The recoverable reserve is the amount that can be extracted economically (ie. at costs which are comparable to current extraction costs) using currently available technologies. A substantial amount of the proven reserves can (and does) occur in geological formations which are difficult to exploit (and hence oil extraction is expensive) or is in very small/poor deposits.

costly than electricity from coal. However, with the long gestation periods and associated cost over-runs characteristic of the industry in India, and the poor performance of the existing nuclear power stations, nuclear power is much more expensive.[8] The government is, therefore, uncertain about large long-term commitments to nuclear power.

Public opposition to nuclear power is also increasing. Though not large or well-organized, the public movements are currently local protests against siting decisions, reflecting more the NIMBY (Not In My Back Yard) syndrome than a grassroots opposition. These movements are delaying future projects and would further exacerbate the problem of time and cost over-runs.

All these factors together make this author believe that despite its potential, nuclear power will not contribute significantly to the energy supply mix in India. The NPCIL programme of 10,000MW of nuclear power by 2000 based on current Pressurized Heavy Water Reactors technology is certainly unachievable and it is the author's assessment that 10,000MW will be about the ultimate nuclear capacity, in place probably by the beginning of the second decade of the next century. At that time, renewable energy will probably start becoming viable for large-scale commercial electricity generation, and investment in nuclear fission technology will not be forthcoming.

Renewable energy resources
The principal renewable energy resources available in India are hydroelectricity, biomass, solar energy, and wind. The potential availability of each of these energy sources is examined in this section.

Hydroelectricity. According to available data, India's total economically exploitable hydroelectric potential is 53Mtoe of annual energy generation, or about 84,000MW at 60% load factor. Approximately 19% of this potential had been developed by the end of 1986-87. While most of the unexploited potential is concentrated in the far north and north-east (about 37Mtoe), low demand for electric power in those regions impedes

---

[8] Public audit of the industry accounts had not been possible prior to the formation of NPCIL in 1986. The financial statistics available since then indicate that investment in projects under construction is double the initial cost estimates. At the same time, the annual electricity generation at the two most recent stations that have stabilized has ranged between 2,935kWh/kW and 5,325kWh/kW (capacity factors of 33% and 61% respectively) over the past five years against the design norm of 5843kWh/kW used in economic calculations.

its development. Over 40% of the potential in the southern states has been developed so far.

While the advantages of hydroelectric power as a reliable and economic generation system are well recognized in India, the exploitation of these resources has been constrained by several factors. These include differences in interstate priorities, long gestation periods involved in construction, financial constraints, and problems of land submergence and resettlement of affected populations.

Biomass. The total area under forest in India was 68.5 million hectares (Mha) in 1952, representing 20.8% of total land area. Total deforestation from 1952 to 1987 was of the order of 4.44Mha. The land area under forest cover in 1987 was 64Mha.[9] On the other hand, area afforested from 1951 to 1986 was 11.5Mha,[10] with the annual rate of afforestation increasing from 0.01Mha (1951-56) to 1.76Mha (1986-87). Assuming a survival rate of 50% in the afforested areas, total afforestation has been about 5.74Mha since 1951, and annual afforestation is presently about 0.88Mha. Consequently, historical deforestation and afforestation are about balanced: afforestation schemes are now probably now maintaining India's forest cover, if not adding marginally to it. Whereas most fuelwood is collected in rural areas, this takes the form of twigs, branches and brush. On the other hand, logs and lops are supplied to the organized urban market. The average production of all forms of firewood from all types of forests and plantations is estimated to be about 2.5 tonnes per hectare.

Estimation of agricultural wastes for energy is complex because of competitive demands for it, principally as fodder. Restricting estimates to non-fodder wastes (rice husk, maize cobs, groundnut shells, cotton sticks, bagasse, and coconut fibre and shell), total production during 1984-85 was about 29Mtoe.[11] The bulk was rice husk (8.8Mtoe) and bagasse (17.2Mtoe). Since bagasse is exclusively used as an energy source in sugar mills, the availability of agricultural wastes for household energy is therefore of the order of 12Mtoe. For resource estimation purposes, domestic energy from agricultural wastes is assumed to be

[9] *The State of the Forest Report-1989*, Department of Environment & Forests, Government of India, 1989.

[10] *India's Forests 1987*, Department of Environment, Wildlife & Forests, Government of India, 1987.

[11] Kaul, op.cit.

about 0.2Mtoe per million tonnes of rice production. Sugarcane production is unlikely to undergo any significant changes. Consequently, industrial energy from agricultural wastes is assumed to stabilize at about 20Mtoe.

The cattle population in India was about 785 million in 1988. Across agroclimatic zones and cattle species, the average annual dung production was about 3.5 tonnes per head of cattle; however, it is estimated that only about 16% of the total dung is collected and used. Consequently, dung energy resources are estimated at about 0.116toe per cattle head. Cattle population in India is now increasing only marginally, and is expected to stabilize at about 800 million. The total annual dung energy availability is therefore assessed at 93Mtoe.

Solar energy. India as a whole is well-endowed with solar radiation.[12] Certain parts of the country, particularly in the west, have average annual resource availability of more than $0.17toe/m^2$ of global solar radiation, while parts of eastern India receive less than $0.145toe/m^2$. The theoretical resource is therefore large: if 0.03% of India's land area were covered by solar cells at 10% efficiency, they would generate as much power as was consumed in 1988. The key constraints on this arise from costs and systems considerations, as discussed below. The pattern of solar radiation is not uniform either geographically or seasonally and a marked decrease occurs with the onset of the monsoon.

Wind energy. Monsoons are also the major seasonal wind circulation generated due to the seasonal land-sea pressure gradients. In general wind speeds are relatively lower in winter over most of the country with mean wind speeds less than 5km/h. In coastal areas, wind speeds are in excess of 10km/h, increasing in spring to a maximum of about 20km/h, and can reach 25-30km/h in mid-summer.[13] As with solar radiation, there are geographic and seasonal variations.

The overall wind energy potential that can be tapped was assessed by TERI at about 235,000MW.[14] Most of this potential occurs in west and

[12] A.Mani, *Handbook of Solar Radiation Data for India*, Allied Publishers, New Delhi, 1980.
[13] A.Mani and D.A.Mooley, *Wind Energy Data for India*, Government of India, 1983.
[14] J.Hosain, 'An Assessment of Potential for Installation of Windfarms in India', paper presented at the PACER conference on Role of Innovative Technologies and Approaches for India's Power Sector, organized by TERI and PFC, New Delhi, April 1990.

south India. About 10,000MW of this capacity can generate electricity at a price less than that of coal-based thermal power stations.

10.3 Socio-economic determinants of energy consumption

The domestic sector is the largest consumer of energy in India, and over 80% of the energy used in this sector is supplied by non-commercial sources, principally firewood, agricultural wastes and animal dung. Though non-commercial fuels dominate in both rural and urban households, there is a broad movement towards commercial fuels with increase in income, and more so with urbanization. Table 10.3 provides estimates of monthly per capita consumption of different fuels in rural and urban households in India in 1977-78. Urban areas used only 14kg of biofuel per capita per month, as compared to 29kg per capita in rural areas, with urban households substituting commercial fuels like coke and kerosene, for crop and animal wastes. Firewood, surprisingly, played an important role even in urban areas: it met more than half of the total gross energy needs of urban homes, similar to the pattern in rural households. The major distinction in the use pattern in rural and urban areas is seen across income levels. In rural areas, no significant change in use patterns was observed across income levels; in urban areas, however, the commercial/non-commercial mix changed from 1:3.7 in the lowest income category to 1:1.7 in the highest income category. Furthermore, useful (or delivered) per capita energy in rural areas is less than in urban areas, and the gross per capita energy consumption is higher in rural areas. A similar conclusion is also true across income levels. The low efficiency of about 8% of combustion of biomass fuels in traditional cookers is the prime reason for this anomaly.[15] Inadequate fuel supply and lack of purchasing power in rural areas are the other major causes of the imbalance.

Daily per capita energy consumption in rural and urban households is approximately 350 to 430kcals, respectively. These consumption norms are low by international standards, and are expected to rise to 520 and 650kcals per capita per day by 2004-05.[16] An important aspect of the consumption pattern is that over 65% of the biomass energy used in rural

---

[15] *Towards a Perspective on Energy Demand and Supply in India in 2004/05*, Advisory Board on Energy, Government of India, May 1985.
[16] ibid.

Table 10.3 Monthly consumption of major fuels per capita in different income groups 1977-78 (rupees)

Income group Rs/month	<3000	3000 to 5999	6000 to 11999	12000 to 17999	>18000	Total average
Rural						
Soft coke (kg)	0.12	0.14	0.47	0.54	0.79	0.19
Kerosene (litre)	0.44	0.40	0.4	0.36	0.35	0.43
Electricity (kWh)	0.20	0.46	0.83	1.28	1.44	0.41
Firewood (kg)	13.67	12.33	13.75	14.33	12.92	13.17
Vegetable waste (kg)	5.08	4.33	5.33	6.92	6.17	4.92
Dungcake (kg)	10.50	11.25	12	13.75	15.5	11.08
Total/month: gross						**115.8**
useful						**9.6**
Urban						
Soft coke (kg)	1.55	2.52	3.83	2.8	2.7	2.61
Kerosene (litre)	0.83	1.04	0.99	1.02	0.83	0.97
Electricity (kWh)	1.01	2.43	4.33	6.56	9.0	2.92
LPG (kg)	-	0.09	0.32	0.78	0.93	0.18
Firewood (kg)	13.89	9.66	6.83	5.68	4.61	9.73
Vegetable waste (kg)	0.92	0.52	0.58	1.28	0.5	0.67
Dungcake (kg)	3.22	2.94	2.87	3.5	1.87	3.0
Charcoal (kg)	0.27	0.31	0.39	0.22	0.23	0.3
Total (Mcal): gross						**91.3**
useful						**11.3**

Source: I.Natrajan, *Domestic Fuel Survey with Special Reference to Kerosene,* NCAER, New Dehli, 1985.

areas is collected.[17] This places obvious constraints on fuel switching as a vast majority of the population does not have the financial resources to switch to commercial fuels even if they are available. However, the percentage of households dependent on collected biomass is expected to decrease with economic development since more households would have the economic ability to purchase commercial fuels, and since increased value of time would encourage a shift from biomass collection to economically more rewarding activities.

Since the average efficiency of traditional cookers burning biomass fuels is 8%, in order to promote energy conservation, the government of India launched a National Programme on Improved Chulhas (cooking stoves) in 1983 under which some 4 million improved stoves were installed during the period to 1988. Preliminary results of an evaluation of the programme found that about 65% of these improved stoves were in use, and resulted in fuel savings of about 25% over traditional stoves.[18] A similar programme has been launched to promote biogas plant at the domestic and community level. While there are about 800,000 domestic plant in use, community-sized plant have not been very successful primarily because the sharing of both gas and costs has not been equitably arranged.

Electricity consumption in the rural household sector is insignificant at present. Electricity shortages have prevented the higher-income groups in rural areas from adopting it as a major energy source and consumption for the highest income is about 0.04kWh per capita per day. On the other hand, per capita electricity consumption in urban areas ranges from 0.03kWh per day for the lowest income group to 0.3kWh per day for the highest income group. Trends indicate that a doubling of income leads to a 75% increase in electricity consumption, with a saturation consumption level of about 5kWh per capita per day. The total commercial energy requirement in the household sector shows a very

[17] *Energy Consumption in Rural Areas of Semi-Arid Agroclimatic Region*, report prepared by the Administrative Staff College of India for TERI, 1988.
[18] V.Joshi, 'Rural Energy Demand and Role of Improved Chulhas', R.K.Pachauri. and L Srivastava, (eds), *Energy Policy Issues*, Vol.4, Tata Energy Research Institute, Delhi, 1989, pp.23-36.

strong correlation with GDP. Electricity and petroleum consumption increase at rates which are greater than the rate of GDP growth.[19]

The industrial sector consumes all commercial sources of energy; electricity, coal and oil. In general, the consumption of all fuels is increasing rapidly, though energy intensity is declining gradually. For example, in the case of electricity, the ratio of consumption with respect to value-added[20] in the industrial sector increased from 1.68 to 2.81 for during the late 1960s on account of the substitution effect due to intensification of electricity use in the industrial sector. After that, the ratio declined, with an average value of 1.64 over the last 25 years; during the late eighties, it was around 1.48.

The major consumers of coal in the industrial sector are cement, fertilizers, paper, textile and brick-making. The intensity of coal use in industry has been declining gradually owing to substitution by oil and gas, as well as due to upgradation of processes and coal utilization technologies. During the 1980s, constraints in supplies of coal to industry encouraged shifts to other fuels, primarily fuel oil and gas as indigenous supplies came onto the market (the elasticity of coal consumption was 0.64 with respect to value-added in industry; down from 0.8 in the 1960s).

Oil and gas have been growing rapidly as industrial fuels, driven mainly by coal shortages and gas availability. Oil and gas utilization intensity decreased during the 1970s and early 1980s, and is steady at about 0.044kg per rupee of value-added.[21]

The growth of the transport sector in India has been marked by rapid growth, with an increasing share of road transport in freight movement, and of cars and two-wheelers (see Table 10.4). The bulk of energy consumption in this sector is in the form of petroleum products. Coal use is expected to become insignificant by the turn of the century as the last coal locomotives are phased out. Energy consumption (of electricity and petroleum products) in the transport sector has exhibited a quadratic growth with respect to GDP.

---

[19] Electricity consumption is proportional to $GDP^{7/3}$, petroleum consumption is proportional to $GDP^{4/3}$, *Report of the Energy Demand Screening Group*, Planning Commission, Government of India, August 1986.

[20] Value-added is the net economic surplus created by the industrial process, that is the difference in the total value of goods produced and that of all inputs.

[21] In December 1990 UK£1=Rupee 35.

Table 10.4 Traffic and energy demand in the transport sector

	GDP (trillion Rs at 1980-81 prices)	Total Traffic Passenger (billion passenger-km)	Freight (billion tonne-km)	Energy Consumption (Mtoe) Petroleum products	Electricity
1980-81	1.22	752	543	12.2	0.19
1981-82	1.3	815	595	12.7	0.21
1982-83	1.34	824	597	13.7	0.22
1983-84	1.44	897	674	14.7	0.23
1984-85	1.5	965	739	15.8	0.24
1985-86	1.57	1090	850	17.1	0.26
1986-87	1.64	1150	893	18.6	0.27
1987-88	1.71	1210	934	20.4	0.33

Sources: *TERI Energy Data Directory and Yearbook 1989*, Tata Energy Research Insitute, New Dehli, 1990; *Report of the Group on Perspective Planning for the Transport Sector*, Planning Commission, Government of India, New Dehli, 1987; *Economic Survey 1988-89*, Ministry of Finance, Government of India, New Dehli, 1989.

10.4 Projections and options to the years 2000 and 2030

This section outlines various possible scenarios for the Indian energy sector, reflecting various degrees of and strategies for carbon abatement. The mix of fuels projected and consequent carbon emissions are shown in Figure 10.3.

Scenario 2000A: Business-as-usual

By the year 2000, the population of India is expected to cross the 1 billion mark, and reach a level of about 1.02 billion. Extrapolating present trends, about 31.2% of this population (324 million) will live in urban areas. The GDP is assumed to grow at the present rate of 5% to be Rs3.06 trillion (at 1980-81 prices) in that year. The percentage shares of GDP accruing due to industry, agriculture and transport are assumed to be 30%, 31%, and 15% respectively.

Figure 10.3 Scenarios for India energy consumption and CO_2 emissions 1988-2030

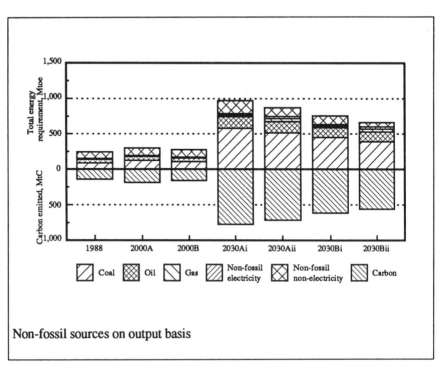

Non-fossil sources on output basis

In the business-as-usual scenario, present energy consumption trends are assumed to continue. Thus, in the domestic sector, the per capita consumption of petroleum products (kerosene, LPG) and electricity would increase by about 10% over the 1987-88 level, while per capita consumption of fuelwood, agricultural wastes and dung would decline by 5%.[22] Coal consumption in the domestic sector is assumed to remain constant on a per capita basis. Daily per capita useful energy consumption is postulated to rise to 450kcals in rural areas and 550kcals in urban areas.

In the industrial sector, intensity of oil use is projected to remain constant, while the intensities of electricity and coal use are assumed to decrease by 10%. The transport sector is assumed to continue to expand

[22] This implies that 15% of conventional biomass cookers would be replaced by energy-efficient ones by 2000.

at the present rate. Introduction of new-generation locomotives and automobiles is expected to reduce energy demand by 5% over the demand projected by the present quadratic relationship of GDP to energy consumption in this sector. No changes in the energy intensity of the agricultural sector are assumed.

The predominant role of coal-based thermal power in the electricity generation mix is postulated to continue with 62% of generation based on coal, 26% on hydro, 6% on diesel, 4% on natural gas, and 2% on nuclear power. The share of natural gas is assumed increase from the present 2% as flared gas is utilized for power generation.

Under these conditions, the primary energy consumption (including biomass) grows by 31% as compared with 1987, and CO_2 emissions grow by 43% because of the increasing role of coal relative to biomass and hydro.

Scenario 2000B: Emissions abatement

Under this scenario, in order to reduce carbon dioxide emissions, improvements in the availability of natural gas and primary electricity are envisioned. Indigenous natural gas production is assumed to increase to the maximum level commensurate with reservoir stability, and its utilization for power generation and industrial steam-raising is promoted. Since both hydroelectric and nuclear power stations have long gestation periods (approaching ten years for hydro, and nearly 15 years for nuclear), there is not much leeway for increasing the share of primary electricity production. It is assumed here that hydroelectric projects are preferentially sanctioned during the next two years so that an additional 1,200MW of hydro capacity are commissioned by 2000.

In addition to this fuel switching, a variety of energy efficiency improvement measures would need to be in place. Ranked in terms of most efficient energy (or CO_2) savings, they would be:

* Continuing the programme of increasing the efficiency of biomass combustion in the residential sector by the rapid dissemination of improved cookers with an efficiency of 12%, assuming one-third of the traditional cookers in urban areas, and one-quarter in rural areas replaced.

* Increasing the efficiency of coal use in the residential sector by 10% by the increased use of efficient cookers and space heaters, through

the dissemination of improved units that are currently available commercially.[23]

* Increasing the average efficiency of coal boilers in industry from 65% to 70%,[24] and of fuel-oil use from 75% to 88%. Decreasing electricity intensity of industry by 10% is also assumed due to the use of energy-efficient motors.[25]

* Upgrading motors for agricultural applications (irrigation, operation of farm equipment, etc.) are upgraded so that average efficiency increases from 70% to 80%.[26]

* Increasing the efficiency of thermal power generation from 28% to 30% because of coal washing, improved operation and maintenance techniques, and reducing transmission and distribution losses from 22% to 20% because of grid stabilization due to introduction of capacitor banks.

As compared with 2000A, these energy efficiency measures, together with fuel switching, would reduce energy consumption by 28Mtoe (9.3%) and CO_2 emissions by 21.6MtC (12.9%), representing increases from 1987 of 19% and 25% respectively.

Scenario 2030Ai: Business-as-usual

Population is estimated to grow to 1.64 billion by 2030,[27] equally divided into the rural and urban sectors. GDP (at 1980-81 prices) is

[23] A.Gadgil, and S.S.Makkad 'Improved Space heating Stoves for Ladakh', *Energy Environment Monitor*, Vol.2, No.2, TERI, New Delhi, 1986.

[24] Currently, fluidized-bed boilers account for about half of the new boiler capacity commissioned every year in Indian industry. This rate of penetration would bring down the coal intensity of industry by 10% as assumed in the business-as-usual scenario; increasing the rate of penetration to over two-thirds would result in the overall average boiler efficiency further increasing from 65% to 70%.

[25] V.Kothari, S.Anand and S.Sabharwal, 'Electric Motors in Industry: Characterization and Energy Conservation Potential', Report submitted to the Department of Power, Ministry of Energy, Government of India, by TERI, 1988.

[26] This would require carrying out relatively low-cost modifications on agricultural pumps, which in individual cases have resulted in savings of up to 50%. However, on a nationwide basis, only about two-thirds of the pumps are assumed to be rectified, and savings in those pumps could amount to 25%. See S.M.Patel, 'Low Cost and Quick-Yielding Measures for Energy Conservation in Agricultural Pumps', *Pacific and Asian Journal of Energy*, Vol.2. No.1, 1988.

[27] Population is projected to increase by 2% per annum during the 1990s, and by 1.75% per annum between 2000 and 2030.

projected to be Rs12.3 trillion, with the sectoral shares of industry, transport and agriculture being 37%, 10%, and 17%, respectively.

Present energy consumption trends are assumed to stabilize around 2020. Thus, in the domestic sector, daily per-capita energy consumption is of the order of 550kcals in the rural sector and 650kcals in urban sector. About two-thirds of cookers burning solid fuels are assumed high-efficiency versions, and biomass combustion is assumed to be almost completely replaced in the urban sector by coal. Biomass continues to be the major energy source in the rural sector.

As a result of this steady growth, primary energy requirements are more than four times those of 1987. Coal consumption is more than seven times the level of 1987, whilst oil and gas use roughly treble. As a result, CO_2 emissions increase by a factor of six, though the per-capita levels are still about a tenth of the current levels in the US.

Scenario 2030Aii: Emissions abatement through fuel switching

Major developmental drilling is assumed to increase natural gas reserves by 100% (over the business-as-usual scenario). At the same time, about 85% of total hydroelectric potential (65,000MW) is tapped. Increased availability of natural gas and hydroelectricity lead to a decrease in coal consumption for power generation. Nuclear power capacity is estimated to peak at 10,000MW for the reasons explained above.

It is likely that technologies for electricity generation from renewable sources of energy (particularly solar photovoltaics (PV)) may become techno-economically viable by 2030. The extent of use would depend on efficiency and cost vis-à-vis that of coal and natural gas. Considering the immense electricity requirement of urban areas, the comparatively low efficiency of solar PV conversion, and the intrinsically low levels of solar radiation, it is currently not possible for solar PV (or thermal solar) to supply electricity in bulk to urban areas without an integrated grid. It is however, quite possible, that electricity in rural areas maybe almost completely supplied by solar PV stations. Consequently, some displacement of coal by solar PV is possible. A large amount of biomass could be substituted by solar energy for cooking and heating applications. Because of the low efficiency of biomass utilization, the biomass requirement would drop by 30% if solar thermal devices replace a quarter of cookers and half of space heaters which use biomass or coal. Wind-farms for electricity generation would probably have an installed capacity of 10,000MW by 2030, and contribute about 45TWh to the grid.

This would displace about 15Mtoe of coal. As compared with 2030Ai a reduction of 100Mtoe (10.3%) in energy consumption, and 56MtC (7.9%) in CO_2 emissions would result from the above fuel switches.

Scenario 2030Bi: Emissions abatement through energy efficiency
The following energy efficiency measures are assumed to be in place:

* New technologies for electricity generation from coal (for example, integrated gasifier combined cycle, pressurized fluidized bed combined cycle, integrated gasifier-molten carbonate fuel cell system) which would raise generation efficiency to 35%, and new transmission and distribution systems (for example, high voltage DC lines, and superconductors) which would decrease line losses to 18%.

* Energy efficiency in the transport sector increased by 50%. Additionally, two-thirds of all commuter trips are made by public transport.

* Efficiency in industry reduced energy intensity by 20% for thermal energy and by 10% for electrical energy.

* All biomass stoves are improved versions with 12% efficiency.

* The efficiency of petroleum and electricity use in the agricultural sector increased to 85%.

These measures would reduce energy consumption by 218Mtoe (22.5%) over the business-as-usual scenario, and emissions by 147MtC (20.8%).

Scenario 2030Bii: Emissions abatement through fuel switching and energy efficiency
Combining the fuel switching measures of 2030Aii with the efficiency measures of 2030Bi gives the maximum abatement scenario 2030Bii, which yields an overall decrease of 290Mtoe (29.8%) in energy consumption, and 196.9MtC (27.8%) in CO_2 emissions compared with the business-as-usual scenario. As a result primary energy consumption increases less than threefold over 1987 levels, whilst the growth in commercial use and CO_2 emissions are constrained to a level 4.3 times that of 1987. Despite such growth, the per-capita levels of commercial energy consumption and CO_2 emissions are still at about one-eighth of the current average in OECD countries.

10.5 Policy options and constraints

The fuel switching and energy efficiency options discussed above require the formulation and implementation of a range of public policies relating to demand management, supply planning and organizational infrastructure of energy services. The nature and scope of these policies are discussed here, along with an assessment of their feasibility in the perspective of the political and economic situation in the country.

Energy demand management

The primary requirement is an *integrated pricing policy*. Prices of all the major fuels in India (except firewood and other biomass) are administered with the goal of pursuing certain social objectives. They do not, in general, reflect costs. Kerosene is subsidized as it is viewed as the major commercial fuel used by low-income households, although it is well known that low-income households may not always get the intended benefits. As a result of the subsidy, kerosene demand has increased, leading to an increased outflow of foreign exchange on kerosene imports. Similarly, electricity tariffs are also lower than supply costs: this is particularly true regarding electricity sales to rural farmers for whom tariffs are the lowest (compared to other categories of consumers), while the costs borne by utilities for supplying electricity to them are the highest. These low tariffs have lead to financial shortfalls for the utility, as well as encouraged the inefficient use of electricity in the rural sector. There has been an attempt, particularly in the last six years, to raise coal prices to reflect costs. However, coal prices are invariably less than costs, though the difference has been reducing over time. Natural gas prices are adjusted so as to maintain rough parity with fuel-oil prices on a calorific basis. The prices of petroleum products, on the other hand, are set by a complex procedure which ensures guaranteed returns to refineries and producers, and also reflects the social priorities of the government in the relative pricing of different petroleum products.

Pricing has not been used as a tool to influence interfuel substitution and energy efficiency. Sectoral financial preoccupations have precluded the establishment of an integrated energy pricing policy based either on market or socio-economic criteria.

Within the national developmental perspective, the aims of an integrated energy policy should be to: reflect the real costs of various fuels to the economy, including depletion costs; encourage energy conservation with a graded tariff structure; promote fuel substitution and renewable energy sources by introducing mill pricing;[28] and incorporate environmental costs in energy prices. Three major macroeconomic effects are expected to occur as a result of the implementation of an integrated energy pricing policy: improvement in the quality of energy supply due to easing of financial constraints on energy suppliers (which would result in better operation and maintenance procedures); encouragement of energy conservation measures driven by increased energy costs; and promotion of interfuel substitution, particularly of coal by natural gas, and of biomass by other renewables.

An increase of average energy prices to marginal costs will probably results in a 5-10% decrease in electricity demand (translating to a 3-6% decrease in coal consumption); and a 5% decrease in primary coal demand. In the case of petroleum products, the relative prices of different products is of crucial importance: currently petrol costs two-and-a-half times as much as diesel (which is priced at marginal cost) and more than three times as much as kerosene. Removal of subsidy on kerosene should reduce kerosene demand by anywhere between 10% and 20%, and a cautious increase in diesel prices could reflect shortages in the economy. Large increases in diesel price are not considered viable because of the associated macroeconomic impact due to increased transportation costs, but small increase could influence a shift in freight movement from road to rail. It is difficult to quantify the extent of this shift, but a rough assessment seems to indicate a 2% decrease in diesel consumption for a 10% rise in its price. For the economy, the level of diesel price rise would essentially be governed by the relative values of the savings in foreign exchange (as diesel is imported at the margin) and the indirect increases in the prices of other goods. As the foreign exchange squeeze becomes acute, diesel price rise becomes preferable.

The marginal costs of natural gas are less than that of coal within certain distance of the well-head. Integrated pricing would encourage natural gas use in these areas, as well as near ports if it is imported. Many renewable technologies are already cost-effective on an economic-cost basis. These include solar hot water heaters, wind electric generators,

---

[28] Pricing in which the consumer pays the cost of production plus that of transport from the production point to the consumer (plus a reasonable rate of return on investment). This contrasts with uniform pricing which envisages spatial averaging of costs so that all consumers pay the same, irrespective of how far they are located from the production point.

solar PV for certain locations, biomass-based gasification (for cooking gas) and electricity generation technologies. Marginal cost pricing of electricity would provide the correct signals for their increased adoption and use.

The second requirement is *appropriate macroeconomic policies*. The government of India has several policies in place to encourage energy conservation and the use of energy efficient technologies. These include the provision for 100% depreciation of energy-efficient equipment in the first year, mandatory reporting of energy-use statistics in the annual reports of industrial units, subsidies for energy audits, and reduced customs duty on selected control-equipment for managing energy use. Despite these steps, energy conservation has not made the kind of impact in India that has been observed in the developed countries since the late 1970s. The major reason for the slow growth of energy conservation is now attributed to the lack of capital.

Policies for providing inexpensive capital for renovation, refurbishment and modernization of industrial units so as to achieve high energy efficiency are required. At the same time, norms and standards for energy consumption in various processes and appliances need to be evolved. These could be coupled with a punitive tax structure to encourage compliance with standards.

A wide range of fiscal policies and instruments are required to check the rapidly growing energy demand in the *transport sector*. Currently, the only macroeconomic tool used to curb petrol/diesel use has been to raise their prices. However, elasticity (especially for petrol) is low as a large percentage of automobiles is part of corporate fleets and often there are no real options available for transportation. Other measures required include taxation on cars and two-wheelers which is inversely proportional to their energy intensity (kgoe per passenger/km), tax credits to companies/institutions that provide mass transport for commuting, and long-term tax breaks and/or low-cost capital for manufacturers developing energy-efficient vehicles.

One of the most important measures for reducing the energy intensity of the transport sector is to provide efficient, comfortable and reliable public transport systems. Para transit[29] should be encouraged by

---

[29] Para transit is intermediate between personalized modes of public transport (eg. taxis) and large public transit systems (eg. city buses or urban railways). Typically, para transit units have capacities of between 5 and 15 passengers and are privately owned.

providing subsidized capital. Innovative fiscal measures are necessary to raise the capital for large public transport projects: these could include low-interest bonds guaranteeing free/subsidized travel on the system, appropriate incentives of capital in return for eventual development of space above/below right-of-way for commercial purposes, and linking the setting up of high value-added export-based industries with capital raising for the system.

A further condition for effective energy efficiency is *policies facilitating technology development*. The foremost constraint to technology upgradation in India is lack of foreign exchange to obtain advanced technologies, as well as to develop these technologies indigenously. Consequently, policies that encourage barter or swaps - goods/services/products for technology, are required. In the past, not many such arrangements have been negotiated, mainly because of barriers of information and capital. Similarly, the suppliers of goods/services/products are often not directly interested in technologies, and the supplier of technology many not be interested in the particular goods/services/products provided. Policies encouraging the setting up of consortia for negotiating these contracts would be desirable: all members of the consortia would be eligible for the export promotion incentives provided by the government. At the same time, technological policies should encourage the indigenous upgradation of technology. Efficiency standards for processes and appliances could be evolved, and manufacturers and users could be encouraged/penalized for adoption/indifference to standards. In addition, the government could identify key areas where technological upgradation is required, and encourage R&D institutions to come together to develop the technology. Some such processes have been initiated in the past year or so (eg. for indigenous development of wind energy generators), but in general initiatives and incentives from the government are lacking. It is also essential that the improved cooker programme and the biogas programme are expanded rapidly and successfully so as to cover the entire population by 2010.

Energy supply planning
The government and public sector organizations largely control energy supply, except in the case of biomass. Recently, the government decided to open the electricity generation sector to private participation; it is still too early to judge the response to this initiative. There is a body of opinion

which believes that this step only postpones the financial collapse of the electricity sector; that nothing short of a complete overhaul of the distribution systems and the tariff structure will provide stability to utilities.

All commercial energy suppliers in India (with the exception of the oil industry) are in financial trouble. Rational planning towards CO_2 emissions abatement will occur only after financial stability is restored. The major reasons for the financial crisis are two-fold: unremunerative prices and large unpaid bills. A chain of events occur that paralyse the industry: the revenue of electricity utilities does not meet costs; operation and maintenance (O&M) procedures are sacrificed, and coal bills are not paid; the coal industry in turn suffers cash flow problems - again O&M procedures are pruned and suppliers are not paid. This also leads, in general, to a decline in the managerial efficiency of public sector organizations.

The separation of capital planning (for expansion) and revenue generation (for O&M) in the national planning process ensures that there is always some capital available for supply expansion in spite of grave scarcity of funds for operational expenditure. This has lead to planning being completely supply-oriented and focused on very short timeframes in order to overcome perpetual (and growing) shortages. This 'tonight timeframe'[30] planning perspective has resulted in expansion of existing technologies (particularly coal and coal-based thermal power) at the cost of efficiency improvements, diversification of supply technologies, and demand management planning.

The options identified above for promoting supply efficiency and fuel switching so as to minimize CO_2 emissions, ranked in terms of cost of energy/CO_2 savings in increasing order would be:

* The afforestation programme accelerated. Presently, the country is at a zero net deforestation level, but increasing population can easily lead to a reversal of trends. Energy plantations around cities be encouraged as a means of meeting urban demand for fuelwood, and agroforestry and social forestry in rural areas to provide the necessary fuelwood for rural consumption.

* Technologies for electricity generation from coal upgraded to maximize efficiency and minimize emissions.

[30] 'Tonight timeframe' promotes a 'more of the same' attitude rather than a complete assessment of available options.

* Developmental drilling for proving natural gas reserves accelerated.

* Along with fuelwood from energy plantations, soft coke should be encouraged as a urban household fuel with appropriate technology upgradation for soft coke manufacture and utilization.

* The forecasting and planning horizon extended to 15 years and a long-term energy policy and strategy enunciated, highlighting the shift from coal to natural gas and renewables, and efficiency in energy conversion.

A major constraint to the above conditions is the socio-economic structure of Indian society which limits the technological supply options that can be effectively utilized to reduce CO_2 emissions. This is particularly true of decentralized renewable-energy technologies aimed at the rural sector, eg. biomass gasification. Biomass gasification produces a gaseous fuel that is suitable for direct use in cooking, or for electricity generation via a gas turbine.[31] Both are feasible technically and economically, but the immense population pressure on land limits the extent of their ultimate penetration. The demand for biomass as a cooking fuel severely restricts its use for electricity generation: the move would be viewed as yet another example of the exploitation of 'common resources' (ie. forest produce) for the benefit of the elite, thus depriving the poor of their traditional rights. The use of gas for cooking, instead of the direct use of biomass, is constrained by the purchasing power of the users. As mentioned earlier about 65% of the biomass energy used in rural areas is collected, rather than bought. A large fraction of biomass users just do not have the economic capacity either to maintain a biomass gasifier, or to pay for the gas from a community gasifier. The latter would suffer from obstacles similar to those faced by the community biogas programme which has been unable to institutionalize the distribution of gas and collection of charges in an equitable, yet economically sound manner. Biomass gasifiers would certainly be adopted by the rural rich but would then have a limited impact on natural CO_2 emissions.

These constraints also restrict technology penetration in much the same way as they constrain traditional supply planning.[32] Pessimistic as it may seem, the most robust strategy for rural economic development rural energy supply, and limiting CO_2 emissions, is vigorous

[31] J.Goldemberg, R.H.Williams, T.B.Johansson and A.K.N.Reddy, *Energy for a Sustainable World*, Wiley Eastern, New Delhi, 1988.
[32] ibid.

afforestation accompanied by transfer of afforested land to the rural landless and development of agro-industries. This would ensure adequate biomass supply and increased purchasing power, which in turn, would lead to the adoption of energy-efficient technologies. This approach, while accepting the low efficiency of biomass utilization in the short-term, moderates the switch from biomass fuels to fossil fuels.

A further major constraint is the limitations of current infrastrucure. The widespread use of new supply technologies, particularly wind and photovoltaic electricity, is limited by the grid capacity and the need for infrastructural enhancements. The variable output of these technologies (linked to the variation in natural phenomenon, eg. wind speed and solar intensity) restricts their share in total grid capacity. Conventional wisdom in Indian electricity planning placed this share at about 10%: a stable grid with a total generating capacity exceeding the demand can, of course, accommodate a much larger share, especially if it contains storage capacity, such as with pumped hydroelectric power.

Exploiting new technologies on a larger scale still might require the development of efficient energy storage routes such as hydrogen generation, transportation and use.[33] The effective deployment of such a technology requires the simultaneous investment in and diffusion of a nest of supporting technologies in order to exploit its potential optimally over the entire economy. While desirable, such a course does not seem plausible in an economy plagued by the 'tonight timeframe' syndrome. The most probable scenario is that while the move towards an efficient renewables-based energy economy could occur, it would exhibit a time lag with respect to the movement in industrialized countries - occurring in India only towards the middle of the 21st century, unless accelerated by major socio-economic restructuring or large-scale capital and technology transfers.

The necessity of technology transfer and financial assistance (in the form of availability of hard currency) for implementing the above policies is a further condition of their success. International cooperation in the energy industry could also help in minimizing CO_2 emissions. Regional trade in natural gas (from Iran, Indonesia, Malaysia, and Bangladesh) could greatly enhance interfuel substitution and decrease

---

[33] See Chapter 1, section 1.5, for a discussion of the issues in integrating variable renewable energy sources, eg. wind and solar on to large power systems, and the possible roles of storage and hydrogen.

dependence on coal. However, national policies have always encouraged energy self-sufficiency for reasons for national security; major gas imports are, therefore, unlikely.

Capital contraints and abatement investment requirements

The central problem of Indian development is that a vast proportion of the population - certainly in excess of 50% - is either unemployed or employed in marginally-productive jobs. Consequently, per capita net resource creation is low, and in spite of the high savings rate in the country (in excess of 20% of the GDP), the per capita annual resource availability is currently a meagre Rs2,700. This is invested in generating employment, as well as for providing amenities (food, shelter, energy) to the population that is unemployed or underemployed. The emphasis of government policy has been on rapid employment generation - and creating a job in the organized sector now costs more than Rs50,000. It is, therefore, politically unacceptable to move capital from programmes for employment generation to those for limiting CO_2 emissions. This capital shortage has long stymied efficiency measures, eg. efficient operation of electric utilities, and energy conservation in industry, even though most energy conservation measures are negative-cost strategies over a period of time.

There are many CO_2 limitation options that are desirable in India for many reasons other than global-warming abatement. Three such major strategies are: afforestation, energy efficiency enhancement, and development and deployment of renewable energy technologies. Each has been individually identified as a priority area, yet capital constraints have limited their impact. For example, there is a stated objective of afforesting 30% of the country's land area. This would be about 109 million hectares (Mha), and currently the area under forest cover is about 64Mha. In the mid-1980s, afforestation was high on the government's agenda, and an afforestation target of 5Mha per year was adopted. Even this relatively modest target could not be achieved, and only 1.75 to 2Mha could be afforested annually in the late 1980s.

In this perspective of the net shortage of capital in the economy, additional programmes for CO_2 limitation would inevitably flounder. These programmes would receive some financial support, but only at present levels of funding. Major limitation programmes would, therefore, necessarily require support from external resources. Such support, on an incremental cost basis, could be linked to a particular CO_2

Figure10.4 Cost curve for CO_2 limitation strategies in India

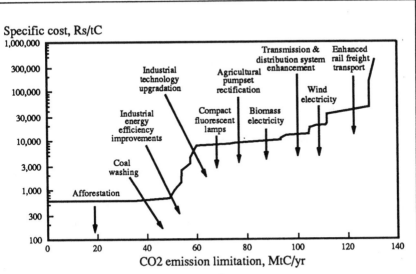

Note: Only major strategies have been identified in this figure. A total of twenty-nine strategies are included in the full analysis

Source: TERI, New Dehli.

limitation programme within the perspective of an overall target at the national sectoral level. TERI has recently initiated a study on the incremental costs of CO_2 limitation strategies and their current potential for emissions abatement.[34] Preliminary estimates indicate limitation costs rising from about Rs600/tC (for afforestation) to about Rs0.4million/tC (for urban metro systems). The total CO_2 emissions limitation potential is judged to be about 90MtC per annum. The cost curve is shown in Figure 10.4. It is the author's opinion that about 20 - 30% of the total potential (apart from afforestation) can be achieved in a ten-year period if both capital resources and policy initiatives are in place. The capital investment for achieving this reduction would be in

[34] A.Mathur, A.N.Chaturvedi, G.Sambasivan, V.Joshi, C.S.Sinha, K.Thukral, R.K.Bose and B.Natarajan, *Strategies for Limiting Carbon Dioxide Emissions in India*, TERI Discussion Paper, 1991.

the order of Rs0.1 trillion, approximately 10% of the GDP of the country. Beyond the ten-year period, it is expected that a snowballing effect will occur as the infrastructure for the three major strategies (afforestation, energy efficiency enhancement, and renewable deployment) would be in place. But although the benefits over time of some measures would exceed the initial costs, that is not the issue: the spare capital is simply not available.

10.6 Conclusions

India has a growing population and a developing economy. The national priority is development for resource creation and employment generation. Global warming is a low priority issue - it is, in fact, an issue in India only because the international debate has potential implications for the Indian development process. The consensus within the establishment in India is that many of the options to be exercised to minimize global warming are desirable for India on other grounds. Thus, the first priority is the emphasis on energy conservation and afforestation. There is also a consensus that energy consumption cannot be decreased: in fact, it will continue to increase well into the middle of the next century.

Accelerated efforts in energy conservation and afforestation require changing emphasis in the planning process, restructuring of the energy industry, and financial and technological inputs. The country is currently in a situation where lack of capital, combined with low energy prices and chronic energy shortages, has created a supply expansion syndrome at the cost of stabilizing and enhancing the efficiency of energy production, conversion and consumption.

Total energy consumption in the Indian economy under the business-as-usual scenario is expected to increase by 60% (over the 1987-88 level) by the year 2000, and then more than treble between 2000 and 2030; CO_2 emissions would increase at a faster rate owing to the growing dominance of coal in the energy mix. Some fuel substitution (coal by natural gas) is possible by 2000, and together with energy efficiency improvements, could reduce energy consumption by 10% and emissions by 12% in that year. Increased natural gas use and promotion of renewables promise energy consumption and emissions reductions of 8% in 2030. Efficiency improvements could lead to energy savings in the order of 22% and emissions reduction of 20% in that year. Both the measures together could yield energy savings of nearly 30% and decrease

CO_2 emissions by 28%. In spite of these measures, energy consumption would still be nearly four times that in 1987-88.

These are substantial savings and benefits for the economy in the long run. The problem in their implementation lies in the social, economic and political costs. The only feasible solution seems to be the injection of a vast amount of capital into the system to simultaneously upgrade supply infrastructure, provide resources for energy conservation, and enhance supply. Following this, price revisions may be more acceptable politically. These would then drive energy conservation and interfuel substitution. The central problem is that accelerating programmes to limit CO_2 emissions requires capital, and it is unacceptable to move capital from programmes for meeting basic needs and employment generation to those aimed at reducing emissions. Abatement may be technically feasible, but it is likely only if supported by external financial and technological aid.

Appendix 1. Units, conventions, and conversion factors

Within the framework of the *System Internationale* adopted by physical scientists, the fundamental unit of energy is the Joule, and the unit of power - the rate of energy conversion - is the Watt, equal to one Joule per second. The rich history of energy has created a plethora of other units which are widely used in energy industries and analysis, where SI units are rarely used. Further difficulties are introduced by the distinction between Gross Heating Values and Net Heating Values (see box), and by varying conventions concerning non-fossil energy equivalence. Common units and conversion factors are shown in the glossary of both volumes. This study uses the following conventions:

* The principal unit of national consumption is the Total Primary Energy Requirement (TPER, sometimes just called the total energy requirement or more loosely, total demand/consumption) expressed in Million Tonnes of Oil Equivalent (Mtoe). This is the most common unit of international energy statistics. Gross Heating Values are used where the distinction between Gross and Net is relevant.

* Electrical output is expressed as Terawatt Hours (TWh)

* In deriving energy statistics for future scenarios, primary electricity (eg. nuclear, hydro, imports) is counted at its direct energy content (output basis), *not* in terms of the fossil fuel which would have to be burnt in its place (input equivalent) - which is about 2.5-3.5 times the electrical output.

This final convention is not standard, but is adopted for several reasons. The efficiency of baseload fossil plant varies substantially between countries and will change with developing technology. Any conversion factor would therefore have to vary over time and between countries. Particular difficulties can arise from converting traded electricity into 'input' equivalents. Using the output basis is more consistent, though less conventional. It is also arguably more realistic, since primary electricity does increase the efficiency of the energy system by reducing the losses from fossil fuel power plant, and hence reduces the primary energy requirement. It does, however, mean that contributions from primary electricity sources - which usually encompass the major non-fossil options - appear much smaller than they would in terms of input equivalents, and they displace much more fossil fuel than appears from a quick glance at the statistics.

Heating/Calorific Values

When hydrocarbons are burnt, the hydrogen is converted into H_2O as steam. If this is condensed to water, it gives off additional energy. The physical energy equivalent of fossil fuels thus depends upon whether this condensing energy is included. Including it gives the Gross Heating Value (GHV), otherwise known as Higher Calorific Value; omitting it yields the Net Heating Value (NHV), or Lower Calorific Value. The figures vary according to the hydrogen content of the fuel, as follows:

> Coal: ratio NHV/GHV = 0.97
> Oil: ratio NHV/GHV = 0.94
> Gas: ratio NHV/GHV = 0.90

One advantage of using Mtoe units for energy is that it limits the significance of this variation - a tonne of oil is a tonne of oil, irrespective of conventions; in relation to oil tonnage, coal and gas statistics differ only by about 3% according to the convention used, and total energy consumption vary little.

Much international energy data is in NHV; US and UK national data, and some others, use GHV, if specified at all. Where physical units and efficiencies are used in the text (as in the detail of the UK scenarios), data is expressed in GHV. This is partly because of the increasing use of systems which do use the latent energy in the steam (notably condensing gas boilers), and which could thus in principle yield efficiencies greater than 100% if expressed on an NHV basis.

Appendix 2. Total greenhouse gas emissions from energy systems: coefficients and implications

For a given consumption of a particular fuel, conversion coefficients are required to calculate the associated emissions of greenhouse gases. In addition to the direct emissions from burning fossil fuels, greenhouse gases may be emitted from other stages of fossil fuel cycles. This appendix summarizes work undertaken to establish conversion factors, and discusses the impact of indirect emissions including non-CO_2 gases.

The standard reference for emission factors, used directly by the IPCC Energy and Industries Sub-group, is work conducted by Marland and Rotty for the US Department of Energy.[1] At the beginning of the EEP project there was some uncertainty about these figures and Marland (personal communication) suggested that in significant areas his own analysis could usefully be updated and cross-checked, so as far as possible values here have been derived from other sources. The analysis is broken down into four components, which are considered in turn:

* Fuel carbon content
* Carbon release coefficients, primary fuel basis
* Carbon release coefficients, delivered fuel basis
* Other greenhouse gas addition coefficients

Studies of the carbon content in fossil fuels were conducted by various supporters of the Programme's work and submitted as unpublished notes. These valuable contributions, by Ian Hughes (British Coal), Andrew Gordon (BP International), John Eyre (Shell), David Fortune (Shell Coal), and Peter Brackley, are gratefully acknowledged, along with earlier contributions by Richard Beresford (British Gas). I am indebted to Peter Brackley for further discussion of the issues.

The carbon in a given weight of fossil fuels, especially coal, can vary widely. That for a given *energy content* varies much less, and all coefficients are expressed in these terms, using gross heating values (GHV).

A2.1 Carbon content of fossil fuels

Natural gas can be readily analysed directly from its chemical composition, using molecular data. The composition does vary

---

[1] G.Marland and R.Rotty, 'Carbon dioxide emissions from fossil fuels: a procedure for estimation and results for 1950-1982'. *Tellus*, 36B, 1984.

Table A2.1 Results of coal composition studies

Author	Source	Reported C-content tC/TJ (dmf, GHV)[*]
Fortune (Shell Coal)	Wide sample	23.5-26.4
Gordon (BP)	Wide sample	23.2-25.4
Hughes (British Coal)	Seyler's Chart (excluding anthracite)	23.2-25.6
Hughes (British Coal)	Coal rank classification	24.0-26.4

[*]dmf = Dry, mineral-free basis; GHV = Gross (higher)heating value

somewhat but the methane fraction is nearly always between 90% and 96%, which leads to a carbon content of about 13.8tC/TJ (0.615tC/toe) for dry gas with a range of ±1%.[2]

As a highly complex mix of hydrocarbons, a *crude oil* coefficient cannot be derived from a molecular analysis. From extensive samples, Marland and Rotty estimated 19.0tC/TJ (0.847tC/toe) ±2%; Gordon (BP) cites 18.5 for a 'light sweet crude' and suggests 19.0 for an average crude coefficient, suggesting a slightly wider range of variation. Most other data offered relates to various *oil fractions*. Gordon (BP) cites products spanning 18.0tC/TJ for gasoline, 18.5 for kerosene, 19.0 for gas oil (with diesel oil 19.2), to 20.0 for fuel oils and heavy oil. Eyre estimates 18.3-19.4 for mogas, 18.8-19.7 for diesel fuel, and 20.2-20.8 for fuel oil. It is likely that various published figures of around 20.0tC/TJ are for fuel oil rather than crude.

For *coal*, Hughes (BC) analysed carbon content in detail using two different approaches; his results are summarised, together with the results of samples from Shell and BP, in Table A2.1. This demonstrates a range of no more than 5% about a central value of around 24.5tC/TJ (1.09tC/toe). Hughes' analysis demonstrates that volatile matter content is by far the most important determinant of variation. Anthracites form the higher end of the range; excluding them gives a range for bituminous

[2] Adjusted dry gas basis: Gordon (BP); Marland & Rotty, ibid.

Table A2.2 Fuel carbon content coefficients

	Carbon content		Range of variation/
	tC/TJ (GHV)	tC/Mtoe	uncertainty
Principal primary fossil fuels			
Natural gas	13.8	0.62	±1%
Crude oil	19.0	0.85	±3%
Bituminous coals*	24.5	1.09	±5%
Other solid fuels			
Anthracites	25.5	1.14	±3%
Wood	27.3	1.22	?
Peat	27.5	1.23	?
Lignite	26.2	1.17	?
Oil products			
Gasoline	18.0	0.80	±2%
Kerosene	18.5	0.83	±2%
Diesel/Gas oil	19.0	0.85	±2%
Fuel oils	20.0	0.89	±2%

*The figure for bituminous coal may be placed more precisely using calorific value by using the equation given in the text.

coals of 23.2-25.2tC/TJ, which can be further narrowed if the calorific value of the coal is known by noting that the variation corresponds to roughly:

Carbon content, tC/TJ = 32.15 - 0.234 x GHV

for GHV (Gross heating value) in the range 31-37GJ/t on dry, mineral-free basis. The range of uncertainty is then of the order of ±1%. Anthracites fall outside this scheme; a value of 25.5tC/TJ ±3% seems suitable for these. The results of these studies are summarised in Table A2.2, together with estimates by Fortune (Shell Coal) of the carbon content in other solid fuels.

A2.2 Carbon release coefficients for primary fuels

The carbon release coefficient for primary fuels is the coefficient for deriving the total carbon emitted as (or rapidly converted to) CO_2 on the basis of fuel production statistics. This is the goal on which Marland and Rotty's principal studies for the US DOE concentrated. It differs from the carbon content in that it needs to take account of non-oxidation of the primary source, and any additional CO_2 released in the fuel production and delivery.

Marland and Rotty cite non-combustion uses for *natural gas* as accounting for 3.4% of production in the US, but most of this is for ammonia production and is soon oxidized: they suggest a maximum of 1% for non-oxidizing applications, plus a maximum of 1% for non-oxidization in combustion. Some CO_2 is released in the flaring of gas which cannot be tapped in the production wells; say 1±1%. The impact of losses in the network are dominated by the greenhouse impact of methane, discussed separately below. It has also been suggested that considerable amounts of trapped CO_2 may be released directly from gas operations: no data were found on this, but it could be significant particularly for fields with unusually high amounts of trapped CO_2.

Oil is applied to a number of non-energy uses. The extent of these applications varies, but typically around 5% may be used for lube oils, wax, bitumen etc; and around another 5% may be used for chemical feedstocks. Although many oils and waxes may be oxidized, not much bitumen is, and this appears to be the dominant factor in this group. For chemical feedstocks, Gordon (BP) suggests that 20% of the input carbon is eventually oxidized, as do Marland and Rotty. Overall, it seems likely that 5-10% of primary oil consumption is not oxidized, but the figure cannot be pinned down further on this data, and is subject to considerable national variation; say 7±3%. Added to this, small amounts may be deposited as soot in burners but for modern systems this is a very small component (other non-CO_2 carbon products, such as CO and evaporation of oil fractions, are soon converted to CO_2 and may have a stronger greenhouse impact than complete combustion, as discussed below). Finally, gas flaring needs to be added. The final figures given in Marland and Rotty suggest that gas flaring accounts for about 2% of total CO_2 emissions from fossil fuels. There is no indication of how this is broken down between oil and gas production: if it is mostly from oil production it implies a penalty of 4-5%. UK statistics show that 40,000BCM of gas was flared at oil fields in 1986, corresponding to about 2% of the carbon in the oil produced. A figure of 3±2% is suggested as an average, with considerable regional variation.

For *coal*, Marland and Rotty estimate that about 4.5% of coal sent to coking plant in the US remains unoxidized, mostly as tar; they suggest overall non-oxidation by this route as 0.8% of coal production. The unburnt fraction in burners is given as at most 1%, and this must be declining, and quite negligible in power stations. SO_2 scrubbing however is essentially exchange of C for S, so that 2%-sulphur coal by weight adds (12/32)x2% of CO_2. Additional small amounts arise from combustion in deposits and waste tips. The net adjustment must be very close to zero.

More significant are the questions raised by processes to obtain synthetic fuels and gas from coal. Unless the by-product is a solid form of carbon (which is usually not feasible), to a good approximation the effective carbon contribution will be very close to that of the source material. In addition considerable energy may be consumed in the conversion process itself, making overall emissions by these routes considerably higher than from direct use of coal (the exception might concern some forms of underground gasification of high-volatile coals, which has been attempted but with very limited success; no data on composition, output and economics were obtained). Synfuels and gasification are discussed by Marland,[3] and I shall not discuss them further here.

Overall, fuel production coefficients seem very close to the fuel carbon content, though in the case of oil particularly this is due to a partial cancelling of non-oxidized applications against additional CO_2 emissions (flaring), with substantial uncertainties in both. The implied coefficients are summarized in Table A2.3.

A brief comparison of these numbers with the work of Marland and Rotty reveals close agreement. The equivalent coefficients they derived, on the basis of reported global primary fuels demand divided by carbon emissions, are respectively 24.99, 17.49, and 13.42 tC/TJ GHV; in all cases within 2% of the central values derived here and within the estimated range of uncertainty. Despite this the global emissions calculated in Volume 1 of this study are about 3% higher than the Marland

---

[3] G.Marland, 'Carbon dioxide emission rates for conventional and synthetic fuels', *Energy*, Vol.8 No.12, 1983.

Table A2.3 Carbon release coefficient, primary fuel basis

	Carbon release coefficient		Range of variation/
	tC/TJ (GHV)	tC/Mtoe	uncertainty
Natural gas	13.6	0.61	±2%
Crude oil	18.4	0.82	±5%
Bituminous coals*	24.5	1.09	±5%

* The figure for bituminous coal may be placed more precisely using calorific value by using the equation given in the text. Coefficients for anthracites and lignites are about 4-7% higher.

& Rotty figures for equivalent years. This appears to be due to differences in the data on primary fossil fuel consumption, which is entirely consistent with Marland and Rotty's own analysis, which identified fossil fuel statistics as the most uncertain factor.[4]

It should be emphasised that the coefficients are averages. Although this average appears reasonably suited to all the countries taken as case studies in this volume (none of the authors suggested they were inappropriate), some countries may differ substantially. For example, the Netherlands has a large petrochemicals industry, which consumes nearly 15% of all the carbon embodied in national fossil fuel consumption, with many products exported. It is also a major port for refuelling of international cargo ships. Emissions attributable to the Netherlands thus depend upon how the boundaries concerning responsibility for CO_2 emissions are drawn. Physical differences in the amount of gas flaring and possibly the CO_2 in gas fields could also create significant differences between individual fields. However, despite such variations, the coefficients in Table A2.3 appear reliable for global and most regional estimates of carbon emissions.

[4] Marland and Rotty op.cit. used UN statistics, and concluded that the uncertainties in this database were of the order of 10% for all fuels, Table 15.

A2.3 Carbon release coefficients for delivered fuels

An assessment based upon the consumption of processed and delivered fuels differs from gross production assessment because (a) non-oxidizing applications are not relevant, (b) statistics may need to be disaggregated according to fuel products, and (c) 'parasitic' energy consumption, such as oil use in refineries, needs to be accounted for as a multiplier on the product use. It is this fuel product consumption coefficient which is relevant to most assessments of policy responses, whether the focus is upon end-use efficiency or upon fuel switching.

Data on parasitic energy for all fuels were quoted in Marland[5] from internal documents by Hannon and Cassler. These are described as showing 'only direct and indirect energy consumption during processing' and refer strictly to 1974 US data. Some figures can be derived from the 'own-use' entries in standard energy statistics tables, though these may represent a subset of the total parasitic use. The author has derived estimates of own-use from entries in the IEA Energy Balance statistics,[6] (which in addition to fossil fuels indicate that own-use in electricity totals 14% of gross production, divided roughly equally between own use in power stations and losses in transmission and distribution). Other own-use examples are derived from UK statistics.[7]

Gas is combusted almost entirely in its original state (after drying & removal of contaminants). OECD average own-use is 8.2%. The figures of Hannon and Cassler show a very large parasitic use of 19%. UK statistics show own-use in gas at 7.5% for 1986. Own-use in the Soviet gas industry is estimated to be about 10% (Soviet case study). Dutch analysts cite a global average indirect CO_2 emissions (apparently reflecting both the own-use and the CO_2 content in natural gas) at a little over 5%.[8] The figures are sufficiently large and disparate that further analysis would be useful, but discounting the Hannon and Cassler data, a broad figure of 8±5% appears suitable for piped natural gas.

[5] Marland, 'Carbon dioxide emission rates for conventional and synthetic fuels', op.cit.

[6] International Energy Agency, *Energy Balances of OECD Countries 1986/7*, IEA/OECD, Paris, 1989.

[7] Department of Energy, *Digest of UK Energy Statistics, 1990*, HMSO, 1990.

[8] P.A.Okken and D.N.Tiemersma, 'Greenhouse Gas Emission Coefficients from the Energy System: Two Methods to Calculate National CO_2-Emissions', Energy Study Centre, Petten, Netherlands, September 1989.

442

Higher figures would be appropriate for gas liquified for transport by ship. Typically 10-20% of the energy of the methane can be consumed in liquefaction; transport may then take a further 0.1-0.2%/day.[9] Further small losses occur from LNG storage tanks.

Oil is transformed into a wide range of products (the carbon content of some of the most important have been listed in Table A2.2). OECD average own-use for oil is 5.5%, and refineries also consume gas and electricity, respectively at about 2% and 1% of the energy throughput. The Hannon and Cassler figures suggest a 1±2% correction for total parasitic use. UK statistics suggest refineries consumption of just over 7% in 1986, a fraction which appears to have remained of similar magnitude since 1973.[10]

A major complication with oil is that the parasitic energy should apply differently to different products. Increasing the proportion of fuel-oil use, for example, would reduce the requirements for cracking and could even reduce overall refineries consumption. Increasing use of middle distillates could either increase or decrease refineries consumption, depending on the existing requirements and the nature of crude oil used. Overall, the uncertainty in how parasitic energy for oil products should be allocated is of at least the same order as the range in carbon content of the main products. Furthermore the penalties are likely to be higher for the lighter products near the top of the barrel, which have the lower C-content. In lieu of better data it therefore appears reasonable to use an across-the-board consumption coefficient applied for all oil products. A figure of about 21tC/TJ (before other factors are considered) would roughly account for the total parasitic use. To this, gas flaring again adds around 4±2%.

For *coal*, the only significant transformation is into coke, but energy is also consumed in mines and in coal transport and handling. OECD own-use appears to be 3.6%. Hannon and Cassler cite 2.2% losses. UK statistics indicate that only 0.15% of coal is consumed by collieries, but that losses up to 3% may be attributed to coke production, and also that coal production consumes around 2% of electricity generation. A figure of 3±2% is taken.

[9] D.Spottiswoode, private communication.
[10] Institute of Petroleum Information Service, *Petroleum Statistics 1987*.
[11] Intergovernmental Panel on Climate Change, *Scientific Assessment of Climate Change*, IPCC/Cambridge University Press, June 1990, Chapter 2.

Table A2.4 Carbon release coefficient, delivered fuel basis

	Carbon coefficient		Range of variation/
	tC/TJ (GHV)	tC/Mtoe	uncertainty
Natural gas	16.1	0.72	±5%
Oil products	22.1	0.96	±8%
Bituminous coals*	25.3	1.13	±6%

*See note to table A2.3

The consequences for the delivered fuel carbon coefficients are shown in Table A2.4. The ranking of fuels is still clear but the range between them is significantly reduced. It should be emphasised these figures exclude questions of combustion efficiency, which naturally depend on the technology used and can vary between different fuels. This may be important in electricity production for example, as discussed in Chapter 3. The impact of the various stages is summarised in Table A2.5.

A2.4 Other greenhouse gases

As discussed in Volume 1, Chapter 1, other gases which contribute to the greenhouse effect can be associated with fossil fuel use: methane (CH_4), nitrous oxide (N_2O), tropospheric ozone (O_3, associated with non-methane hydrocarbon (NMHC) emissions and NO_x), and the indirect impact of carbon monoxide (CO). By weight, these are all negligible in comparison with CO_2, but they are much more powerful per molecule, with radiative impact relative to CO_2 of over 20 for methane (see below) and 290 for nitrous oxide.[11]

Nitrous oxide is projected to account for perhaps 5% of future radiative forcing, but improved understanding of releases from fossil fuels and from biomass burning suggest that both these are negligible sources.[12]

[12] Studies published in 1988 demonstrated that earlier estimates of N_2O release from these sources had been distorted by contamination of sampling flasks. The IPCC estimate that both fossil fuel and biomass combustion account at most for a few per cent of global N_2O sources (ibid).

Table A2.5 Summary of results for estimating carbon emissions from fossil fuels[1]

Fuel	C content tC/TJ	tC/Mtoe	Uncertainty/ variation	Non-oxidation correction, %	Additional CO_2, %	Parasitic use, %
Gas	13.8	0.62	±2%	-3±2%	1±1%	10±5%
Oil	19.0	0.85	±5%	-7±3%	4±2%	8±5%
Coal[2]	24.5	1.09	±5%	-1±1%	1±1%	3±2%

Notes: [1]Carbon release coefficients on primary fuel basis are obtained by adding columns 1+2+3. Coefficients on delivered fuel basis are obtained by adding 1+3+4. For total radiative impact, other gases may need to be added (see text). [2]Bituminous and brown coal. Anthracite has a C-content of 25.5tC/TJ, lignites may be higher; other factors are as for bitumous coal.

CO helps to form tropospheric ozone and competes with the processes destroying methane in the atmosphere, thus extending methane lifetimes. The IPCC estimate that fossil fuels account for about half of global CO emissions, but the subsequent interactions are so complex that it is as yet impossible to quantify the radiative impact of this. Emissions of CO reflect limitations in the design and maintenance of combustion systems, and are starting to decline in the US and perhaps Europe and Japan.[13]

Unlike other greenhouse gases, the contribution from tropospheric ozone is hard to estimate because it is a short lived gas with localised concentrations, the implications of which also vary with its height. Hansen[14] estimated that it might have contributed 10% of total radiative forcing during the 1980s; the IPCC concluded merely that it might be significant but could not be quantified at present. 10% is of the same order of magnitude as the contribution from CO_2 emissions from

[13] IPCC, *Scientific Assessment of Climate Change*, op.cit., Chapter 2.
[14] J.Hansen et al, 'Global Climate Changes as Forecast by the Goddard Insitute for Space Studies Three Dimensional Model', *Journal of Geophysical Research*, 93-D8 pp.9341-9364, 1988.

Indirect CO_2 emissions from non-fossil sources

There has been some debate about indirect emissions from primary (non-fossil) electricity sources, due to energy use in plant construction, and from the thermal processing of nuclear fuels.

A study by Mortimer examined these issues. In general the study confirmed that the full-cycle emissions from all non-fossil sources are a very small fraction of fossil fuel emissions, the largest being nuclear power (PWR reactors) with indirect emissions at about 4% of the emissions of a coal station. Most of this arises from the thermal part of the fuel cycle, dominated by ore separation, for which Mortimer states the thermal energy requirement as:

$$(611300G\text{-}360)/(24900G\text{+}700) \text{ x electrical output}$$

where G is the ore concentration in per cent U_3O_8. Mortimer notes that (if the equation holds) this does set a limit to the ore concentration useful for CO_2 abatement; exploiting ore concentrations much above 0.01% would emit as much CO_2 as a coal station. Not surprisingly this is equally important as an economic limit. Mortimer estimates that this would limit the extent to which nuclear power could replace fossil fuels on a large scale (excluding fast breeders) to a few decades at most.

However, uranium resources are probably larger than this assumes (see Chapter 1), and there are some opportunities for improving the efficiency with which uranium is used (apart from using fast breeder reactors), and probably lowering the energy requirements of ore extraction. With respect to present policy at least, other constraints on nuclear seem much more important, though the CO_2, energy and economic consequences of exploiting very low-grade ores does introduce some uncertainty concerning nuclear's long-term potential without FBRs.

N.Mortimer, 'Aspects of the Greenhouse Effect', Friends of the Earth, London (Proof of Evidence to Hinkley Point C Inquiry); 'Nuclear Power and Global Warming', *Energy Policy* 19(1), Jan/Feb 1991

D.M.Donaldson and G.E.Betteridge, 'CO_2 emissions from nuclear power stations - a critical analysis of FOE9', *Atom*, No.400, UKAEA, Feb 1990.

the transport sector, but is probably on the high side (perhaps reflecting too much the situation in the US). An added layer of uncertainty is the immense complexity of ozone chemistry and sources, though emissions of unburnt hydrocarbons are clearly important (NO_x and CO also play a role). Anthropogenic emissions are largely associated with transport (catalytic converters will greatly reduce emissions) and the solvent industry, but as yet it is impossible to quantify the effect of this, and because the emissions depend upon the combustion and control technology, they have to be related to specific uses and general coefficients are not applicable. However, it is possible that non-CO_2 emissions from cars without catalytic converters add considerably to the greenhouse impact of the CO_2.

NO_x emissions from aircraft may also be important relative to their CO_2 emissions, because the lifetime of NO_x is greatly extended in the upper troposphere. Another emission which may have a significant radiative impact - this time a negative one - is sulphur, through its suspected role in helping to form clouds which reflect sunlight. All these issues need clarification.

But by far the greatest concern about non-CO_2 emissions from fossil fuels has concentrated upon methane, especially from natural gas. Three issues need to be disentangled: the relative importance of methane as a greenhouse gas; the implications in terms of 'significant' emission rates from different sources; and various estimates of leakage rates from fossil fuel systems.

Molecule for molecule, methane has much more radiative impact than CO_2. Furthermore it is implicated in ozone formation, and can be carried up into the stratosphere where it reacts to form water vapour, another strong greenhouse gas. Comparison with CO_2 impacts is complicated by the fact that methane has a much shorter lifetime than CO_2, so the relative impact depends on the timescale considered; over a hundred-year period, the IPCC estimate the 'global warming potential' of methane, including indirect effects, to be 21 times that of CO_2 for a given mass (or 13 for molecular comparison); for a 20-year horizon the figure is 63.[15] The IPCC estimated that total 1990 emissions of methane were a little over 1% of CO_2 emissions, and that these emissions would contribute

[15] IPCC, *Scientific Assessment of Climate Change*, op.cit., Chapter 2.

respective 15% and 61% to the total radiative forcing from 1990 emissions over the next 100 years.

The sources of methane are many and varied. The estimates of Cicerone and Oremland[16] are the main source quoted in the literature, and were used by the IPCC. They indicate very large uncertainties, with the best defined source subject to a factor or two uncertainty, ranging up to a factor of 10 for some others. Their central estimates suggest that coal mining accounts for about 6% of global methane emissions, and natural gas about 8%. Unless natural venting of fossil methane is much larger than expected, these figures are not consistent with the results of isotopic analysis which suggest that about 30% of atmospheric methane is derived from fossil sources, and a subsequent meeting concluded that the evidence pointed towards the upper end of the range.[17] Even at this upper limit, the total radiative impact of fossil methane emissions accumulated over the next 100 years is about a tenth that of the direct CO_2 emissions, though over a twenty year horizon it would be about a third.

However, from the energy policy perspective, the key question is how methane emissions may affect the relative contribution of different fuels. Using the IPCC estimate, the full radiative impact of a 1% methane leakage from natural gas accumulated over 100 years would be equivalent to about 13% of the direct CO_2 impact; leakages much greater than this would become highly significant, especially with respect to shorter-term impact.[18] Unfortunately the statistics do not appear adequate to establish for certain the significance or otherwise of methane leakage. Cicerone and Oremland made a central estimate of 45Mt and 35Mt methane from gas operations and coal respectively, which compares with worldwide production of about 1,000Mt natural gas and 3,500Mt of carbon in coal.

[16] R.J.Cicerone and R.S.Oremeland, 'Biogeochemical Aspects of Atmospheric Methane', Global Biogeochemical Cycles, Vol.2 No.4, December 1988, pp.299-327.
[17] Environmental Protection Agency of Japan/US-AID/US Environmental Protection Agency, 'International Workshop on Methane Emissions', Washington DC, October 1990.
[18] For example, Rhode (H.Rhode, 'A comparison of the Contribution of Various Gases to the Greenhouse Effect', Science, Vol.248 pp.1217-1219) estimates that 'natural gas is preferable to other fossil fuels in considering the greenhouse effect as long as its leakage can be limited to 3 to 6%'.

The most contentious issue has been that of leakage from natural gas systems. The Cicerone and Oremland figures suggest leakage of several per cent of global throughput, even after allowing for methane from oil production (which is part of the 45Mt). Other studies have suggested similar orders of methane leakage from particular systems, some of which have been critiqued in a broader discussion by Stern.[19] The most coherent and detailed analysis of which the author is aware is that of Mitchell *et al* for the UK system,[20] which 'estimates a Low, Medium and High leakage rate of 1.9%, 5.3% and 10.8% respectively. The authors are confident that the leakage rate is above 1.9% and consider it more likely that the leakage rate is between the Medium and High case'. However, even this had to rely ultimately on a single 20-year old source for estimating the bulk of leakage, from pipes on old systems as measured at the time of conversion from town gas to natural gas.

Such figures contrast sharply with estimates from current gas industry analysts. A study by the Alphatania Group[21] details statements and studies across the full range of operations and many different countries and concludes that methane leakage cannot be greater than about 1% of throughput worldwide, and suggest that many higher estimates arise from basic misunderstandings of gas industry 'unaccounted for' statistics. Furthermore there is a financial element: in the UK, for example, a leakage of 2%/yr would imply financial losses of perhaps £100m/yr, which is more than half the total British Gas expenditure on mains and services, and should make tackling leakage a high financial priority.

Clearly estimates from gas industry analysts are not consistent with those of many independent studies. The estimates span the range from making methane leakage negligible to making it sufficient to offset most of the CO_2 advantage of natural gas over other fuels - depending on leakages from oil and coal operations. Atmospheric isotopic analysis cannot distinguish between different fossil sources, but tends to suggest leakage rates well above 1% unless other sources are much higher than

---

[19] J.Stern, *European Gas Markets: Challenge and Opportunity in the 1990s*, RIIA/Dartmouth, Aldershot, 1990, Appendix III.

[20] C.Mitchell, J.Sweet and T.Jackson, 'A Study of Leakage from the UK Natural Gas Distribution System', *Energy Policy*, November 1990.

[21] D.Spottiswoode et al, 'Methane Leakage from Natural Gas Operation', Paris: Cedigaz, Institut Française de Pétrôle, November 1989.

currently estimated. Certainly, if industrial estimates are anything close to correct, the 'missing sink' of carbon appears to be paralleled by a 'missing source' of fossil methane.

Estimates of emissions from coal are rapidly become as contentious as those from gas. Globally, coal-bed methane emissions appear comparable to those of gas. Mitchell's gas study was followed up by an analysis of UK coal arguing that coal industry statistics also underestimated emissions.[22] Coal-bed methane indeed could be a significant energy resource, and much as for gas the implications of higher leakage figures is that greater efforts to capture methane rather than vent it could be justified.

The debate is unlikely to be resolved until all details of gas, oil and coal industry estimates are publicly available, direct measurements improved, and a better understanding obtained of overall methane cycles. Fortunately, the uncertainties seem less significant concerning future developments. First, if further measurements do identify substantial sources of methane loss, it will almost certainly make financial sense to deal with them. Second, the losses from marginal increments in production through old systems will generally be less than the average losses (though, as Mitchell et al point out, this will depend somewhat on the nature and location of the new demand). Third, new gas systems tend to use pipes and valves with very much lower leakage rates - and leakage from new systems would doubtless be further reduced if there were added incentives to do so. The Alphatania study[23] states that 'our estimate of leakage for new supply would be around 0.05% .... for incremental volumes through existing systems the figure would be lower'.

Viewed from this perspective, methane leakage is more an issue which might (and should, if environmentally significant leaks do exist) marginally increase gas industry costs than a fundamental reason for discounting the environmental benefits of gas. On the basis of the various statistics, in fact, there are few convincing grounds for believing the marginal leaks associated with gas expansion, at least, to be any higher than for oil and coal. In each case, while current average methane leakage may well add 5-25% to the 100-year radiative impact of the CO_2 emitted, the impact for future emissions from marginal increases are likely to be much less, especially if efforts are directed at reducing leakages.

---

[22] C.Mitchell, 'Coal Bed Methane in the UK', *Energy Policy*, forthcoming 1991.
[23] D.Spottiswoode et al, 'Methane Leakage from Natural Gas Operation', op.cit.

With further research it might be possible to derive meaningful coefficients to cover non-CO_2 emissions for particular applications where the non-CO_2 impacts may be particularly significant, such as air transport, cars without catalytic convertors, gas through old pipeline systems, and coal from methane-rich mines without methane recovery. But in view of the wide uncertainties and, more pointedly, the great variation in non-CO_2 emissions according to the nature of the energy use and technology employed, it appears impractical to derive general emission coefficients to cover non-CO_2 gases, and improbable that doing so would significantly alter policy conclusions.

A2.5 Conclusions

Coefficients for the carbon content of fuels can be derived to within a few per cent accuracy, and those for estimating the CO_2 emissions from primary fossil fuel statistics are also quite precise. For policy-related research the significant uncertainties concern (a) the parasitic energy consumption in gas, oil, and primary electricity conversion, including the way in which this should be apportioned among different product sectors; (b) the scale of methane emissions from coal and gas production; and (c) the extent and sources of gas flaring. The overall uncertainties in the CO_2 end-use coefficients are of the order of 6%. For a few particular end uses (particularly in the absence of measures to remove non-CO_2 exhausts) these may be swamped by uncertainties concerning the impact of other non-CO_2 emissions.

Finally, the numbers point to possible policy implications. Gas flaring, parasitic energy use in the energy industries, methane leakages, hydrocarbon emissions, and possibly NO_x from aircraft are all potentially significant sources of greenhouse gases. Reducing some of these emissions may give a much simpler way of starting to tackle the greenhouse problem than major measures in fuel switching or demand management. But none are of sufficient magnitude to alter the ordering of the fossil fuels, or the basic concentration on CO_2 as the primary determinant of long-term radiative impacts of energy activities and, indeed, of all anthropogenic greenhouse gas emissions.